Book One

Idealism and Materialism

Second Edition

K Kobayashi

This book is a treatise on history coupled with the author's interpretations.

Strictly Literary™,
PO Box 242,
Scarborough, Queensland, Australia, 4020.
www.strictlyliterary.com
Phone: 0413 004 138
First published by Strictly Literary, Australia, in 2016

Copyright © 2016 Kiyoshi KOBAYASHI. All rights reserved. Apart from any fair dealing for the purposes of private study, research, criticism, or review, as permitted under the Copyright Act, no part of this book may be reproduced or transmitted in any form or by any means, electronic or mechanical, including photocopying, recording or by any information storage and retrieval system, without prior permission in writing from the publisher. The moral right of the author to be identified and to have his text preserved is asserted. Enquiries should be made in the first instance to the publisher.

First Published 2016

Second Edition 2020

ISBN: 978-0-9923297-8-5

The author K Kobayashi is issuing the following series of books:

Book One *Idealism and Materialism*
Book Two *Religion*
Book Three *Communism*
Book Four *The Third Prophecy*
Book Five *The Sexual Laws*

Though the series is a coherent unit with the unified purpose, each book is designed to be read independently from the others. The first three books are preparing for the proposal and the last book is augmenting the proposal. His core proposition is in Book Four *The Third Prophecy*; in fact it can be expressed in one simple sentence 'To love a child is not to make one'.

He proposes the love which is the most beautiful and the strongest the humans will ever know; and unless this love is stronger than the love between the sexes the proposal does not make any sense. People imbued with this love gladly discard everything else including their sweethearts. As the concession to an idealised state of being single the sweethearts, unmarried, may remain friends to have sex with precaution against pregnancy. Buddhists and Christians have always taught their adherents to be single all their life. The author firmly believes that marriage has been the greatest curse of the human race. Men and women suffered tremendously through marriage all these millenniums still they could not work out the way out. Only the love of the Third Prophecy leads the ordinary people to stay out of marriage with the unwavering conviction.

This love when adopted by an individual will fulfil what the first (idealism; and religion as crystallisation of idealism) and second (materialism; and communism as an extreme form of materialism) prophecies promised but did not deliver in full to the humans and human societies. This love when adopted by a society as a whole will fulfil not only the first and second prophecies to the full but also will solve many serious problems the humans have had all these millenniums as well as the humans may have in the future. The acceptance of this new way of life by the bulk of the population will result in hugely reduced population with the predominantly beneficial results to the humans. This leaves one serious problem for the ordinary single men and women, that is, how to solve their sexual problem. The author proposes the solution of this problem mainly addressed to single men in Book Five *The Sexual Laws*. He expounds the solution getting the idea from 'mind only' developed by the Buddha; the mind only concept is explained in Book Two *Religion*.

The author wants to prove beyond reasonable doubt that the arrival of the societies dominated by this new way of life is inevitable in the future provided the humans act according to the survival instinct as they have done all these millenniums. Since his message is contrary to the people's way of thinking in the past and present, he thinks that the ordinary people at present do not comprehend the message of the Third Prophecy, and it will take one century for the general public to fully appreciate its teaching and live according to its creed.

Contents

Introduction to Series

The introduction of a book is normally a brief preliminary explanation to lead readers to a better understanding of the book. However, since there are five books in this series, each with its own messages, I realised that I must have a rather lengthy explanation to orient readers. Though the main message I want to convey is in Book Four *The Third Prophecy,* the series is a coherent unit and I would like to say a few words about that too.

Preface

When I was a child, ten or eleven years of age at the time, I read a narrative from European--Greek or Italian--classical history and remembered its passages in part. A commanding general uttered the following remark just before engaging in a decisive battle: 'If god wants me to live, let me win this battle!' That battle cry was so strange that it was beyond my comprehension: 'What was god? Why did he ask for the assistance of god at the critical moment? In what way would god help him if god would at all?' These puzzles, etched upon my mind, stayed in my consciousness for many years. Years later I could not even recall what the outcome of the engagement was nor if he further lived or not. I was to be given the answer in an unexpected and extraordinary fashion.

My incomprehension in the above paragraph clearly shows that my environment--familial and social--was totally non-religious and materialistic. I did not have any reason to deviate from the setting of my childhood and adolescence. I believed in practical matters of life such as manufacturing industry, utilitarianism, economics and politics; they are mostly termed materialism in this series of books. I did not see any reasons why the other aspects of life such as religion, idealism and arts should exist. In fact I used to mock these latter activities as well as the people who were engaged in them. Marx's saying that religion is the opium of the masses went down well with me. I thought before entering the university that only communism could solve the various problems of the society, though I had only a rudimentary understanding of communist theories at that time. My attitude towards life was narrow and one-sided to the extreme.

My life view was to change drastically for the rest of my life. I would have kept the virtually same view if I had been reasonably happy. At the time of my university life my career was in total jeopardy and I was in a state of shock and despair. My narrow outlook did not give me any escape from the situation I was in. Out of this extreme suffering, the concept of the Third Prophecy was born in my mind and has grown since then. However, this new way of thinking by its nature did not lighten my distress: I was still shell-shocked and did not know what to do.

I read many books in random in an effort to console myself. I read literature as arts, and I became submerged in arts to such an extent that I could not comprehend why people wanted wealth. By sheer chance I got hold of a book called *The Imitation of Christ* (1441), a devotional book. I came to know that the author was a devout Christian and disclosed his intense religious feeling. He exhorts people to cast aside the worldly affairs which are false and ephemeral in order to live in the spiritual world which alone is real and lasting. I derived an immense consolation out of reading this book, which became an introduction to my religious experience. To look back at me around this time, I drastically changed my life view and looked for spiritual matter in life rather than practical matters I had sought before. The reason for this change was obvious; temporal matters of life did not give me any relief and I had to rely on spiritual guides from the nature of the suffering.

The Imitation of Christ is extensively read and it is often cited that this book is most popularly read after the Bible in the Christian world. The author, commonly quoted to be Thomas A Kempis though it seems that is not the case, emphasises many times in the book that unless a person goes through an agonising trial in life, that person is incapable of understanding deep insight into life. Times of trouble best discover the true worth of a man; they do not weaken him, but show his true nature (Thomas A Kempis 1952, p. 45); In this life men are tried like gold in the furnace (ibid., p. 45; Wisdom 3:6); He is not worthy of high contemplation who has not suffered some trials for God's sake (Thomas A Kempis 1952, p. 80).

The following verses, which also impressed me around that time, are similar to those in the last paragraph: I read books randomly from desperation not confining myself to Christianity. The Lord disciplines those he loves, as a father the son he delights in (Proverbs 3:12). Everyone who calls on the name of the Lord will be saved (Joel 2:32) If a person believes and takes refuge in the Buddha, the Thus Come One will never deceive him [*The Lotus Sutra*; a Buddhist canon] (Watson 1993, p. 36). By degrees, little by little, from time to time, a wise person should remove his own impurities, as a smith removes [the dross] of silver [*The Dhammapada*; a Buddhist canon] (Narada 1993, p. 199). Time shows us who is worthy of our affection, and adversity better than prosperity [Aristotle] (Harbottle 1897, p. 533). The righteous, therefore, can endure difficult circumstances while hoping for easier ones; but those who have done wickedly have suffered the difficult circumstances and will never see the easier ones (2 Esdras 7:18). How swiftly passes the glory of the world! (Harbottle 1897, p. 189) These messages hit the right inner chord with me. Tension between contradictions produces thinking and energy. People under extreme suffering which normally comes from the contradictions they cannot resolve are forced to think.

The exhortation in the sporting training 'No pain, no gain' seems true even for the development of the mind. Also there is a Chinese saying: A fierce wind knows the strong plant. The author of *The Imitation of Christ* thought it to be wrong to seek any other consolation but in God. The book not only opened a new value in me but destroyed the old value cherished since my birth. I extracted a great deal of pleasure out of the book, though I still felt often times miserable and unhappy with my lot. I read between the lines that the author himself went through a distress similar in intensity under different circumstances from my experience. He even commented Jesus Christ must have gone through the tremendous suffering only to come out with the unshakeable convictions: No man feels so cordially the passion of Christ as he who has suffered such like things (Thomas A Kempis 1982, p. 136); Our Lord Jesus Christ himself was not for one hour of his life without suffering (p. 137).

I also found the following verses in the Bible. See, I have refined you, but not like silver; I have tested you in the furnace of adversity (Isaiah 48:10). Who among you fears the Lord and obeys the voice of his servant, who walks in darkness and has no light, yet trusts in the name of the Lord and relies upon his God (Isaiah 50:10)? Share in suffering like a good soldier of Christ Jesus (2 Timothy 2:3). One measure of human greatness may be the ability to suffer.

The New Testament gives out the verse 'Be imitator of God, therefore, as dearly loved children and live a life of love, just as Christ loved and gave himself up for us as a fragrant offering and sacrifice to God' (Ephesians 5:1-2). And there is another verse 'Be imitator of me, as I am of Christ' (1 Corinthians 11:1). I have come to believe that the title of the book

The Imitation of Christ was taken from these verses which summarise the essence of the book.

After many years, I gained in a foreign country what I had originally wanted in my country. I believe that this fact fulfilled what the Bible says: … for though the righteous fall seven times, they will rise again; but the wicked are overthrown by calamity (Proverbs 24:16). High moral standard on my part in some ways—I misbehaved badly in other ways--before my religious experience makes the above fulfilment even more befitting. My trial times in my life were gone for good. I believe not many people would have had such a suffering to come out alive and good. I don't have any vigour left in me to go through such an ordeal at my advanced age; however, the religious zeal is still firmly with me.

The extreme suffering changed me forever and inspired me with the deep religious insight as well as the concept of the Third Prophecy. I resolved to write books primarily to make public the latter concept in the fourth book of this series and the rest is the supporting evidence. Books One to Three are the bases before the exposition of the concept and Book Five is the support after the exposition.

I don't try to preach people since the concept I am to disclose in Book Four of this series will, I firmly believe and explain by various means, prevail naturally assuming the humans will act on survival instinct, in a century to come and become the common belief of the human race. Hence the purpose of this series is more exposition than persuasion. Some earth scientists tell us from the available evidence that we live between the ice ages, and the next ice age will be fully set in within one generation of the humans once it comes. I would say similarly the concept developed in Book Four of this series will be fully set in the economically advanced countries within one generation once it comes possibly after the global catastrophe, the kind of which the humans have never known and the depth of whose sufferings the humans have never experienced. Karl Marx prophesised the inevitable arrival of communist society in the wake of capitalism; however, he did it on the premises many of which are erroneous as I expound in Book Three *Communism.* The communist countries in the past did not and could not put into effect the communist doctrines, and communism even in its height of influence did not spread to the advanced capitalist countries.

I also believe that unless a person goes through sustained unbearable suffering, the person is unlikely to understand the deep meanings of such creeds as Buddhism, Judaism or the Third Prophecy, all of which are products of extreme sufferings. Among the huge number of Buddhists and Christians through the history of human kind only a small number lived according to their creeds. People understood the teachings presented according to their experience in life and unless they went through torment they could not understand the deep significance of their religions. However, this series of books centres on the practicability rather than the deep meanings. Readers would be the judge after going through this series if I made an empty boast.

This series of books deviates considerably from the usual book writing practice in a few points.

Readers may find it odd that quite often in the process of the exposition, the viewpoint changes from the impersonal to the personal explaining my personal experience. Readers may attribute the changes to my immature way of writing since it is a rule of writing a book that the personal point of view should not change throughout. I emphasise that this series of books is the reflection of my life experience, and hence I present my experiences to tie the exposition close to my life. Also I use the conclusions drawn in one book of this series in the other books strengthening the unity of the series, thus I have to change the viewpoints from this consideration too.

I explain a few other odd aspects of the series in the introduction to follow.

Outline of Series
This series of books consists of:

Book One *Idealism and Materialism*
Book Two *Religion*
Book Three *Communism*
Book Four *The Third Prophecy*
Book Five *The Sexual Laws*

The topics of the series wildly range from history (Book One) to religion (Book Two) to economics (Book Three) to new way of life (Book Four) to sex (Book Five). Like most of the books in a series readers can read each book independently from the others. However, some topics discussed are parts of the whole and readers may wonder why I present them in one of the books, not knowing the overall setup. Their presentations make sense only from the perspective of the series. People further ask questions such as:

- Why did I write the series of books in a setup so grandiose as to be out of focus and beyond anyone's capability?
- Why did I write on the subjects for which I am not professionally trained? knowing that I am a qualified engineer with the main experience in ammunition manufacture and did not receive any tertiary education in the disciplines expounded in the books except for economics.

I am to answer the above queries in the following eight paragraphs.

The only reason why I wanted to write a book at all was to reveal the concept of uncontaminated love towards my children, which is the theme of the Third Prophecy. I have come to believe that to love a child is not to make one on the premise that that is what is best for a child. However, this love is hard to convey per se and even more so since it goes against the public belief of the past and present. This concept came out from my extreme mental agony. It is impossible to convey by the laying of the words the acute suffering and what came out of it to readers. Hence, people without any trying experience in life, when they hear about this love, will most likely say, 'I had never heard such an absurd thinking' or 'The author must be mad to make such extravagant claims: If any individual practise the above truth expressed in a simple sentence that person will live the life realising the full potentials of the two prophecies (idealism and materialism) among other benefits. Moreover, if the bulk of a nation follow the truth that society will make available further benefits and the humans will be saved from extinction' or 'He is contradicting himself. He said in another context that the survival means are multi-focal.' In order to forestall these kinds of misunderstandings, I present the other books of accessible themes to establish a rapport between readers and myself. I am hoping that readers may find one or two books in this series interesting and be encouraged to go on to read *The Third Prophecy*.

Only the Third Prophecy has the capacity to override the overwhelming urge to get married in the same way only the proper growth of the part of the brain has the capacity to override the overwhelming fear of the nerves. Willpower simply does not have the ability to overcome both the urge and the fear which are in fact in higher order than willpower. The third prophecy has the stronger dictate than the urge to get married, and people imbued with this love have no problem to be single all their life. Love of the third prophecy sits on the higher plane than the consideration of happiness or unhappiness; wealth or poverty; love of sweethearts. In other words love of the third prophecy is like the order from the highest authority in an organisation.

Before I go onto further dissertation let me assure readers that many of the historical events have surprisingly simple causes. The quest for the discovery of new routes to the East by the West Europeans in the 15th century was to make money as for the Industrial Revolution in Europe in the 18th and 19th centuries, through trade for the former and through production and trade for the latter. People were not interested in the maintenance, let alone the expansion, of the Roman Empire and the British Empire at the closing phases of these empires when they stopped making money. The fundamental drives of the expansion of the Mongol Empire in the 13th and 14th centuries were the acquisition desire by the Mongol soldiers of wealth and women: they obtained both of them through pillages, tributes and trade. The crusade zeal by the Europeans in the 11th-13th centuries was more to do with trade rather than religion. I make clear these points in this series of books. There are so many private firms, sales and production, in the society today; the primary, if not the only, purpose of these establishments is to make money, which is the manifestations of materialism. All these drives are simple but rooted in the self-preservation and pleasure seeking of humans.

Further I wanted to prove to myself and hopefully to readers that the acceptance of the Third Prophecy by the general public in the not distant future is inevitable. I make this claim because ultimately the survival of the human race hinges on it: I believe that the survival instinct will decide the human destiny as has done through the past millenniums. The minority who do not believe in this new way of life will maintain the population. People can stay away from marriage, which has been the curse for all these millenniums for the majority of people, only through this new teaching. People have described marriage as a blessing for all these millenniums through general conversations, literature and the mass media, mostly ignoring the sufferings in marriage and child rearing. Buddhism and Christianity teach people to be single to lead the religious way of life to the full: it is the means to achieve the higher end, and it is the core theory of their creeds. Confucianism does not preach abstention from marriage. The Third Prophecy centres on children, which are the only focus of the teaching. Also this book shows how the human developments have been defective, not realising the full benefits of idealism and materialism in the absence of the new prophecy. It shows using both historical evidence and logical inference how the new thinking will correct various deficiencies of the human race.

The arrival of the Third Prophecy is inevitable provided the survival instinct guides humans. A small number of people completed idealism in several parts of the world at the early classical era. Subsequently several societies integrated idealism into the social institutions. Materialism also bloomed in several European nations to spread to the world in the modern context. Not all the nations embraced idealism and materialism, which were in fact effective survival means. It is hard to answer why the rest of the nations did not adopt these ideologies as their way of life for survival. Is it racial? Is it the environment people were placed? Will the Third Prophecy spread eventually to all the nations on earth? Or will it appear only in a few nations as the dominant ideology? It is hard to answer these questions but I resolutely believe that the Third Prophecy is the answer to the fundamental problems of the world and many of my queries.

The subject matters dealt other than the Third Prophecy have fascinated me with varying enthusiasm, having direct bearing on my life. On the foundation of the interests I read hundreds of books spending a quarter of a century since I resolved to write the books, both to make them interesting and informative to readers and to make me free from the accusation that I wrote on the subjects I didn't have the expertise about. I unwaveringly feel that the number of the years spent and the number of the books read are not enough to write the kinds of the books I am working on. Since this series covers a large range of topics, I cannot help the books becoming eclectic, that is, selecting what seems best from the various sources and lacking in-depth and first-hand research in many topics. I build on what the other people researched and presented.

This approach resulted in some obvious flaws. Statements on the same subject appear from the different sources arising from the different context. Also a statement from one source often contradicts from another source. My efforts to reconcile the difficulties were not necessarily successful. The experts in any human endeavours have different opinions, and it may be appropriate to give different versions. Besides, if I give only one version, I am siding with that version without knowing the full extent of the matter; to cite only the version which suits my line of argument is not quite right. I am to give an example from the Chinese civil service examinations expounded in this introduction. Some scholars said that the examinations were only the facade to perpetuate the dominance of the governing nobility with some exceptions. Some scholars said that the system made the successful candidates the core of the governing body. I gave both versions in the text, leaving readers wondering what the true state was.

The truth may have lied in between on this matter. Some departments and some eras, seeing the institution was vast and long lasting, strongly exhibited one aspect and the others the other aspect, depending on the prevailing conditions, particularly on the strengths of the reigning emperor and the nobility. Also I am rather suspicious the raw data presented in the past reflected the correct family connections. Plenty of historical information concerning the successful examinees and their family backgrounds is available, especially from the Ming era onwards. Some modern researchers expressed grave doubt as to the full extent and some bias on the extent of the information. How did they define the governing nobility? Did it depend on the possession of the large tracts of lands? Did it depend on the examination pass of the family members? Did it depend on the holding of the government posts? Did the researchers in the historical China have the full access to all the information they needed?

It is rather strange that the more I learn about the subjects the more interesting they get and the more ignorant I feel about them; and the more I write the more topics to write about come out. Still I tell to myself I have to finish the books before I get too old or die. If a considerable number of readers find some of the books other than *The Third Prophecy* enjoyable, I will be fully rewarded in this context.

One thrusting notion in this series of books is that humans are led by the survival instinct manifested in the dogmas that are to follow, though people may not be aware of this fact. It is easy to see that for Book One to three, survival is the fundamental basis of the exposition. The main theme of Book Four is also survival though readers may be at a loss until they go through the details. The laws governing sex in Book Five is also surprisingly survival. The properties of metals are decided by the atoms and their means of bonding. Similarly the natures of the group or nation are decided by the individual desires for self-preservation and the relationships of people within the group or nation as well as the relationships of the groups or nations.

Another notion I continually adhered to is that I address these books to the average or common or ordinary readers, hence naturally the conclusion drawn from the laying out the common sense is also the common sense. I do not pretend that these books are scholarly treatise. I do not define the average readers in this series. Sometimes I refer to most readers or majority of readers to mean the same idea. The average people as the subject of Book Five *The Sexual Laws* are not in the extreme two ends, though this is a tautology. The average men cannot stop having sex with or without women, and do not rape or murder to satisfy their sexual desire. Only the superman can practise total abstention of sexual activities and thoughts. I don't see any sense in defining the average using the statistical terminology since this series of books does not rely on statistics to proceed with the argument: I usually use the statistics only to reinforce the premise presented. What readers find in this series is a factual common sense. For example, idealism and materialism of Book One start along the common notion of the concepts, not on the philosophical definitions of the scholarly books, and thence proceed to academically acceptable definitions. I leave out some theories of Buddhism which are hard to understand or suspect of values. Some theories of Christianity and Communism are also left out being suspect of values. Certainly heroes or intellectual giants are not average but the masses have to understand them before they can be the leaders of their claims within the society. If the geniuses are beyond the comprehension by the bulk of the population, which happened, I am sure, often through the course of the human history, they do not exert much influence within the society. It is true that the main proposition in Book Four and some thoughts on Book Five are contrary to common belief; however, I put meticulous care such that people with today's average intelligence can understand them without much difficulty. Hence the average people can carry out the messages with ease once understood.

Some readers may find some of my presentations rather hard to understand at the first reading. However, after a few readings they will find that the messages are all common sense, the difficulty, I surmise, being in following unfamiliar factual details.

It is interesting to explore this point a bit further. Beethoven produced many kinds of music and the general public enjoyed his vocal works, orchestral music and piano works. However, the bulk of the music lovers could not appreciate some of his chamber music and one critic commented that Beethoven went beyond the scope of general understanding. We can find another example in the people's desire to have children. As I expound in conjunction with Chinese dynastic cycles in Section 2, Chapter 2, Book Four, the governing elite of Communist China did not realise the serious problem of the overpopulation until after Mao's death in1976. They went ahead with the implementation of One Child policy realising the seriousness of the overpopulation. The Chinese public ignored any scholars who publicly had voiced the opinion that it was better to suppress the population growth before 1976, rather through the history of China, as far as I can ascertain. The Chinese scholars in the historical China knew that the fundamental cause of the dynastic changes was overpopulation, though in the historical narrations they mentioned the specific reasons for the changeover of the particular dynasties in accord with the evidence available. Also some scholars stressed the spiritual side of the Chinese people and maintained that the dynastic change was due to the failure to maintain the Confucian values in the society. That is to say, some scholars in China narrated Chinese history from the temporal point of view and some, from the spiritual point of view. In the Bible, the narrations are centred on the will of God, that is, on the spiritual viewpoint.

Though I designed each book to be read on its own, there is some glue to connect all the books into the whole set. The development of the books goes something like this. Many historians have wondered why China lagged so much behind the West in the modern era in spite of the fact that the former was far advanced than the latter in the classical and medieval eras of the European classification. Chapter 5 Possible Causes for Rise of Europe and Decline of China tries to fathom into the underlying causes of this historical fact. During the Sung period (960-1279) China was possibly ahead of Europe technologically as much as five centuries (Harris 1999, p. 38). More than half of the basic inventions and discoveries upon which the modern world rests come from China (Temple 1986, p. 9). The superiority of the East over the West is shown in the indications such as by a large number of inventions including three greatest inventions in human history by the Chinese, by the Huns' incursions to the West in the fourth and fifth centuries and also by the expansion of the Mongol Army into Russia and Eastern Europe in the 13th and 14th centuries. Western Europe was saved from the Mongol conquest by a fortuitous circumstance. For the detailed treatments see Section 4, Chapter 2. The opposite trend in the modern era is shown among other indications in the superior material cultures especially military equipment, manifested in the process of colonisation of the East by the West European nations in the 19th century. I expand this historical happening in Chapter 4. In the process of delving into the reasons I noticed that the above expression 'China was advanced' must be qualified by the word materialistically and it seems, judging from the comparative historical developments of the East and the West, that Europe was superior to China since the classical era in regard to the spread of idealism.

Book One focuses on idealism and materialism, though these ideologies are only two among the several manifest dogmas of human race. Idealism is the theories of everyday life, focusing its attention on the mind; materialism is the theories of everyday life, focusing its attention on the objects. I have stressed in this series of books that acquisition of necessities of life, sex, religion, idealism, materialism, racism, nationalism, sexism and arts dominated the human minds as distinct ideologies together with non-ideological means of survival, and both decided the course of human history. Idealism may be the means how to live successfully for the individuals and the societies, and in practice shown as ethics. The crystallisation of fear and suffering may be religion, which I expound in Book Two. Idealism and religion are strongly bonded and it is impossible to separate the two in practice, though they are entirely different in essence as I show for Buddhism and Christianity. An extreme manifestation of materialism may be communism, which I appraise in Book Three. In the latter book I propose the concept of Partial Communism which aims to overcome the deficiencies of capitalism by incorporating some communistic doctrines into capitalism. The economically advanced countries are trying to do away with racism and sexism at present.

The main contrasts in Book One are China proper and Western Europe, and idealism and materialism; in Book Two Buddhism and Christianity; in Book Three capitalism and communism. I have kept these contrasts in mind and used the results as much as practical in writing this series of books. Masters and Johnson were more impressed in the course of their sex research with the similarities of men and women than the differences which the general public often emphasise. For this aspect of the research, refer to Section 14 Sexual Differences between Men and Women, Chapter 1, Book Five *The Sexual Laws*. Analogously, I was more impressed with the similarities both between China proper and Western Europe and between Buddhism and Christianity in the course of my investigations than the differences which the general public often emphasise. In the course of explaining religion, for example, Buddhism, I quote another religion, for example, Christianity. Readers may find this presentation strange. I place an emphasis on each unity of idealism and religion. I highlight the differences in the clearly defined manner. All these similarities are surprising, but came about naturally and inevitably, not by accident, because many human activities consciously or subconsciously stem from and lead to survival instinct. Survival is the focal point, if not all, of human thoughts and decision making processes.

I expound next the central theme of this series of books in Book Four *The Third Prophecy*. The concept 'To love a child is not to conceive one', though quite simple once understood, tells us a great deal about the past and future of the human race. I organise this series of books such that The Third Prophecy gives the answers to the fundamental questions posed in Book One *Idealism and Materialism*. It argues that the general public have not received the full benefits of the first two prophecies, that is, idealism and materialism. Idealism failed to achieve the general practice of its teachings in the course of human history in spite of its splendid theories. The teaching 'Love thy neighbour', the essence of idealism in practice as I understand, has never been the dominant feature of the human existence through the course of civilisation. However, the West fared comparatively better in this respect because of the institutional advantage to effect idealism, and it seems that the West was ready for the next stage of materialism at the end of the medieval era. People in the West could not satisfy themselves with idealism and paid attention to materialism as their leading doctrine in due course. The different manifestations of idealism between China proper and Western Europe came from the different institutional setup which embraced idealism in their societies.

The social practice of 'Love thy neighbour' was incomplete throughout the human history of the world, though the idealism itself was completed by the early classical era, Book One (Section 1, Chapter 1) defining the era classification.

Some concepts of idealism go against natural instincts of people. Education centred on idealism tends to encourage suppressing natural passions such as the desires for wealth, one manifestation of materialism, and sex. For example, the Islam Scriptures state that the acquisition of wealth and women is the vanities of the world (Qur'an 7.169).

When Plato proposed the state rule by the philosophers in his *Republic* in the early classical era, not only the state but the philosophers meant differently to him as they do to the modern people. Similarly the concept 'Love thy neighbour' beyond different places and different eras--the ancient era lasted thousands of millenniums--had different presentations and connotations to the ancients as has to the modern people. I explain these points in A, Section 3, Chapter 7, Book One. We tend to understand the concept in the literal sense. I have come to believe that 'Love thy neighbour' for the ancients really meant 'Love one another', leading to ethics or morals directed to the fellow human beings not restricted to the neighbours. I found that the concept is the set expression of the Bible, and the ancient Greeks made some use of it. Certainly some people over the world used the expressions in contradistinction to the above general usage. The reasons for my adopting the ancient use will become clear as readers go on reading the text.

Confucianism stressed reverence among the family members especially filial piety, which resulted in the strong family ties still observable in the Chinese families today. The families were the ubiquitous social units in the Confucian contemporary society as in any other societies, though the firms and the state bureaucracy were also prominent units in China. The ancient Greeks sought justice in their society. Asoka (c. 265-238 BC) of India enjoined his officials--the evidence indicates he really meant it--to attend the needs of common people and to dispense justice impartially. This instruction is applicable to any society, past and present. Asoka was guided by Buddhism. Islam encourages charity. The book of Zechariah says, 'Do not oppress the widow or the fatherless, the alien or the poor' (Zechariah 7:10). These are the manifestations of 'Love thy neighbour'.

The Bible (Exodus 20:12-7) well expresses the essence of the concept 'Love thy neighbour', as I use in this series of books as the ancient people did, in the following concrete form:

- Honour your parents.
- You shall not murder.
- You shall not commit adultery.
- You shall not steal.
- You shall not give false testimony.
- You shall not covet your neighbour's possessions.

Similarly *The Dhammapada,* a Buddhist canon, discloses the following ten kinds of evil to avoid: killing, stealing, sexual misconduct, lying, slandering, harsh speech, vain talk, covetousness, ill-will, false belief (Narada 1993, p. 45).

The central theme of Confucianism is ren (jen), usually translated as benevolence or love. As I explain in Section 2 Various Religions, Chapter 1, Book Two *Religion*, it is more fitting to give it an active rendering of 'Love thy neighbour' rather than the above static meaning:

As a matter of fact I cannot make a distinction between ren (jen) and 'Love thy neighbour' and they mean the same idea.

Christianity and Buddhism go beyond the concept of 'Love thy neighbour'. In fact the core theories of these religions have little to do with idealism in spite of the fact they spare a large part of their teaching on idealism, that is, 'Love thy neighbour'. I explore the essence of these religions in chapters 2 and 3, Book Two.

Development of Idealism (Judaism, Christianity and Islam)

I am to explain why and how idealism developed in conjunction with Judaism, Christianity, Islam, and under the next subhead, Confucianism; since these strands of thoughts start the series forming the bases of the comparison between Western Europe and China proper in this book. The doctrines of Christianity and Buddhism come to sharp focus in Book Two *Religion.*

Preliminary Remarks

The Buddha lived ?563-483 BC; Confucius, 551-479 BC; Socrates, ?470-399 BC. It is amazing that these three sages were virtually contemporary people, living in 6th or 5th century BC. Books One and Two expound the teachings of these characters together with those of Jesus Christ (?4 BC-?AD 29) and Muhammad (?AD 570-632).

Karl Jaspers, a 20th century Western philosopher, saw a turning point in human history in the 6th century BC. In this century lived the Buddha, Confucius, Zoroaster, Deutero-Isaiah and Pythagoras. The appearance of the wise men with their idealism marks the end of the ancient era. The surprising uniformity of idealism the world over means that idealism is the fundamental laws of human existence, and the reason for its painfully partial success is the starting point of this series of books. The consolidation and dominance of idealism in medieval society follow the diffusion of idealist doctrines in the classical era. Materialism characterises the modern era. The era classification of Europe corresponds well and justifies the above developmental statements of idealism.

I expound the following lines of thoughts in Section 2, Chapter 1 Birth of Religion, Book Two *Religion.*

It is a general rule that people produced great arts when the society as a whole went through joy and happiness from the social (political, economic. military etc.) events. The Greeks produced great and varied arts when they learned how to express their oral language in writing and formed the city-states in the eighth century BC, and further won the crucial wars against the Persians in the fifth century BC and the Greek cultures came to the full bloom. The Greeks were proudly conscious that they lived under democratic rule whereas the Persians under tyrannical rule. The English brought the flowering of the literature, a form of arts, in the Elizabethan era when they entered the peaceful era from the religious wars in England and achieved naval victory against the fearful enemy Spain. In the process the English made the English language respectable in the contemporary European society where Latin (international language, and language of learning) and French (upper-class and prestige language) prevailed. The Puritans opposed the promotion of literature, which supports the view that religion and literature are quite different originating from different causes. Flowering of fantastic English literature had much to do with interest and encouragement by Queen Elizabeth I and was virtually confined to her reign, though she also encouraged the other forms of arts such as paintings, potteries and decorative arts.

The T'ang dynasty is together with the Sui dynasty credited with unifying China against the fearful northern barbarians. The T'ang dynasty (618-907) was the high point in Chinese history characterised by marked cosmopolitanism, though the rebellion (755-63) led by An Lu-shan brought the large scale destruction and broke the prestige of the empire. T'ang era is said to be the golden age of Chinese literature, especially in the form of poems. Unfortunately these highly refined poems can be understood only after mastering the Chinese characters though we can appreciate history, various ideologies and even prose literature produced in China at the various eras through good translation.

I am to reinforce the last statement by my personal experience on *Strange Stories from a Chinese Studio* (1740) written by Pu Songling. He was born to a poor merchant family in 1640. He earned his living as a private tutor most of his life. He passed a bachelor's degree (Xiucal) before he was 20 but failed many attempts in examination to get a master's degree by his neglect of standard fields of academic study and also possibly by lack of social standing. This gives us the idea that the examination system was defective in some ways. He eventually obtained a master's degree (Gongsheng) when he was 71 by his achievement in literature, not by passing the examination. The English title of the book given is grossly inadequate. Reading the book gave me so much pleasure that I simply did not want to go to bed. I learned later from various sources that many people had the same experience. I did not get any pleasure reading English translations; it is simply not possible to translate the beauty of the original Chinese. This book is the most impressive book I read in the use of language in all my life.

There are two sets of great epic poems in India composed in Sanskrit: *Ramayana* was composed c. 300 BC recounting the feats of Ramachandra, and *Mahabharata* was developed over the centuries and reached its present form c. AD 400. Appearance of *Ramayana* coincides with the establishment of the Maurya Empire by Chandragupta Maurya which unified north and south of India for the first time. The present form of *Mahabharata* appeared during the reign of Chandragupta II (c. 380-c. 415), one of the most powerful emperors of the Gupta Empire. It is an important source of information for history and Hinduism. The earliest version was composed c. 400 BC, and a few empires rose and fell till the establishment of the Gupta Empire. Though *Mahabharata* deals chiefly the struggles between two rival families, it contains many separate episodes and describes the development of Hinduism.

On the opposite end the people had to devise religion and idealism when they felt extreme fears and sufferings from various causes. They could not solve the unbearable sufferings with all the means they knew. The primitive people called for the help of gods when they felt powerless against such forces as the overwhelming powers of nature or deadly diseases or fearful enemies. In an effort to appease gods they sacrificed humans and animals, built various monuments and prayed carrying out various rituals. The Chinese produced Confucianism and Daoism when their society was in a political turmoil. Buddhism came forth when the society in India was in political disarray. The Greeks developed idealism represented by Socrates, Plato and Aristotle when their city-states went into decline and the Greeks desperately fought among themselves.

Extreme sufferings do not come often to any people in the same way they do not to any individual. Normally these exceptional sufferings last only a few generations to any people. This can be contrasted with the formation of arts which can span a lot longer or shorter. The nature and depth of sufferings and joys precisely decided the nature and depth of religion and arts; it cannot be otherwise. The great religion and arts were the products of deep sufferings and extreme joys respectively. The Greeks showed their talents characterised by not only the various forms of arts but the diverse fields of scholarship lasting for centuries. The Greeks came into contact with the high cultures in the Mediterranean world through trade, and by their unique social structure and mental vigour (libido) absorbed these cultures and made their own. It is well known that Athens, a port city-state, was culturally vigorous and Sparta, a land-locked city-state, did not develop refined culture for lack of sea trade, through their existence from ancient to classical periods.

We can find a great artist or a great idealist in the society which was not going through extreme joy or suffering at the time; however, they did not reflect the society and did not have a large number of followers.

I have come to the conclusion that Judaism's origination was of racial cause rather than of social cause, though it was also based similarly on the fears and sufferings of the Jewish people.

Judaism

The Jews feared and agonised in the different way from the Greeks, Chinese and Indians. The above observation can be inferred not only from the lengths taken to form religion and idealism but the nature and depth of the doctrines. The Greeks, Chinese and Indians formed their religion and idealism in the matter of a few generations when they went through sufferings though certainly the doctrines were based on the traditional cultures. The formation of Judaism spanned for a few millenniums while the Jews were under continuous sufferings. It is said that the creative era of Mesopotamia ended around 1500 BC when the Indo-Europeans invaded the Middle East; Mesopotamia is adjacent to east side of the Levant. The Levant is the Promised Land cherished by the Jewish people, though the Old Testament often uses Canaan, the southern part of the Levant. However, the creative genius of the Jews lasted a long time after the demise of Mesopotamia; in fact the Jews creativity did not diminish till the AD first century when the New Testament was completed, that is, all through the compilation of the Bible. The reason might have been the Levantines benefited from the trade and were culturally active as long as the trade flourished since the Levant was open to the Mediterranean Sea on the west side, though the Bible does not mention the trade benefit. Also Judaism shows the intense adoration for God as well as the deep insight into the human natures and relationships, and history, all of which the Jews tried to unravel through the workings of God. The aforementioned religion and idealism other than the Bible disregarded social events such as politics and economics which were the source of the woes at the formation stage. Socrates and Confucius made some comments about politics. These religions other than the Bible mentions gods, Heaven and the Law rather incidentally which do not form their core teachings.

The Jews' sufferings originated in the evil life of the bulk of them. It caused social unrest, and in relation with the neighbouring peoples the Jews faced with the pogroms lasting for millenniums. The prophets among the Jews preached the fellow Jews that they had to depart from their evil way of life and follow the teachings of God, which was the fundamental drive of Judaism. The Bible contains the best of the books written over the few millenniums. This fact also explains why the Bible is esteemed as the best book ever written, The Jewish state survived with so many interruptions. It is true that the Jews saw the formation of their state in their history and they composed literature from joy and happiness. However, the Hebrew Bible as a whole is a religious book arising from the agony of the Jewish people, and also contains racism to preserve their identity. Hinduism also has an element of racism arising from the conquering by the Indo-Europeans over the native Dravidians, and the Hindus thought the caste system integrating classism and racism was a divine order. Idealism, religion and arts are the survival means the humans devised over the millenniums. Plato posited that humans are social beings, and the foregoing observations underline his contention.

Idealism is the domain of the human affairs. Religion is the domain of the absolute, the ultimate and God. The difference between the two is hard to make in practice and I have to ignore the distinction at times. For example, The Wisdom of Solomon (1:4) says, "... because wisdom will not enter a deceitful soul, or dwell in a body enslaved to sin". The argument that this is idealistic or religious is a nonsense.

The Old Testament addresses to the Jews advocating the concept that the Jews are the God's elect or chosen people, though the book does not follow the notion in some parts. The concept is characteristic of the Jewish people and expressed clearly in the Old Testament. For example, Deuteronomy 7:6 reads: For you are a people holy to the Lord your God; The Lord your God has chosen you out of all the peoples on the face of the earth to be his people, his treasured possession. Possibly this idea can be said to be defensive racism of the Jews. Yahweh or Jehovah of the Old Testament is God of the Jewish people and addresses only to the Jews. As a matter of fact, in the ancient world it was a norm that a tribe had gods of its own creation, being isolated and having its own language.

The New Testament and the Qur'an (Koran) had to modify Judaism, emphasising the equality of all the peoples before God, to become the universal or world religions. God of the New Testament and the Qur'an addresses to all the peoples of the world, thus removing the racial element of Judaism.

The evil life of the Jews caused serious social unrest and fear within the Jewish community. Also the peoples surrounding the Jews did not recognise that the Jews were God's chosen people and saw only the evil deeds of the Jews and attacked them for being Jew, threatening the very existence of the Jewish people and the Jewish community or state. The latter was in fact the brute expression of racism directed to the Jews. As the consequence the Jews agonised, which further reinforced the idea of the chosen people. Possibly pogroms gave birth to the concept in the first place. The notion of pogrom was ever present in the consciousness of the Jewish people and appears in many parts of the Old Testament. For example, Genesis 1:8-14; 1:15-21; 1:22 refer to it, and the book of Esther as a whole deals with a pogrom and the favourable resolution for the Jews. The Christian scholars established the story of Esther as a figment of the imagination in spite of the elaborate and detailed setup of the Persian court and the later celebration of the Jewish holiday Purim originating in the story. A small number of the Jews, who were called seers or prophets, preached the people to change the wicked thoughts and life to lead to the salvation, and to prevent the onslaught of pogroms.

I would say that pogroms were the racial reason together with the social unrest to develop Judaism. The prophets being agonised delved into and discovered the fundamental laws of human existence. They realised that life and the world reduced to the relationship of God (Truth) and the devotees rather than idealism which deals with the relationship among the devotees. The former relationship formed the basic tenets of the Jewish faith, and subsequently the Christian and Islamic faith.

This is the clue to understanding Judeo-Christian-Islamic faith. The harsh Jewish society did not allow to embrace idealism. We can see this facet of faith in the history of Catholic and Protestant conflicts, and also the recent brute actions of Islamic State. They have maimed and murdered people in the name of their religion.

The concept of gods appeared universally all over the world. However the acute fears and sufferings felt by the Jewish prophets prompted the deep insight into the human natures and the social phenomena, which they expressed in the Old Testament and later in the New Testament. The prophets lived according to the precepts of God (Truth), whereas the bulk of the Jews did not follow the words of God (Truth). We may think that the prophets should not have agonised over the conducts of the fellow Jews; however, possibly they prayed so fervently in search for the answer that they were able to produce such an impressive work called the Bible. It is often said that the Bible is the greatest book ever written by humans.

The Old Testament has been the survival guide for the Jews, and possibly without it the Jews and their state would have been wiped out from the earth in the course of history as happened to many other peoples now forgotten.

Pogroms have been the continued and bitter experience for the Jews all these millenniums--in fact all through their existence from their appearance on earth to the present. Many Christian communities forced restriction in regard to occupation and domicile on the resident Jews. The Jews often served as money-lenders, which the canon laws forbade the Christians to engage. The reason why the creative genius of the Jewish people ceased after completing the Old and New Testaments is that the Bible was already a completed religion and did not have any need to develop further. In fact the majority of the Jews thought that the Old Testament was a completed faith in itself and did not see any reason why they should advance it further to satisfy their religious cravings. After the compilation of the New Testament, the oral tradition among the Jews was committed to writing to become the Oral Law or Talmud, and also Midrash was compiled. The former deals with Jewish religious laws and the latter a homily on passages of the Hebrew Bible. Most Jews no longer consider that the Oral Law was divinely inspired.

Unlike Christianity and Islam, it is difficult to define Judaism. Judaism has no unitary canon, and various books purport to represent Judaism, and many Judaic practices and beliefs are not even written down, and the Jews practise ceremonies, rituals and holidays of their own. However, there is a general consensus that the Hebrew Bible, sometimes the Talmud added, is the canon of Judaism: the Hebrew Bible was originally written in Hebrew though a few of the books, in Aramaic. The Old Testament is the designation by the Christians and the first part of the Christian Bible, and somewhat different from the Hebrew Bible; however, I always refer to the Old Testament when discussing Judaism on the belief that the substance of the argument does not change. I also do not pay any attention to the different Bible presentations of Catholics and Protestants.

As far as I know no nation other than the Jews took up Judaism as their national religion except in conjunction with Christianity. The large numbers of the Jews living outside the Jewish state have held fast to this religion all these millenniums. There are about 14 million Jews worldwide today, and they live in Israel (4 million), in the US (4.5 million) and in the former Soviet Union (2.2 million).

The Babylonian Exile of 605, 597, 586 BC under Nebuchadnezzar II of Neo-Babylonian Empire was the first so-called Diaspora (dispersion of the Jews among the gentiles) when the parts of the Jews--at least one eighth of the population in the kingdom of Judah including the biblical authors Ezekiel and Daniel--were deported into slavery to Babylonia. Cyrus the Great (?558-529 BC) of the Persian Empire, after conquering Babylonia, permitted the Jews to return to Palestine; some Jews stayed behind voluntarily. During the Hellenistic-Roman period at least one million Jews lived in each of the following regions: Syria, Asia Minor, Babylonia and Egypt. Among these Egypt had the largest Jewish population, and historically most prominent. Alexandria represented the large concentration of the Jews who made up 40% of the population in the first century BC.

Julius Caesar exempted the Jews from the military service. The Roman government allowed the Jews to continue to practise their faith among the Jews widely scattered in the Roman Empire in the New Testament times.

Another Diaspora followed the destruction of Jerusalem by the Romans in AD 70. It has been said that Diaspora (meaning the Jews living outside of their home land Palestine) was greater than the Jews in Palestine (present-day Israel). Since Nerva's reform in 96, the practising Jews paid tax but the Christians did not.

One persistent tension among the Jews under the Roman rule was due to the heavy tax burden on the impoverished Jews. The New Testament has a story (Matthew 22:15-20) illustrating that the Jews paying tax to the Roman government was a sensitive issue.

The number of Christians was insignificant in Judaea or Judea--both are Roman designation for Judah--in the New Testament times. The Christians did not practise the obligation of military service for the Roman Empire. The conflict between Judaism and Christianity grew sharper from the second century onwards.

Christianity

Obviously only the survival reactions from the sufferings of the Jews coming from the evil life and against the onslaught of pogroms are insufficient to explain the compilations of the New Testament. Under the Roman rule the majority of the Jews felt that the Old Testament contained enough teachings to live on. Many Jews were determined to fight against the Roman occupation. However, it became obvious that the Romans were so powerful that the Jews could not shake off their rule. A small number of the Jews were encouraged by the new teaching by Jesus Christ and saw the opportunity to expand their faith in the Roman Empire, compiling the New Testament. They focused the New Testament on Christ, thus Christ had to be God-like without a blemish. We can see the parallel in the adorable portrayals of Adolph Hitler based on nationalism and racism, and Mao Zedong based on communism (an extreme form of materialism), when the German people and the Chinese people were desperately fighting for their sheer survival. After their deaths the failings of these characters and doctrines were exposed.

These Jews, a tiny fraction of the Jewish population, intuitively knew, in spite of the fact they suffered under the Roman rule, that the Roman Empire held a good future development and took a bet that their faith would have a good prospect of preservation in the same way some mothers would feel that their babies would have a good prospect of happiness with good husbands. Chapters 2-8 of Daniel in the Old Testament refer to the Roman Empire as the last empire before the arrival of the kingdom of God--the Jews were not under the Roman rule at the time--hence it is not surprising that the Jews under the Roman rule looked up to the empire to continue their faith. This was the political reason why the New Testament was written in the first place. The later history confirms that their judgement was correct. Though the authors did not openly express the above aspiration in the New Testament obviously in order not to antagonise the Romans, there is sufficient evidence to support the notion:

- The narration of the New Testament starts after the Roman conquest of the Jews and does not refer to its process; there is a time gap of 4 centuries between the last of the Old Testament and the first of the New Testament, thus avoiding a possible conflict with the Romans. There are a few references in the New Testament that the Roman occupation of the Jewish state was a sensitive issue.
- Some scholars say that the New Testament was originally written in Hebrew or Aramaic; however, there is no concrete evidence for their claim. Even the claim is justified, it does not alter the argument presented in this paragraph. It is popularly believed that the New Testament was written in the Koine, common Greek of the time, which many of the peoples in the Roman Empire understood in spite of the fact that Jesus Christ spoke Aramaic (originally the language of Aram, present day Syria), the lingua franca of Palestine in the New Testament times. However, the written Hebrew as a sacred language of Judaism did not lapse. Aramaic was the mother tongue of Jesus Christ and closely related to Hebrew, and both are Semitic language. It seems he also spoke Hebrew or Greek depending on whom he was speaking to. Today Hebrew is the national language of Israel. Latin was an official language in the Roman Empire, though the East Roman Empire changed the official language from Latin to Greek. Anybody aspiring in the Roman government post had to master Latin or Greek while anybody aspiring in high culture, Greek. Though the creative period of the Greek culture ended a few centuries earlier, the Greek language was a prestige language giving people the inspirations in the various fields. The empire was half Roman (or Latin) and half Greek as the common languages apart from

the indigenous languages as for Aramaic in Palestine. Thus the Roman Empire became the transmitter of Greek culture to later centuries. The Christians used Greek as their liturgical language well into the 3rd century. The use of the Koine for the New Testament rather than any other language would have secured the maximum readership within the empire.

- All the authors of the New Testament were careful not to criticise or attack the Romans and the Roman Empire. Four Gospels absolved the guilt of Christ's crucifixion from the Roman governor and placed the blame on the Jewish mob. I detail the circumstance in Section 2, Chapter 1, Book Two *Religion*. Also Paul left out all references to Jewish nationalism. It was the strong tradition of the Old Testament to lament and fiercely attack the foreign domination of the Jews. The prophets in the Old Testament preached that the conquest of the Jews by a foreign power as well as pogroms were an abominable evil resulting from the lack of faith in Yahweh. Though the authors of the last books of the New Testament were aware of the Roman persecutions of the Jews and Christians, none of them referred the matter in their books.
- Since many peoples lived in the Roman Empire, the authors had to stress the equality of peoples in order to spread the faith within the empire. The equality of the various peoples of the New Testament replaced the concept of God's elect of Judaism. Yahweh or Jehovah in the Old Testament is God presiding only over the Jewish people, whereas God in the New Testament presides over all the peoples on earth. Namely the New Testament removed the racial component of Judaism, though the New Testament suggests that Jesus Christ was race conscious as well as nationality conscious.
- Paul was born a Roman citizen. All the missionary journeys made by him were within the empire. He made a trip to Rome via a few places in AD 59-60. Paul had earlier addressed *Romans* (AD 57) to the Church of Rome and made systematic exposition, containing many important theological themes.
- The Old Testament is hard to understand in some parts, and lay followers needed the professional priests to interpret. Further, to appreciate some parts of the Old Testament requires a good knowledge of history in the Middle East. Hence the New Testament without the difficulties of the Old Testament had to be presented to spread the teachings among the various peoples in the Roman Empire. I entered Christianity through the New Testament, the Old Testament being hard to understand.

The compilation of the New Testament was really a revolution within the confines of both Judaism and the Jewish Kingdom, the latter of which was within the Roman Empire. In the broad perspective, I believe, the different presentations of the New Testament from the Old Testament are insignificant except for the racial concept of Judaism.

The Christian scholars generally agree AD 50 was the earliest year when the first book of the New Testament, Matthew or Mark, was written. The last book of the New Testament Revelation was written circa AD 95, when the Christians were entering the time of persecution as the Roman government came to adopt harsh measures. The New Testament is a coherent unit under one direction as I mentioned earlier. All the above evidence points to the strong possibility that the authors wrote compulsively even if we doubt they met to discuss the outline of the books during the half century.

I also have some doubt about the reason to crucify Jesus Christ as narrated in the Gospels. The Roman government could have been afraid of the spread of Christ's teachings while he was alive and even after his death to eventually conquer the Roman Empire. The authors of the New Testament tactfully organised the Testament to centre on Christ hiding their true intents aforementioned.

Pompey, the Roman general, captured Jerusalem in 63 BC, and Augustus incorporated Judaea into a Roman province in AD 6 and respected the Jewish customs taking into account their celebrated nature. The reigns of Jewish kings elected from the family of the Hasmoneans had been disastrous and the Jewish people accepted Roman suzerainty with relief (Eliade 1982, p. 264). Jesus Christ was born in 6 or 5 or 4 BC and the New Testament was written under Roman occupation.

Nero, a Roman emperor, executed many Christians accusing them of starting the Great Fire in Rome in 64. This is the first recorded Christian persecution. Titus's legions crushed the Jewish revolt against Roman occupation in 66-70. Hadrian savagely put down another and last insurrection in 132-5. (p. 264) The Zealots refused to recognise the authority of the Romans, encouraging the armed conflicts against the Roman rule and resulting in the above two large scale engagements. The Zealots was a fanatical political party rather than a religious organisation. Though the Christian scholars later identified some disciple of Christ as a Zealot, the Christians made up only a small number of people at the time even in Judea. The Zealots drew their inspiration from the Old Testament as well as nationalism to overthrow the Roman rule from their homeland.

The people within the Roman Empire at first did not know much about Christianity and were generally tolerant. Then the persecutions started as the number of the Christians increased. Fundamentally, the monotheism of Christianity was incompatible with the pagan practices and the emperor worship of the Romans.

Systematic persecutions of the Christians began under Diocletian, a Roman emperor, in 303, and reached their peak under Galerius and Maximian. However, the religious toleration spread thereafter in the Roman Empire. The Roman governing body realised that there were so many Christians that they could not suppress: the Christians numbered 5 million out of the total population of 60 million in the empire by the end of the 3rd century. West Roman Emperor Constantine converted to Christianity in 313. The two emperors Constantine and Licinius (East Roman Emperor) signed the Edict of Milan in 313 guaranteeing the religious toleration for the Christians in the Roman Empire. They wanted the Christians on their side in the aspiration to become the sole emperor among the seven emperors who had shared the same ambition in the early 4th century. Constantine subsequently defeated Licinius in the battles in 324 and became the sole emperor. Emperor Theodosius, born in Spain of Christian parents, prohibited the pagan (non-Christian) worship within the Roman Empire in 391 and ordered all people to attend Christian services in 392, making Christianity the official religion of the empire. Thus the Christianity spread within the empire, thence to Europe and beyond.

Accordingly the Jewish faithfuls enacted the spiritual conquest of the Roman Empire in a few centuries as the authors of the New Testament had envisaged. It is rather strange to note that during the century after the conversion of Constantine, the religious riots continued and the most prominent among them were the Christian sectarian strife rather than the pagan persecutions against the Christians or the Jews. The emperors assumed the right to interfere and often did so. However, in the reign of Theodosius, Pope Damasus and St Amrose protested saying that the state should restrict to the secular arm and further the church had the right to judge the emperors. This protest initiated the conflict between the state and the church.

The Bible had the advantage of presenting various approaches and different theories but they were not consistent in some parts, which gave rise to the difficulties and the different interpretations. Let us introduce examples. The author of *The Imitation of Christ* proceeds his religious thinking from the concept of afterlife. If the author had not believed in afterlife some of his religious thinking would have been a void. Some books of the Bible do not support the existence of afterlife. He exhorts himself ceaselessly to attain the eternal salvation; however, he also at times stresses that only the grace of God effects the salvation. The author is blissfully unaware of these different presentations of the Bible. In fact the Bible presents various beliefs.

Though the Qur'an's presentation and beliefs seem consistent, it, on close examination, presents considerably different styles and contents. There were certainly the doctrinal controversies in Islamic theology; however, the serious differences were more political such as whom to appoint as the caliph successor.

Jesus's ministry lasted perhaps three years and most of what he said came from the Old Testament. The New Testament relied heavily on the person of Jesus Christ and his miracle works to proceed on the foundation of Judaism. Christ told to the persons who received the miracle cures to keep quiet about them (e.g., Matthew 8:1-4). I thought it rather strange when I first read—the Bible does not state the reason—but it seems he had a few good reasons. It is unreasonable to expect that the recipients of miracles should not tell about the cures; what happened was contrary to Christ's instruction. Many miracles performed by Christ were similar to those by Elisha in 1 and 2 Kings. Christ's main attraction, as I see, was not so much the verses he quoted but he lived according to the teachings of the Old Testament and his life could be equated with his teachings, thus fulfilling the essence of Judaism in his person. Hence he was accorded the title of the Son of God in the New Testament, and some Christians have regarded him like God and some God itself.

The gospel of Christ was repeated four times to cover up the lack of documentations. The author John wrote (John 21:25): Jesus did many other things as well; If every one of them were written down, I suppose that even the whole world would not have room for the books that would be written. The author must have been aware that the information available about Christ was scarce and made the above defensive statement, to console himself or counteract any comment that might arise in the future. The Qur'an, though as bulky as the New Testament, makes a similar excuse in the verse 18.109: If the ocean were ink (wherewith to write out) the words of my Lord, sooner would the ocean be exhausted than would the words of my Lord, even if we added another ocean like it, for its aid. My Lord in the above sentence does not refer to the prophet Muhammad but refers to God generally, hence the sentence does not present any difficulty. Still the Qur'an relies on the repetitions for emphasis as well as for multiplication.

I make the doctrine 'Love thy neighbour' (ethics) as the central plank of idealism of the various religions. Judaism, Christianity, Islam, Buddhism, Greek philosophy and Confucianism all uphold the doctrine, and these faiths at times make a general statement that we have to conform to the above doctrine because it is the way of God or Heaven. In Book Two *Religion* I make clear that idealism is only one way of reaching to the absolute or the ultimate and is not the core theory of Buddhism and Judaism, hence, Christianity and Islam.

The Bible, especially the New Testament, clearly states the reason in the way the authors believed. Be holy because I, the Lord your God, am holy (Leviticus 19:2). Since God is holy, we must be holy to draw near to God (1 Peter 1:16). Everyone who has this hope in him purifies himself, just as God is pure (1 John 3:3). Dear children, do not let anyone lead you astray. He who does what is right is righteous, just as God is righteous. (1 John 3:7) Whoever does not love does not know God, because God is love (1 John 4:8). Dear friends, since God so loved us, we also ought to love one another (1 John 4:11). If we love one another, God lives in us and his love is made complete in us (1 John 4:12). God is love. Whoever lives in love lives in God, and God in him. (1 John 4:16) Do not love the world or the things in the world. The love of the Father is not in those who love the world; for all that is in the world--the desire of the flesh, the desire of the eyes, the pride in riches--comes not from the Father but from the world. And the world and its desire are passing away, but those who do the will of God live forever. (1 John 2:15-7)

In fact, everyone who wants to live a godly life in Christ Jesus will be persecuted, while evil men and impostors will go from bad to worse, deceiving and being deceived (2 Timothy 3:12). Jesus Christ faced persecution for his conviction, and Paul met fierce oppositions in spreading Christianity.

The Mahayanist Buddhists answer thus: It is because we are all one in the Dharmakaya [the ultimate truth or absolute reality] and because when the clouds of ignorance and egoism are totally dispersed, the light of universal love and intelligence cannot help but shine in all its glory. And, enveloped in this glory, we do not see any enemy, nor neighbour, we are not even conscious of whether we are one in the Dharmakaya. There is no 'my will' here but only 'thy will', the will of the Dharmakaya, in which we live and move and have our being. (Suzuki 1973, p. 48)

I have come to understand that God is equated with Truth and Truth with God. God is not someone existing in heaven directing the human affairs--except in the sense of the figure of speech. God is the universal truth which has worked for both the believers and non-believers among the various races since the creation of the universe. Whether people believed in God or not, Truth was there irrespective and worked its way through human life. If people follow Truth, they are sure to reap blessings; if people go against Truth, they are sure to reap curses. These observations are virtually the definition of Truth. If Truth does not have these concrete results we should not bring out God or Truth. Some people saw Truth and some did not. All the arguments in this series of books proceed on this basis and this premise has not contradicted all my religious experience. As I point out in Section 1 Quiddity of Judaism-Christianity-Islam, Chapter 2, Book Two *Religion*, it looks that this interpretation goes against some of the biblical narrations. However, my overall assessment is that this interpretation enhances the worth of the Bible. The idea is similar to that of Spinoza who identified God with the universe. Also one idealist contention that Truth is the whole or the absolute supports the concept. Yahweh of Judaism, God of Christianity, Allah (meaning God in Arabic) of Islam, Heaven of Confucianism and Greek gods in Mount Olympus are all truths though presented from the different cultures or angles. Jesus Christ was so close to Truth or God that he was virtually identical with Truth or God. Hence the statement Jesus Christ was God (Truth) does not cause any problem. Also this interpretation enables people to learn about other religions (they are all truths) and promotes the harmony among the religious of different faiths. Buddhism refers only to the Law or truths but not to God, as far as the essence is concerned. The Buddha said, 'Follow my teachings not as taught by a buddha, but as being in accord with truth'. Truth is everywhere the same and is attained through the removal of ignorance. (p. 56-9)

When we suffer we are close to God (Truth). When we indulge in pleasure we are away from God (Truth), and naturally we do not pay attention to the matters important to us and we are punished accordingly. Refer to Psalms 73:27-8 and 145:18. Also the Bible says, 'He is a holy God; he is a jealous God' (Joshua 24:19). Hence those who suffer can see Truth more clearly than those who indulge in pleasure. Deeper sufferings for longer periods lead to deeper truth and the more intense pleasures for longer periods lead to mundane philosophy.

Jesus Christ and Muhammad were born in the middle of the classical era of the former and the late classical era of the latter and spread their faiths. However, as far as the doctrinal teachings are concerned they made little contributions to Judaism. I have found few concepts in both the New Testament and the Qur'an which do not appear in the Old Testament. Only the last of the Old Testament 'Malachi' was written after 500 BC. In this series of books, the ancient era ends in 500 BC, and the classical era extends from 500 BC to AD 600. The majority of the Jews rejected Christianity (Acts 13:46).

Islam
The Roman Empire extended to Judaea, and to Mesopotamia though only for a brief period, but did not ever control central and southern Arabian Peninsula. Aelius Gallus, under Augustus, opened the Red Sea to Roman use in 25 BC and recognised the Arabian Desert as the suitable frontier. When Muhammad made an appearance in Arabia at the end of the 6th century, the Western Roman Empire was no more, and was a history. Muhammad showed his genius not only in adapting the teachings of the Bible suitable to the Arabs and in preserving the fundamentals of the Bible but in formulating policies as a religious leader. Though there is ample evidence that the Old Testament went through many revisions over the centuries, there is no suggestion that somebody altered the New Testament and the Qur'an (the Koran) once they were written down. We have to realise that before the invention of printing all the manuscripts were copied by hand, resulting in the discrepancies not only inadvertently but from the well-meaning corrections. Though the Bible was available in the Arab world at the time the Arabs had a strong resistance to read it. Yahweh or Jehovah in the Old Testament addresses only to the Jews who were hostile to the Arabs. This is the political foundation to develop the Qur'an for the Arabs. The widespread social unrest and tribal divisions in the Arab world at the time became the trigger. For details see Section 2, Chapter 1; Section 1, Chapter 2, Book Two *Religion.*

The Arabic language in the written form developed through the earlier centuries and acquired the definite form as we know today in the course of the AD 6th century, before the appearance of the Qur'an.

The Arabs and the Hebrews, both being the Semites, are racially and linguistically close: this fact is rather surprising seeing the strong enmity between these two peoples through the millenniums till present. I suspect that there may have been also rivalry over trade. Arabic and Hebrew languages in written forms are phonetic and used to write from right to left. A small amount of learning can overcome the language difficulty, both oral and written, between the two languages. Most Semitic languages including Arabic and Hebrew wrote from right to left in the historical past; however, it seems that some of them changed from left to right in the way European languages wrote.

The Old Testament in Hebrew and Greek, and the New Testament in Greek were widely available in the Arab world before the appearance of Muhammad; however, the Bible in the Arabic language did not appear till the 9th century. We often hear that Muhammad was illiterate and heard the verses of the Qur'an from the angel Gabriel and Muhammad's followers wrote them down. There were many Christians living in Arabia at the time; some were even of Muhammad's own clan. Muhammad had many opportunities to converse with them at home and on his travels.

The New Testament and especially the Qur'an were made easy to understand. The Qur'an has a single format of poems, whereas the Old Testament adopts several formats. Further, one messenger, Muhammad, in his life time presented the Qur'an in the Arabic language, whereas the scores of authors living apart scores of centuries wrote the Old Testament; and the scores of authors wrote in the time span of a half century, the New Testament. For these reasons the Qur'an has the advantage of consistency apart from being easy to understand. We made idea of the Qur'an easy to understand and remember (Qur'an 54.17). However, the special branch called Qur'anic exegesis was developed for the correct interpretations of the Qur'an, though the canon itself was untouched by any criticism and esteemed to contain no mistake, being the infallible words of God. The Muslims are proud that they don't need the priest class to understand the Qur'an. As a matter of fact Islam disapproves monasticism (Qur'an 57.27). Christian monasteries in the Middle Ages had the other functions of catering for the poor and the sick, which was made possible because many people donated money and lands wishing their salvation.

The New Testament originates in the Old Testament as the former contains, as most of the Bibles make clear, many of the verses of the latter as the authors judged as relevant and important. In the similar fashion the Qur'an makes use of the Old and New Testaments not attributing the sources as one messenger of God, Muhammad (Mohammad), judged proper. I am to present next a summary of this aspect of the Qur'an.

The Qur'an does not deviate from the strict monotheism of the Bible (e.g., 10.66, 98.6), utterly rejecting polytheism and idolatry of pagan worship prevalent in the Arab world at the time and makes the prohibition of idolatry as the pillar of Islam (e.g., 29.25, 31.13). The Qur'an describes God as all-knowing and all-powerful, and repeats its attributes in the similar phrases (e.g., Ali 2001, 2.115, 4.85, 6.101, 8.41, 8.42, 9.15, 15.25, 22.40, 35.44, 41.39). It also makes rare reference to omniscient and omnipotent of God (ibid., 6.96, 54.55) The Qur'an makes the concept of paradise and hell the important teaching of Islam (e.g., Qur'an 11.103-8, 35.33-7, 39.72-3). We may summarise the cardinal teaching of Judaism and Christianity in the precept that you shall love the Lord your God with all your heart, and with all your soul, and with all your mind (e.g., Deuteronomy 6:5; Matthew 22:37). However, this teaching is hard to understand and altered to submission to Allah in Islam, though the Qur'an makes some references to love of Allah; Islam means surrender. Submission to Allah and the various expressions used in the Qur'an such as all-knowing and all-powerful of Allah do not carry the full meanings of love of God in the Bible and omniscient, omnipotent of God as the Christian scholars enunciate. Love of Allah plays a minor role in Islam; whereas it plays the major role in the Bible. This evidence among others leads us to conclude that the Qur'an sacrifices the depth of the Bible; however, the former gains in easiness and practicability. Muhammad cleverly used the sentiments of the Arabs in these matters to gain acceptance. The precept of 'Love thy neighbour' is prominent not only in Judaism and Christianity but also in Islam. Islam upholds the view that only God is Truth (e.g., Qur'an 10.32, 10.36, 22.62) and urges the followers to choose the good and not the evil (e.g., 30.41) and to avoid the worldly pursuits such as wealth and progeny (e.g., 7.169, 8.28, 28.60). The Qur'an (5.69) even expressly supports the Old and New Testaments betraying the denigrating remarks against the Jews and Christians later to be cited in this introduction.

However, Islam places different emphases on some creeds of the Bible. The Bible recommends moderate drinking (e.g., Sirach 31:27; 1 Timothy 5:23), but there is no reference to gambling though it prohibits excessive drinking (e.g., Isaiah 5:11). It seems that drinking and gambling were not serious problems in the Jewish community while the Bible was being formed. Whereas in the Arabic community drinking and gambling were acute problems when the Qur'an was being formed. There were constant fightings among the people as the result. Hence Muhammad placed strict prohibition on the two vices (e.g., Qur'an 5.90-1). One scholar commented that after the spread of Islam people stopped drinking and gambling, and fighting ceased and the people lived harmoniously. Buddhism also prohibits drinking and gambling.

The Bible commends prayers as well as alms giving with the accrued benefits (e.g., Proverbs 15:8; Tobit 4:10; Matthew 6:2-13)--Jesus Christ also prayed and advocated alms giving, whereas these two activities are central themes of Islam. The verses similar to the following verses appear repeatedly in the Qur'an:

And be steadfast in prayer;
Practise regular charity;
And bow down your heads
With those who bow down in worship.
(Qur'an 2.43)

Islam does not recommend the mere formality of worship and charity but the followers must put heart and soul into them to gain spiritual benefits. The Qur'an 107.4-7 refers. This can be understood well if we reflect that we have to put heart and soul into learning or physical exercise or whatever else we undertake in order to gain real benefits—we get the benefits according to the natures and degrees of efforts we put in. The concordance is assured whether we believe in religion or not.

Buddhism also makes the distinction of the worldly giving and supramundane giving. If people give away their properties however generous they may be, that is the worldly giving if they are tied by the notions of self, recipients and gifts. Only when they leave behind these notions, they practise the supramundane giving. (Conze 1975, pp. 198-99)

We find the following passages in the New Testament. The holy one to be born will be called the Son of God (Luke 1:35). And those in the boat worshipped him saying, 'Truly you are the Son of God' (Matthew 14:33). And I myself have seen and have testified that this is the Son of God (John 1:34). These passages refer to Jesus Christ and the Son of God is a figure of speech, possibly a metaphor. The following interpretation by Muhammad on this point is amusing. How can he have a son when he has no consort (Qur'an 6.101)? They say; God has begotten a son. Indeed ye have put forward a thing most monstrous. (Qur'an 19.88-9) For it is not consonant with the majesty of God that he should beget a son (Qur'an 19.92). The referral to Jesus Christ as Son of God in the New Testament is a metaphor; whereas Muhammad interprets the Bible in the literal sense.

Christianity and Islam go against some aspects of the religions they originate from. Unless the new religions are superior to the old teachings there are no gains in introducing them. The New Testament repeatedly denigrates the Sadducees and the Pharisees of the Jewish sects. It also places the blame on the Jewish mob for the fact that Christ was crucified. The Qur'an makes the similar references against some followers of the Bible. In blasphemy indeed are those that say that God is Christ the son of Mary (Qur'an 5.17). They do blaspheme who say: God is one of three in a Trinity: for there is no god except One God (Qur'an 5.73, 4.171). Christ the son of Mary was no more than an apostle (Qur'an 5.75, 4.171). Take not the Jews and the Christians for your friends and protectors: They are but friends and protectors to each other (Qur'an 5.51). To the Jews we prohibited such things as we have mentioned to thee before: We did them no wrong, but they were used to doing wrong to themselves (Qur'an 16.118). Qur'an was compiled centuries before the crusades by the European Christians.

The Arabian Nights' Entertainment (*The Thousand and One Nights*) is a collection of about 200 folk tales in the Islamic culture, and its nucleus was of Indian origin though later enlarged. Its earliest reference was the 9th century fragments. The tales refer to all the Christians and in a lesser degree the Jews as sinners and criminals without any hope of redemption. Its authors are unknown. It is a composite work of popular stories developed over several centuries with material added later haphazardly. The work took the present form in Arabic about 1500. We note that the crusades lasted from 1096 to 1291 with the likelihood that anti-Christian statements were added to the stories during and after the crusades.

King Shahryar, a leading character of the stories, is said to be modelled on Caliph Harun ar-Rashid (786-809). He is the fifth caliph of the Abbasid dynasty, and the Islamic Empire with its capital Baghdad prospered under his rule. Many stories narrate his magnificent wealth and palace. He fought many battles against the Christian Byzantine Empire, sometimes leading the army himself. Thus, all in all, it makes sense that we find many anti-Christian sentiments in the stories.

Here are some examples from *The Thousand and One Nights*. The author calls a Christian a dog and son of a dog (Mathers 1953, p. 345). The author wishes that Allah confound and burn a Christian in the fire of His hell and torture him until the end of time (p. 351). A miserable Christian decayed with vices (p. 368). In the beginning Allah created the Fire and shut it within seven different regions of the Globe. In the seventh region Allah put the overflow of the Jews and Christians and this region was by far the worst. (p. 476) The Qur'an is a religious book whereas the Arabian Nights are literature written for entertainment.

Islam denied the divinity of Jesus Christ as Arius (c. 250-c. 336), an Alexandrian priest, and Nestorius (died ?451), a Syrian churchman, did not equate Christ with God. However, in the overall assessment, Islam, as for Arianism and Nestorianism which offered different interpretation on the status of Jesus Christ but were not so radical as to be called a revolution, is based on the Old and New Testaments and does not challenge the authority of the Bible. As a matter of fact Arianism played an important role, not as a creed itself but as a form of Christianity in shaping the destiny of Europe as the text will make clear. The council of Ephesus condemned Nestorianism in 431, and subsequently the faith spread to India, China, Egypt, Central Asia and the Middle East. As I see, Islam is the second revolution by the Arabs within the confines of Judaism. Islam spread in the Arab world and beyond.

There are two more revolutionary movements of Christianity among the Europeans. The Great Schism between the Church of Rome and the Church of Constantinople came rather symbolically by the mutual excommunication in 1054, culminating from the fundamental differences on creeds, culture (Latin vs Greek) and politics over several centuries. Byzantium (the former name of Constantinople), embracing millions of people with diverse ethnic background, was held together by three bonds: Christianity, Greek culture and Roman political heritage (The Editors of Time-Life Books 1988, p. 58). In 1095 Alexius I Comnenus, the Byzantine Emperor, asked for the help of Latin Pope Urban II when his empire was in dire strait from the threat of the nomadic Seljuk Turks. In response the pope called for the First Crusade, one reason being the hope to unite the Eastern and Western churches. The split has lasted to the present day in spite of many attempted reconciliations such as the further crusades, and the annulment of the excommunication in 1965.

The Reformation in the 16th century was another revolution, splitting the Church of Rome which had been noted for its strict control. The Bible itself was not challenged but its interpretations, the church authority and the religious service came under scrutiny. The Catholic and the Protestant Bibles of today have only minor differences, except that the Catholic versions include the 14 books of Apocrypha as appendix to the Old Testament, whereas most Protestant versions do not. In point of fact the King James Version (1611) composed by the Anglican Church included Apocrypha.

Thus Judaism went through four revolutions; however, it is significant that the fundamentals of Judaism were unchallenged though certainly it had disputes and controversies as to its interpretations. We find in the Old Testament all the fundamental concepts of this strand of religion. These observations lead to the conclusion that the four revolutions were in fact more political than religious.

The religions preached by the two prophets, Jesus Christ and Muhammad, made inestimable contributions to the advancement of human kind. The religious faith thus consolidated its position and became dominant in the medieval times (600-1492) in the Western world, and the 7th century onwards in the Arab world. In medieval Europe Christianity as idealism was the basis of the general education, and the church as an institution of their own hierarchy was the centre of the spiritual power in contrast with the governments which were the centres of the temporal power. The church buildings (designated as temple in many other cultures) and the government buildings (designated as palace in many other cultures) were separated and had different functions. The Bible says that money is the root of all kinds of evil (1 Timothy 6:10). The fact of the matter was that the church and the government could not carry on without money apart from the desire for money of the people who worked in these institutions. Similar development took place in China with the modified time frame and with some notable differences.

I am sure that readers are familiar with the church establishments as the vehicle of maintenance and propagation of idealism; hence I do not have to elaborate here. Book One (Section 3, Chapter 1) explains how the church came to dominate European society in the medieval era. I am to outline next Confucianism and the Chinese civil service examinations to give some idea to readers how the system was designed to uphold the cherished idealism in China. I added the relevant information of the Roman Empire, the European nations and Egypt for the sake of easy understanding and comparison. The comparisons clearly indicate that they all strived for survival as individuals and empires, though responded differently under the different settings they were placed. Most of the individuals correlated their survival with the survival of the empires they came under. Without proper knowledge of the fundamentals of both Christianity and the church we do not have good understanding of European history. Similarly, I have come to believe that without proper knowledge of the fundamentals of both Confucianism and the Chinese civil service examinations we do not have good understanding of traditional Chinese history.

Confucianism (Idealism) and Chinese Civil Service Examinations

Idealism was formulated in the early classical era in several parts of the world and subsequently became the educational basis of Europe in the form of Christianity, Greek and Latin cultures; and of China in the form of Confucianism, Daoism (Taoism) and Buddhism. A small number of Chinese emperors favoured Daoism or Buddhism, which became the examination topics to recruit the public servants under these emperors. However, Daoism and Buddhism, though they were quite popular among the general public in China through her history, were rather exceptions as the examination subjects, and Confucianism was the norm in the successive celestial empires. Buddhist Sangha in China institutionally corresponding to Christian Church in Europe had a minor influence on the Chinese society in comparison with Christian Church on the European society.

Confucianism was the teaching by Confucius (551-479 BC). I explain his ethical teaching in Chapter 1, Book Two *Religion.* There were two prominent followers, Mencius (?372-?289 BC) and Hsun-tzu (c. 300-c. 230 BC), though when these two characters were born Confucius was dead at least a century. They were contemporary people, Mencius being older, and formulated Confucianism differently and became ideological adversaries. The difference stemmed from the issue of human nature.

Mencius proceeded with his thought from the premise that human nature is good. He stressed morals, righteousness and democracy; and education was to strengthen the minds. He preached to the contemporary princes that they should cultivate virtuous personal conducts and humane government forsaking the policies of force and intrigues. But he fell on deaf years. He was thought to be an orthodox Confucian, though *Mencius* is the collections of his sayings extending beyond Confucian virtues to the principles of the government policies. Whereas Hsun-tzu proceeded with his thought from the premise that man's nature is evil. He stressed Legalism, propriety (rites and rules), and authoritarianism and totalitarianism, and education was to discipline the human nature. He reasoned that since man was born for a fondness for profits, goodness is the result of conscious activity. Accordingly the Confucians preached the moral teaching and the importance of education; the Legalists advocated the legal stipulations concerning punishments and rewards.

Hsun-tzu has the credit of remodelling Confucianism after the aforementioned framework of his. He also argued after extensively studying the ideologies of 12 eminent philosophers that Confucianism and Legalism are ideologically different, and every thought had defects.

He preached the strong need for the social constraints, and the uniform ideology by the central authority. Confucianism and Legalism were contradictory in some sense but Hsun-tzu formed a logical link between them.

Legalist theoretician Han Fei-tzu (d. 233 BC) and Legalist statesman Li Ssu (?280-208 BC) were Hsun-tzu's students. Han Fei-tzu was a member of the ruling family of Han, a weak warring state, but he was the greatest of the Legalist philosophers in Chinese history. Shih huang-ti (c. 260-210/9 BC), who unified China for the first time in 221 BC, had admired his writings well before he became an emperor. The above emperor of Ch'in launched an attack on Han in 234 BC, and the ruler of Han dispatched Han Fei-tzu to Ch'in for a negotiation. Li Ssu conspired and had Han Fei-tzu imprisoned on a charge of duplicity and made him drink poison to end life. Possibly he was afraid that Han Fei-tzu, his former schoolmate, may gain the emperor's favour ahead of himself by virtue of his superior intellect though Han Fei-tzu had a speech defect. Li Ssu as the Grand Councillor to the emperor carried out the policies. Many of the Legalist policies the emperor adopted were earlier initiated by Lord Shang (d. 338 BC), chief minister of the state of Ch'in, who wrote lengthy Legalist measures to strengthen the power of the ruler.

The Chinese bureaucracy was firmly established during the Ch'in regime whose guiding principle was Legalism. The Chinese people rejected Legalism after the demise of the Ch'in Empire, and the ideology had never regained its dominant status in the Chinese society. However, Legalism survived in China in the Legalistic administrative practices and the penal codes of the laws by sheer necessity till the strong Western influence in the course of the Manchu dynasty. The Confucian scholars were dominant in the Chinese imperial administration since the Sui era onwards but they had to adopt on the side Legalist measures of the emphasis on authority, efficient administration and strict rules. Also the imperial government, though it upheld Confucianism in the official capacity, had to adopt Legalist dogmas in enforcing one law within the boundary of the empire. The Chinese central government had to have the unified ideology of Confucianism, the unified scripts and the unified laws for its survival. Similarly Europe from the medieval era well into the modern era strived to have the unified church dogma, the same language of Latin and the unified church laws for its survival. The Confucians practised such measure as the separation of the court and the government. The court punished the law breakers for the purpose of education from the viewpoint of Confucianism, and for the purpose of punishment for the past offence from the viewpoint of Legalism.

Today's legal system has the above two functions and we use legalism in the sense of strict formulation of and adherence to the laws not referring to any political dogmas.

In retrospect, the success of the bureaucracy in China may have been due to the fact that the Confucians in the administration accommodated some Legalist measures in the prosecutions of their duties. That is to say, they compromised and took the middle path on this matter rather than strictly adhering to their Confucian creed. In fact the middle path is an important teaching of Confucianism as I explain in C Middle Paths, Section 3, Chapter 7.

I also refer to the following observations in the text to follow. The political dominance of Legalism lasted only 15 years ending when the Ch'in Empire collapsed in 206 BC. Daoism and Buddhism made brief political dominance in China.

In Europe the church organisations and the state organisations were separated to the present day since the church was formed based on Christianity. The pope and the church dictated the church matters, and the temporal politics whenever they had a chance for their gains. The politicians, some of whom were certainly Christians in the truest sense, dictated the states. The politicians executed their duties according to their understandings under the policy directions of their governments. This mode prevailed even under the Roman Empire since Constantine Christianised himself and the empire.

China developed the bureaucracy to carry on the business of running the government and the meritocratic examination system to man the bureaucracy. The two preconditions of the existence of bureaucracy in any nation were the system of writings and the literary class. Further, the running of bureaucracy required both record keeping and knowledge on the specific fields of administration.

The Enlightenment philosophers of 17th-18th centuries in Europe favoured to introduce the examinations modelled on the Chinese civil service examinations into the European nations. The concept of the scholar officials and also religious tolerance in China were the major attractions. The idea that only the persons who passed the examinations were entitled to hold the government professional positions was unknown through the history of Europe up to that time. However, it seems that the philosophers did not have the full pictures of the examination system in China, though it became the model of the most governments of the world in the subsequent years. The East India Company in India adopted the qualifying system to prevent corruption and favouritism. Then the United Kingdom adopted the system 1870 onwards and the United States of America 1883 onwards; they were qualifying rather than competitive as carried out by the Chinese government. Virtually all economically advanced countries followed suit.

The adoption of the bureaucratic system in the governments above mentioned was a culmination of ever expanding government in the modern era of these countries. In the medieval Europe only the pope had the effective administration to enforce his will within both the church organisation and the secular kingdoms, and the national governments in Europe simply did not have the financial resources to set up the large administration. Towards the end of the Middle Ages and onwards, the European governments obtained the taxing power to establish standing army and bureaucracy with various administrations. The bureaucracy collected tax and carried out the government policies trying to balance the total incomes and total expenditures.

As ancient Greece and modern England created the tradition of representative democracy, so China contributed to the world the bureaucracy integrating the examination system whose fundamental principle was to recruit and promote people for merits rather than the family background. It is strange to note that when China realised the examination system was obsolete at the late 19th century and subsequently abolished it with the bureaucracy intact, the West took up the idea of examination on their bureaucracy with notable differences. The West imposed the specialised examination subjects with the qualifying setup, while the Chinese imposed Confucianism as the topic of the examinations with the competitive setup.

In China the literary class who got the high pass marks in the government examinations centring in the Confucian classics were as a general rule appointed to the government posts since the Sui dynasty. If we had imposed this idea in Europe, the literary class who got the high pass marks in the government examinations centring in Christian doctrines were appointed to the government posts. This thinking is strange in the modern society. However we have to take into account of the following facts. Idealism represented by Confucianism, Daoism and Buddhism in China was completed subject as much as Christianity, and Greek and Roman literature in Europe were. Whereas the subjects such as politics, economics, science and technology became mature only in the modern era of the European designation, and a large number of the European literati recognised that they were the subjects of serious concern and relevance within some sections of the society. Certainly some literati of the East as well as the West made serious study of the non-idealist subjects before the modern era; however, they were not the general knowledge required for the running of the public service. Thus the European nations decided these non-idealist subject pass as required to fill the public service posts towards the end of the 19th century. The bottom line was that these subjects in the modern setting became indispensable for the practical life and hence the running of the public service.

Though it is true that we cannot place too much emphasis on the morals in the executions of the duties, we can assume that most of the jobs are filled by people capable of doing the duties in the past as well as in the present society. 'Love thy neighbour' also leads people to do their jobs with zeal. The job well done not only in the private industries but the governments make the recipients happy. Aggregate of the ethical persons in the society makes all the difference on the performance and progress of the society.

The two prominent institutions of exuberant bureaucracy and strong family units marked the traditional Chinese society. The ardent Confucians argued through the centuries that these two pillars of the Chinese society were similar in many respects and should be guided by Confucianism. The adoration for scholars characterised China, which often resulted in weak defence and conquests by the neighbouring nations, unlike the Roman Empire which glorified in military strength and conquests of territories. China relied on bureaucracy to maintain its successive empires and the Roman Empire on military force with strict disciplines, though any empire needed the bureaucracy and the military. It has been the general rule that only the military conflicts resolved many serious disputes between the states. The state had to have the military to enforce its laws and to repel any challenges from both within and without its borders. The Roman Empire in fact had a highly sophisticated network of administrative offices, the officials being appointed by custom and the judgement of superiors, and the bureaucracy conducted tax collections and administration. These two empires stood on two legs of the civil service and the military as for any other empires and nations. The two services carried out entirely different functions of the government, and the personnel attributes required to fill in the positions were also entirely different.

The pope and the Christian church have never constituted a state, nor a kingdom, nor an empire. Since the establishment of the Christian church it had the administration but not the army. However, the church condoned the military orders such as the Templars (began in c. 1119), the Hospitallers (recognised by the pope in 1113), and the Teutonic Knights (founded in 1189-90) for the crusades, in the similar way Japanese monasteries nurtured warrior-monks for protection during critical social unrests.

Similarly in the earlier millenniums, Egypt, apart from the army, had the bureaucracy noted for its efficiency contrary to our low opinions of the bureaucracy in general. The fact that the Egyptian civilisation lasted for three millenniums and the Egyptians built huge pyramids and magnificent temples among the other notable creations gives ample credence to the above statement. As a matter of fact the bureaucracy may have been the real cause of the flowering of the Egyptian civilisation by governing the society orderly and efficiently while maintaining peace within the borders on the foundation of huge amounts of crops harvested. We can surmise from the evidence that the tax rates on the farmers were low--normally about 10% of the yields--and the corvèe labour was not harsh excepting for the duration of the huge projects such as pyramid buildings. Because of the annual flooding of the Nile River the farmers harvested a tremendous (4 to 5 times more than on the rain-fed soil) amount of crops; besides the tax rates were fixed according to the level of the anticipated flooding, not the amount of harvested crops as was done in the past and present in practically all over the world. Consequently the Egyptian farmers were willing to work getting ample reward for their extra efforts. Today's bureaucracy may learn from the Egyptian proficient organisation. I detail how the ancient Egyptians built the pyramids in Section 4, Chapter 7, Book One in conjunction with materialism.

The amount of crops harvested depends on soil and weather more than any other factors. The silt carried by the Nile River is extremely fertile. Warm and hot weather was assured from the end of the flood in November to the June harvest of the following year.

Defeating Antony and Cleopatra at the naval Battle of Actium in 31 BC, Augustus became the undisputed leader in the Roman Republic. He became an emperor in 27 BC with the enormous authority concentrated in his person. He carried out various reforms and also ushered in the Pax Romana. Among the various reforms, he broke up the huge army no longer required and set up the standing army and established the imperial civil service manning with equities. Equities were the wealthy class of citizens who originally formed the cavalry in the Roman army. Hadrian (117-138) further expanded the civil service and consolidated the bureaucracy. Constantine (312-337) also rapidly increased the civil service, which was at least 50 times the civil service under Caracalla (198-217).

Diocletian (244-311) separated the empire's civil and military services, and established the most bureaucratic government of the Roman Empire. It is estimated that he doubled the number of men in the civil service including provinces from 15 000 to 30 000. This gave one imperial official for every 1667 to 2167 inhabitants depending on the population estimates. This can be compared with one bureaucrat for every 15 000 people in 12th century China. (Diocletian-Wikipedia, the free encyclopedia)

By this time the emperor's authority was theoretically absolute. However, ironically, the corruption within the civil service and the shielding of the real state of affairs from the emperor made him less effective--almost powerless in some respects--in carrying out his duties and reforms.

The huge civil service marked Chinese empires. The bureaucracy in the successive celestial empires played such a crucial role in the society that the Chinese thought it natural to present paradise and purgatory with the bureaucracy in a similar way the Christians thought it natural to present heaven and hell with angels and devils. The Roman Empire was renowned for its gigantic military apparatus with its extremely high participation rate in the military and also with the need to procure the food supply to feed the large number of soldiers. The Roman army had between 9 and 16 per cent of male citizens in normal times and 25 per cent at times of crises. A large number of slaves--between 2 and 3 million by the end of the first century--were exempt for military service and many of them worked the land for food production. The economic base of both empires was agrarian and both governments' main economic concern openly stated was agriculture, though in fact both relied on trade for prosperity and revenues. In sharp contrast with the above observations, the Jews wanted to maintain their identity and state through the faith in God, as I stated earlier in conjunction with Judaism.

The Romans were famous road builders. We often hear that all roads lead to Rome. The fact that Appius Claudius Caecus began Appian Way, the highway in Italy, in 312 BC, a few centuries before the Roman Empire was established, gives us good insight how the Roman Republic and the subsequent Empire needed the good transport system. The Romans had to have good roads not only to transport soldiers and supplies during war time, but also to unify the empire, for example, to exchange information and to transport commercial goods during both peace and war times.

The governing elite in both empires believed in physiocratic concepts. We can detect mercantile policies in the Roman Empire based on the belief that trade was the source of wealth, though the commercial and industrial activities were completely subordinated to the need of agriculture. The policies of the successive Chinese empires were unambiguously physiocratic based on the belief that land and agriculture were the source of all wealth, and the merchants and artisans were looked down in the Chinese society. Certainly the Chinese carried out the trade (interregional and international) vigorously as any other peoples since the trade was the important source of wealth. However, the Chinese government placed all kinds of restrictions on trade such as imposing perennial heavy taxes or banning to build the seagoing ships in some era. It is interesting to note that the policies of the physiocrats and mercantilists are not the modern inventions as the economic books make us believe but these historical empires conducted the relevant policies.

Scattered states marked the medieval Europe with regional languages, and Latin as an international language, though it was unified religiously by Christianity. Similarly the Chinese thought it to be ideal through the centuries before the modern era that a Chinese emperor ruled a unified state with the same written language under the Confucian disciplines, though the unification by a Chinese emperor was interrupted for many centuries through the Chinese history.

Idealism was fostered by the state in China, unlike by the church in Europe, as well as by the scholars who were versed in Confucianism and had high positions within the governing bureaucracy. The Chinese government even nominated prominent scholars by whom the Confucian classis should be interpreted. By the Ming times the Sung philosopher Zhu Xi (Chu Hsi) was nominated as the orthodox. It was the duty of the government to keep records of the events and history, and as a consequence the bureaucrats left a vast amount of the historical records for later generations. Most bureaucrats were Confucians and naturally they interpreted, and I am sure some altered, the documents according to the Confucian ethics. In the same way the Jewish scholars interpreted, and some altered, the Old Testament according to their religious faith and the new historical happenings.

The different attitudes concerning the maintenance of the Roman Empire and the Chinese empires possibly came forth not so much from the life views of the governing elites but from the necessities. Small numbers of the elites could have expressed dissenting views but the majority must have overwhelmed them as is always the case. We can say that the necessities formed the life views. The Confucians opposed the military whether they were in the government posts or not, and both before and after the Confucian dominance of the government in the Sung era; however, the necessities proved to be stronger than the doctrinal dictates. Once the Chinese empire was unified the incumbent government disbanded the armed forces--I could not find any document supporting the view that money saving was the fundamental reason--and beefed up the military only when there was a national emergency. Whereas the senators always had the urge to expand the Roman territories using the military might though some emperors curbed the expansion move. The governors were appointed, many of whom were the senators, to oversee the conquered provinces, which commanded both wide discretionary power and huge wealth.

We can see the different emphasis in nature too. Some fiddler crab has a tiny claw and an enlarged claw with differing usefulness, the difference stemming for survival. We are at a loss why the other crabs do not have this enormous imbalance in the same way why the other empires did not display the imbalance of military and bureaucracy as the Roman Empire and the Chinese empires displayed.

It is not that the Roman Empire made light of the administrative or bureaucratic arm. The expansion and consolidation of the empire clearly displayed that the Romans were also proficient in this field. In the first place the main reason why the Romans ventured into the empire building was to collect taxes from the conquered territories, which the administration conducted efficiently.

The successful campaigns brought treasures and slaves to Rome, and the colonised territories, taxes. Gaius Marius reformed the Roman Army in 107-100 BC, and the landless citizens could join the reformed army. Before this reform the freeholders of lands made up the bulk of the army. The generals always had to reward the soldiers after the successful campaigns. These new arrangements resulted in dramatic change. The soldiers did their utmost to win the battles, and the generals were assured of their support and eager to open new campaigns driven by ambitions and monetary rewards.

Also the Roman Empire was so to speak open in many frontiers, and the military attacks by the neighbouring or even discontent subjugated peoples would have followed any perceived weakening of the Roman defence. This had been the normal state of the affairs for the Roman Empire since its establishment till its demise when the Western Roman Empire collapsed in the year 476. Even during the Pax Romana from 27 BC to AD 180, the Roman Empire was constantly engaged in wars in spite of the fact that general peace prevailed for more than 200 years. Augustus inaugurated the Pax Romana.

Augustus tried to conquer Germany but suffered the humiliating defeat at the battle of the Teutoburgerwald in AD 9. This defeat convinced him that the empire reached its natural limit and adopted non-expansion policy since then. After his death in AD 14 the empire continued to expand another century. Peace promoted trade aided by the use of the extensive road networks.

In contrast, the successive Chinese empires had closed fronts, once unified, except the northwest where the Great Wall was laid for the defence purpose against the steppe peoples. As I explain in the text (Section 1, Chapter 1) the Eurasian steppes acted as the population pump forcing out a large number of people not continuously but sporadically through the millenniums, which resulted from the changes of the weather pattern. Dry north with easy access by horsemen was much easier to overrun than wet south. It is well quoted in the Chinese literature that the terrain in the south is low and the foot soldiers have a great difficulty in carrying heavy loads especially if it is raining. (Temple 1986, p. 83) In the eighth and ninth centuries (during the T'ang period) China experienced threats of incursions from Tibet and stout resistance from the Nanzhao natives in Yunnan, but they did not result in the long term loss of territories. In this period the Turkic-speaking Uighurs settled in the far west of province of Gansu but were friendly to China. (Ostler 2006, p. 141)

Historically no kingdoms nor any peoples in the south posed any serious military threats to China. This observation is reinforced by the fact the historical migrations of the Chinese because of the overpopulation were mainly to the south. However, since the mid-1950s the Chinese government sponsored large scale migrations to Inner Mongolia, that is, within the Chinese border. Also we hear the recent reports that the Chinese were encouraged migrating to Tibet (southwest): the government judged that it was easier to expand to Tibet than to south-east Asia in the current political environments.

For these reasons it was not necessary for the traditional Chinese empires to maintain a huge army during peace time but they organised the sophisticated bureaucracy to run the country. Reduced military spending meant less tax on Chinese people and more government civil expenditures, which led to the stable government and society. The civil service examinations to man the bureaucracy persisted with some interruptions and modifications through the successive Chinese empires until the early 20th century. The examinations centred on Confucianism helped unify the Chinese people not only in believing in the perpetual system but the sense of common belief in Confucianism. The use of the common and universal Chinese scripts and also the fear of the northern barbarian incursions did similar tasks. The Chinese celestial empires, though punctuated by dynastic changes, lasted a lot longer than the Roman Empire: they existed both before the establishment of the Roman Republic which gave way to the Roman Empire and after the demise of the Eastern Roman Empire in 1453. Refer to Section 2 China's Dynastic Cycles, Chapter 2, Book Four *The Third Prophecy* for the fundamental reasons why the Chinese imperial dynasties had to collapse and start anew.

I made contradictory statements concerning the defence of the Chinese empires. I stated that the Chinese empires did not have to keep strong defence force once unified, yet they were characterised by the weak defence and overrun by the powerful northern barbarians. Why then didn't the elites in the government, civilian and military, by the direction of the emperor build the strong army when they needed? When the foreign power threatened the empire, the ruling body beefed up the army without any doubt. However China simply did not have the military tradition and the soldiers occupied low place in the social hierarchy. Hence the military build-up lacked the planning and executing enthusiasm, the competent officers and the disciplined soldiers.

As I stated earlier, Legalism became out of favour in the Chinese society after the collapse of the Ch'in regime; however it coupled with Confucianism survived in the bureaucracy and the law. Legalism did not become a dominant idea even in the military after the Ch'in dynasty. Its emphasis on authority and strict rules was not enforced in the military: the military as a whole did not have the will to comply though a small number of the military personnel of upper and lower ranks might have wished otherwise.

I am to cite an example of the sorry state of the army in China, taken from the early Ming era. One family in six was supposed to be a hereditary military family, and 2.7 million such families were registered. The soldiers assigned on garrison duties often had to do other works on the side because the officers pocketed the pay and used them as personal servants. They ran away, but the officers did not mind as long as the soldiers were on the payroll, and the officers kept the pay. Though in 1520 the metropolitan battalions numbered 380 000, the real strength was 20 000. (Milston 1978, p. 212)

The Great Wall of China which became the corner stone of defence for the succeeding empires not only symbolically but practically highlights the weakness of the Chinese defence. Even with the existence of the wall the Altaic hordes kept the northern China's population on the perpetual fear. The Chinese hid behind the wall hoping that it would give them the protection from the nomads. The Chinese knew how to make gunpowder as early as the 7th century. However, the Sung dynasty used firearms for the first time at the early 12th century, when the Sung court had to move south under the Jurchen invasions over the wall and the Sung army could not get enough supply of horses being cut off from the horse pastures. We can see the peaceful nature of the Chinese by the delay of adoption of explosives for military use since their invention—as long as 5 centuries. The Southern Sung Empire used firearms against the Mongol army in the 13th century but eventually succumbed. The Mongols in turn adopted firearms. Firearms did not decide the outcome of the battles until the 15th century in reference to Western Europe.

Though Confucius died believing himself as a failure, he became a symbol of thought within two centuries, and Confucianism became the subject of Chinese civil service examinations lasting for two millenniums with some interruptions. From the AD first century his temple was found in every town. The civil service examinations centred on Confucianism and conducted in classical Chinese scripts kept the cohesion of the body politic, Confucianism being the common language, common cause and policy guidance.

Though we can see the embryos of bureaucracy in the Shang time, the bureaucracy in China as we know was established during the Qin (Ch'in) period (221-206 BC). The recruitment into the bureaucracy during the Ch'in regime was based on the recommendations by the local officials. In fact this was the traditional way of appointing the officialdom in China. With the passage of time, the emperor acquired more power and authority to appoint the officials for the government. The Han dynasty (206 BC-AD 220), reorganising the centralised and bureaucratic empire of the Ch'in, introduced the examinations mainly to grade the officials already in the civil service or appraise the recommended officials rather than the recruitment purpose.

From the early Han period onwards through the successive Chinese imperial dynasties, Confucianism became the foundation of education and scholarship in China. In the year 136 BC, Emperor Wudi (Wu-ti) (140-86 BC) by the advice of the prime minister Dong Zhongshu (Tung Chung-shu) (179-104 BC) set up five Erudites of Five Classics at court and proclaimed

Confucianism be the state cult. Five Classics were equated with Confucianism at the time. They were *Classic of Poetry, Classic of History, Classics of Changes, Records of Rites,* and *Chronicles of the Spring and Autumn Period.* Though most of the above classics existed before Kongfuzi (Confucius), he is attributed to writing or editing some of them. His own statements collected in *Analects* (*Lun yu*) were not admitted into the canon at this time. In 124 BC, Imperial University was established in Ch'ang-an, the capital of Han, to train and test the government officials, accepting Five Classics as its core curriculum. Wudi greatly extended the Chinese empire and made Confucianism the state religion. He saw education as the way to strengthen his empire and also the newly educated class as his faithful subjects and an ally against the old aristocratic families. In Europe also the interest in the ancient Greek and Latin classics really dates from the founding of the universities in the twelfth century.

The corpus of Confucian Classics changed over time. *Analects*, the most revered sacred scripture in the Confucian tradition, was compiled by the disciples of Confucius. In addition to *Analects,* three canons *Mencius, Great Learning,* and *Doctrine of the Mean* became of central importance in Confucianism. Chu Hsi (1130-1200), the Neo-Confucian scholar, compiled them into Four Books, which were to be used as introductory texts to Confucianism. *Mencius* elucidated the ideas of Mencius, a Confucian thinker. *Great Learning* and *Doctrine of the Mean* were two chapters of *Records of Rites*, a voluminous anthology. Chu Hsi, as a proponent of Neo-Confucianism, met the fierce oppositions in his life time; however, the emperor ruled in 1237 (posthumously of Chu Hsi) that Four Books, Five Classics and the commentaries by Chu Hsi should be the bases of the civil service examinations. This ruling prevailed since then until the system was abolished in 1905.

The Confucian idealists defended both the feudal order and the ruler and ruled classes. Confucius insisted that the class distinction should be based on intelligence, ability and moral character, that is, by merits. This ideal was in sharp contrast with the feudal hierarchy, though the feudal society was in the process of decay at the time. He regarded the rule by the wise and virtuous as the very foundation of the good government. (Ho 1976, pp. 4-5) He also maintained that only through education people could form moral character and did not recognise any other ways such as innate intelligence or birth. In contrast Plato emphasised the genetic factors, the in-born differences between people, for general intelligence. Up to the life time of Confucius, education was a monopoly of the hereditary feudal nobility and he proposed the equal opportunity of education irrespective of social origins. (p. 6)

During the reign of Han Wudi the government began to employ the Confucian trained graduates of National University, earlier cited as Imperial University in Ch'ang-an. As a matter of fact during the late Chou dynasty the tradition of scholar statesman was established, though the examination system to qualify men for office was still unknown at that time. The idea was similar to Plato's which stated that philosophers should govern the state.

The Sui dynasty (581-618) adopted the Han examination system in a more systematic way, resulting in what we understand as the Chinese civil service examinations. After the demise of the Han dynasty in 220, China degenerated to political fragmentations, and the hereditary aristocracy controlled the political offices in central, provincial and local governments during the disunion. This very problem persisted through the succeeding Chinese empires, and the desperate need for the civil service examinations remained for the emperor to check the privileged families who continually amassed military power based on the wealth derived from land and expected to hold all the important posts in the bureaucracy. Another fundamental reason why the examination system perpetuated through the imperial dynasties since the Sui era was the cost factor, though this aspect was not in the open as far as I can ascertain. The government wanted to save huge amount of money and administration associated by transferring the education from the public sector to the private tutorials. The public education entailed establishment and maintenance of a large number of school buildings as well as training and employing a large number of teachers. Not only did the government save money but they made money by selling the examination titles through the history of the system.

When the Sui ruler, Emperor Wen-ti, restored the order in China in 581, the power of aristocracy constrained the emperor's power to appoint officials. The second emperor, Yang-ti, established the civil service examinations for recruiting the government officialdom and made it a rule to use only the degree holders to fill the vacancies in government posts. During the Sui era it was established that the Ministry of the Civil Affairs be responsible for the appointment, training and dismissal of officials; the Ministry of the Rites, for examinations. The Bureau of Records in the Civil Affairs kept all the records necessary of the individual: the examination records, experience, assessments etc. The terms of office were three years for all government posts and the merit ratings were drawn up at the end of every three years together with the recommendations for appointments and promotions. Thus the Minister of the Civil Affairs became most powerful man in China in many ways except for the emperor, though these recommendations were not the only bases for appointments and promotions.

There were also imperial favours, transfer from the other services, and the hereditary rights, that is, the hereditary aristocrats recommended their own son or a relative for appointment. The degrees and the government posts were also sold for profits. This was particularly pronounced when the government wanted money urgently as in emergency of rebellions or wars. The subsequent dynasties employed these systems with minor modifications. However, with the passage of time money became increasingly important. 1451 onwards money could be directly translated into the degrees, offices and official titles. 1850 onwards money became the main determinant of higher statuses in China, overshadowing academic qualifications. (p. 256) The underlying reason must have been the widespread rebellions in the 19th century forced the suspension of the printing of classics and the civil service examinations. These facts are the clear indications that the Ch'ing dynasty was in chaos and heading for its termination.

The imperial government of China in need of the public servants to fill the government posts instituted the examinations which were strongly focused on Confucianism. The Confucian scholars thus selected and posted adored scholarship and disdained intensely the armed forces and trade, all of which became the characteristics of the Chinese bureaucracy through the ages. The examinations were competitive rather than qualifying, that is, the quota was set to a large number of applicants and the provisions for fair competition were made. The latter fact is shown in that during the Ming era, nearly half of those who passed the highest level examinations did not have any official connections. The competition was fierce and became fiercer with the passage of time. Naturally the corruptions among the examiners and the cheatings among the candidates occurred. Also some men inherited or purchased official posts, bypassing the examinations. All public offices with the exception of the throne itself were theoretically open for the degree holders of the civil service examinations. The succeeding Chinese emperor, even having risen from humble origins, needed the bureaucracy to govern and wanted to see his subjects scrambling for the public offices, himself being secure.

Many families with the strong sense of unity, even poor, supported financially and otherwise the brainy members of the family to study and sit for the examinations. The high pass marks rewarded not only the candidates but the other members of the family in terms of honour and finance. If a candidate passed Provincial examination, his entire family was raised to scholar gentry: the members of this family were exempt from labour service and some tax. It seems that the title was accorded differently in later dynasties. During the Ch'ing era, the holders of Local examination high pass, not the ordinary pass, were called gentry (Lai 1970, p. 2). In the order of merit, Provincial pass was above Local pass and below

Metropolitan pass and Palace pass. These levels of the examinations were established during the Sung era. Only men who passed the examination could sit for the next higher examination. The qualifiers of Metropolitan and Palace degrees were entitled to the official positions which were quite lucrative. Once held a government post, the official was recognised as such even after retirement, often being entitled to the various government benefits.

I would like to define briefly the gentry used in conjunction with the Chinese civil service examinations. During the later dynasties the gentry's position and qualifications were formalised (Chang 1974, p. xiii). The gentry used here is different from the term used, say, in England. The English gentry are the class of people of high birth just below nobility, whereas the Chinese gentry apply only to a particular generation, not hereditary. He is either a regular who passed the government examinations or irregular who purchased the status with less prestige and privileges. As the number of candidates were much larger than the quotas, usually one to two percents passed the higher level examinations (p. 11). The gentry in historical China formed the distinct upper stratum of society in contrast with the commoners: the society expected the former to act as the leaders of the latter in many fields of social activities. The upper gentry who held the titles of Metropolitan and Palace were much smaller in number compared with the lower stratum gentry, and only the former was directly entitled to the official government posts (p. 21). Some gentries were landowners; most, literati; some, the government officials who carried out their duties under the general directions of the emperor. The gentry had the almost magical power backed by political, economic and social privileges. In the European industrialised societies, the qualified (professional and of trades) persons carry some prestige apart from the obvious right to the employment; however, the prestige is very much constrained and only within their profession compared with that in China under the civil service examinations.

Among the privileges, the gentry had exemption from the corvèe and personal tax but not from the land tax and other taxes on property. The corvèe exemption extended to the members of the gentry family. Stipends and other subsidies were provided for further educational advancement. Moreover, the gentry using their influence often delayed the payment of tax and even at times evaded the payment altogether. (pp. 37-41)

The gentry cooperated with the government officials to carry out the government administration and sometimes took actions independently of the government officials. The gentry obtained the profits of the government administration, and in some cases the gentry used their own money to finance the project. In all these the gentry's practical strength lay in the fact that they were the local leaders. (pp. 49-57)

When the government forces were weakened, the gentry members became the military leaders of their local and regional military organisations. During the Taiping Rebellion, the gentry even moved into the field of taxation. (pp. 66-9).

The gentry came to make up about two per cent of the population in China during the Ming period (Milston 1978, p. 202), though the gentry is loosely defined and does not state if they held the official positions or not.

The central government created the gentry, deciding the examination subjects, how they are rated, how the examinations are conducted and the frequencies and quotas of passes. However, the gentry had an enormous power in the Chinese society that looked independent of the government organisations. There is some evidence that the reason why the government sold the title of gentry was, apart from the monetary consideration, to exploit the rivalry between the regulars and the irregulars. (Chang 1974, xiii-xxi)

After the conquest of China the Mongols suspended the civil service examinations in the north from 1237 and in the south from 1279, and reintroduced the system in 1315 which ensured the Mongol admission into high offices. The Mongol government did not accept the serious use of the examination system and hence allowed the growth of the local lordship. Ironically, these regional powers became strong enough to unseat and expel the central government from China in half a century since the reintroduction of the system.

Also the Manchu (Ch'ing) government set the equal quotas for the Manchus though the Manchus constituted only 3% of the population. Though the Chinese outnumbered the Manchus among the most distinguished degree holders, the latter outnumbered the former in the highest civil service posts. (Menzel 1963, p. ix) The Manchu language remained in the government documents until the fall of the dynasty in the early 20th century; however, all the Manchu descents were speaking in Chinese within 150 years since the conquest. The Manchus and Chinese became indistinguishable, despite the various government policies to try not to assimilate the Manchus into the Chinese society.

The governing elite, especially the emperor, wanted bureaucracy to be manned by capable and loyal persons, both of which, they reasoned, could be achieved by persons proficient in Confucianism. Thus one justifying reason for instituting the Chinese imperial examinations was a meritocratic strategy; the able men should occupy the public service rather than the men with special or inherited privileges. The Confucians were by the nature of Confucianism conservative and loyal to the governing bodies. Generally the Confucian Classics were thought to form the basis for good citizens. There was also an enduring dispute as to how to devise meaningful tests for practical qualities: the examinations were often criticised that they had no relation to the ability to govern.

China changed from the matrilineal system to the patrilineal system where the family descent was traced by male line at an early stage, probably during Longshan (Lung-shan) culture, though virtually all communities of the world did at some stage. Longshan culture was at Neolithic stage and dates back to 3000 BC. Women were excluded from the rites of the ancestor worship, the examination system and the public positions (Roberts 1998, p. 14). All three functions were crucial in carrying out the duties in the Chinese society. Law made the latter two exclusions. There were brief periods in the Chinese history that women were allowed to sit for the civil service examinations and hold offices in the bureaucracy.

During the Han era, Six Arts (music, archery, horsemanship, arithmetic, writing, rituals and ceremonies) and Five Studies (military strategies, civil law, revenue and taxation, agriculture and geography, and Confucian Classics) became the examination syllabus. Also the subjects such as poetry, history, administration and government came to be the topics for examinations during the Tang (T'ang) era but they carried far less prestige than Confucianism. By the Ming times only the Confucian Classics were tested; history, and literature such as poetry and essays were tested as parts of the Confucian doctrines in the same way the Christian Bible contains history, and literature such as poetry and narrations as the vehicles of conveying the theological dogmas. The non-idealist subjects were looked down as specialist and technical.

In today's normal use in the public sector, military service is contrasted with civil service. The military service examinations existed in China alongside the civil service examinations with the similar forms of setup. The holders of the military examination pass were accorded the status of gentry as for those of the civil service examination pass but with the low esteem. In the military examinations the main focus was on outdoor martial skills such as archery on horseback or on foot, bow bending, halberd brandishing and weight lifting. There was also a test of scholarship on the military classics. However the military, the government and the society poorly received the graduates of these tests. In the army the war trained soldiers were most highly regarded for promotion especially if they made good contributions for victory. The graduates of the military examinations were supposed to go no higher than the unit commanders. Chiefs of staff, generals, and minister of war were normally selected from the professional soldiers or the degree holders of the civil service examinations.

Even today the government of any country very much constrain the running of the public service in sharp contrast with the private sector, and the public sector has the arms of civil service and military service. In the historical past the Roman Empire emphasised the military, and the Chinese empires, the civil. In both empires the immediate necessities compelled the highest ranking officers in the government to place the above emphases, not for brief periods but for virtually all their existence. Hence the insight into these public services give us good understanding on the respective empires.

The examination benefits were available for many centuries in China for the gifted to be appointed to the important offices; however, the great majority of posts had always been occupied by the members of the upper class (Harris 1999, p. 37). These statements have been the points of controversy by the scholars. Many scholars say the civil service examinations were the motive force of the social mobility in China as was evidenced by many eager young men to obtain the degrees and the government posts as well as by its long existence spanning over the succeeding dynasties, native and foreign. Some scholars say that the system was only a façade to hide the self-perpetuating setup of the aristocracy with some exceptions. As a matter of fact, the emperor appointed the upper echelon of the officialdom. The emperor chose the top perhaps one per cent officialdom out of his clans, the distinguished characters or his favourites, irrespective of whether they held the degree or not. These appointed officials became new aristocracy. In the early era of the T'ang dynasty, the upper echelons of officials were largely recruited from aristocratic families of the Sui dynasty, but a small number (less than 10%) were selected for their literary talents through the examination system started by the Sui. (Murowchick 1994, p. 135) Thus the T'ang emperors had a need to strengthen the examination system to combat the powers of the hereditary aristocracy.

From Emperor Taizong (T'ai-tsung) (626-649), the second emperor of the T'ang dynasty, onwards the civil service examinations were held regularly. Empress Wu (690-705), for example, during the T'ang era (618-907), promoted the scholar-officials through the examination system in preference to the noble and wealthy classes many of whom had held high offices. She could count on the loyalties of the new appointees rather than the incumbents. (Harris 1999, p. 30) She was once an imperial concubine and only woman ever to become the official ruler of China. She bore four sons and a daughter to the reigning emperor, and through her incredibly bold machinations she secured the official title of the empress and exercised her authority with competence. By the end of the T'ang dynasty, the non-hereditary scholar-gentry who passed the examinations formed the bulk of the bureaucrats displacing the old aristocracy, thanks to her policies.

Empress Dowager Cixi (Tz'u-hsi) in the Ch'ing era, though she was the real power behind the throne, was not an empress in the official capacity. She was a low-ranking imperial concubine, but bore the emperor's only son thus came to importance and power.

Under the Sung era (960-1279), the civil service examinations took the mature form and the Confucian scholars established themselves as the China's ruling class, variously called gentry or scholar officials--in fact a new aristocracy of merits, thus freeing the dynasty from the dependency on the old aristocracy. The degree holders made up almost all high level officials in the Sung dynasty, thus the graduates formed the largest group in the civil officials for the first time. In the period 1165 to 1173, the total Chinese civil officials consisted of:

3000-4000 of high class
7000-8000 of low class
(Menzel 1963, p. 7)

These figures do not include the large number of the non-professional government employees. During the Sung era it was established that the examinations be held every three years. The wealth of the Chinese people dramatically increased in this period and as a consequence, the number of candidates and degree holders increased correspondingly. The Buddhist fervour was at its height from 4th to 8th century in China; however, Confucianism triumphed during the Sung period, backed by the dominant scholar-officials. (Harris 1999, p. 111)

The Ming dynasty just after the departure of the Mongols from China had only 5400 civil officials (central, provincial and local) totally with the population of 65 million. Bad administration and heavy taxation marked the Mongol rule, which are often cited as the reasons of their failure in China.

The current public service in Australia (federal, state and local) is similar to the traditional Chinese bureaucracy. The employees in the Australian bureaucracy are divided into the salaried permanent staffs holding the designated positions, and the wages. The permanent staffs obtain the positions by virtue of firstly passing the examinations imposed by the relevant and recognised course, secondly possessing the necessary experience and skills and thirdly coming on top of the merits, that is, competition. These are the official criteria in the gazette; however, there are also the other criteria which decide if the applicants are successful in getting the job or not: some are in the open and some, hushed up. The huge expansion of public services characterises the modern industrialised nations. In fact the bureaucracy in such country as Australia with its 20 million population in the year 2003 is incomparably large compared with the historical Chinese empires. The total number of people employed by the governments in Australia (federal, state and local) is slightly over 1.5 million in the year 2003.

The population of China is estimated to be about 410 million in 1850 (the Taiping Rebellion lasted from 1850 to 1864) and the following figures give the degree holder percentages among the population.

Local (2%)
Provincial (0.18%; 527 000 civilian and 212 000 military)
Metropolitan (0.0065%; 16 000 civilian and 12 000 military)
Palace (0.0009%; 2500 civilian and 1500 military)
(Outline of XIX-Century Chinese Civil Service Examinations. weber.ucsd.edu/~dkjordan/chin/hbcivilservice-u.html)

The scholar-gentry among the degree holders were known to be mandarins since they strived to learn 'official speech', a version of Mandarin, to communicate with people with other regions. As a matter of fact, 70% of the Han Chinese speak various dialects of Mandarin today.

The dominance of Confucianism did not break in China until 1905. The Ch'ing Empress Dowager Tz'u-hsi announced in 1901 the establishment of a new school system for the entire country and the abolition of the examination system, under the pressure from Chinese intellectuals. When the Western ideas flooded into China in the 19th century, the civil service examinations were deemed unfit for selecting the scholar officials who could not cope with the new ways. Thus the mandarin class was choked off the new blood. The Qing (Ch'ing or Manchu) imperial dynasty terminated in several years, that is, in 1911/1912.

The Chinese communists, as for the Russian communists after their successful revolution in Russia, were distrustful of the bureaucracy just after the successful revolution in China. However, the communists of both countries realised that they had to have the bureaucracy to implement the revolutionary goals, and adapted the bureaucracy to suit them. This observation among others indicates that the communist theoreticians were totally out of touch with the realities. In China, the important positions in public administration were manned by new cadres and old cadres, the designations indicating the official entry date into the revolutionary movement. In Russia the Bolsheviks kept the bureaucrats of the old regime except for the top positions, and some bureaucrats gave their services grudgingly and the others wholeheartedly. Many Bolsheviks were indignant that the bureaucracy still dominated the soviet society. Pondering the state of Russia in 1922 after having a stroke, Lenin noticed to his regret the strong growth of bureaucracy. (Kenez 2006, p. 50)

Overall Evaluation of Chinese Civil Service Examinations

As a general rule the number of the degree holders of the civil service examinations, academically obtained or purchased, increased and hence their influence within the government increased with the passage of time. As a rough rule, the authority of the emperors in China strengthened with the passage of time. It may not be right to draw the conclusion that these facts, simple and scanty, are in cause and effect relationship. As a matter of fact the authority of the Roman emperors grew stronger as time went on. I mention in the text the ineffectual emperors emerged from various specific reasons for both empires; some are by the emperors' failings and some, by the circumstances beyond emperors' control. Contrary to the above observations the decentralisation was the definite trend with the passage of time in the ancient Egyptian society, and consequently the reigning pharaoh's authority ever diminished after the firm pharaoh's hold on power in the Old Kingdom. The above passages are referring only to the authority of emperor, and the rise and fall of the empire may be a different matter.

Theocracy is the rule of God, a form of the government controlled by a deity, in practice, by a religious leader. Its examples are pharaonic Egypt, Vatican City, and Tibetan government in exile. Also the leaders of the Jews in the Old Testament were the religious heads and carried out the temporal duties as well, and in effect the government was theocracy.

Caesaropapism (Caesar and pope) is the idea of combining the secular government and the church, as happened in history, with the state supreme over the church. The Byzantine emperor had the authority over the church from the 6th to 10th century and appointed patriarch of the Eastern Christian Church. The Eastern Church did not have the power to enforce the tithe obligation unlike the Western Church, and its authority and finance were not as strong as the Western Church. These resulted from the high probability that the people under the Eastern Church were not as religious as those under the Western Church: the latter, Catholic and Protestant, was independent of the secular governments financially and administratively. Caesaropapism is most frequently applied to the Byzantine Empire but also used to describe Russia after acquiring Christianity from the Byzantine Empire and before the communist revolution, and England after the establishment of the Anglican Church.

In today's organisations the unions can resist the arbitrary rule of the management, private or governmental. In the similar manner the church organisation resisted the arbitrary rule of the emperor or the king under caesaropapism.

In traditional China, emperors had the functions of carrying out both the sacrificial duties and the reigning duties. The emperors had the authority to decide which idealism (Confucianism, Daoism or Buddhism) should be the subject of the public service examinations to man the bureaucracy. As a matter of fact the majorities of emperors favoured Confucianism. They even decided how Confucianism should be interpreted. In Caesaropapism the church had the organisation to resist the power of the emperors but Confucianism did not have the organisation except in the sense that the successful Confucians were in the state bureaucracy. The state bureaucracy was under the strict control of the reigning emperor, and rather strangely Legalism rather than Confucianism governed its organisation. All these facts pointed to one direction of absolute power of the monarchs in China.

I drew the following conclusions in regard to the Chinese civil service examinations from the known facts:

- Military force was necessary to defend the dynasty and to enforce the will of the governing body but the emperor had to have the bureaucracy to govern and maintain the country.
- The emperor needed the degree holders to fill the central, provincial and local government posts with able and loyal body of men. The emperor exerted his influence to appoint the degree holders in defiance of the pressures from the hereditary aristocracy. Actually the contrast is not sharp. The sons of the hereditary aristocracy sat for the examinations and some passed the examinations and held the degrees. Also the degree holders together with the emperor's clans, distinguished persons and his favourites appointed to high posts became new aristocracy.
- The degree holders in turn looked up to the emperor and the government for appointments for their avenue of social mobility. The government services were traditionally esteemed as the most honourable and lucrative careers in China.
- Confucianism triumphed over non-ideological disciplines such as science and technology and also Daoism and Buddhism in the execution of the Chinese civil service examinations in a similar way Christianity triumphed over non-ideological disciplines and also Greek and Latin cultures in the medieval Europe. Confucianism emphasised on human nature, not on observations of nature, though Neo-Confucianism placed an equal emphasis, which was lost as time went on.
- At least one reason why China lagged behind Europe in technical matters in the modern era is that science and technology were not seriously considered as the topics of the civil service examinations. This came to be established with the passage of time. This in turn came about from the fact that the emperor relied less on science and technology for his success and survival but more on Confucianism which emphasised conservatism and loyalty to the emperor. There is also a popular belief in China that mathematics was the occupation of merchants; and science and technology, that of the specialist working class. Astrology and alchemy were nurtured in the ancient China as in the medieval Europe and both subjects were thought to be the embryos of science. The technical branches such as the constructions of palaces and temples, ships and dams were always in the guidance of artisans, not of the degree holders in China. In traditional China, the success in trades, industry, finance, science and technology was viewed as of secondary importance. The Confucian value supported and the civil service examinations reinforced this idea. The emperor had to respond to the popularity among the general public for the examination system to be successful.
- There is no question that the examinations produced men who were proficient on calligraphy and composition, that is, literary competence. The examinations imposed,

though centred on Confucianism, compositions of poems and essays. There was also no question that the students had to go through self-discipline and self-cultivation in the process of learning.

- Who passed the degree examinations and who were appointed as the examiners and such things were the hot topics of the conversations among the intellectuals and the populace through the ages of the Chinese society. Hence the emperor had to make sure to maintain the high reputation of the examinations that the examinations were fair with the minimum corruption among the examiners and the minimum cheating among the candidates. The re-examinations were introduced to enforce the fairness. Also the Palace examinations were introduced to minimise the collusion between the examiners and the candidates. The collusons led to the faction formation within the government departments. Successful candidates owed lifelong gratitude to the examiners and formed a group or faction around the examiner. The assessment always involved subjective judgement apart from the objective measures. The examiners could magnify the former resulting in pass or failure marks. This formed the basis of collusion. The emperor himself supervised the Palace examinations to ensure the fairness and loyalty to him.
- The emperor and the government officials were well aware that education was vitally important for the empire but cost money. China placed education and teachers in high esteem as nowhere else in the world. The civil service examinations cost far less than the government sponsored schools. The public education reached its zenith during the Sung era and ever since it went into continual decline. During the Ming and Ch'ing times, the university in the capital and the government schools in provinces were name only because no teaching took place there. (Miyazaki 1976, p. 124) The government saved a huge amount of money by shifting the education from the public school to the examination system. This created a dichotomy. The examinations were to give equal opportunity for everyone. However the cost factor resulted in favouring the wealthy and aristocratic families who could afford to pay for the private tutoring for many years. Thus the commoners were disadvantaged crucially from the monetary point of view, which became one criticism of the examinations. Hence the private academies and the public schools provided stipends to students, though limited in scope. (Ho 1976, pp. 202-3)
- The Chinese imperial examination system went through the evolution with so many criticisms and reforms, and reached the final form in the Ch'ing era. However, when faced with European cultures, it was judged to be useless and abolished in 1905 and the dynasty (the last of the imperial dynasties) itself collapsed in several years. Thus the Chinese discarded the Confucian and imperial dominance in the early 20th century, while the Europeans discarded the Christian and feudal dominance centuries earlier.
- The emperor made sure that the number of official positions was far less than the number of degree holders such that he and the relevant ministries could pick and choose among the competing degree holders. Hence only the highest degree holders, that is, those of the Metropolitan and Palace passes, were more or less guaranteed the officialdom.
- The ideals of the Chinese education may be ranked as character, ability and technical skills in sharply descending order. The examinations may measure intellectual ability, but not character and integrity effectively. This is one source of bitter criticism of the examination system.
- The examinations were open to all people except for those whose families were engaged in the mean occupations such as slaves, servants, prostitutes, entertainers and lictors (Menzel 1963, p. 22).

- The upward social mobility during the Ming-Ch'ing periods for the commoners, that is, people without wealth or aristocracy, was greater in China because of the civil service examinations than those in the contemporary or even modern Western society.
- The examinations had deficiencies, and merit ratings and sponsorship or recommendation were used to plug the holes of the deficiencies. Merit ratings measured energy, zeal and ability in the actual performance of duties. Sponsorship or recommendation focused its attention on character and integrity, the ideals of officialdom.
- Confucianism stressed person, family and state in terms of governing. Hence it makes sense that it was chosen as the examination subject, the pass holders of which were to govern people. The objects of Daoism and Buddhism are on person only and more to do with self-cultivation for its own sake. Hence they were chosen as the examination subjects only when the reigning emperor had a special interest in either of them. They were exceptions to the general rule of Confucianism as the examination subjects.
- The Confucian scholars, once safely in the civil service, naturally supported the prestige of Confucian learning; and being conscious as an elite class, tried to suppress the military and merchants. These became the policies of the succeeding imperial governments in China till the early 20th century with some exceptions such as shown by the southern Sung and Mongol governments.
- The officials, qualified or unqualified, and the qualified scholars together with their families were exempt from corvèe. Many wealthy families not in this class used their influence to have their names removed from the tax registry. Thus the tax burden fell on people lower in the economic scale, especially on the peasants. Nevertheless it was the custom in China that the gentry spent a proportion of their income for education, the arts and even public works in their own region.
- The bureaucrats made up the outside party and the eunuchs, the inside party; the outside and the inside referring to the relative location in reference to the palace. The rivalry of the two parties was fierce and persistent through the history of the Chinese empires, and particularly so when the central authority represented by an emperor became weak.
- Since the imperial China did not allow any organisation other than literary and educational, Confucian scholars and bureaucrats through history formed at times a political group on the pretence of literary society. The most famous of these groups was the Tung-lin Academy formed towards the end of the Ming dynasty. It aspired to political reform and fiercely opposed the dominance of eunuchs in the government. However, the eunuchs won over this movement under the inept emperor; they destroyed the Academy in 1625. (Milston 1978, p. 214) Contrary to the above observation, the growth of commercial towns created a large number of town dwellers with common interests: they combined in protest movements on occasions, especially against ever increasing taxes during the late decades of the Ming era.
- The Chinese imperial government was highly centralised with an emperor at the apex, and only the high ranking officials who were qualified were able to initiate policies or actions.
- The gentry were the carriers of Chinese culture and teachers of schools. In the 19th century when the Westerners came to do the trade and business, the gentry hated them since they were a threat to the gentry's dominant positions in China. The gentry resented the missionary's role of teaching and criticism of their culture. They felt demeaned when they had to deal with the Westerners.
- Emperor Wudi of the Han era initiated the proto-Chinese civil service examinations which would become the major check on the despotism of the emperors and would last 2000 years. This emperor was as a matter of fact extremely autocratic though he was genuinely interested in learning and literature.

Chinese Imperial Examination Establishment Carried Critical Defects through Its Entire Life. It looked that the Chinese imperial examinations had established a meritocratic system in China and served well the need of the Chinese bureaucracy. However, autocracy, not democracy, started and maintained the system hence they embraced the fundamental flaws therein. When China was unified, the emperor was the sole authority within China, and idealism (Confucianism, Daoism and Buddhism) simply did not have the organisation to withstand the emperor through the ages. The emperor (politics) and idealism do not go together. This is often expressed as politics and religion do no mix. The Byzantine and Russian Orthodox churches and the Anglican Church were under the control of monarchies: however, these churches had strong organisations to curb the tyranny of the monarchs. The Chinese monarchy, which lasted from 221 BC to AD 1912 with some interruptions, was based on Legalism not on Confucianism; an emperor's will and edict overriding any other institutions and laws with virtually no restrictions. Legalism in this context meant that the bureaucrats had to act according to the rules or the laws. However, Chinese history shows some exceptions to the above general rule such as the dominance by the eunuchs, the weakened court, or when the empire itself was breaking up.

The civil service examinations became the tools of governing, and the government set the examination system to suit them. Also the government saved the huge amount of money by transferring the public education to the private tutorials, and sold the titles for large profits.

The system promoted good bureaucrats, and punished any dissenting or non-performing bureaucrats by blocking their promotion or even by dismissal. The reigning emperor had the authority to dismiss, jail or execute anyone in the service except the prime minister by tradition. The Chinese adoration for bureaucracy was based in part on the efficiency of the administration the people experienced in their daily lives and in part on the opportunity for the recognition and advancement for the common people.

Confucius died a few centuries before Shih huang-ti became the first emperor in China, and Confucius did not deal with the proper conduct of emperor. However, Confucius lectured on the ideal relations of the ruler and the ruled. Later Confucians expected an emperor to act as father of people as well as to rule by moral examples; people in turn were to show filial piety to the emperor. *Analects* does not specify what people can do if the emperor rules tyrannically. Still the Confucians depended on the institution of legalist monarchy for their existence. When Empress Dowager Tz'u-hsi decided to abolish the civil service examinations in the early 20th century, there was no organisation which was strong enough to resist the decision. A large number of Confucian scholars with successful careers were in the public service under the strict control of the Dowager. If they had aired any grievance they could have been dismissed or sent to jail. In point of fact the strong demand for the abolition came from the Chinese intellectuals, though some Confucian scholars being conservative and threatened to lose their privilege opposed the move. The Dowager made the decision of terminating the examination system seeing that Japan with the new educational system based on the European model had defeated Russia.

In Europe the scattered and independent states during the Middle Ages did not have the power to override the authority of the pope and the church with their strong and universal authority backed up by the ownership of huge tracts of lands and the wealth. Idealism in China was under the rigid control of the reigning emperor.

Apart from the observation in this article about Confucianism under the imperial institution, there were other defects. The Confucian bureaucrats excluded science and technology from examination topics when they acquired dominance in the bureaucracy and the society. Confucianism was conservative and against reform and made light of science and technology. It always looked down on the military, its personnel and institutions. It was also against the trade, regional and international, and placed all kinds of restrictions on them: it was especially against the international trade which disturbed their set social hierarchy. At the end of the 15th century the Chinese government banned building the oceangoing ships and also their nationals leaving the country. Thence China lost the unchallenged naval supremacy in Asia which she had established since the first half of the 15th century following the maritime expeditions by Admiral Cheng Ho. However, these bans were largely lifted by the mid-17th century. Emperor Ch'ien-lung issued an edict in 1757 restricting foreign trade to Canton. Since the government revenues from trade were considerable, the government restrictions were not always effective. There was no question that the international trade was the vital element of development not only economically but technologically and culturally. It seems that the Chinese government absorbed foreign ideas without inhibitions until the Sung era, when the Confucians triumphed in the public service and felt secure in the dominance. This is the period when China's technological superiority peaked over Europe and from this era onwards the superiority lead gradually diminished.

There were other factors for the Confucian officials to dislike the international trade. The Confucian scholars reasoned that China was a vast country spanning from the dry north to the subtropical wet south and there was no need to import the products from abroad; the products of the various regions and the inter-regional trade satisfied the needs of the entire population. Also the Sino-centric notion which settled in the Chinese minds, scholars and non-scholars, from the Shang era (the 18th to 12th centuries BC) to the present day, made the importations of not only the various products but the various ideas rather difficult, not in the absolute terms, throughout the Chinese history. This refers to the attitude of the entire population compared with the attitude of the Confucian officials and the government earlier mentioned.

The government saved a huge amount of money by adopting the examination system rather than public schooling. The government had the opportunity and the authority to sell the examination titles when they needed money. This problem became especially acute in the course of the Manchu era. It was well known that the Manchu candidates were no match for the Chinese candidates in the performance of the examinations. This fact must have accelerated the sales of the titles and led to the eventual abolition of the examination establishment by the reigning Manchu Empress Dowager.

Idealism, Materialism and Third Prophecy in Historical Context

High moral standard and the capability to do the jobs are two separate issues. The ethical persons are not necessarily good at doing their duties. However, if the society as a whole stands on high moral levels, that society are on the track to build an advanced society in the long course of history. People in this society will do their jobs properly and expose any problems to the open, which other people may try to solve immediately or in the future. As far as my experience goes we can solve the various problems of our responsibility, that is, the officers-in-charge can make sure they can eliminate the problems within their responsibility within the rules given in the organisation. We often hear through the media of mismanagement or accident. In many cases people responsible did not do the job properly. After the event these people do their best to try to evade the responsibility and to place the blame on somebody else. This is also a moral issue.

The practice of idealism, as reflected in the daily life of the majority people, was incomplete in both Europe and China through their history in spite of the fact that a large number of people of both regions were interested in and studied idealism. Comparatively speaking, the Europeans practised idealism successfully due to the advantageous institutional settings in their society aforementioned. I have come to believe that the degree of success has more to do with the social institutions embracing idealism and the people's attitude rather than the inherent values of idealism. In the medieval Europe, the conflicts between the church and the state or spiritual power and temporal power are well documented. At first the church took the upper hand and then gradually the states became powerful. After the start of the modern era in 1492, the states asserted their dominance. This transition reflected people's growing disillusionment with and even resentment about Christianity and the church establishment. The institutions such as the state bureaucracy in imperial China and the church in the medieval Europe were to uphold idealism, and people in turn looked up to them as a unifying force of society. There were no conflicts between idealism and the state in China as happened in the medieval Europe: Chinese emperor represented both spiritual power and temporal power, apart from conducting ceremonial duties. Idealism was totally under the control of the state, particularly of the emperor as the apex of the state organisation in China. Even when the states became dominant in the modern era of Europe, the states did not have the total control of the church establishments and ideologies. For further information refer to 'Introductory Remarks' of Chapter 3.

In the European context, Hebraism was the core idealism represented by the establishment of the church in the mid-classical to medieval era; in China Confucianism was the basis of the civil service examinations in the time setting of its own. The European church embraced monasteries, friars, cathedrals and parish churches. The Chinese government consisted of central, provincial, and local organisations conducting the examinations and their guidance. Greek and Latin cultures did not form any institutions of social dominance in Europe; neither did they become one of the bases for the overseas expansion. They were the arts, philosophy and science in the society and were not the object of faith. Christianity was the popular faith. Confucianism was chosen ahead of Buddhism and Daoism in China as the examination subject because the former promoted loyalty within the government and the society, apart from the inherent nature of the subjects earlier mentioned. While China was left behind in material aspects of culture in the modern era, Europe surged ahead heaps and bounds in this field. Europe took up where the Greeks left off in the theories of material culture in the late ancient to classical eras, especially mathematics and science developed in Alexandria during the Hellenistic era.

Europe went through the Renaissance from the mid-fourteenth century to mid-sixteenth century. The main interest of the Europeans was idealism before the Renaissance, and materialism after the Renaissance. The 1400s and early 1500s were the age of the great explorations and discoveries for the Europeans. The discovery of the North American continent in 1492 started the Commercial Revolution and some historians date the modern era from that year. Paradoxically the European expansions into the various continents of the world brought the most rapid expansion of Christianity. Religious and political movements in Europe of the 16th and 17th centuries that began as the challenge to the Roman Catholic Church are called the Reformation.

Europe made cataclysmic developments in the various fields including foreign trade and agriculture between 1500 and 1700. This placed Europe crucially in advance over China, and was possibly the reason why the industrial revolution broke out in Europe and not in China. Many scholars wondered why the industrial revolution did not start in China. In fact it started in Britain in the mid-18th century when it possessed huge overseas colonies and was making further expansion.

The Enlightenment is a 17th-18th century intellectual movement stressing the new reasoned approach of life style, and encompassed philosophy, politics, economy and science among others.

A number of national academies of science in Europe were laid in the 17th century, which may be a part of the Enlightenment. Outstanding among them were the Royal Society of London (1660) and the Paris Academy of Science (1666). The Industrial Revolution started in Britain in 1760 on the theoretical foundation built in the 17th and 18th centuries. The radical change in how commodities were produced came from the huge demand for them mainly from the colonies. The changes were effected naturally, not by government initiatives, but by the people with little academic background in search of profits. Subsequently the Industrial Revolution spread to many parts of the world. The government mostly sponsored these revolutions such as in Germany and Russia.

Also in the field of politics revolutionary developments took place in Europe and America and they manifested as wars and revolutions:

Seven Years' War (1756-63)
American War of Independence (1777-81)
French Revolution (1789-99)
American Civil War (1861-5)

These events and many other events brought the European and American powers to the ascendancy and helped form the modern democratic European and American societies.

Book One explains why idealism ceased to dominate institutionally in China and Europe, which resulted in the weakening or the abolition of the institutions, and Book Four explains that only the new way of thinking can overcome the difficulties in applying not only idealism but materialism. I point out that the core practical manifestation of idealism, that is, 'Love thy neighbour', has never been the general rule of the above societies, though comparatively speaking Europe was more successful in integrating the said ideal into their society than China. I say only after people love their children more than their sweethearts do they unfailingly learn to practise 'Love thy neighbour'. It cannot be otherwise in terms of logic, strength and practice.

At the material level a similar reasoning unfolds. The ultimate aim of materialism is that the bulk of the population lives in comfort materialistically, though the wealth owned by individuals can achieve the aim partially at least without the development of science and technology. Only science and technology can produce high-tech commodities, sophisticated medical treatments and technologically superior military forces. In spite of the tremendous development of science and technology up to the present, many people of the world live in poverty and even the fortunate have to struggle to keep the good material living they enjoy. The bulk of the world population have not received the full benefits of materialism and only a small percentage of people are really wealthy. I claim that only the new philosophy can overcome these difficulties and the majority of people will enjoy materialistically comfortable life under the spell of this new way of life. The average readers should be able to understand the reasoning as the text discloses.

I have come to believe that idealism and materialism have no inherent defects. According to the principle of sufficient reason, there must be some reason even to the historical happenings. So we must find the reasons why people have not received the full benefits of idealism and materialism. The Third Prophecy focuses its attention on the common observation of everyday occurrences and looks at these in an entirely different light. The family institution is the main theatre of the Third Prophecy. Idealism was the basic attitude of life, and Karl Marx' main concern was firms and states. The family may be the unexpected theatre of revolution I am proposing. Let me remind readers that idealism and materialism were unexpected ideologies when they each appeared in the history of the human race. The universal change of this common happening concerning families gives rise to a sea change, that is, complete and radical transformation of society. The series concludes with the book on sex which is one basic requirement of human beings and sex is the only major drawback associated with the new way of thinking. I believe I have found the solution to this problem.

I present the series in a historical context. Many historians believe that human history developed in stages in the same way infants develop in stages. They start crawling, walking and talking by a certain age, and they grow to discover an ego and then mature sexually, each stage exhibiting clearly. Sigmund Freud formulated the psychological stages of infant development; the oral stage, the anal stage, the phallic stage, the latency stage and puberty. Section 1 Sexual Desire, Chapter 1, Book Five *The Sexual Laws* details these phases. Freud insists that each child have to go through each gradation satisfactorily for proper development. If the child does not resolve any stage adequately, it exhibits problems after growing up. The child may also be stationary in one stage in its outlook or thinking, and does not develop any further. The child if exposed to constant fear does not grow mentally and the arrested growth impedes the proper development of personality. Section 7 Cure of Nervous Problems, Chapter 1, Book Four *The Third Prophecy* refers to this problem and the curing technique.

In this book, the historical developments of ancient, classical, medieval and modern eras are clearly defined in the European context. Karl Marx divided the economic developments of human society into primitive, slavery, feudal and capitalist periods, and proceeded with his argument. The classification suited his economic dissertations. In this series of books as a whole it is argued that humans lived in barbarism without any guiding notions or principles and then idealism (the First Prophecy) flowered first in several parts of the world. There are a few preconditions for the development and flowering of idealism. I mention these conditions in Section 1, Chapter 7, Book One. Several places of the world satisfied these conditions towards the end of the ancient era. The era classifications of Europe may broadly stand for the formation and diffusion (classical), consolidation and dominance (medieval) of idealism in the similar development in China with a different time frame. Then materialism (the Second Prophecy) dominated civilised societies in the modern era. The bulk of economically advanced human societies at present are on the second stage of development, as the spectacular advance in science and engineering testifies. I propose in this series of books that humans have to go on to the third stage, possibly the last stage, in coming years if they are to have a sound future. Only after the introduction of the Third Prophecy, idealism and materialism will come to fruition for individuals and societies. Idealism and materialism are the survival means of humans, and the individuals and societies which integrate the Third Prophecy will master idealism and materialism in practice. Furthermore the human race cannot survive unless this entirely new concept, as the fourth book of this series explains, comes forth and becomes the dominant ideology among the world population.

The emergence of Europe in the modern world was inevitable, though nobody had anticipated. The emergence of materialism as exhibited as the mass production of commodities backed by science and technology was also inevitable, though nobody had anticipated. People may mock the concept of the Third Prophecy when they hear about it, but I absolutely believe in a similar way that it will become the leading ideology of the human race and will govern the human destiny. I place my strong conviction when I use the term 'inevitable' in conjunction with historical events. I am aware of one scientist's conviction that if the clock of the evolution were turned back humans may not become the dominant species, that is to say, the dominance of human beings was not assured.

The arrival of the Third Prophecy as a dominant ideology is sure to come. I base my assertion on the following particular argument apart from the broad assumption that humans cannot survive without the introduction of this new thinking. Idealism and materialism have not delivered their promises fully. The prevalence of idealism has been confined to general education and the institution, and its core teaching of 'Love thy neighbour' has never been dominant among the general public. It is true that idealism was only one branch of general education even after idealism established itself as institutionally dominant. For example, *The Thousand Nights and One Night* says that education consists of fair writing, Qur'an, geometry and poetry (Mathers 1953, p. 186).

In spite of the institutional dominance of idealism, people before the modern era did not know why idealism did not permeate their everyday life. Only after people learn to love their children will they learn to love their neighbour: it cannot be otherwise. Similarly people today in spite of the prevalence of materialism in their daily life do not understand why they have to make daily struggles to maintain their material comfort, many of them being worried about the depletion of natural resources and environmental damages. In other words, the teachings of the First and Second prophecies will not become the rule of society until the Third Prophecy becomes the rule. Only the Third Prophecy, as Book Four discloses using various arguments, explains the reasons for the partial success of and fulfils what idealists and materialists cherished.

The love of the Third Prophecy is stronger than the love between sexes. Otherwise, the whole argument will end in nonsense. When a couple fall in love and marry and have children, they will forget the love of the Third Prophecy. Similarly Jesus Christ preached love of God (Truth) which should be stronger than love between sexes, and taught to abstain from marriage.

I claim that the ideological governance of the Third Prophecy among the world population is sure to come in the next one hundred years or so. There is no indication that this ideology will dominate the world and I have put my meticulous argument supporting the premise in the text. However I have some philosophical reservations as to why idealism and materialism were the controlling ideologies in shaping the history of human kind. The other survival forms of religion, racism, nationalism, sexism, and arts were also strong and universal human traits but were predominant in the specific arenas and eras. Also the rates of development of the various races are different. Some peoples of today are at hunting and gathering economy. Some peoples today still look at religion as their prime concern. To tell these peoples that they have to go to the next stage seems nonsensical. The argument of the stage developments from idealism to materialism to the Third Prophecy does not sound right looking at these peoples.

Further as I studied the world history, Europe in the late 15th century did not look as if it would push aside the other three (China is one of them) regional powers which seemed to have as much chance as Europe, and come out on top. The fact of the matter was that Europe achieved the world hegemony peaking at the nineteenth century and is on the wane at present. I put aside the philosophical doubts and look at the history as it was. I conclude that the reasons why the scholars did not see the strong growth of idealism, materialism and Europe before each came to prominence is that they were not competent enough to foresee the future. The scholars must come up with the valid reasons to justify its inevitable ascendancy. Book One *Idealism and Materialism* details how materialism and Europe surged ahead in the modern context and also refers to other theoretical possibilities for the underlying reasons for these historical facts.

If I claim that idealism, materialism and the Third Prophecy are the means of survival for humans, why did people not skip the first stage or even the first two stages and go onto the third stage? Humans have to go through each step satisfactorily. For example, babies have to learn to crawl before they can walk. Also, Freud asserts that infants must go through each psychological stage satisfactorily before they can go onto the next stage. Also the developmental stages of the embryo in the mothers' womb are the compressed evolution to humans starting from the crude form of life; human embryos show the stages of developments in a compressed evolution from our remote ancestors. In both cases development traces are compressed and definitely not skipped.

The different stages deal with the different aspects of human development. Walking is different from language acquisition though walking comes before language acquisition. People, individually and racially, must go through each stage adequately; otherwise they carry problems into the future. It is well known that a speech defect acquired during infancy is often carried through life unless treated correctly. Also people are aware that what they did not master at school shows up as a difficulty in later years. Europe went through the stage of idealism tolerably as manifested not only in its institution but among the populace to be ready for the next stage of materialism. China's passage through idealism as conducted by the government institution carried fatal defects through the centuries. I make a proposition in Chapter 5 that these defects were possibly the cause of decline of China in comparison with Europe in the modern setting.

It is not that Europe did not have institutional imperfections but the nature of the defects was such that Europe developed normally while Chinese defects impeded the normal development of their society. We find parallels in the development of children. Most children grow normally though they—probably all—have some problems; however, some children do not grow normally since their shortcomings are pronounced.

Europe did not have any politically unified authority until the modern era since the end of the Roman Empire though it was unified religiously under Christianity. I explain these observations along with the possible causes in Section 1, Chapter 5 in conjunction with the development of Europe. I also refer to it in 'Introductory Remarks' to Chapter 3 European Middle Ages (600-1492).

The Industrial Revolution and the subsequent expansion into the world by the West European nations and the USA were not accidents. I am to present the following historical factors for the eruption of the Industrial Revolution in Europe. For further details refer to Section 1 Background of Communism, Chapter 1, Book Three *Communism*.

Europe experienced expansion from the middle of the 11th century after the defensive 9th and 10th centuries as the result of the Viking raids. Towns and trade began to revive, new lands were being cultivated, the frontiers of Europe were expanding--the crusade was only one attempt--and the population was increasing. Between 1000 and 1300, the European population overall increased at least twofold. The revival of city life and the recovery of commerce went hand in hand; industry and commerce were natural partners. The city was the centre of industry and also a ready market for merchants.

The expansive mood was also afoot within the confines of Europe. The population increase forced the clearing of waste lands and cultivation of new lands. In Spain the Christian reconquest from the Muslims was pressing forward from the 11th century. In Germany the Saxons made war against the Slavs, expanding their settlements to the east. They pushed further to the south too, into Austria and Bohemia. Even more striking than these developments may be the establishment of a single province of northern France, Normandy. It was a remarkable achievement that the Normans conquered England in 1066 with its impressive results later to be explained in the text. Restless aristocrats made the conquest and no peasant immigrants came in their wake. (Keen 1991, pp. 87-9)

European commerce emerged in strength in the early 13th century. Cloths were the main export items. The towns of Flanders were the great centre of the cloth industry. Flanders was a powerful medieval principality extending along the coast of the Low Countries because it was at the strategic trade routes. The skilled artisans stationed there wove wool brought from England, Spain and Scotland. The merchants brought the cloths to the Levant and bought the goods most in demand in Europe. They were silks and spices from the orient via the Red Sea and the Persian Gulf from China and the Indies. Throughout the medieval period the townsmen of Italy--particularly Venice, Genoa and Pisa--excelled all others in trade and consequently in wealth. Money was freely circulated and became a vital source of wealth rather than land which had been esteemed as the only source of real wealth. The contact with other societies brought the Europeans to the consciousness that they were unified under one society of Europe with Christianity as a guiding dogma. The contact also brought them new ideas which they were prepared to assimilate and spread. (pp. 90-3)

In the course of the Renaissance (from the mid-14th century to the mid-16th century) Europe more than compensated for the population lost due to the Black Death. Also the national governments acquired the taxing power and set up the armed forces and the national administrations. Europe went through the Scientific Revolution initiated during the Renaissance, and discovered the New World followed by the Reformation (completed in the mid-17th century) to be ready for further expansion into the world. The Enlightenment is another European intellectual movement spanning from the 17th century to the 18th century. Industrial Revolution started in Britain in the middle of the 18th century and spread to continental Europe and North America and many parts of the world.

In the field of shipbuilding, European development was also spectacular, and together with the improved navigational techniques paved the way for the world exploration and exploitation. By about 1200 the European shipbuilders adopted rudders on their ships. During the 1200s the Europeans began to build deep-hulled galleys and replaced oars with sails. The deep-hulled ships were faster and more suitable for the high seas than the conventional galleys (with oars or sails) which had navigated extensively in the Mediterranean world as cargo, passenger and war ships from the ancient era. The European ships carried naval guns since the mid-1300s but the guns as a weapon of war were not effective at this stage. Galleons, large sailing ships typically square-rigged with three or more decks, appeared in Europe in the mid-1500s and served as warships and merchant ships, and became predominant by 1600. Both the English ships and Spanish ships that clashed in 1588 were galleons.

In the medieval era, many wars fought in Europe were in the name of religion. However, in the modern era, nationalism in conjunction with materialism was the basic drive of wars by the Europeans and it thrust them into the world. The individual nations of Western Europe took the initiative and there was no unifying governing body behind the expansion. The nations cooperated or fought depending on the circumstances. Also the European expansion to the East and the world was initially trade purpose only, that is, the desire for wealth accumulation, assisted by the hunger for knowledge of new lands and new products, and for religious zeal. However, seeing that the East in particular did not cooperate for trade, the European nations resorted to subjugation and colonisation of the East and the world making use of their superior armed forces with large manpower. It has been established that Portugal and the Dutch Maritime Empire could not expand as much as the peoples, the policy makers and the colonists of these countries hoped because of lack of the populations, which most likely these peoples were not aware of at the time. For detailed treatment, see Chapter 4 Rise of Europe and Decline of China in Modern Setting, Book One.

The Industrial Revolution in Europe brought materialism to high level and the sharp increase of the European population both of which became the cause and the backup of the European further expansions into the world. Europe mastered the stage of materialism to dominate the globe in the course of the 19th century though commercial capitalism was in force three centuries prior to industrial capitalism realised by the Industrial Revolution. Only after the Industrial Revolution was well under way in Europe, that is, after the middle of the 19th century, West European nations tried to exploit China which looked formidable under one emperor with the vast area and resources, human and natural. Even at the time no single

European nation dared to challenge China and they coordinated their efforts. See the text for further development.

At present the industrialised nations dominate the world; the industrialisation is the logical consequence of materialism.

Survival Strategies

Distinct Ideologies as Means of Survival

The distinct human ideologies are in fact a part of the manifestations of the survival as individuals and groups. I listed them before as acquisition of necessities of life, sex, religion, idealism, materialism, racism, nationalism, sexism and arts. The necessities of life are the highest order. With their absence everything else does not make any sense, resulting in the nonexistence of meaningful cultures. Many regions of the world lacking the necessities of life did not develop meaningful ideologies, though certainly all the survival strategies existed in crude forms. Karl Marx proceeded his argument based on this notion. However, once the necessities of life are satisfied humans seek the other ideologies eagerly, and his argument failed on this point.

In this series of books, the survival instincts of both the individual and the species are assumed and form the bases of the discussion. The overriding concept of survival is the starting premise of the various human activities, in fact of all the living creatures, and manifested as the means of survival. These human activities can be further sub-grouped into individual level and group (family, firm and nation) level. Some activities are pronounced in the former; some in the latter. When the society faces serious survival challenge, some means of survival come forth strongly and become prominent for the individual and the society. I would say that Nazism (focused on nationalism and racism) gripped the German people in the 1930s because their survival was at stake.

I earlier mentioned that Judaism (focused on idealism, religion and racism) came into being when the Jews and the Jewish state were threatened to be wiped out from the face of the earth all through their history. The Germans and the Chinese in the modern setting reacted differently. The nature and depth of the sufferings and the different social and racial settings must explain these different responses.

The concept of survival is inherent in all living things and we do not have to question why that is so and only how they attain their survival makes sense. Survival is an instinct, an instinct of self-preservation; all the living things we now see act according to the survival instinct. All living things from the low mode of life such as germs and plants to high mode of animals and humans consist of cells and we can say that cells have the ingrained will to survive. I do not think the biologists will ever see this strong will by looking into the structures of the cells. I could not come up with the reasons behind such a strong feeling. We will never know the reasons however hard we may try. This instinct comes from the observations of life and the world. We have to accept that all the cells want to survive. This series of books starts from the premise that the human beings are geared for survival and think and act accordingly.

We can imagine an individual or a group of people in the past which acted otherwise. These small number of people did not even seek the fundamental survival modes such as learning to acquire the necessities of life in a proper way and the concept of 'Love thy neighbour'. These people would have sunk to the level of animals or died out hence they are not our consideration.

The proposition that the various human thinking and activities are the means for survival seems to satisfy us convincingly, though they may not look that way on superficial observations. For example, two low desires of the humans for wealth, one manifestation of materialism, and sex can be shown to be instinctive and based on self- and species-preservation, though people desperate for these desires may not think so. For many young men, the above inclinations show up as the desires for a good job and pretty girl friends, not caring much about everything else. The desire for wealth stems from the desire for security and comfort, which in turn originate in human weakness. It is obvious that the inordinate desire for wealth is as bad as any other addictions and should be avoided. Men's desperate need for sexual partners is the survival instinct to lay sperm in good-looking females, though men do not reflect this fact every time they are sexually aroused. I also found that sexism was in fact the opposite side of the same coin as the strong male sexual drive for women: Women have survived using their beauty, not relying on anything else until recent years. For details of this aspect of sex refer to Section 14 Sexual Differences between Men and Women, Chapter 1, Book Five *The Sexual Laws.*

Animals have the desire for sex but don't have the desire for wealth. Humans have had a strong drive for sex. Humans in the process of evolution acquired the desire for wealth together with many other survival plans.

What is survival? If people are hungry they naturally want something to eat. If suffering is mental, people naturally want a teaching to lighten the distress. The Old Testament explains it in terms of faith in the Almighty and consequent physical existence in the hope of the cessation of fears, sufferings and pogroms. If people follow the teachings of the Testaments and their way of life, they will be as numerous as sands on the seashores or stars in the sky. This is the survival technique the Jews developed over the millenniums against the social turmoils and the onslaught of pogroms both of which in turn originated in the evil life of the bulk of the Jews. Buddhism has no social messages and does not create any creed that leads to the continuation of any human beings including the Buddhists, though this is really a strange outcome given the starting premise of survival. Charles Darwin defines the survival of plants and animals in terms of the suitability to the environment. The species suitable biologically to the particular environs are to multiply and the other species, to die out. He emphasises the survival for the physically fittest or natural selection and does not refer to the moral strictures which are not pronounced even in the animal kingdom any way. His ultimate concern is the physical continuation of the plants and animals of the species and not of the individuals. Plants and animals change on biological levels to adapt to their environment, which is evolution. Some people posited in a similar way that humans individually and as groups have to change to adapt to their environment culturally. Failure to change for plants, animals and humans is retardation, biological or cultural, and eventual extinction.

Karl Marx taught that the survival of humans lies in economics, and the acquisition of the means of production by the state: his communist theories were a part of materialism. Adolf Hitler declared that nation and race were the aim and means of the survival as the nations and the species, and the individuals were not important in the process: his doctrines were in the spheres of nationalism, racism and totalitarianism.

In this book the survival goes further than the physical existence of the individual or the species, and I delve into the success or failure of individuals and groups. I also refer to the ideological, as mentioned, and non-ideological, to be mentioned under the next heading, means of survival for the individuals and groups.

Another characteristic of these manifestations is that some ideologies such as idealism, materialism in the sense of science and technology, and arts must be taught in contrast with sex, materialism in the sense of the various possessive desires, racism, nationalism, sexism which people acquire naturally and instinctively. Certainly some of the latter concepts can be taught to modify or strengthen the legitimacy of the ruling idea. For example, in Nazi Germany and South Africa during apartheid, racism and possibly sexism were taught at school to justify their social structures.

Manifestations of survival are in fact so closely linked in the lives of humans that they are hardly independent entities. For example, we may think that idealism has nothing to do with arts, which is true as far as the essence is concerned, yet the religious establishments systematically used various arts (literature, buildings, paintings, sculptures, music etc.) to impress people. Racists and sexists also point out their achievements in the various fields such as idealism, science and technology, and arts to strengthen their claim of racial and sexual superiority. Racism often leads to sexism. Nazis were racists as much as sexists and it is strange to me that some females support Nazi causes.

Some techniques, though they all have to do with survival, are not listed as the ideologies. I am at a loss as to the reasons why I present some means of survival as ideologies and some non-ideologies. The distinction is flimsy and one of convenience. This series of books proceeds on the assumption that human actions are geared mostly for survival and in the process of quoting I cannot enumerate every survival technique. Some means of survival can be classed as good or bad; overt or covert; abstract or concrete; permanent or temporary. After the spread of the Third Prophecy, some means of survival such as idealism and materialism will become dominant and some virtually obliterated.

Non-Ideological Means of Survival

These are separate from the ideologies as the means of survival but are no less important and widespread.

Humans are curious animals, and coupled with the desire for survival developed a vast amount of knowledge in vastly different fields, apart from the knowledge associated with the ideological means of survival aforementioned. Psychology, logic, history and sociology, to mention only a few, obviously belong to this class of knowledge, that is, knowledge in the non-ideological means of survival. Do politics and economics belong to one or the other classes? There are many subjects which pose this question; however, it is nonsensical to try to classify human knowledge in this way.

Conflict and war have been the mainstay of the survival of individuals and groups. Many people train their body fearing physical attacks, and many nations perceiving foreign threats adopted militarism. A German man I knew well used to tell me that people's aggressive behaviours distressed him. The reason for aggressiveness is that these people received aggravation in the past and when they have an opportunity to express aggression, they do so. Even if he is in Germany, he has the similar exposures as we all do. This is the means of survival but I believe it will mostly disappear together with conflicts and wars after the introduction of the Third Prophecy in the social scale.

Likes and dislikes are another means of survival. If a person likes music and particular music, it is hard for us to see that it affects the survival of that person. However, likes and dislikes can affect the choice of manifestations and hence they should affect survival. If a person chooses idealism rather than materialism simply because that person likes idealism, it would affect his or her survival.

Also the acquisition of wife and family is hardly an ideology. So is the acquisition of friends. So is the acquisition of qualifications and jobs. If a man loves a woman dearly, he wants to be with her and nothing else matters. Similarly if a person really wants a qualification and a job, he or she casts aside everything else in an effort to obtain them. To be qualified in a profession or to have a good job can constitute one's means of survival. So is the acquisition of language, oral skills and written communication skills. The Third Prophecy concerns itself with families and children, and readers have to read Book Four to understand why a new look at these universal but rather insignificant units in society would bring fundamental changes in society. The Buddhists and Christians in their truest sense cast aside spouse, family, friend, qualification, job and wealth.

A huge number of thinkers through human history put enormous amount of effort into thinking and debating about idealism of individuals; production and economics of firms; and idealism, religion, economics and politics of nations; however, they have not spared much thought about the families. Book Four's main concern is families and children and I argue that their absence in the bulk of society will decide the future of mankind.

Lie and cheat. Dogs eat dogs. Machiavellianism. Might is right. These are all tools of survival and universally used in the society the world over. They all go against the concepts of idealism and will greatly reduce under the Third Prophecy.

The majority of people want to be happy, which is not an ideology. Happiness comes and goes to all people. When the Greek city-states were in decline, sometime after the Peloponnesian Wars (431-404 BC), the Greeks' main concerns were the happiness and security of their individual lives rather than those of the polis states of the earlier era. When people acquire what they want they feel happy for a while. We often hear happiness lies in contentment.

People as individuals and nations strive also for dominance, honour and fame. Dominance and honour show, among other indications, as the ranking or the pecking order in families and firms for the individuals, and in the international politics for nations.

Diligence is an important feature of survival: diligence tends to lead to success on any matter; and laziness, the opposite of diligence, tends to lead to failure on any matter.

Sigmund Freud put up the theory that the pleasure principle regulates mental events, and the human mind has the dominant trend to pleasure avoiding unpleasure. However, another instinctual impulse, as repression, opposes this strong and inherent inclination, though how the two opposing forces work is not well understood. Also a separate instinct of self-preservation (the reality principle) works against the pleasure principle and forces unpleasure on the human minds. (Freud 1961, pp. 4-5)

Challenge to Survival Principle

I pointed out earlier that many human actions stem from or head for survival consciously or subconsciously. In other words some human activities do not contribute to survival. This comes in part from the complexity of humans and human societies, in part from the deficiencies in survival techniques though most of them are carefully conceived and well developed, and in part from the fact that survival is not the only reason for human existence. Even animals seek pleasure at times after they satisfy their survival needs. The net result is that humans created both the multitudes of survival techniques, and the pleasure modes that do not lead to survival.

Satisfying the necessities of life is the fundamental means of survival, and in its prosecution people obtain various degrees of pleasure. Many people strive to satisfy five senses, though it goes against religious teachings. A large number of people spend enormous amount of money in the effort. Good food, good clothes and good houses are the main concerns of these people.

I am to cite a few examples to show the deficiencies of survival techniques. Religion deals with rules governing human thinking; it still does not explain other aspects such as how the world was created, how to cure bodily sickness or how to build strong military. Karl Marx built the communist theories which were based on many erroneous premises, which I explore in Book Three *Communism*. We may find another example in Hitler's racial theory. He placed a heavy emphasis on nation and race to try to explain human existence. He did not want war with Britain and America whose people, he reasoned, were akin to the Germans still he ended up fighting with these nations. Also he thought the Russians were racially inferior but the Russians fought incredibly valiantly in Stalingrad from virtually hopeless situations and forced the German capitulation. The evidence points that after this defeat Hitler realised he could not win the war though his rhetoric was otherwise. The Battle of Stalingrad, the first major Russian victory, was the turning of the tide in favour of the Russians: the Russians were losing the war before and winning after. His racial theory could not explain these major historical events he himself went through. The fact that Karl Marx centred his theories on materialism and Adolf Hitler on nationalism and racism is a defective oversimplification of life and the world in themselves. Humans have strongly exhibited these survival traits as individuals and groups for millenniums, but they are not sufficient to explain the totality of human existence.

Many of the human activities originating in pleasure seeking do not have the purpose of survival. Many people indulge in tobacco smoking, gambling, drinking alcohol and taking various narcotics. Many religious doctrines which are survival means, teach their adherents to keep away from the above indulgences. Humans undoubtedly act in the guidance of pleasure principle at times.

Sex has a double character of pleasure and survival. Sex gives tremendous pleasure and this is the way nature ordained to preserve the species. I stress both the survival aspect of sex and its pleasure in Book Five *The Sexual Laws*. Sex is a survival instinct for men to lay sperm in the female bodies and many look for young and pretty girls to maximise pleasure and survival. However, a small number of men who are homosexuals look for men to have sex though sex drive itself originates in survival. These men are acting only on the pleasure principle. The behaviour of gay men make sense only in the light of the sexual laws expounded. Also the acquisition of wealth has a double purpose of pleasure and survival. It is interesting to note that two prominent human activities of sex and acquisition of wealth have two purposes of pleasure and survival ingrained in them. This may explain why these two pursuits have governed humans so strongly and persistently for many millenniums.

Other principles are also at work. Some people cannot help being stupid. Lying is undoubtedly a survival technique but some people may lie so silly that people can prove they are lying. Some people are simply intent on destroying other people's good wishes, though it is hard for me to see in this case if they are acting on survival principle or pleasure principle.

Every human being acts sometimes on survival principle and sometimes on pleasure principle. Some people choose one over the other consistently, and that characterises them. Also we have to take into account of the time frame: Some people choose one over the other in certain times of their life. Pleasures are often seen as recreation, that is, not the purpose but the means to enhance various survival activities: people are trying to justify pleasures.

Concluding Remarks

Apart from the inherent difficulty in conveying the concept of love to readers, there is another practical problem associated with writing *The Third Prophecy.* The love of the kind I preach is hardly a topic for a book and, as far as I know, nobody has written a book on this subject. Book Four cites a small number of people who have expressed the idea in the East and West. Normally when people write a book they have a large number of reference books at hand, as was the case for the other books in this series. However, I did not have any books I could consult except for fragments from the various sources for *The Third Prophecy* hence I had to use all my skills to expand the concept in a way acceptable to most readers.

I started writing the book on the Third Prophecy in 1989 when I was 45 years of age. Originally I planned to write one book with five chapters. However, I realised it would be more interesting if I developed each chapter into one book so that people could read each book on its merit. The subjects of all of the five books interested me--some from childhood and some after growing up--and I want to pass that fascination to readers. On the process of expanding, I reckoned that I would need 20 years in total to finish all the books, when I would be 65 years of age. As a matter of fact it took me 25 years to complete the books.

Preface to Book One

Many historians wondered why in material culture China lagged so much behind Europe in the modern era in spite of the fact that the former was far in advance of the latter in the pre-modern era, and further speculated that the industrial revolution should have happened in China rather than in Europe. Some ventured their opinions on this matter; however, I don't think any of them gave correct answers to the query raised. When I was inquiring into the possible causes, the distinction of idealism and materialism came to the fore. In the course of human development through history, idealism and materialism were the two major preoccupations of humans, if not all. The two divisions adopted may explain the nature of the progress of human civilisations and also give some clues why the well-advanced culture of China stalled to be eclipsed by the late comer Europe.

Human history is marked by major events such as taking up the agriculture, formulating idealism, the industrial revolution, and the dominance of the nations which adopted these modes of life. Also the reasons why these events took place give us insight into history. I present the book in the fashion to highlight the major events.

Arnold Toynbee concluded that race theory or environment theory on its own does not explain the cause of the human history (Toynbee 1962, p. 59).

The West Europeans ventured into the world in the middle of the 15th century and engaged in trade to make money, a manifestation of materialism, and this phase is called commercial capitalism. The further West European expansion into the world followed the Industrial Revolution, another manifestation of materialism. The Industrial Revolution of the 18th century onwards gave the West Europeans the military superiority backed by the increased population. This book tries to unravel the reasons why materialism bloomed in Europe in the modern era.

In comparing the East and the West in this book, I use the terms superior and inferior in a common sense manner, which does not stand scholarly scrutiny of a philosophical or scientific nature.

- Life is better than death.
- Happiness is preferable to unhappiness.
- Strive for wealth and avoid poverty.
- Success is desirable than failure.

All the above propositions are correct according to the common notion of our everyday life. However, philosophical treatises seriously challenged all these assumptions, and many thinkers in the East as well as in the West proposed that the opposites of the above premises were in fact desirable for the ultimate benefits of the individuals and the societies.

The opinions of these philosophers may have been right; however, the number of these people was insignificantly small. The average people who formed the bulk of the population did not understand the intricate theories which may be right in the absolute terms. The bulk of the population decided the course of the civilisation which this book is trying to unravel.

In the similar logic many readers would justifiably object to the manner I apply the terms superior and inferior in this book. They might argue that we cannot grade one current of civilisation above another and doing so is unscientific; all the civilisations are different as much as all individuals are different. Even the military victory does not indicate the victor is superior to the loser as human beings but simply means that the former prevailed in military context over the latter at a certain location and time under the given conditions. I am to offer a couple of examples. When the Romans conquered the Greeks in the second century BC, the former acknowledged the cultural superiority of the latter. Also when the northern peoples repeatedly invaded China through history, the Chinese always thought that they were culturally superior to the conquering barbarians. I am fully aware of the limitations on the use of these terms. This book is by no means a scholarly thesis but addressed to the general public and designed to introduce and expound the concepts of idealism and materialism which are to lead further to the subsequent subjects in this series of books.

In 'Introduction to Series', I make a point that humans act, consciously or subconsciously, according to survival techniques developed over the millenniums or the pleasure principle at times. I also express that the survival motivations rather than the pleasure principle played the major role in forming the history of human kind.

This book on history stresses the roles played by idealism and materialism. Readers may naturally ask what roles other survival techniques played in forming the histories of China proper and Western Europe. There is no question that all the survival techniques acted out, more or less, directly or indirectly. For example, once a new emperor established a Chinese empire, the eldest son of the emperor was to become the successor. The Chinese people did not doubt the setup even though it was sexism. Also the ancient to classical Greeks built a culture, one of the highest in the human history, on sexism and racism; they barred women and foreigners from the cultural activities. Further, the Christian church during the medieval era manoeuvred against the regional powers to preserve and increase its authority, though some of its policies were not in accord with the biblical teachings. All the survival techniques are in evidence in the history of the world as much as they are in today's societies, and people have made decisions accordingly.

I explain the reasons in 'Introduction to Series' why idealism and materialism are the two major motifs in the development of China proper and Western Europe. For more details readers have to go through the text to follow.

Chapter 1 East vs West

Section 1 Era Classifications and Prehistory Humans

Era Classifications

I use the historical eras of human development in this book in the following modes as in *The Cassell Atlas of World History* (2001). This classification applies only to Europe. However, in the absence of proper classifications for the other regions I use the same designations to indicate, what I consider, the parallel eras of these regions.

- the ancient world (4 000 000-500 BC)
- the classical world (500 BC-AD 600)
- the medieval world (600-1492)
- the modern world (1492 onwards)

  Note: Antiquity is sometimes used to denote the far distant past, especially, the time preceding the Middle Ages in Europe. Primitive is also used to indicate pre-writing or prehistory.

There is another developmental classification which focuses the attention to the most advanced forms of tools and weapons in use in an era:

- Palaeolithic Age (Old Stone Age)
  The period of the emergence of primitive man and manufacture of unpolished chipped stone tools, about 2.5 million to 3 million years ago until about 12 000 BC. Speech developed between 400 000 and 100 000 BC, though the scholars still debate vehemently about it because oral language did not leave concrete evidence as written language did (Rietbergen 1998, p. 6).
- Mesolithic Age (Middle Stone Age)
  The period between the Palaeolithic and Neolithic, in Europe from about 12 000 to 3000 BC, characterised by the appearance of the microliths, small blade tools of flaked stone.
- Neolithic Age (New Stone Age)
  The cultural period that lasted in South West Asia from about 9000 to 6000 BC and in Europe from about 4000 to 2400 BC and was characterised by primitive crop growing and stock rearing and the use of polished stone and flint tools and weapons.
- Bronze Age
  A technological stage between the Stone and Iron Ages, beginning in the Middle East about 4500 BC and lasting in Britain from about 2000 to 500 BC, during which weapons and tools were made of bronze and there was intensive trading. Around 3000 BC the horse was domesticated on the Russian steppes north of the Black Sea. This age marks the migrations of peoples with wheels, wagons, horses and chariots.
- Iron Age
  The period following the Bronze Age characterised by the extremely rapid spread of iron tools and weapons, which began in the Middle East about 1100 BC. The use of horses and chariots was widespread.

There is another classification coming from social evolution, which Lewis Morgan sets up (Whitehouse and Wilkins 1986, p. 10; Marx and Engels 1970, p. 209).

- savagery (or band society): The dominant life support for savages is hunting and

gathering.
- barbarism (or tribal society): The dominant life support for barbarians is farming.
- civilisation (or state society)

I am to refer to these broad classifications on occasions.

Clyde Kluckhohn proposes that as a rule of thumb a civilisation must possess at least two of the following three features (Whitehouse and Wilkins 1986, p. 10):

- a town of more than 5000 people
- writing
- a monumental ceremonial centre

Temples were the most prominent buildings of ancient civilisation, indicating theocratic society. There were a number of priests and priestesses looking after the various affairs--worship and sacrifices to the temple god--around the temple. The elite, of family or intelligence, of the society formed the priesthood. However, even after the secularisation took place, the temple buildings were still prominent buildings, as classical Greece and Rome exemplified. (p. 99)

The appearance of temples marked the end of barbarism--the absence of culture--and the beginning of civilisation. Around the time of the appearance of temples appeared the various cities. The word civilisation derived from *civis*, a Latin word for city dweller. (Davison 1993, p. 16)

Unless persons can read and write, we can hardly call them educated. Similarly unless people have a system of writing, we can hardly call them civilised. I adopted the formula 'human society with writing system = history or civilisation' in this series of books. Prehistory is an era of human habitation before the use of writing. The scholars must rely on archaeological evidence to learn what happened before people used the writing which was invented in or imported to the region. We don't know anything about the idealist culture before writing was invented: idealism in the pre-writing or prehistory or pre-civilisation era can only be guessed at. Stones for implements and weapons and the other artefacts found used in the prehistory are all parts of material culture.

We generally regard the advent of writing as marking the transition from barbarism to civilisation. Its evolution from the earliest pictograms to modern alphabets is a complex story.

Systems of Writing:

The pictographs of synthetic writing
    Drawings or picture writing
Analytic writing
    Single words were then isolated and symbols were invented.
    Ideograms; symbols that represent ideas or objects as for Chinese
    Cuneiform; wedge shaped characters as for Sumerian
    Hieroglyphs as for Egyptian
Phonetic writing
    Sounds were codified.

(Reader's Digest 1983, p. 86)

In more developed pictograms, the images could be used in an abstract way or combined to express more complicated ideas.

We can divide the archaeological records—the totality of surviving material traces of the human past—into three broad types of evidence:

- human remains
- artefacts and sites
- ecofacts; prehistoric deforestation and soil degradation

(Taylor 1996, p. 10)

Prehistoric arts may not represent what prehistoric people did in general terms, though they certainly represent the artists' thoughts. Gas chromatography analyses chemical residues in the artefacts such as bowels or utensils, and we can ascertain what was in them.

Early Humans

There are scientists who believe that modern humans evolved separately in different parts of the world. However, DNA analyses support the theory that hominids, modern man and its extinct precursors not including apes, evolved in one area of Africa and gradually spread across the globe. (Brooks, Fowler & Adams 2000, p. 25)

A Swedish botanist, Linnaeus, came to believe in the early 18th century that all humans were part of the same species, though he also presented sub-classifications for races or subspecies of humanity in conformity with the public perception that there were diverse humans on earth.

The Sahara Desert today is without vegetation and inhospitable except in scattered oases. This desert was not always like this. William Calvin, a neurobiologist, concluded that the Sahara worked as a population pump. During the wet periods the Sahara sustained a large number of people who lived on the abundant games available. When the dry periods set in the Sahara returned to uninhabitable desert, forcing the bulk of the population to emigrate. (Wells 2003, p. 108) In assessing the scale of migrations thus generated we have to take into account the following facts. The Sahara Desert is the largest desert in the world, occupying over a quarter of the African continent and stretching 9 100 000 square kms at present. The pump acted over millions of years. We know well that favourable weather increases flora and fauna enormously in any region, which in turn increases the human population in proportion.

Hominids evolved over millions of years and gradually spread over the world. The four main groups are: *Australopithecus*, *Homo habilis, Homo erectus* and *Homo sapiens*. *Australopithecines* are the oldest known hominids and their fossilised remains, the oldest being four million years old, were found in Tanzania, Africa. *Homo habilis* (handy human) appeared in sub-Saharan Africa two millions years later; they are supposed to be the first true humans. *Homo erectus* (upright human) appeared 1.7 million years ago in Europe and Asia. *Homo sapiens* (wise human) started to flourish 200 000 years ago at around the time when *Homo erectus* died out. (Martell 1995, pp. 10-1) *Homo sapiens sapiens* had peopled virtually the entire globe by c. 11 000 BC. They are the subspecies of *Homo sapiens* and refer to all existing people.

The palaeontologists can classify hominids and determine the approximate years of their existence from fossils. However in the past they could not figure out scientifically how the higher stage hominids evolved from the lower stage—local evolution or migration from another region. DNA techniques are helping them to solve this problem.

One favourable weather pattern resulted in a population explosion in Africa prior to 50 000 years ago according to the mitochondrial DNA results (Wells 2003, p. 100). When the dry periods set in the surplus people had to move out of Africa. Thus major migrations by Upper Palaeolithic modern humans (*Homo sapiens sapiens*) took place 50 000 years ago and they moved to the Middle East which was really an extension of north-eastern Africa. Also we must remember that these peoples did not live in the houses as we know but migrated following the herds of animals, sometimes spurred by the sense of adventure and instinct. A small number of them migrated to Europe. However, the bulk of the people spread out to Eurasian (Asian) continent and further to the ends of the earth over the next 30 000 years. (p. 106)

These people entered China through Central Asia between 40 000 and 10 000 years ago. The different migration periods seem to account for the split between northern and southern Han Chinese, who are still genetically and linguistically similar. The northern China had been inhabited by their distant relatives Peking Man, *Homo erectus*. (p. 119) These hominids lived in a series of caves at Zhoukoudian (Chou-k'ou-tien), near Beijing (Peking), from 600 000 to 230 000 years ago.

We may imagine that the emigrants from the Sahara Desert must have been black; however, that was not the case. The weather pattern at the time was entirely different from the present. This fact also explains why the bulk of the people in the Middle East followed the steppes to the north in the Eurasian continent, which we think must have been really cold.

The distinctions of race, that is, Africans, Asians and Europeans, or the skin colours of peoples are recent phenomena that accentuated during the last Ice Age (100 000-12 000 BC). For instance, sinodonty—the distinctive tooth pattern common to north-east Asia and Americas—first appeared in the fossils less than 30 000 years old. Besides, before agriculture was established peoples moved freely and frequently and any distinguishing features disappeared into the mixed population. (pp. 191-2)

Milutin Milankovitch, a Serbian mathematician, proposed in the 1940s that three orbital variations change how the sunlight is distributed seasonably and geographically over the earth:

a precession (wobble) of the earth's surface
a variation in the tilt of the axis
a variation in the path of orbit

Most climatologists agree that the above three cycles probably altered global temperatures at regular intervals throughout the earth's history, and brought the glacial periods. (*Encyclopedia World Book,* 1983 edn, sv, Axis of rotation.) Certainly the above changes are not the only factors affecting the earth's climate; however, the other factors are considered to be temporal and regional for the past climates. Recently it has been the hot debate that the increase of carbon dioxides in the atmosphere due to the burning of fossil fuels is causing the global warming. Some scientists do not agree with this proposition.

Emigrations from Eurasian Steppes

The Eurasian Steppes are a belt of grassland stretching some 8000 kilometres from Hungary in the west and Manchuria in the east. Most steppes receive annual rain fall of between 25 and 51 centimetres and do not permit the growth of trees, being characterised by hot summers and cold winters. They are suitable for grazing livestock, though they allow limited growth of crops. Though the Eurasian Steppes separate into segments, horsemen can cross the barriers without any problems.

The Eurasian Steppes are broadly separated into the Western Steppes and the Eastern Steppes, the Altai Mountains separating the regions; and Manchuria. Peoples of the Western Steppes always through known history had the motivation to migrate to west or south seeking milder climates and more rainfall. Similarly the peoples in the Eastern Steppes which provided a harsher climate than that of the Western Steppes were under strong and constant urge to move to west or south; or east, that is, Manchuria or northern China.

The population the steppes could support was far fewer than that the cultivated lands could. Once the upper limit of the population was reached the surplus herders had to move out unlike the farmers in the cultivated lands where the extra work could absorb the extra population to a considerable extent. Another feature of the steppe life was the recurrent problems for the grass and water rights, and it was the perennial practice that the herders resorted to fightings. Thus the skills in fightings and the worship of the warriors marked nomadic life. All of these factors paved the way for migrations out of the steppes and conquests of non-nomadic peoples.

In the north of the Eurasian Steppes lay the forested regions which were even more forbidding for human habitation than the grasslands. The forest peoples, hunters and gatherers, tended to migrate into the steppes thus becoming nomads.

The land cultivations were carried out around the oases scattered in Central Asia. The oasis dwellers had a different way of life from nomads, and the former enjoyed a more civilised and easier life than the latter. It was a feature of Eurasian history that nomads raided the oases for booty or for occupation. Another feature was the trade between the two sectors since they offered different commodities. It is conjectured that nomads initiated the trade routes called the Silk Road.

There were grasslands stretching from the Caucasus Mountains to Asia Minor and further to the Middle East. There were several passes through the Caucasus Mountains. These facts, and also the strong evidence that the weather in Central Asia was a lot milder than at present, explain the reasons why hominids in the Middle East migrated to Central Asia rather than to Europe. They followed the games on the familiar steppes to the north. As a matter of fact the migrations not only from the south to the north but in the opposite direction happened repeatedly through history, especially after horses made the journey easier. Hence the various races mixed in Asia Minor and the Middle East: predominantly Semitic in the south; and Indo-European, Turkish and Mongol in the north.

The nomadic people of the southern Russian steppes spoke Proto Indo-European language (common ancestors of all Indo-European languages) from around 5000 BC, though they did not leave written records, and were called the Kurgan people because of the enormous burial grounds (called kurgans) they left.

The Kurgan people embarked on a broad wave of expansion c. 4500 BC. The Kurgan culture spread west c. 4000-3500 BC. They made a second wave of expansion c. 3500 BC. Their presence was traced to Danubian Europe in the period 3500-2300 BC, and they arrived in the Aegean and Adriatic regions after 2300 BC. They also occupied a wide area from eastern central Europe to northern Iran c. 3500-3000 BC.

These Indo-Europeans were warlike and lived on steppes feeding cattle, sheep, goats, and they were as mobile for easy migrations as for any other steppe dwellers. They domesticated horses around 3000 BC. The steppe dwellers began to keep horses besides their livestock sometime before 2000 BC. They drank horse milk and ate horse flesh. Europe's fertile fields with temperate weather became the great attractions for the Indo-Europeans of the plains of central Eurasia. About 2000 BC the Indo-Europeans with their superior warrior might overran the farming and fishing populations of the European peninsula. Around 1700 BC wheelwrights learned to make spoked wheels suitable for use on wheeled wagons and chariots. The chief beneficiary of the invention at the initial stage was the Indo-Europeans, who soon after overran the entire Middle East, and India around 1500 BC. Their use of horses for wheeled wagons and chariots gave them a decisive advantage over the infantries of the other people of such as hunters and gatherers or cultivators. The use of chariots for warfare spread to Europe; and to China by the 14th century BC during the Shang dynasty.

Another revolution came about soon after 900 BC: Men learned to ride horses. It was a tremendous advantage for swift movement during both peace and war. Horses gave not only a decisive edge in combat but made the swift communications and assemblies of armies possible. Thus horses gave a decisive advantage to the steppe peoples over the sedentary peoples in mobility and in military engagements. Only the grasslands were perfectly suited for raising horses; and the agricultural people had to feed their horses grains, raising the costs and restricting the number of horses, thus it was cheaper to import horses. The Indo-Europeans on the steppes raised a large number of horses by reducing the number of cattle, thus they were again the ones who got the most benefit from this revolution.

The use of stirrups was found in India around 500 BC, though they were only looped ropes. There is some evidence that the stirrups of our understanding may have been used in Assyria as early as 850 BC, thence the horsemen spread them throughout the Eurasian Steppes.

People in Europe adopted stirrups c. AD 500. Stirrups united horse and rider, and cavalry became more effective. It is induced that the introduction contributed partially, if not totally, to the spread of feudalism by elevating the role of knights. Surprisingly the Romans before the collapse of the Western Roman Empire did not use stirrups, though the Roman cavalry in the movies ride on the saddles with stirrups. The introduction of stirrups to Europe above quoted seems late. The fact of the matter was that stirrups were such a simple device which came out of the simple need that the scholars hardly agree by whom, where and when they were invented and spread out. It may also be possible that the people of different places and eras discovered the use independently from others.

The Eurasian Steppes worked as a population pump in a similar way as the Sahara Desert did in earlier eras, both regions covering huge tracts and spewing out a huge number of people for millenniums. In both cases the basic underlying feature was the change in weather pattern. However, we notice that some aspects of life on the steppes were different from those on the Sahara Desert. Since the herders depended on animals, the steppes, though vast, could support only a limited number of humans in contrast with the cultivated lands. Herders sometimes cultivated lands thus becoming semi-nomads. Also some on the steppes engaged in hunting games. Just as in the Sahara Desert the weather controlled the number of animals and humans in the steppes. Good weather of heavy rains and warm air for some years produced a large number of animals and humans. Bad weather forced herders to move around. It is not hard to speculate that a large number of people unable to find enough pastures left the steppes looking for a better life. These pastoralists were migratory and ready to move. This was true even before horses were available. There is no statistical evidence to support such speculation: we do not know how many people lived in the Eurasian Steppes. However, the history of the steppes and the researches by scholars tend to confirm the speculation.

Known history shows that when a capable leader emerges people are willing to cooperate not only in the steppes but also in any other places such as empires, nations, institutions or any groups of people. This is the natural reaction of people since their instinct tells them by following the capable leader they can increase the chance of survival, in terms of not only good life but also life or death. The following paragraphs mention a few prominent leaders of the steppe peoples who played a dominant role in history.

The Xiongnu (Hsiung-nu) formed the empire in Central Asia from the late 3rd century BC to the AD 2nd century, modelled on the Chinese empire. The Hsiung-nu exchanged their horses for Chinese grain, silk and other luxuries.

The Huns, possibly Turkish origin, arrived from the east. Some historians claim that the Huns descended from the Hsiung-nu but the evidence is tenuous. They crossed the Don about AD 370 and occupied the westernmost steppes. This predatory power brought the flights of the Germanic peoples who broke through the Roman frontier in 376. In fact the migrations lasted for half a millennium, on and off. The Hunnish people under the strong ruler Attila (reigned 434-53) built an empire on the Western Steppes. However upon his death the Germanic tribes revolted, and the Huns disappeared as a distinct political entity. In the confusion ensued the Roman Empire came to an end in 476 and the Germanic peoples became the rulers of the Western provinces of the empire.

A powerful new Turkish confederacy, headquartered in the Altai Mountains, was formed in 552. The Turks (Turkish people) claim that they descended from the Hsiung-nu. It covered a huge geographic range extending from the frontiers of China to the Caspian Sea. These Turks were skilled in ironwork and used their own runic scripts. Though disputed succession tore the confederacy apart and it ultimately dissolved in 734, still it played a major role in history after, as before, the dissolution. The ferocious Turks put to flight the peoples of the steppes, and these refugees--Avars, Bulgars, Khazars, Pechenegs and Magyars--migrated to the Balkans and central Europe, and established Bulgaria and Hungary. In the ninth and tenth centuries the migrations of the steppe peoples into Eastern Europe slackened; in part the European peasantry moved out to the east and in part the Turks moved to the Middle East. The Turkish tribes arrived within the realm of Islam of the Middle East after about 900 in such a large number that they exercised decisive military force. Sufism of Turkic origin came to the fore among the esoteric Sufi orders of Islam. Turkic is a branch of the Altaic family of languages including Turkish and Tartar. Turkish became the language of the Middle East together with Arabic and Persian.

The Arab Muslims had raided the western coast of Indian sub-continent in the 7th and 8th centuries; and invigorated by the Seljuk (of Seljuk Turks) Muslims the Muslims raided into India in the year 1000, and within two centuries established Muslim control over northern India. On the other flank the Seljuk tribesmen defeated the Byzantines at Manzikert in 1071, and established their occupation of the grasslands in Asia Minor. The Seljuks created a Turkish empire by the late 11th century. These developments triggered the crusades. However, the crusades could not contain the Turkish onslaughts permanently. Osman founded the Ottoman (of Ottoman Turks) dynasty in the early 14th century. The Ottomans succeeded the Seljuks as the leaders of the struggles against Christendom towards the end of the 13th century, and continued to advance their frontiers. By 1683 all the Balkans and Hungary were under Turkish rule. All the Turks with a few exceptional tribes became Muslim.

The Mongols in the Eastern Steppes came into a sudden prominence under the leadership of Genghis Khan (1162-1227). By incorporating defeated enemies into their army the Mongols achieved remarkable conquests. Thus the Mongol army dominated all the Russian principalities except Novgorod by 1241, most of the Middle East by 1260, and all of China by 1279. However, succession problems, not military failure, proved to be the undoing of the huge empire. Towards the end of the 13th century the empire fragmented though it maintained ceremonial unity. After the death of Kublai in 1294 it discarded even the pretended unity. The separate parts of the empire went their own ways, and began to break up as the subject peoples asserted their independence.

The Mongol Empire constituted the apex of steppe history. The emigration of people from the steppes--a pattern that played the dominant role in Eurasian history since 4500 BC with regard to the Indo-Europeans--diminished after the Mongol eruptions. The most likely fundamental cause underlying the military and succession problems was the recurrent infection of bubonic plague due to the spread of the disease among the burrowing rodents of the steppes, and as a result the population in the steppes did not increase markedly apart from the unknown effect of the weather. The Manchus from the Manchurian steppes conquered China in 1644. This was the final eruption of nomad military resources. Also the European and Chinese artificers developed powerful handguns by about 1650, and the steppe peoples with the limited knowledge of explosives were no match to the sophisticated gunfire by the beginning of the 18th century.

Early Migrations and Settlements of Peoples in Europe

Europe was accessible from Africa, the Middle East and Asia with few obstacles to impede migrations. The weather is mostly temperate except in the extreme north. *Homo erectus* which evolved a million years ago in Africa entered Europe between 800 000 and 500 000 years ago and further migrated into Asia. They were hunters and gatherers at the stage of the Old Stone Age, and made use of fire. Between 80 000 and 60 000 BC, the Neanderthals (*Homo sapiens*), a more advanced species, emerged in Europe and throughout the Old World. They were also hunters and gatherers and used fire but died out around 30 000 BC. Around this time *Homo sapiens sapiens*, often called Cro-Magnon man, appeared in Europe, migrating from the Middle East and the Caucasus. This species also originated in Africa and had large brains and were much like the modern humans. They had a complex social structure and relied on tools and brains for survival rather than the brute force of the Neanderthals. Divisions into nations were more recent events and did not show any sign of the divisions around this time. The cave paintings of Lascaux in France and Altamira in Spain are dated to the late Cro-Magnon period, 15 000-10 000 BC. The paintings show the bison, boar and wild horse. (Berg & Litvinoff 1992, pp. 19-21)

According to DNA analyses the majority of Cro-Magnon (*Homo sapiens sapiens*) came from Central Asia and only a minority came directly from the Middle East. It was concluded that the modern Europeans are descendants of Cro-Magnon. (Wells 2003, p. 154) However, scientists no longer use the term Cro-Magnon but designate them instead anatomically modern human or early modern human, noting that these people were the same anatomically as the modern human. The Indo-Europeans (*Homo sapiens sapiens*) were related to Cro-Magnon; however, it seems that the latter emigrated out of the Eurasian Steppes so much earlier than the former that scholars today cannot ascertain.

During the 1800s linguists identified the similar languages that were predominantly spoken in India and Europe. Linguists and anthropologists further researched where the Indo-Europeans came from. The Indo-European homeland was traced to north of the Caucasus Mountains hence the Indo-Europeans are also known as the Caucasians.

Once people settled in one area and commenced agriculture they were reluctant to move. Agriculture could absorb increased populations by intense labouring, but occasional famines resulted.

The most recent Ice Age began about 100 000 years ago and reached the coldest period between 23 000 and 14 000 BC. *Homo erectus* and *Homo sapiens* were on the move long before the last Ice Age started. The reasons for the emigrations are cited as overpopulation in their old habitat, natural disasters such as flood or drought, and simply a yearning for adventure. Also in the thick of the Ice Age the sea levels became low resulting in easy migrations. The sea level was much lower during the Ice Ages, possibly as much as 125 metres than it is today: Britain was linked to the European mainland; Scandinavia to Denmark; and the Balkans to Asia Minor. (Martell 1995, p. 17) A part of the people in Central Asia migrated to Siberia and further to North America in the past 20 000 years. Asia and North America were connected by land at that time, and people simply walked across from Asia to North America where people had never lived before. People further migrated to

South America. The sea between southeast Asia and Australia became small and shallow, and people sailed across to Australia around 60 000 to 53 000 BC. (pp. 13-4)

Mammoths, large hairy Ice Age mammals, had ranged widely across Europe, Asia and North America, but died out around the time the Ice Age ended. They retained heat not so much by their thick hairs but by the bulk of their bodies, that is, less surface area relative to their volume, heat being lost through the surface. They were slow and ungainly and became easy prey for humans. The last Ice Age ended about 12 000 years ago, and the warmer climates dominated the continents since then and farming became possible.

As the Ice Age ended the ecology radically changed too. Dense forests replaced large parts of the tundra and steppe, yielding different types of food. Generally warmer climate yielded plentiful of food; pigs and deer in the woods; seals, water fowls and shellfish near the coast. As a result the population was generally on the increase, though when farming started in the later stage in some parts of the globe, there was a sharp increase of population in these regions. People had to adapt to the new environment for survival. Consequently people in Europe learned the techniques of farming from those in the Near East by the seventh or sixth millennium BC. The earliest evidence was found in the Balkans. In the New Stone Age farming of cereal crops and raising of livestock became widespread in Europe. Agriculture brought the surpluses of food, population growth, and the development of social and religious institutions. (Rietbergen 1998, p. 16)

Section 2 First Civilisations and Their Transmissions

We use the East and the West today in various contexts depending on the circumstances to which people focus their attention. In this book we are primarily comparing China proper with the Western European countries, two currents of civilisation. We can identify China proper and Western Europe as not only geographical but cultural and racial units though neither of the two is homogeneous under close inspections. In spite of the fact that there are dozens of nations competing in the European continent, to our surprise, only a few countries in Europe played a leading role at one time in such fields as politics, economics and arts.

There are other dimensions of contrast when we talk about the East and the West. Greece, as for Rome, is a secondary civilisation, taking cultures from the surrounding nations. These civilisations were, comparatively speaking in the long history of human kind, late comers and secular from the beginning. The ancient Greeks (the Westerners) took many ideas from the Near East as is symbolically manifested by their adaptation of the Phoenician alphabets, though as a matter of fact the Ugarit alphabets were the early form of the Phoenician alphabets. They also learned sculpture from the Egyptians and architecture from the Levantines but they insisted on interpreting every foreign influence on their own terms. These Greeks in their height of culture felt superior to any other peoples around them in spite of their cultural debts. In the ancient to classical Greece, the citizenship was a privilege and closely guarded. They henceforth instituted imperialist policies towards their neighbouring nations though they had a renowned democratic system within the Greek city-states. The ancient to classical Greek imperialism came from cultural pride rather than military strength; classical Roman imperialism came from military strength.

One reason why the Romans (the Westerners) were at first reluctant to embrace Christianity was that the religion originated in the Levant (the East) and the Romans had some aversion to the region. Today we associate Christianity with the Western world.

We also contrast the East and the West in relation to the former communist world and the Western world.

Adolf Hitler declared in *Mein Kampf* (1925) that all the human material culture, that is, all the results of science, technology and inventions, were almost exclusively the creative results of the Aryans. The Aryans as he meant referred to the Germanic race which was flanked by the Latin race in the south and west and by the Slavic race in the east, in the European continent. The Aryans occupied and still occupy as the dominant people in north and central Europe, North America and Australia among other places. He further stated that the Germans should expand to the east, motivated by the considerations of communism, race and vast living space (Hitler 1992, pp. 262-3, 598). Unfortunately for him and the German people, when he spelt out while in prison the intention to conquer Russia in the above book, he did not take into account the climatic consideration and also the incredible resilience of the Russian people, both of which combined produced disastrous results for the German armies in the early 1940s.

The Aryans, as Hitler conceived, are the same people that Tacitus, the Roman historian, described as the Germanic tribes in *Germania* (AD 98). Tacitus wrote that the Germanic people posed the greatest threat to the security of the Roman Empire. His basic supporting line of the above proposition was the moral discipline. The contemporary Romans were morally lax, whereas the Germans possessed the simple virtue though mingled with some primitive vices. Sure enough the German tribes a few centuries later overran the Roman Empire, and then expanded to the northern Europe and overseas. (Dudley 1968, pp. 218-27)

Hitler, if he had travelled to England and realised about the prejudices against the Germans by the English, might not have propounded his racial theory so shamelessly. If he had lived in England for a while and received a rather cold treatment, he might not have mistreated the sojourners in his country while being a prime minister. Also though Hitler was an Austrian he fought in the western front under the German army during World War One. Hence he did not have the experience of fighting with the Russians of incredible resilience in mental and physical capacity as well as the bitterly cold winter in Russia. It is on record that he inspected his army around Moscow during the Russian campaign during WW II. He desperately wanted to avoid war with Britain and America whose people, he thought, were racially akin to the Germans, and besides these countries being highly industrialised would have made the formidable opponents. His wishful thinking came to naught in the course of the war, which points to the possibility that he based his racial theories on the mostly wrong premises.

Without a doubt Hitler was aware that religion and idealism made their greatest advances by the non-Aryans but did not mention this fact in his book because of the embarrassment to his line of argument. He believed and wrote that the Aryans made the greatest contributions to inventions and material culture, which was in fact his critical mistake.

As far as his conviction about the human material culture was concerned, it was what Hitler wanted to believe and the German people wanted to hear, being more emotional and ignoring what really happened in the course of human history. In fact nothing could be further from the truth.

Hitler made his error in judgement criteria he used. He mentioned only the material aspects of civilisation. He did not take into consideration the idealistic views of human achievement, which are, I believe, more fundamental to the existence of human society, although he wrote in another context that there is no true higher development of man without idealism (Hitler 1992, p. 275). He was also wrong because he did not identify any time frame in the superiority criterion: the comparable levels of civilisations are not fixed but variable with time. He, getting the ideas from his daily experience, concluded that the Aryans were the major contributors to the material culture in the modern context, which is in itself questionable. He wrote:

> When the nations on this planet fight for existence—when the question of destiny 'to be or not to be' cries out for a solution—then all considerations of humanitarianism and aesthetics crumble into nothingness; for all these concepts do not float about in the ether, they arise from man's imagination and are bound up with man. When he departs from this world, these concepts are again dissolved into nothingness, for Nature does not know them. And even among mankind, they belong only to a few nations or rather races, and this in proportion as they emanate from the feeling of the nation or race in question. Humanitarianism and aesthetics would vanish even from a world inhabited by man if this world were to lose the races that have created and upheld these concepts. (p. 162)

He also wrote that the two queens of all the arts are architecture and music (p. 275).

Hitler was possibly ignorant of the fact that the hegemony of world affairs by the Western Europeans had already passed the peak and was definitely declining when World War One was over. At the latter half of the nineteenth century, the machine industry ceased to be the monopoly of Europe. Only the careful analyses would have revealed this historical truth at the time, though it is clear to us today. World War Two accelerated the process of European decline, though he was the one who precipitated it in the hope of world hegemony by the German people.

His boast was a brag of a young pretty girl over the old and ugly women who had been beautiful centuries ago, seen better times, and made major contributions to the human cultures.

It seems that what a community as a whole wanted determined the course of human history. These aggregate desires originated in the survival instincts of individuals.

People want various things in life. They must have necessities of life; food, clothes and shelter. Animals may be content if they have food and shelter and copulation: many wild animals jealously guard their territories but these are only the means to secure the afore-mentioned necessities. Humans by their nature want something more once they have the necessities of life. They hanker for sex, wealth, authority, dominance and popularity which are often said to be what all humans want. When people have these things they are supposed to be happy; when they haven't, unhappy. Particularly sex and wealth are what all people desire instinctively. These desires do not have to be taught and they naturally fascinate and grip humans. People are racially conscious, too. People act according to nationalism and sexism. People also value arts. Most people are equipped to think in terms of idealism and materialism (in the sense of solving various problems with the use of material), which learning greatly alters. Idealism has to be taught before people can live according to the set teaching.

Kongfuzi (Confucius) said, 'Wealth and rank without justice are no more to me than floating clouds' (Chien 1979, p. 113), indicating he wanted wealth and rank. The popular Chinese proverb says concerning what men want, 'On top of men, on top of horses and on top of female breasts': the first item indicates rank, the second wealth, the third women. Montaigne wrote the following passage in his *Essays*; he refers to valour and fidelity and contempt for riches but we can imagine the idea applies to anything we desire:

> I do not think that any citizen of Sparta glorified either in his valour, for this was a universal virtue in their nation, or in his fidelity and contempt for riches. No reward falls due to a virtue, however great, that has passed into a custom; and for that matter I do not know whether we would ever call it great when it was common. (Montaigne 1965, p. 276)

Plato ranked corporeal or human goods in this order: health, beauty, strength, riches (p. 45).

Epicurus said that being rich is not alleviation, but a change of troubles (p. 43). In truth not old age alone, but every weakness, according to Aristotle, is a promoter of avarice (p. 281).

The following peoples made contributions to the world in their respective spheres by their talents and diligence; however, some passed their vigour centuries ago and some millenniums ago and they all can be said at present figuratively speaking in the old age:

- The ancient Egyptians set up efficient bureaucracy and created unique material culture matching with their uniqueness of race, language and religion. Their approach to engineering was practical and ingenious with an emphasis on aesthetics, and the Western Europeans adopted many of their creations in the course of history.
- It is said that agriculture started in the Middle East. Due to the ideal conditions for agriculture and habitation the various peoples, whites, yellows and blacks, struggled to survive in the Middle East in the ensuing centuries, resulting in the adoptions (created in this area or imported from the other regions) of many important ideas. This area is often called the cradle of civilisation.
- The ancient to classical Indians gave out Hinduism and Buddhism, both of which are centred around religion and idealism.
- The ancient to classical Jews formulated religion and idealism in the form of the Bible.
- The ancient to classical Greeks were proficient in wisdom. The Greeks excelled not

only in idealism but in their analytic approach to science. They also showed their talents in the other various fields such as history, politics, arts, science and even psychology. The democratic government they created was only one manifestation of their wisdom. The West Europeans took up the Greek's scientific approach at the Renaissance among the other borrowings.
- The classical Romans created a huge empire, and by conquering nations preserved their cultures as an important heritage to humans, which would otherwise have been lost. The Romans excelled in their own right in such practical knowledge as laws, government, architecture with wide spread use of concrete which they invented, and art of warfare with sophisticated weapons and siege technology. The concrete used was a mix of volcanic ash and lime to bind rock fragments.
- The classical to medieval Chinese made many notable inventions and created meritocratic bureaucracy, both of which became important legacies to the modern western nations. They also developed the ethical system which is idealism by definition.
- The Arabs blazed like a star for half a dozen generations particularly in the field of science after the appearance of Islam in the early 7th century.

[The Italians and the English together with the other Western Europeans became the dominant people in the modern world, as detailed in sections 1-4, Chapter 4.]
- The Italians displayed the abundant fertility at the Renaissance ushering in modern Europe. The Renaissance was a wide ranging movement, encompassing materialism and the applications of idealism.
- The English came out brilliantly in literature in the sixteenth century, and outmanoeuvred the other European nations politically and economically in a few centuries, and built a huge empire outside Europe, initiating the Industrial Revolution on the way.

Explanations to the above list. The above classifications of ancient, classical and medieval refer to the European context; however, I use them in the text to denote the eras parallel to Europe in the absence of proper designations.

The list can go on with the stretch of imagination. For example, the Germans and Austrians perfected music through Haydn, Mozart and Beethoven around the turn to the nineteenth century; modern jazz music is an African innovation. Music does not seem to be important in forming the destiny of human beings; it is a form of arts.

Though categorised separately in the above inventory, material culture and inventions are probably interchangeable and refer to material objects rather than ideas or concepts. The cradle of civilisation of the Middle East refers to ideas or concepts as well as material objects. The Egyptians were a lot earlier in their prosperity than the Chinese and both civilisations lasted for more than 3000 years, though their cultural vigour was at times low. It is interesting to note that the two cultures, Egyptian and Chinese, which relied on noted bureaucracy and more on material objects than idealism lasted the longest.

Originally the Romans were one of the three groups of the Italic people, and founded the Roman Republic. Italic denotes ancient language or people of the Indo-European family and includes Latin (or Roman), which became dominant in the city of Rome. The city of Rome grew to be republic and empire. During the Roman Empire the genuine Romans were only a small part of the Roman population. The cohesion of the empire was political and economic, rather than racial. Rome as used in the Roman Empire came to mean the capital city controlling the empire, Latin language, citizens of the empire rather than race.

Though the huge empires such as Roman and British were complex and showed many features such as I mentioned as survival means in 'Introduction to Series', one of the fundamental drives of empire building was making money. When these two empires stopped making profits, the people were no longer interested in conquests and administration, and the empires ceased to exist. There are some philosophical doubts if all empires in human history had the same motive of money-making for their existence as these two empires clearly showed in their closing phase. In fact I will mention in the subsequent text that European nations acquired colonies or formed empires in the modern setting for reasons other than money-making. However, it is certain that the industrial revolution came into being to make money. We also know that the purpose of perennial trade, manufacturing and service industries is profit.

Every individual and race had to strive for survival and dominance as it has to today. Penalty for not doing their best was often financial ruin, subjugation or oblivion for both individuals and races.

I expound the Jewish and its derivative faiths, Christian and Islamic, and Buddhism in Book 2 *Religion*. Section 2, Chapter 1 and again Section 4, Chapter 7 of this book refer to the Egyptian and Chinese history. Further Book 2 deals with the Confucian classics and the Greek philosophy. Sections 2 and 3, Chapter 1 of this book refer to the Greeks and the Romans in the ancient and classical eras. Chapter 4 of this book refers to the Italians, the English and more generally the West Europeans in the modern setting. Book 3 *Communism* deals with communism as an ideology and its spread in Russia and China.

The Old Testament refers often to Canaan, which is the ancient name given to Palestine. This is the Promised Land cherished by the Israelites (the Jews) while in Egypt. They eventually conquered and occupied it, as the Bible narrates, during the latter part of the second millennium BC.

The Near East includes the area called the Fertile Crescent, a region stretching from the Mediterranean Sea through the Dead Sea to the Persian Gulf. This area has the suitable soil and climate for growing crops. The western edge of the Fertile Crescent is the Promised Land held dear by the Jews. The Fertile Crescent has the suitable average rainfall to grow corn, watered by the rivers, Jordan, Tigris and Euphrates. Here the agriculture with the cultivation of wild cereals, mainly wheat and barley, was widespread about 10 000 years ago (8000 BC). A fundamental reason for these developments was the far-reaching global change in climate that occurred after the end of the last Ice Age, some 12 000 years ago. One theory goes that the agriculture with the necessary techniques diffused from this region to the rest of the world. (Williams 1987, pp. 25-6)

Another recent theory states that the agriculture developed in the following three areas independently:

- South-West Asia including Egypt; 8000 BC onwards
- China; 5000 BC onwards
- Central America; 1500 BC onwards

The Chinese civilisation may have started from the second millennium BC. The earliest known Chinese writing dates from 1600 BC. The civilisation of the Near East is much older than that of China and possibly triggered it.

Herodotus, 'the father of history' in the western world, learned about culture and history through extensive travels because there was not much written information available in his fields of interests around 5th century BC. The role of geographic factors in human history fascinated him. (Riasanovsky 1977, p. 8) Soon after 464 BC, Herodotus, a Greek historian, began to wander the Greek and Persian world. He visited Egypt around 450 BC and recorded what he observed in Book 2 of his *History*, which is a rich source of information for us. The *History*, thus composed, certainly gives the impression that he wrote up from the travel notes. (Freeman 1996, p. 155) The *History* primarily centres on the struggles between the Greeks and the Persians. However, he also wrote about geography, history and peoples he got to know. His works give us the most detailed picture of the Greeks. (Roberts 1973, p. 16) Herodotus looked into the reasons why a historical event took place, and he did his best to achieve an even-handed approach with the scarce information available to him.

Hippocrates (460?-370? BC), a Greek physician known as 'the father of medicine', was also active during this period. Polybius (?205-?123 BC), a Greek historian, also relied on travelling to collect the data necessary to write on history. (Mercer 1996, p. 150)

For the Jews, the past was a record of the relationship between people and Yahweh. They compiled it into what we call the Bible. For the Egyptian state, the past was in the possession of kings to be manipulated to protect their own possession. The Chinese reverence for the past emerged as fine historical records such as by Sima Qian (Ssu-ma Ch'ien) (c. 145- c. 86 BC) and Ban Gu (Pan Ku) (AD 32-92) (Harris 1999, p. 171).

There is in China an interesting parallel to the foregoing episodes. Ssu-ma Ch'ien wrote *Historical Records,* which is often compared with *Parallel Lives* by Plutarch (AD ?46-?120). Both authors narrated the lives of the heroes or leaders of the time on the belief that the accurate descriptions of their lives would make contemporary history. Ssu-ma Ch'ien travelled widely on government missions, often accompanying the emperor on his journeys or touring the country collecting material for his records. He created a new historical form, which subsequent generations in China imitated though there had been a great deal of historical writings in China before him. His works were forceful, systematic and comprehensive. His records were accurate as far as he could ascertain and he avoided falsehood and hypocrisy. (Chien 1979, p. i)

The above view by Ssu-ma Ch'ien and Plutarch can be sharply contrasted with the communists' view that the masses made human histories.

The thrust of contrast in this book is between China proper and Western Europe. It is certainly hard to believe, looking at the old woman (China), that she was once pretty many centuries ago and that fact does not impress us at all. China was once a beautiful girl who did not know that she would become old and ugly. Both the East and the West in their prime should have known that one day they would not be pretty any longer, which should have lessened their arrogance at youth and the pains of old age and possibly prolonged their prime time. Beautiful girls, knowing they must age, should look at old women the same as themselves rather than regard them as something different and despicable.

Egypt

When Herodotus visited Egypt in the fifth century BC, priests said to him, 'Egypt is the gift of the Nile'. The Nile River flooded over the banks each summer to deposit millions of tons of sediment on the flat plains along the river, though excessive flooding at times caused destructions and a loss of properties and lives. The fact that water carried a large amount of black silt, rich in nutrients, for many thousands of years amazes us but this is a geological process observable in other major rivers. Lake Victoria is the largest lake in Africa and the chief reservoir of the Nile River; and spring rains, especially in the Ethiopian Highlands, and melting snow brought the flooding of the river. When the flooded water receded the farmers cultivated the soil to produce food. The rainfall was so poor in the lower reaches of the river that they would have been arid without the deposit the flood carried. Silt properly controlled produced four to five times of crops of what rain-fed earth would produce, which was further assisted by warm to hot dry weather from planting to harvesting. The farmers repeated the same process every year to harvest ample food with minimal labour. Thus the Egyptians were able to devote their time on what we call cultures. By 3000 BC the people in Egypt spoke one language and shared common religious beliefs.

The following are today's data. Though we cannot make a definitive statement that the amount of the rainfall over today's Egypt has been about the same in the past five millenniums, we can obtain at least some idea what the Nile River would have been like during ancient Egypt.

The Nile River is the longest river in the world spanning 6650 kilometres. Highlands characterise eastern Zaire, Uganda, Kenya and Ethiopia with the large amount of the erodible rocks and soils of high nutrient for farming. They are in central Africa, and the first three countries are under the equator. These regions receive 150 centimetres or more rain annually. Lower part of the Nile River receives less than five centimetres of rain annually. The mountains in Kenya and Ethiopia have glaciers and are covered by snow for much of the year. The south-west monsoon brings a lot of rain to those mountainous regions for 7 to 8 months (March to October) annually, and the north-east dry winds (November to early March) prevail and bring dry season annually. Naturally the rains on the highlands run to all directions; the water going north and the overflow of Lake Victoria form the Nile River. The salient landscape in the African continent slopes down to the north from these regions to the Mediterranean Sea.

The Egyptians are of the Hamitic family of Afro-Asiatics and not Arabs and have no close relatives racially and linguistically, and produced correspondingly a unique culture. The Egyptians have spoken Arabic since the Arab Muslims conquered Egypt, that is, the AD 7th century.

The recent excavations by scholars revealed that the Old Kingdom collapsed because the Nile River ceased flooding for some years. Scholars reached to the obvious conclusion that this was because sufficient rain did not fall in the upper reaches of the Nile River. They also theorised that the ancient Egyptians must have believed that the pharaohs who were ultimately responsible for the welfare of the people did not have the divine power to cause flooding. Coupled with political failures people lost respect for the order, and the Old Kingdom fell to be followed by the First Intermediate period and the Middle Kingdom. The Old Kingdom was known for the absolute power of the pharaohs and key administrative posts were held by the members of the royal family, which the later pharaohs aspired but could not attain.

No foreign domination took place in Egypt until the Hyksos ruled the northern Egypt for over a century towards the end of the Middle Kingdom. The Hyksos occupation was an aberration resulting from the weak Egyptian pharaohs, unthinkable up to that time for the proud Egyptians with the sense of superiority ingrained. Thus the Middle Kingdom terminated, and the Second Intermediate period and then the New Kingdom followed. The Late period came after the New Kingdom. Decline and chaos marked the Late period, to be followed by continuous foreign occupations, and Egypt was never to regain its former vigour and glory.

When the Aswan High Dam was constructed in the 1960s the Nile flooding stopped, and the dam, releasing floodwaters when needed for irrigation, brought several other benefits, the chief of which was the potential for generating hydroelectricity. Obviously it brought adverse effects as well such as trapping a large volume of sediment behind the dam wall.

Unlike the Middle East nearby, Egypt was well-defined by the desert, the Red Sea and the Mediterranean. Until the invasion of the Hyksos (1674 BC), Egypt experienced no danger from outside. Despite the proposition to be expounded next for the Middle East, it is interesting to note that the geographically well-defended Egypt was a centre of glistening civilisation parallel to the Middle East.

Central to the lives of the Egyptians was a religious belief which differed from any other we know. The afterlife, or resurrection, was not spiritual but a concrete mirror of this life, depending not on ethical conduct but on religious rituals conducted by the priestly class or on the command of the pharaoh. They needed perfect bodies for resurrection, which explains mummification of the dead. They believed in various gods, from which they picked and chose, though some were central to their lives. For example, the pharaohs were thought to be divine and the human form of the sun god Ra, and theoretically had absolute power. Religion determined how the government and society should be.

Only the pharaoh could intercede with the gods, and he was the only one who could minister in the temples. In practice since there were so many temples he designated a high priest in each on his behalf. Over time the temple establishments came to employ tens of thousands of people. During the New Kingdom Amun, a god of Thebes associated with the sun, became so powerful that the status of this high priest rivalled that of the overseer. (Brier & Hobbs 1999, p. 68) The title of overseer was used by every senior- or middle-ranking official in every level of the administration; however in some cases, as in the above reference, overseer referred to vizier. In the 20th dynasty (1196-1070 BC), last of the New Kingdom, it was estimated that one-fifth of the population worked in one way or another for the religious establishments which controlled one-third of all the country's land.

The Egyptians were conservative and abhorred change, and felt superior to other nations expecting the pharaohs and the governments to behave as such. By the Early Dynastic period writing became integral to the Egyptian administration. Thus bureaucracy with the literate class came into being.

People had to go through an apprenticeship to enter the professional classes such as scribes and priests. The scribes and priests taught their sons to read and write, though there were schools in the temples. It is estimated that only five per cent of the total population was tolerably literate. The scribes and priests wanted their sons to escape the misery of manual labour and passed their skills and their professions to their sons.

The government employed a large number of public servants with literate skills, i.e., scribes. The bureaucracy thus created recorded diligently Egypt's resources, human and produces. As far as we can work out the highly centralised government was efficient and effective, even in the matter of taxation. The government controlled international trade, the reason being that many items such as copper, tin and timber were so important that trade could not be left in private hands. Record keeping of produce and manpower, tax collections and the absolute rule by the pharaohs made possible the construction of the huge pyramids. (Hellum 2007, pp. 3, 66)

The sense of superiority also manifested itself in plundering expeditions to foreign countries. The Egyptian army marched south into Nubia for gold and north to Syria for cattle and slaves, and they returned with booty, which they shared among themselves and the pharaoh. They were not interested in the empire building outside Egypt and repeated the expeditions many times. The Egyptians never recorded the battles they lost, and glorified repeatedly the victorious battles. For instance, Egypt did not have the record of the Hyksos invasion; also Ramesses II boasted that he won the battle against the Hittites at Kadesh in spite of the fact he did not win. Though the Sumerians sailed the Persian Gulf to trade with India, the Egyptians were unwilling sailors and played little part in opening up the Mediterranean Sea.

Egyptian society consisted of royalty, free citizens, serfs and slaves. Royalty, a tiny percentage of the population, wielded all official power through the pharaoh. A large number of free citizens consisted of government officials, priests, soldiers and civilians. Slaves could be bought or sold individually, but serfs belonged to the land hence they changed hands only when the land changed hands. Large scale slavery did not exist in the early days of the Egyptian civilisation when the pyramids were being built. During the New Kingdom when Egypt made military conquests, a large number of the prisoners of war became slaves. (Brier & Hobbs 1999, pp. 70-3) The Exodus story happened around this period and the Hebrews were enslaved and forced to work on building sites.

As time went by hundreds of appointments the pharaoh had to make became hereditary, that is, a father's responsibility passed to his son. Also landholdings passed into private hands by virtue of the successive cultivations by the same family being recognised by the courts. The pharaoh ceded the royal holdings to the temples for various reasons. Powerful pharaohs reversed the trend, but the overall trend that royal holdings decreased as the dynasties progressed was unmistakable. Moreover, it was customary that the pharaoh paid directly or indirectly the priests for their sustenance and donated a portion of war booties to the temples.

Marriage in Egypt was a social institution by which people wanted to maximise the number of their children because there was ample food. Since as many as 3 to 4 children out of 5 did not grow into adulthood, girls were married as soon as they were physically mature, that is, at 12 to 14, to ensure the longest fertility period. Men were adults at 15 and allowed to marry. Successful marriage produced anything from 10 to 15 children. Most men and women did not live beyond thirty.

Egypt carried out agriculture from 8000 BC onwards. The Egyptian civilisation emerged in the valley of the Lower Nile. Pharaonic (or dynastic) Egypt is generally assumed to have started when Narmer from the south unified the Upper and Lower Egypt c. 3100 BC and ended in effect at the last native pharaoh, Nectanebo II, in 343 BC. The pharaohs ruled by divine right, and religion became the backbone of Egyptian society throughout its history. Scholars normally add two more dynasties, the Second Persian rule and the Macedonian rule. The Macedonian rule was tied with the Ptolemaic dynasty, which ended with the suicide of Cleopatra in 30 BC.

An Egyptian priest-archivist named Manetho who lived around 300 BC and is often called 'Father of Egyptian history' separated Egyptian history to dynasties which designated rule by families. He further grouped dynasties into major divisions. His system is the base of today's classification. Modern historians normally divide with some variations (often confusing to us) the ancient Egyptian history into: Predynastic, Early Dynastic (First, Second and Third dynasties), Old Kingdom, First Intermediate period, Middle Kingdom, Second Intermediate period, New Kingdom, Late period and Ptolemaic period.

The historians are at a loss why all three pharaohs who unified Egypt and started Old, Middle and New kingdoms after each chaotic period came from the south; the next paragraph gives out the most likely reason. People of two lands (North and South) understood each other but spoke with different dialects. Throughout its ancient history Egypt effectively operated with two capitals, Memphis in the north and Thebes where Karnak Temple, dedicated to Amun, is located in the south. Many pharaohs meticulously promoted unification and all the evidence indicates that this was successful. For example, many pharaohs wore at times the Red Crown of the North and at times the White Crown of the South. The Egyptians always referred to their country as the Two Lands and to the pharaoh as the Lord of the Upper and Lower Egypt. In fact no exact border existed and the Upper Egypt even stretched to Memphis. However, it seems that people did not forget which part of the country they originally came from throughout Egypt's 3000-year dynastic history rather like the Australians, new and old, today do not forget where they originated.

The Egyptians as a whole were a proud people and inward looking and did not care what was happening outside their country, though these aspects changed with the coming of the Macedonians. The Upper Egypt stretched around the Nile River and was surrounded by hostile barbarians who lived in arid areas and longed for the well-watered area in the vicinities of the Nile River. These people were ever on the look out to invade and occupy the well-watered area, hence the Egyptians in this region in turn were prepared for battles and war-like. Whereas the Lower Egypt was open to the Mediterranean Sea and had the land connection to the Middle East, and the people were engaged in trade through these routes from necessity and profit. These two cultures clashed on contact.

From the unification of Egypt c. 3100 BC, possibly by Narmer (the last king of Predynastic period), Egyptian civilisation went from strength to strength in every sphere of the arts, sciences and technologies, reaching its zenith during Khufu's reign (2589-2566 BC), the second king of the Fourth Dynasty (2613-2498 BC). A century after the unification Egypt developed a complex national government, peculiar religious establishments and written language. They owed a great deal to Narmer. He established Memphis as the national capital which remained the seat of the government for much of Egypt's history. He formed the government with the powerful pharaoh at the top and this form of government characterised the long lasting civilisation of Egypt as we know it.

During the Old Kingdom (2686-2181 BC), Egyptian civilisation really came of age, as the construction of pyramids clearly shows. The Fourth Dynasty, the first dynasty of the Old Kingdom, witnessed the apogee of pyramid construction; Djoser's Step Pyramid at Saqqarah, the Great Pyramid of Khufu at Giza; and the Pyramid of King Khafre and the Great Sphinx thought to personify King Khafre both at Giza. Khufu and Khafre were said to have been particularly harsh in oppressing people during their pyramid construction.

During the Old Kingdom Egypt did not require a large standing army because it did not feel threatened in isolation and also the unification of the Upper and Lower Egypt was successful and peaceful. It had only small army units and militias. At the time of crisis the pharaoh called on the nomarchs to provide military forces. The nomarchs were rulers of nomes, the city-states or provinces scattered all along the Nile River. The nomarchical system came into being during the Second Dynasty of the Early Dynastic period. There were 22 nomes in the Upper Egypt and 21 in the Lower Egypt. The pharaoh appointed nomarchs from members of the royal family; however, as time went by the positions became inherited, contributing to the decentralisation of the state. Theoretically the pharaohs owned all the land in Egypt. The nomarchical landholdings were separate from the royal landholdings from which the pharaohs derived considerable revenues. In the Third Dynasty the position of vizier came into being; one vizier for the north and one for the south. The pharaoh appointed to this position, at least during the Third and Fourth dynasties, a prince of the royal family who was second only in importance to the pharaoh and responsible for every aspect of civil administration. However, the heads of the treasury and tax departments reported directly to the pharaoh. (pp. 66-7)

Montuhotep I, the southern king, started the Middle Kingdom (2125-1550 BC) by unifying the upper and lower Egypt and nominated Thebes, his hometown, as his capital abandoning the old capital Memphis. This pharaoh built his huge funeral complex on platform surrounded by columns in front of cliffs, since he came from a part of Egypt with different funeral traditions from the Memphite kings. The vizier of Montuhotep III became a pharaoh, though he lacked royal blood, after confusion. He became Amenemhat I and nominated a site near Memphis as his capital. He came from a town where people worshipped Amun, and this god became the chief god of Thebes and in effect of all Egypt.

Amenemhat I started a great new dynasty which sparked a renaissance of huge temples and tombs. (pp. 14-6)

The period from the 20th to the early 19th century BC in the 12th Dynasty was the zenith of Egyptian literature and craftsmanship. The mud brick fortification walls of the Middle Kingdom fortress at Buhen (Nubia) predate their later medieval European counterparts by some 3200 years.

People called the Hyksos invaded Egypt and ruled northern part of the country for more than a century (1663-1555 BC). They established their capital at Memphis but their dominion did not extend to the upper Egypt which the Theban dynasts had firm control though they were subservient to the Hyksos. Though the invaders, mixed Semitic-Asiatics, were less cultured than the Egyptians--in fact they were illiterate and besides were vastly outnumbered, they won because of the use of horses and chariots, neither of which the Egyptians had seen. The Egyptian forces from Thebes eventually defeated the Hyksos, ending their domination. Still they learned from the invaders and set up the chariot divisions which formed the heart of the army ever after. (pp. 206, 209) They also learned the art of making bronze, a metal harder than copper from the Hyksos. The Egyptian army, now aptly called the standing army with better organisation and equipment, looked beyond the northern borders and came to dominate the Middle East. The overall scheme was the same as the tradition dictated, and the Egyptian army battled for pillage and withdrew as soon as they plundered, not interested in making an empire. The army shared the booties among themselves after they subtracted the pharaoh's share.

Because the invasion and expulsion of the Hyksos occurred at about the same era and have similarities to the stories of the Bible in regard to Joseph, his families and the Exodus, some scholars conjectured that the Hyksos were really the Israelites. Still the hypothesis does not satisfy some historical evidence.

The wealth of Egypt under Amenhotep III (1386-1349 BC) of the 18th Dynasty came not from the spoils of conquest, as it had under Tuthmosis III (1504-1450 BC) of the same dynasty, but from international trade and an abundant supply of gold.

Many royal lands were passed, from the 18th Dynasty, that is, the start of the New Kingdom, onwards to the temples which the priests controlled; thus the priesthood became so powerful to become the rivals of the pharaohs. (Hellum 2007, pp. 8-9, 12)

> By the end of the reign of Amenhotep III, the temples were so rich that they had become political and economic rivals of the king (Freeman 1996, p. 39).

Amenhotep III tried to curb the growing power of the priesthood of Amun, god of Thebes. The next pharaoh, Akhenaton (1350-1334 BC), his son, took the matter further and practised a monotheistic cult of sun-worship, the Aten, though the worship of the Aten was nothing new in Egypt. His cult was monotheism and did not recognise any other traditional gods in Egypt. He moved his entire court from Thebes to a desolate location near modern Tel Amarna. By the sun-worship the pharaoh tried to do without the intermediate priesthood. He then went ahead with dismantling the priesthood and closing temples. His actions made many people unhappy. People kept worshipping the traditional gods in the hiding; thousands of priests were thrown out of job; the army were kept idle while Akhenaton preached love and peace. When he died his cult also died: his revolution lasted only 17 years and did not leave any lasting imprint on Egypt.

Akhenaton is said to have composed *Hymn to the Aten*, which may, it has long been noted, be the possible source of Psalm 104 of the Old Testament. The sun or Aten in the above hymn transposes as Lord of the Psalms.

Akhenaton's only surviving daughter married her half-brother, who became the pharaoh Tutankhamen. He moved back to Thebes and restored the old religion, deserting the holy city and monotheism of his predecessor.

Ramesses (Ramses) II gathered one of the greatest fighting forces ever assembled in Egypt--20 000 men--against the Hittites. The Hittite king, Muwatallis, assembled an even greater army--37 000 man and 2500 chariots. They fought for the control of the region, especially of Syria at the time. They fought one of the greatest battles of the ancient world at the city of Kadesh on the Orontes River in 1299 BC, both armies suffering crippling losses. They sued for peace with the Hittites still in possession of Kadesh. Ramesses sealed a peace treaty 16 years later with Hattusilis III, succeeding king, Ramesses marrying a Hittite princess.

Ramesses III (1187-1156 BC) fought battles including the famous sea battle against the Sea Peoples, and stopped their further southward advances. The Sea Peoples referred to the confederacy of sea raiders, the second wave of the Indo-European migrations into the east Mediterranean. They invaded through the Balkans and Italy to Anatolia, Syria, Palestine, Cyprus and Egypt towards the end of the Bronze Age. They were especially active in the 13th century BC. They destroyed the powerful Hittite Empire in Asia Minor and devastated Syria, and threatened to invade Egypt by land and by sea in the late 19th Dynasty, particularly during the reign of Ramesses III of the 20th Dynasty. They settled in Palestine as Philistines. During the reign of 31 years, Ramesses III further organised an expedition to Punt for incense and another to Sinai for turquoise.

The steadily increasing power of the priesthood of Amun at Thebes came to a head under Ramesses (Ramses) XI (1098-1070 BC). The Amun priesthood came to own two-thirds of all temples land in Egypt, 90 per cent of all ships and 80 per cent of all factories. Their grip on the state's economy was paramount. *The Book of the Dead,* referring to the particular document in this context, was the joint funeral papyrus of Herihor (1080-1074 BC), High Priest of Amun, and his wife.

King Necho (610-595 BC) pre-empted the Suez Canal by almost 2500 years when he had a navigable canal dug. Cleopatra had ships dragged overland from the Nile River to the Red Sea. (Hughes-Hallett 1990, p. 31)

The Achaemenid (Achaemenian) Persians, led by Cambyses II, took charge of Egypt in 525 BC, when the Saite dynasty had collapsed. Under Darius I, the digging of a canal linking the Red Sea with the Nile commenced. It has been suggested that over-taxation was the major cause of the Persian Empire's downfall. (Cotterell & Morgan 1975, p. 159) Alexander the Great defeated the numerically superior Persians in Anatolia, then marched to Egypt where the Egyptians welcomed him as a saviour and proclaimed him as pharaoh.

Ptolemy I, Alexander's boyhood friend at Pella and later his trusted general, became god-king of Egypt in 305 BC. He built the Lighthouse of Alexandria, though in fact it was completed in Ptolemy II's reign, and the Library which became a great centre of learning. The Lighthouse is one of the Seven Wonders of the ancient world. The Ptolemies in their final days introduced money to Egypt. The Egyptians had relied on complicated barters for exchanges of the goods before the introduction of money into their society.

With the death of Cleopatra Egypt became a province of the Roman Empire. Egypt was useful not only as the granary of the empire--the staple diet of the Romans and the Egyptians was bread--but the source of wildlife, gold and building stones. The Romans exercised a brutal labour system to run the mines for maximum profits, and imposed heavy taxes on the Egyptians.

When Emperor Constantine converted to Christianity in 312, Egypt, being a province of the Roman Empire, became a Christian nation and remained so for the next three centuries. The Coptic Christians, controlling Egypt, destroyed the ancient Egyptian cultures so thoroughly that not even one person could read hieroglyphs. Only after one millennium and half, the Frenchman Jean-Francois Champollion deciphered the language of the great civilisation and published the results in a book in 1825. (Jackson & Stamp 2003, p. 115)

Middle East (or Near East) before Prominence of Greeks and Romans

The Near East is often said to be the cradle of civilisation, which is not an accident. It does not mean that all the ideas for cultures originated in this region: many ideas flowed into this area. This location had geographical and climatic advantages with the additional advantage of fusion of races for survival and development.

The Tigris and Euphrates rivers were subject to violent floods; however, silt properly managed produced four to five times of the amount of crops to have been produced on rain-fed earth, further assisted by warm to hot weather after planting the seeds. In fact an extensive network of irrigation canals was created. This area was also the right location for trade. Even today the location of any business has a vital importance; however, the location for some trade has lost much significance through the development of the various transport systems. The area was also a melting pot of races resulting in both fusion of ideas and fierce struggles for survival. This area was a glistening lure for the neighbouring peoples. Another people would have easily conquered continually changing patterns of cultures with poorly defended borders if the resident peoples were unprepared. (Freeman 1996, p. 59) The Semitic peoples had earlier settled in the Middle East and subsequently the fusions of races took place:

- the Whites from Central Asia
- the Negroes from Africa
- the Yellows from Asia

The most prized area of the Middle East is the Fertile Crescent. Its central to eastern area is Mesopotamia. The American Orientalist James Henry Breasted (1865-1935) popularised the term ‘Fertile Crescent’. The development of radiocarbon dating technique since 1948 confirmed the age-old belief that the first civilisation in the world history started in the Fertile Crescent. Some scholars claim that Egypt has a history as ancient and magnificent as the Fertile Crescent. Some scholars esteem the Nile Valley of Egypt as its extension. The Fertile Crescent is crescent-shaped spreading from the Levant on the Mediterranean coast through Mesopotamia to the Persian Gulf. The Near East has a largely flat landscape of rich soil with suitable rainfall for easy irrigation and farming unlike the nearby desert and mountains, and unlike Egypt where the farmers needed the annual flooding to bring rich soil from the upper Nile River since annual rain fall was too poor to sustain profitable farming. The Fertile Crescent was an ideal place to settle for another reason: wheat, barley, sheep and goats were abundantly in the wild.

Mesopotamia refers, not to people or civilisations, but to the region between the rivers Tigris and Euphrates and is mostly inside present-day Iraq. The base of the economy of this region was efficient farming and consequent trade of the surplus food and luxury items utilising rich soil and efficient transport of the two rivers. Several civilisations flourished in this region in the ancient times. Sumer referred to the southern Mesopotamia; Akkad (later known as Babylonia), the middle; Assyria, the northern. People today use these geographical designations of Sumer, Akkad (Babylonia) and Assyria only in the context of history. Towards 1500 BC the creative period of Mesopotamia ended (Eliade 1978, p. 83).

The Tigris and Euphrates rivers originate in the mountains in the east of Anatolia. The water flow of these rivers comes mainly from the snowmelt in the spring of the Taurus and Zagros mountains where widespread snow falls during winter. The tributaries have extremes of heat in summer and cold in winter. During winter the mean temperature in the region is well below freezing, and agriculture comes to a halt. The seasonal rainfall peaking between March and May melts the snow and further rainfalls supplement the snowmelt on the way. Most of the huge amount of water and silt carried by the rivers does not reach the Persian Gulf but evaporates or runs into the extensive water catchments for irrigation and marshes on the way.

Seasonal wind flows explain the above weather pattern. South-easterly winds from the Arabian Sea move up the Arabian Peninsula becoming predominant in winter and spring; they are cool and damp and bring cloud, snow and rain. During summer the north-west winds, warm and dry, become predominant, and move along the Taurus Mountains to Mesopotamia and to the Arabian Sea.

Mesopotamia lacked defensible frontiers, and the rapid movements of peoples and the bewildering changes of kingdoms marked its early history. The peoples in the outer regions such as the Syrian Desert and the Zagros Mountains migrated into the higher culture or better life of Mesopotamia and became assimilated with the native population. The powerful Assyrian and Babylonian armies did not have the targets to attack with the migrating nomads. These nomads did not have the leaders nor the cities nor the permanent habitations. By the 10th century BC the Aramaeans and the Chaldeans abandoned their nomadic life and the former settled in the Levant and the north Mesopotamia and the latter in the south Mesopotamia. Once settled these former nomads lost the above advantages and were assimilated into the native population. But the Aramaeans kept their culture and language, and the Aramaic and its alphabets became common in the region by 500 BC.

I mentioned the various reasons why the Middle East had to be the cradle of civilisation. Egypt was also an important source of ideas and innovations. Egypt had a different setup from the Middle East, though both had high agricultural yields because of the inundations of the large rivers in the regions.

Egypt was geographically well defended unlike the Middle East. The Egyptians were unwilling international traders unlike the peoples in the Middle East. The same language and same people marked Egypt except for the Hyksos occupation of the northern Egypt towards the end of the Middle Kingdom. The continuous dominance of Egypt by foreigners at the end of the New Kingdom happened when the Egyptian empire was at an end. Bewildering changes of the peoples and languages marked the Middle East through its history.

The question may reduce to the following. Developments of the Middle East around the Fertile Crescent were expected. So why did Egypt play such a prominent role in the developments of human kind in the field of material objects given its environment? Were the surplus crops produced after the annual inundation of the Nile River so huge that this negated any adverse effects? Egypt and the Middle East are geographically close and are connected by land, hence did the peoples and ideas freely move between the two regions? According to the Old Testament there were no restrictions on the movement of people, though this observation goes against the proposition that Egypt was geographically well defended. Were the ancient Egyptians geniuses? The Egyptians were characterised by practicability coupled with aesthetics, hence did they push their culture to such a height? Did the bureaucracy, which controlled Egyptian society, govern so successfully bringing peace and stability that the Egyptians directed their attention to what we call culture? It is hard to answer the query convincingly. We don't know the reasons why a certain phenomenon takes place even in the field of science. This might be one area where we simply don't understand, manifesting the fascinating features of history, societies and humans.

The nomads in the desert renewed themselves by absorbing other Semitic peoples: the Amorites (c. 2200-2000 BC) renewed themselves as the Aramaeans (c. 1200-1000 BC), who in turn renewed themselves as the Arabs (800 BC onwards). The nomads moved constantly on horses, their distinct assets for mobility and warfare, and became sedentary when they saw a chance for a better life. According to one theory, the Bedouins in the Arabian Desert domesticated Arabian horses as early as 4500 years ago. Thus horses were widely available among the nomads by the late third millennium BC. By the end of the second millennium BC camels gave the nomads the ability to travel the desert. 'Bedouins' simply meant desert dwellers in the ancient world, and the Bedouins were engaged in trading, hunting, crop production and animal husbandry. Today the term Bedouins invariably refers to the nomadic Arabs, and almost all of one million Bedouins are Muslims and speak some form of Arabic.

Bedouins spewed out of the desert into cultured areas and took the names of the Amorites, the Aramaeans and the Arabs. It is conjectured that the drying up of farm lands forced them to leave their home lands. We must understand that people risked their lives through many of migrations in history and only critical problems such as overpopulation, starvation, or tribal fights led to the migrations.

When the Ice Age was drawing to a close, the Middle East went through an intensive climatic change. The weather changed from continental to Mediterranean, and brought long dry summers and short wet winters. This favoured the growth of wheat and barley and heralded the short lived Natufian culture which preceded farming in this region. The Natufian was named after the first site where it was uncovered, Wadi an-Natuf in Israel. This culture centred on gathering cereal plants. (Wells 2003, p. 149)

> As for the Natufians themselves, their skeletons show them to have been small-boned people about five feet tall, with long skulls and delicate features. The bearers of the Natufian culture, Mesolithic in character, appeared in Palestine and chose a sedentary existence. They utilised the wild cereals as foodstuffs and began the domestication of animals. All the above activities led to the increase of population and the development of commerce. (Eliade 1978, p. 33) Perhaps they were among the ancestors, still undifferentiated, of later Semites and Hamites. Or typical Mediterraneans? But this entire area (the Near East) has been a melting pot for the peoples and civilisations which have seeped into it from its continental hinterlands—starting with the very earliest interbreeding of *Homo Sapiens*--so that the Natufians were probably thoroughly hybrid already. So were elements on their culture, ... (Grant 1969, p. 17)

After 9000 BC the eastern Mediterranean summer became increasingly drier, which reduced the yield of cereals. The Natufians in such place as Jericho had to resort to planting the gathered cereals, thus the 'Neolithic Revolution', as an archaeologist V Gordon Chile coined, started. (Wells 2003, p. 150)

Thus people in the Middle East started to grow wheat and herd wild sheep and goats about 9000 BC, and in the next 3000 years they learned to keep livestock; mainly pigs and cattle. Annual rainfall was enough to grow crops and provide pastures for animals. Certainly the amount of harvest depended on the weather; however, at the time of poor harvests they resorted to gathering and hunting hence minimised the chance of starvation.

The Semitic people moved from Africa into southern Mesopotamia around 5000 BC and engaged in farming taking advantages of the favourable conditions.

The Sumerians (of unknown racial origin), who probably migrated from Anatolia to southern Mesopotamia (Sumer), built the first civilisation in human history. They introduced ox-drawn ploughs around 4000 BC. Circa 3500 BC they invented wheels which were used for pottery and transport. They also invented the first known writing c. 2900 BC, at around the same era as the Egyptians did. They built city-states; Uruk and Ur by the Euphrates River were the most important at the time. Uruk was probably the first city ever built by humans and had a population of 50 000 by 2700 BC. Each state consisted of a city and its surrounding countryside. Each city with ziggurats and mud-brick houses was independent with its own ruler, priests and merchants. A ziggurat was a link between heaven and earth designed to be the temple of the gods.

The Israelites were one of groups of Semitic peoples who established themselves along the western part of the Fertile Crescent around 2500 BC. This is the era when Genesis of the Bible is supposedly referring to by oral tradition, though the commitment to the writing took place much later. King Solomon initiated the recording of tribal traditions, and by the time of his death in 922 BC solid foundations of the so-called Bible had been laid, though it was to go through many revisions over many generations (Davison 1993, pp. 19, 21). The dominant race in the Near East was to be the Semites, that is, the Jews and Arabs. The Jews and the Arabs, though they are racially and linguistically akin, are still fighting today in the same way the Bible narrates of the historical past. Many Jews were dispersed since the biblical times and lived outside Palestine to the present day.

The Akkadians from the north led by King Sargon of Agade conquered Sumer c. 2350 BC. His native tongue was Akkadian, not Sumerian, and he became the emperor of south Mesopotamia, establishing the world's first empire. His dynasty died out c. 2150 BC as the result of internal strife and foreign invasions. Though the city of Ur tried to regain Sargon's empire but fell to the Elamites, invaders from the east. As the Amorites, the nomadic people from the Syrian Desert, gained strength, Sumer became a part of the Babylonian Empire. The Amorites set up a number of small kingdoms, among which Assyria and Babylon became dominant in the next one and half millennia of Mesopotamian history.

Babylon became the chief city of the Amorites c. 1900 BC. King Hammurabi, an Amorite ruler, reigned, 1792-1750 BC, and conquered Mesopotamia. The Kassites, from the Zagros Mountains in the east, invaded and ruled the city of Babylon, 1595-1155 BC. The Chaldeans took over the city of Babylon in 900 BC. The Assyrians conquered Egypt c. 671 BC, but were expelled from Egypt in 651 BC. The Assyrian power entered into terminal decline in the 630s BC. The Babylonians defeated the Assyrian army, 612-605 BC, and Assyria disappeared from history for good. Nebuchadnezzar II, Chaldean, and Babylon became the world power, and he as the king of the Neo-Babylonian Empire ruled, 605-562 BC.

The Hittites in Asia Minor and the Philistines in the Levant as we are familiar through the Bible were Caucasians. 'Originating somewhere between the Carpathians and the Caucasus, these people (the Hittites) had arrived in Asia Minor shortly before 2000 BC, during the huge wave of assaults from the north which extended from India to western Europe and affected the destinies of the entire Near and Middle East.' (Grant 1969, pp. 72-3) The Philistines after being repulsed from Egypt in 1180 BC settled in the Canaanite enclave. 'In about 1000 BC, the Aryan tribes from the Caucasus overran the Levant and settled in two separate kingdoms: the Medes in the north and the Persians in the south.' (Reader's Digest 1983, p. 140) The

Medes migrated from Central Asia into Iran c. 850 BC, and the Persians migrated from Central Asia into southern Iran c. 750 BC.

Hittite farmers settled in Turkey c. 2000 BC, and Hattusas became its capital in 1550 BC. The Hittite Empire reached its peak, 1350-1250 BC. The Hurrians founded the Mitanni kingdom about 1550 BC and controlled most of the northern Mesopotamia for two centuries. However, the Hittites attacked Mittani and sacked its capital around 1348 BC and the Assyrians conquered Mittani by 1300 BC. The Assyrians and the Sea Peoples attacked the Hittite Empire in 1250 BC, and the empire coupled with poor harvests declined circa 1200 BC. Assyria growing from the city-state of Ashur reached greatest power, 744-727 BC. Assyria conquered the Hittites in the 8th century BC, after which the Hittites lost their identity. Sargon II of Assyria broke the power of the Urartu kingdom around Armenia and expanded his dominions with the campaigns against the Chaldeans (who had seized Babylon), the Elamites and the Hebrews. The Elamites were possibly Negroid and pushed by the Aryan invasions and faded out of history.

The Persians (the Indo-Europeans) formed a small nation near Babylon. Achaemenes was the founder of the Persian monarchy. It was in the reign of Cyrus the Great when Persia rose to the status of an empire. Cyrus became leader of the Persians in 549 BC, and conquered Media, Ionia and Lydia, thus creating the first Persian Empire. Cyrus destroyed the Babylonian Empire in 539 BC, thus ending the imperial tradition almost 2000 years old and creating the largest empire the world had ever seen up to that time. The consolidation of the empire owed much to his policies of moderation. The tribute tax was moderate, and he did not interfere with the local customs, religion and the government. Darius I, a junior member of the Achaemenid house, reigned, 522-486 BC, and conquered parts of Egypt, and took over the Indus Valley area as well. Though the rebellions by the Ionian Greeks were put down in 494 BC, Darius was determined to punish the mainland Greeks for aiding the rebellions. The Persians invaded Greece but were defeated at the Battle of Marathon in 490 BC. Xerxes failed in another attempt to conquer Greece in 480 BC. The Persian Empire entered the period of slow decline. Alexander the Great destroyed the Persian Empire in 333 BC.

After the death of Alexander the Great the Persians again began to control their lands, resulting in two dynasties of Parthian and Sassanian. The Parthian dynasty ruled Persia c. 240 BC-AD 226. A son of the high priest Sasan destroyed Parthia and founded the Persian Sassanian dynasty in AD 224. Muslim Arabs invaded and destroyed the Sassanian Empire in AD 637.

After the demise of the Babylonian Empire, the Mesopotamian civilisation lasted for some centuries; however, it gradually declined under the influence of Persian, and later Hellenistic rulers, and died out by the beginning of the Christian era.

Though people such as the Sumerians, Elamites, Urartians and Hittites in the Middle East spoke different languages, they wrote their language in cuneiforms (wedge-shaped letters), which were originally designed to represent meanings rather than how they sounded. Sumerian cuneiforms were the forerunners and models of various other cuneiforms in the Middle East.

The *Epic of Gilgamesh* was a universal literature and three versions, Sumerian, Babylonian and Akkadian, circulated widely. This is a moving tale of the quest for immortality and its failure. Interestingly this epic narrates a flood story familiar to us through Noah in the Old Testament. (Eliade 1978, pp. 62, 77)

One striking feature of the ruling languages in the Middle East is the continuation of the sister languages of Akkadian, Aramaic and Arabic, all of which are Semitic languages. All Semitic peoples came out of Africa in prehistoric times and were nomads before settling in the Middle East. The city-states in Sumer enjoyed unprecedented riches and cultural brilliance in the third millennium BC, which prompted invasion from the king of Akkad. Akkadian cuneiform writings were based on earlier Sumerian writings as were all the other cuneiform writings in the Middle East. Sargon I, the first Assyrian king, spoke Akkadian. Aramaic took over as a lingua franca as Akkadian declined around 600 BC. Darius of the Persian Empire decreed that Aramaic, not Persian, be the administrative language of the empire in the six century BC though Aramaic was not the language the Persian royalty spoke: Aramaic was the common language of the Near East under the Assyrians too. Thus Aramaic spread far and wide in the Middle East, and even to Egypt and the banks of the Indus. (Ostler 2006, pp. 35, 47) When Alexander conquered the Persian Empire the Greek language replaced Aramaic, though Aramaic remained the international language in the region, not so much as the spoken but written form. Arabic made its way with the coming of the Muslims after 630, and even today the classical Arabic is used in Muslim prayer and broadcast to an audience of well over 200 million souls.

Persian, a highly literate and prestige language, made resurgence in the tenth century, though it was overlaid by the Mongol language from the 11th to 15th century. Persian became the principal official language of the Indian administration from the thirteenth century to the nineteen century when the British colonised the country. (p. 108) Persian, or Farci as it is called today, is still spoken beyond the borders of Iran—in Afghanistan, western Pakistan, Tajikistan; and by the Kurds.

Not all the peoples in the Middle East were focused on the Fertile Crescent. The Phoenicians were traders, and settled in the cities of Phoenicia, the western coast of Palestine or present-day Lebanon. They lived in a dozen or so independent cities, the most famous of them being Byblos, Sidon and Tyre. Phoenicia was a linguistic or economic unit more than a political unit: there is no record that they formed even a league. (p. 44) They sent trading expeditions far and wide from the middle of the 2nd millennium BC, established Carthage in North Africa, circumnavigated Africa and traded with Britain and the Baltic. Phoenician shipping dominated Mediterranean shipping for most of the first millennium BC. On the way the Phoenicians spread their alphabets to the Greeks and the Romans who eventually became masters of the Mediterranean world. Possibly without the acquisition of alphabets from the Phoenicians the Greeks and the Romans would not have achieved the prominence in history. Phoenician was spoken on the coast of Lebanon until the first century BC, when Aramaic replaced it; in North Africa until at least the AD fifth century.

In the 6th century BC by virtue of enforced exiles of the Jews to Babylon, Hebrew ceased to be the vernacular among the Jews. Aramaic became widespread as the Babylonian Empire spread; Aramaic was the standard language in the empire. As a consequence the Jews spoke Aramaic, though written Hebrew as a sacred language of Judaism has never lapsed. (p. 70)

After 3000 years of shifting power, the control of the Middle East passed to the Greeks and the Romans. The Parthians held sway for a while. The Arabs, Turks and Mongols succeeded in governing this area in the past, and the bitter contests still carry on in the 21st century with the complex mix of religion, racism and nationalism.

Greek Civilisation

The Indo-Europeans lived as nomadic pastoralist tribes from present-day Poland and Hungary through southern Russia to Central Asia and western China by 5000 BC. They farmed, raised cattle and horses and moved around in wagons drawn by oxen. A huge number of people, the West Indo-Europeans, migrated out to Europe between 4000 BC and 2000 BC. The East Indo-Europeans who had lived in north Afghanistan and spoken Indo-Iranian dialect migrated to the Middle East and India between 1500 BC and 1100 BC. The West Indo-Europeans who had lived in the north of Caucasus Mountains pushed aside or absorbed the earlier inhabitants of non-Indo-European origins in Europe as they migrated. Only a few pockets of non-Indo-Europeans remain in Europe today. Notable examples are the Basques, Finns, Estonians and Hungarians. Many of the Basque people, to illustrate, live in the autonomous Basque Country in Spain bordering France: the Basques are of unknown racial origin but definitely not Indo-European. 660 000 people speak the Basque language today among 2 million inhabitants of the autonomous region.

It seems the major motive for their migration from their homeland was reduced pastoral feed for their animals due to climatic changes, which occurred irregularly over the centuries. Good climate, even for one year, produced good pasture to feed the cattle, which in turn resulted in increased population. It was the norm in antiquity the world over that people produced as many children as they could like the animals do. Thus favourable weather for several years resulted in a population explosion. When the weather became unfavourable the region could not support much of the population and a large number of people had to leave looking for better pastures. It is known that the emigration from the north of Caucasus Mountains lasted for millenniums.

The second wave of Indo-European migration during the fifteenth and fourteenth centuries BC was notable for its destruction. Peoples swept through the Balkans and Italy conquering many kingdoms in the eastern Mediterranean and moved further to the west. The Egyptians called them 'sea raiders' because they came from the Mediterranean Sea.

The Indo-Europeans (or Caucasians) had the identifiable same language origins and a social hierarchy of priests, nobility warriors and farmers. Their society was geared for war. They retained their social distinctions after migrating into a conquered territory. In India this tripartition developed into the caste system, whereas the Greeks and Romans discarded social hierarchy at an early stage of development. These facts and other evidence indicate that they moved in large numbers and suppressed any resistance with warrior might.

If we look at the history of Europe for the past 3000 years we notice the changing fortunes of five closely related Indo-European races; Celtic, Greek, Latin, Germanic and Slavonic. The Celtic peoples existed as a distinct identity from the 2nd millennium BC to the first century BC, and they lived in vast areas of Europe--Greece, northern Spain, France (as Gauls; and later as Bretons in Brittany), northern Italy, central Germany, the British Isles (as Britons; and later as Welsh or Scottish), Ireland (later as Irish) and central Eastern Europe but they were not unified politically. Scholars could not establish if the Celtic people migrated into Europe or the descendants of the original inhabitants. Though the Celts were warlike they did not eliminate or submerge the people in their path and coexisted with them. This was a pattern among the Indo-Europeans. Military conquests rather than peaceful migrations mark the dominance and spread of these five Caucasian races; however, the original inhabitants and the conquering people coexisted.

The Greeks lived in Greece at least in the early third millennium BC. Formerly scholars believed that three main waves of migration took place into present-day southern Greece and the island of Crete: The Ionians from Asia Minor from 2600 BC; the Achaeans from the north and north-west of the Greek mainland about 1500 BC; the Dorians from the north-western part of the Greek mainland after 1200 BC. However the archaeological evidence no longer supports this theory.

The Phoenicians developed alphabets--representing 30 basic sounds out of the hundreds of symbols which were originally pictorial representations. Alphabets were a simple way of writing down the various languages spoken in the course of trade which their prosperity depended on and they were famous for. (Reader's Digest 1983, p. 82)

For any language the number of distinct phones (phonetic sequence indicated by square brackets [ ]) is typically between 40 and 60 (Greenberg & Ainsworth 2006, p. 4). Humans have a limited capacity to articulate different sounds and at the same time they have to have a sequence of sounds to distinguish different meanings. The above number is a compromise between the two requirements.

The Phoenician alphabets contained no vowel signs and hence the Greeks had to modify these alphabets to express their vowels. The most important borrowings by the Greeks from the East may be this adoption and modification of the Phoenician alphabets. By c. 720 BC, the Greeks had fully established their alphabets. (Grant 1969, p. 150)

It seems that the Greek language was spoken five hundred years before the first Homeric text was made. Greek is one of the families of Indo-European languages which originated from a common source in the area north of the Black Sea and travelled westward into Europe. These invaders entered Greece about 2000 BC and became dominant over local languages. (Freeman 1996, p. 81)

In the ninth and eighth centuries BC, as Greece emerged from the Dark Ages, the focus was trade with the East. Four centuries later Alexander the Great launched an attack on the East. Though it seems that the Greeks had some prejudices to the Orient, the Greeks absorbed so much from the East through trade and contact with craftsmanship. (pp. 97, 100)

In the eighth century BC, there came a dramatic transformation in Greece. Suddenly the Greeks went through rapid social, economic and cultural changes, complete with an increase of population. They gained the means to write ideas around the eighth century BC. By the end of the eighth century, the Greeks established the polis and Greek states as we know them. (p. 85)

Homer (c. 800 BC) and Hesiod (8th century BC) were credited with the epoch-making books which became the models of subsequent Greek culture. The former poet has the credit for *Iliad* describing the siege of Troy, and *Odyssey* describing the ten-year homeward wandering of Odysseus after the fall of Troy; but he could not have written since he was known to be blind. It is generally agreed that the *Iliad* and *Odyssey* evolved over many centuries, originally as songs. (p. 87) *Iliad* was probably recited by 1000 BC, though in a cruder form, but it was not written down until perhaps 700 or 600 BC (Wells 1925, p. 170). Homeric poetry took permanent shape when it was written down, taking the ideas from the oral transmission (Levi 1980, p. 60). The latter wrote *Works and Days* dealing with the agricultural seasons, and *Theogony* concerning the origins of the world and the genealogy of the gods. The Greeks took many ideas for these books from the neighbouring peoples, especially Ugarit myths, direct or through later intermediaries. (Grant 1969, p. 77) 'And the succession myth, told in Hesiod's *Theogony*, whereby the supreme god (Zeus) ousted his father (Cronus), was not original to the Greeks, but had been borrowed from West Asia.' (Cotterell 1993, p. 16) The Homeric poems had incomparably the greatest single influence on the Greeks until the end of Greek antiquity. The above works of Homer were Alexander the Great's favourite reading.

In the ancient and classical Greece, pupils were encouraged to learn poetry, particularly that of Homer, as a means of absorbing moral values. The idea is similar to modern European society where pupils are encouraged to read the Bible to absorb moral values. It seems that Homeric poems obtained many of the ideas from *The Epic of Gilgamesh*, a favourite of the Sumerians. *Theogony* of Hesiod has parallels in the earlier Hittite epic of *Kumarbi.* (Freeman 1996, p. 63-7, 188)

The tragic dramas of Aeschylus, Sophocles and Euripides declared their eastern inheritance more clearly, since the myths with which they were concerned contain a large quantity of elements as oriental as the sphinx encountered in Sophocles' *Oedipus*. Yet the Greeks thoroughly assimilated these debts, again, although recognisable; ancient Greece had completely absorbed its gifts from the east and made them its own. In architecture too, the Greeks thoroughly absorbed the eastern contributions. (Grant 1969, pp. 204-5)

Solon laid the foundation of Athenian democracy in the early part of the sixth century BC. In the 5th century BC, the Greeks were at the height of their achievements in all fields. (Toynbee et al. 1968, p. 69) In particular, in Athens and some other Greek cities, democracy as an institution established from the ideals reached its climax in the fifth century BC (Guthrie 1975, p. 148).

It is interesting to note that after the Greeks repelled the Persian invasions of 490-479 BC, the Greek culture came to full bloom. The Greeks lived under democratic constitutions, but the Persians lived under arbitrary rule:

> All subjects were the king's servants, and he was the source of all justice, possessing the power of life and death over everyone (Spielvogel 1991, p. 54).

Through the struggles and victories of the Persian Wars, the Greeks acquired their true identity, though only between 30 and 40 of the seven hundred or so Greek cities participated in the struggles against the Persians (Freeman 1996, p. 165). After the victory of the Persian Wars, the Greeks enjoyed 50 years of peace and they rebuilt their city-states devastated by the conflicts. Athens at the time of Pericles had a total free population of about one hundred and fifty thousand which comprised of 40 000 citizens and women and children; plus 70 000 slaves. This golden age of the Greeks came to an end in 431 BC, at the outbreak of the Peloponnesian War. After passing the peak of vigour as city-states, Socrates, Plato and Aristotle made their contributions, inquiring primarily why the Greek culture had passed their glory, though Aristotle went far beyond that.

The Koine, the Attic Greek, gradually replaced the 20 dialects in Greece after the 4th century BC. The Greek language, as the Koine, became the international language in the eastern Mediterranean. The Roman Empire and the Christian Church adopted it for over a thousand years. Its dominance lasted as long as peoples recognised the cultural and technological superiority of the Geeks, and the peoples turned their attention elsewhere when the Greeks ceased to be their inspiration.

Well into the Roman era, the peoples within the empire--including the Romans and the Greeks themselves--thought the Greeks to be intellectually on higher ground than any other peoples; however, by the 2nd century BC the Greeks lost all cultural vigour, and the relationship between the Greeks and the Romans became more like a marriage. The Greeks eventually came to possess the mind of slaves.

Henryk Sienkiewicz in his historical novel *Quo Vadis?* refers to the Greeks as intellectually much higher than any other peoples. However his novel is set on the Mediterranean coast in the AD first century. Though Greek was a prestige language and also the Greek culture had a formidable influence in the Mediterranean world at around the time, the creative vigour of the Greeks had ended a few century earlier.

There is an interesting parallel to the demise of the classical Greek world with the modern Europe. World War One like the Peloponnesian War in the classical Greek world was a tussle to decide who was the most beautiful or dominant in the region. The acquisition of territory was only one reason why the European powers participated in the Great War. The girls wanted to be beautiful for the sake of beauty and also attracting the boys. The nations wanted to be beautiful for the sake of beauty and also dominating the region. I do not see much difference in the aspirations and fights between girls and European nations. In both cases the ultimate aims were survival. World War One may have been Europe's desperate struggle to reverse the tides of their flagging fortunes. The Europeans fought the modern imperial wars, as Lenin pointed out, for greater shares of markets in both raw material and manufactured products. When both of these conflicts were over the hegemony, political and cultural for the Greeks and political and economic for the Europeans, was over and none of the combatants were as beautiful as they were before the wars.

The Bible says:

> Your heart became proud on account of your beauty, and you corrupted your wisdom because of your splendour. So I threw you to the earth; I made a spectacle of you before kings.
>
> (Ezekiel 28:17)

There are similar passages in Ezekiel 16:14-43 and 27:3-36.

Though Sparta (a land-locked country with no effective navy) and its allies were victorious against Athens (a naval power) and its allies at the Peloponnesian War, Sparta collapsed a few years later from exhaustion. Just before the Peloponnesian War, in the middle of the 5th century BC when Pericles was the leader, Athens was at the peak of her political and cultural supremacy. At the end of the Peloponnesian War, which lasted nearly 30 years, the Greek city-states were exhausted materially and mentally and were on the decline.

'It is something of a paradox that the Greeks, admired as founders of democracy, derived much of their wealth from the exploitation of slave labour in the mines under conditions of cruelty and degradation such as few barbarian states have ever equalled and could scarcely have surpassed; small wonder that they revolted in AD 103. The Roman record was no better until the Flavian reforms of the AD first century....' (Williams 1987, p. 71)

In the fourth century BC, Alexander from Macedonia, the northern periphery of the Greek world, conquered the Greek city-states. The world of the Greek polis and freedom was over to be replaced by cosmopolitanism. Greek culture still kept living in the Alexander's empire in a new form. The cities Alexander founded, especially Alexandria founded in 331 BC, exhibited vitality of the Greek tradition fused with regional characters. Alexandria in the Nile delta utilised its position to become an important trading port as well as a centre of learning. (Rietbergen 1998, p. 34)

Alexander the Great (356-323 BC) of Macedonia built an empire encompassing the Greek world, and the regions from Asia Minor and Egypt to India. No other peoples in that region around that era fought battles more often than the Greeks, often among themselves, and the Greeks acquired experience in warfare and developed superior tactics. Coupled with Alexander's genius for war and politics no army could withstand the onslaught of the Greek army at the time. This is based on the observation that the qualities of the weapons used in the region and era were almost at the same standard. Napoleon was a genius in warfare but made a serious mistake in politics and economics as shown in the declaration of the Continental System which eventually led to his downfall. The period of these regions from the death of Alexander to the defeat of Anthony and Cleopatra (30 BC) is called the Hellenistic Age, noted for high achievements in scholarship, science and the arts. Cleopatra, last of the Ptolemies, committed suicide failing to seduce Octavian who entered Egypt after the naval victory of the Battle of Actium in 31 BC.

During the Hellenistic period, Athens remained the centre of moral philosophy. However, the Ptolemaic dynasty with its outlying possessions around Egypt held the central position in the Hellenistic world. Alexandria dominated the intellectual life of the enlarged Greek world. (Cotterell 1993, pp. 49, 69) It was the focal point of mathematics and science. The three great mathematicians of the Hellenistic world, Euclid, Archimedes and Apollonius were all based in Alexandria. Greek culture decayed during the late Ptolemaic dynasties in the second century BC, when the Alexandrian Museum decayed. The cultural vigour of the Greeks started in the 6th century BC and ended in the 2nd century BC, and lasted roughly for four hundred years. (Wells 1925, p. 362)

Trans-Eurasian Land Routes and Sea Routes

The material culture and the ideas spread by the movements of the people, by conquests and trade (Bowden 2002, p. 19).

The Chinese overproduced silk through the centuries, which was the fundamental drive for the continued use of the Silk Road. Obviously there was a strong demand for silk on the other pole of the roads, and the profit motive of both sides is assumed. The silk producers would have sold all their products within China with reduced price and longer time. One benefit of export for the silk industry was to keep the price of silk high in China. The situation of silk export dramatically changed when European ships with huge cargo capacity visited the Chinese ports for trade in the 19th century.

In the course of looking into the relationship between the East and the West, I realised that communication between the two regions dated back a lot longer and was far more important than I had anticipated. This explains the fact that the cultural levels of the Eurasian continent as an aggregate were distinctly higher than those of the pre-modern American continent, Australia, and the African continent excepting for the Mediterranean coast.

In the ancient to classical times, northern Africa was an integral part of the civilised world of the Mediterranean. Plato dismissed the Egyptians describing they were avaricious in one context; however, he acknowledged in *Timaeus* that the Egyptians were the repositories of ancient wisdom in contrast to the childlike Greeks. Also Aristotle commented that Africa always had been showing something new.

We can look at the roads around the Mediterranean coast as the extension of the Silk Road. Also the Mediterranean Sea in itself was important trade routes since antiquity as we can judge from the fact how eager the Romans were to control the territories surrounding the sea which exhibited high cultures. Read the next section 'Europe under Roman Empire' for details.

If the trade routes between the East and the West were well developed from antiquity, why didn't China and Europe develop uniformly? This book stresses the unequal developments of the two regions. The answer is that when the Europeans were shown advanced knowledge in various fields in the pre-modern era they like toddlers were not mature enough to comprehend and utilise it. Similarly when the Chinese were shown the advanced knowledge of Europe in the modern era, the Chinese were figuratively too old to be interested. It is known that the Chinese willingly absorbed foreign cultural influences until the Sung era, when the Chinese lead over the West became greatest in terms of wealth and technical expertise and the Confucian control of the government became undisputed.

Traders from the East as well as from the West used land and sea routes in order to make profits through trade. However, the Christians travelled to China for missionary purpose. It is well established that the Buddhist canons reached China from India through the trade routes. Also the government diplomatic missions from both sides crossed the continent, for example, for military alliance. Some people explored the regions for tourism, adventures, and expanding their knowledge, scientific or otherwise, on the other side of the continent.

Land routes and sea routes were complementary rather than competitive before the modern era. Travellers took into account of various considerations in deciding which routes they should take: cost, time, safety, purpose, amount of cargo and so on. For example, travellers used the sea routes when there was a local disturbance on the way such as war or famine. Marco Polo travelled to China by land but returned by sea. However, the growth of maritime trade gradually eclipsed the importance of land routes since the 16th century. Also the Chinese government preferred sea trade because it was easy to monitor and tax in the nominated ports. The Chinese government closed private trade through maritime routes from around 1368 for three centuries. When maritime trade was resumed, it was mostly concentrated in Guangzhou (Canton).

The Silk Road between the Middle East and China, possibly India included, as often shown by text books were the major routes. Besides the major routes there were many minor routes which merchants used.

The Middle East was the nexus of trade routes in terms of both land and sea connections to three continents since the earliest times. It is a land junction to Asia, Europe and Africa. It has easy access to Africa and Europe through the Mediterranean Sea, to Asia and Africa via the Red Sea and Persian Gulf. The tea trade between the Indus civilisation and the Persian Gulf area during the late third millennium BC is historically documented (Burenhult 1994, p. 126). Between 1600 BC and 500 BC, bronze articles together with a technique of making bronze of Western Asia travelled to Shang China. Only after 500 BC, when horse-riding became way of life, did the distinct nomadic lifestyle develop throughout Central Asia. The regular exchange of the gifts between the kings to cement the alliance between China and Persia and the other kingdoms on the way eventually led to commercial activities (Boulnois 2005, pp. 59, 69, 145).

Alexander the Great opened up the land and sea routes between the Mediterranean coast and India at the early fourth century BC, which would never sever completely. The unification of the regions was achieved initially by the migrations of the Hellenes (an old name of the Greeks), by the Greek language and the Hellenistic culture. During the Hellenistic period, the different Greek dialects became united as the Koine. The Koine of Hellenistic times was a popularised version of Attic, a dialect of Ionic spoken in Athens. Common Greek (the Koine) was spoken and written from India and Iran to Syria, Palestine, Italy and Egypt. The Greeks had continuing relationships with Palestine since the Late Bronze Age; however, only after Alexander's victory in Palestine, did the Hellenistic culture attain formidable influence in this region. The Koine was the language used in the translation of the Old Testament (Septuagint)--which was made in Egypt from c. 280 BC--and used in the New Testament as well (Grant 1969, p. 214).

There is convincing evidence that China had trade contact with nomadic pastoralists further west in Asia such as the Scythians by the third century BC (Ebrey 1996, p. 68).

Since the very earliest times, Asia and Europe were interwoven by the ebb and flow of peoples or by the necessity of trade. As far as the trade was concerned, there was a symbiotic relationship existed between the nomadic societies and China proper (Roberts 1998, p. 18).

> The Chinese had overland trading links with the Middle East and Europe before the birth of Christ. They were exploring the east coast of Africa long before the Europeans rounded the Cape of Good Hope. (Cotterell & Morgan 1975, p. 19)

Trade between China and the Roman Empire brought the zenith of the silk route activities around AD 200. The routes were connected to the Roman roads leading even to Spain. Naturally when the Roman Empire declined the trade of these routes declined too. The Silk Road reached another peak in the 7th century when China and Sassanian Persia formed two poles of the commerce with friendly relations (Boulnois 2005, p. 255). Unfortunately there are no data quantifying the amount of traded goods.

The Great Silk Road of the Middle Ages spanned thousands of kilometres between China and Persia or present day Iran. Both endured to be political and economic centres for many centuries and acted as the destinations and the transit poles of not only traded goods but the various ideas such as religion, inventions and even arts. Nomadic merchants explored the trans-Asian route--precursor of the Silk Road--many centuries before. (Reader's Digest 1983, p. 157)

The Silk Road denotes the transcontinental commercial routes between China and the coast of the eastern Mediterranean through Central Asia and India, and does not refer to the sea routes from the coast of the east Mediterranean to India and China in the normal usage. Goods were transported between the eastern Mediterranean and the Roman Empire, later to the Byzantine Empire, and later to Europe, by the Mediterranean Sea. There were further sea routes between the east Mediterranean and India through the Red Sea or the Persian Gulf. (Boulnois 2005, p. 97) Though sea transport was much cheaper than land transport, it seems that land routes and sea routes were not in competition but were complimentary until the discovery of the American continent and the sea route to India around the African continent. After the 16th century parts of European trade went to North America, and the Europeans traded with the East around the Cape of Good Hope. This trend accelerated as the Europeans built bigger and faster ships with guns on board, and later they built steam ships which traversed the ocean. Land routes gradually faded into insignificance. (pp. 367-69)

We expect that every government on the routes of the Silk Road protected trade and traders for their own goods during peace time and possibly even during war time, though obviously they could not control the behaviours of every citizen and every combatant, foe or friend. Trade raised the revenue for governments and brought prosperity for the community just as every nation today protects tourism industry for revenue, prosperity and reputation. Also local merchants plied their trades assisting travellers in many ways. Any person might have made a huge profit by travelling to certain locations on hearing of trade opportunities. For example, differences in gold values were often enormous and they could have made a fortune by buying and selling gold at the right places. Though Australia is noted for mining industry today, in point of fact tourism is as big as mining.

Caravans consisted of hundreds or even thousands of animals, a host of people such as merchants, servants, monks and artists accompanied by armed escorts. Oasis settlements along the way supplied food for people and feed for animals, and other necessary articles. The journey lasted from several months to several years and a merchant caravan progressed on average 25 to 30 kilometres a day. Caravans transported all kinds of marketable commodities; textiles and dyes, weapons, gold, gems, medicine, aromatic substances and even slaves. There were all kinds of trading methods, crisscrossing the Eurasian continent for profits. Some merchants carried the marketable merchandise from their home land to a fixed destination. Some merchants carried gold, buying and selling goods on the way for profits. The only thing that counted to them all was what amount of profit they made when they returned home out of a certain hardship and duration taking into account of safety.

Before the world went through the industrial revolution, it was the rule that demand exceeded production at least in international markets, which was the strong base for trade. When industries were fully developed in Western Europe in the middle of the 19th century, production often exceeded demand, which also became a strong impetus for trade: China and India imported a large amount of cheap textiles from England. However, the overall trend was that the West did not have the commodities China wanted; hence the former had to pay with gold and silver to trade. In spite of the above observations silk was consistently overproduced in China before and after the industrial revolution in Europe, which gave a strong impetus to export it to the West.

The Silk Route:

> Silk, on which China held a virtual monopoly, was known to the Greeks from the 3rd century BC. Merchants acquired silk from Chinese dealers who traded in Turkistan markets. (Reader's Digest 1983, p. 188)

> The existence of the Silk Road does not imply direct contact between East and West. Goods were conveyed in stages by successive carriers, few if any travelling the entire distance. (Williams 1987, p. 21)
>
> The intrepid traveller and adventurer Zhang Qian had been the first Chinese to make contact with the western world, during the Han dynasty. The epic journeys he undertook between 138 BC and 115 BC opened up an overland route from China into Eastern Europe, via Persia--the route later known as the Silk Road. Previously [officially], China's only trading contacts had been by sea with Japan and India. (p. 236)

The above mission directed by Emperor Wudi (Wu-ti) was more for a military alliance rather than trade purpose. The Xiongnu (the Hsiung-nu), who were thought to be the ancestors of the Huns, a theory now contested, threatened China and the emperor wanted an alliance with the remote tribes who would attack the Xiongnu from the rear. The curse of nomadic incursions into China was fundamental through the succeeding dynasties until the modern day. The nomads were hunters and breeders of animals and exhibited a simple way of life, whereas the Chinese were sedentary land cultivators and a tempting lure for the nomads, exhibiting a complex way of life. The Xiongnu, the Turks, the Mongols and the Manchus all followed the same pattern.

The Spice Route:

> As early as the first century BC, Greek and Roman traders went by way of the Red Sea to India and beyond to acquire spices from the East (Reader's Digest 1983, p. 188).

Betraying our expectation, the southern part of the Arabian Peninsula had suitable soil and rainfall for agriculture. Sizable farming was carried on there from ancient times. Apart from agriculture, in the southern coastal mountains grew two varieties of gnarled, scrubby balsam trees. The resins that oozed from their trunks, frankincense and myrrh, were among the most precious items of the ancient world, and were used as incense and perfume. The Old Testament often refers to them though it does not say where they come from. The Arabs, since the ancient Roman and Greek eras, traded these resins with gems, textiles and spices from India and China, sailing the Indian Ocean with lateen rigged Arab dhows. (The Editors of Time-Life Books 1988, p. 20) Generally, rich nations, as for rich people in a community, make good customers. When Rome reached its greatest prosperity, it imported a great quantity of frankincense and myrrh, which grew almost exclusively in the southern end of the Arabian Peninsula.

Overland transport was slow and expensive but sea transport faced serious hazards from piracy and weather changes. R Duncan-Jones estimated that during the Roman period carriage costs by sea were a fifth of those by river and one twenty-eighth of those overland. (Freeman 1996, p. 452) Live cattle are perhaps the only commodity for which transport is more expensive by sea than by land (Smith 1991, p. 355).

Silk manufacture remained a Chinese monopoly until the AD 5th century when its secrets began to be learned in Central Asia and Persia. When Marco Polo returned from China to Venice at the end of the 13th century, sericulture (the rearing of silkworm for the production of raw silk) was already flourishing in Italy. The Italians controlled not only the silk manufactured in Italy but the silk trade from the Middle East, and exported the silk to France, Germany and England. King Louis XI of France established the silk industry in France in the fifteenth century. (Boulnois 2005, pp. 370-2)

The Chinese exported not only silk, but lacquer, cups and bowls, and spices. Porcelain made in China was made from a clay of such superior quality that liquid inside could be seen through it. None of the above items were necessities of life and only luxury items were worth transporting such a vast distance for sizable profits. Some scholars attributed the weakening of the Roman Empire to the drain of gold in exchange for Chinese luxuries. (Murowchick 1994, p. 32)

China was a sedentary land cultivating country and always lacked horses for military purpose through the generations and imported horses from Western Asia. Also the Chinese demand for Western glass was strong from the beginning of the Christian era.

Along the trade routes crisscrossing the Eurasian continent—the Silk Roads is only one of them, apart from commercial goods people flowed. These people carried their arts, skills, technology and even ideas and religions. Nestorian Christianity spread from Europe to China; Islam from the Middle East to China; Buddhism from India to China. Religious canons had to be translated by experts in religion as well as in two languages before people could appreciate them. This may be the reason why the religions spread only to some regions rather than all over. For example, we have no record that Buddhism spread to Europe at these times, in spite of the fact that commercial goods freely flowed.

The Buddhist canons were first translated into Chinese during the reign (57/58-75/76) of Han Ming Di (Ming-Ti) (emperor of the Han dynasty) by the Indian monks, Kasyapa Matanga and Dharmaratna. In the middle of the 2nd century, Buddhism started to make rapid inroads into China. In the early fifth century, a monk called Faxian travelled to India and brought back Sanskrit texts unknown in his homeland and then devoted his time to translation. Also about the same period an Indian monk, Kumarajiva, accomplished the extraordinary feat of translating Buddhists texts into Chinese. (Boulnois 2005, pp. 210-6) Hundreds or even thousands of Buddhist canons have been in popular circulation.

Nestorianism prospered in Mongol China. Under Mongol rule on the Eurasian continent, land communications were quite safe. The Yuan government wanted to use Nestorianism for political ends. The Roman pope was eager to spread Nestorianism in the east, though the Roman Church had outlawed this religion. France and England were keen to form an alliance with the Mongols against the Muslims. (p. 364)

After the demise of the Roman Empire the land trade between the East and the defunct empire largely ceased; however, the Arabs and the Chinese used the sea (monsoon routes) connecting the Middle East and China for trade. Muslim Arabs deeply resented the intrusion of the Europeans into their trade routes. In modern times, the interest of the Europeans in the East was originally in trade only but as they ventured into the East, they realised it was impossible to make profits through trade without direct political rule since they were dealing with so many nations of the various life views. It paved the way for a dominion lasting 300 years. (Roberts 1973, p. 46)

The travel time from China to Iran on land by a merchant caravan was six months to one year (Boulnois 2005, p. 87). It took about forty days to traverse the ocean by ship from Egypt, a port on the Red Sea, to India, assisted by the monsoons. A large number of vessels--over one hundred--sailed in convoys for safety. (Wells 1925, p. 299) It took five months by sea from Siraf in the Persian Gulf to Canton in China in the 10th century (Boulnois 2005, p. 303). Trade was not only the source of wealth but were the source of intellectual and artistic stimulation in pre-modern times. Trade was also an important means of exchanging ideas. Good traders had to know the latest technology in the distant land and brought it home for sizable profits. Profit margins were high for successful businesses, in part to compensate for the high risks involved in travel and transport.

The Semitic people (a branch of Afro-Asiatic) to this day have a well-developed sense of trade and accounting. They developed alphabetical writing through trade and account-keeping. Modern computation is largely their credit. The modern numerals are Arabic; the Arabs (a subfamily of Semitic people) adopted Arabic numerals from India c. 760. Modern arithmetic and algebra are essentially Semitic sciences. (Wells 1925, p. 112)

The Sumerians (of unknown racial origin) kept accountancy records consisting of numbers, dates and pictures of objects in clay tablets by about 3000 BC. Around the same time the Egyptians (Hamitic people, a branch of Afro-Asiatic) first inscribed on stone and later painted on wall and on paper quite different pictorial signs called hieroglyphics. The Sumerians developed cuneiform--stylised designs--from original drawings. The Sumerians and the Egyptians further developed signs representing not images but sounds. (Davison 1993, p. 14)

The Chinese invented and modified certain techniques, but it is indisputable that proto-historical China received numerous cultural elements of Near Eastern origin. The development of Chinese Neolithic culture and metallurgy came about as a result of dissemination of agriculture and metallurgy from the Near East. (Eliade 1982, p. 4) The notable Chinese discoveries and inventions are the later development.

> A 9500 BC copper pendant from Shanidar, Iraq, is the oldest known metal artifact .... By 6000 BC, unsmelted copper was being used in the Middle East; smelted copper first appeared about 4500 BC .... The Hittites were probably the first to smelt iron, around 2000 BC. (Reader's Digest 1983, p. 245)
>
> Bronze (an alloy of copper and tin) was produced in the third millennium BC in Anatolia before the Hittites came. The Iron Age began in Anatolia towards the end of the second millennium BC. (p. 103)
>
> The metal seals made during the second millennium BC by the craftsmen on the Iranian plateau were found in the steppes of southern Russia, and even as far east as the fringes of China (p. 16).

There is nothing new of the Chinese adopting the foreign material culture. EH Schafer states in his book that some of the Chinese material culture was in fact borrowed from alien races (Schafer 1967, pp. 16, 34, 41). I am to present a few examples in the following paragraphs:

Water-raising wheels for irrigation were in use in China from the second century, in the Middle East and Greek world from the first century BC; however, they could have originated in India (Milston 1978, p. 168).

> Probably stimulated by the Indian toe stirrup, the foot stirrup appeared in China in the second century BC, a thousand years before it reached Europe. It made Chinese cavalry a rival force to the Huns for the first time, fusing horse and rider into one immovable force. (Cotterell & Morgan 1975, p. 75)

There were no chairs in ancient China: they came from India. During the T'ang (Tang) period the Chinese adopted chairs in the Chinese way of life.

Persia seems to be the source of the first wind mills and the knowledge travelled east to China where the Chinese built quite differently.

Cotton was cultivated in India and then introduced to Central Asia and, to China during the Han period.

Iran had a long tradition of woollen products, particularly carpets, and exported to China and elsewhere.

Chinese silk and Greek bronze were found together in the tomb of a prince in Stuttgart who lived in the 6th century BC (Levi 1980, p. 19).

Petra is a good example of trade between the East and the West. The Arabs established cities along the caravan trade routes about 400 BC, the most important of them being Petra and Palmyra. Petra was an ancient city in the south of present-day Jordan and capital of the Nabataean Kingdom. Petra prospered through trade:

> Ideas flowed along the trade routes, with military and technical knowledge, along with artistic and architectural traditions. Petra absorbed some, profited from all, and went on to devise its own cultural amalgam of East and West. (Reader's Digest 1983, p. 185)

Petra flourished for a half millennium--from about the 4th century BC until the AD early 3rd century, though the Romans conquered the city in AD 106.

The Europeans towards the end of the medieval era were eager to find new sea routes to the East. The Muslim Turks overran the Middle East from the 11th century, and trade along the land routes became uncertain. The crusades were to capture the Middle East for vital trade links, among other reasons, as long as the East-West trade flourished. The Mongol Empire fragmented in the 1300s and overland trade became increasingly difficult and expensive. At the close of the medieval era the Europeans were capable of building large ships with large cargo capacity and large capital available and had competent navigational techniques, though they were no match for the Chinese in these matters. After the 16th century the Europeans used long-ranged gunned sailing ships and relied on sea routes. English ships could carry 360 tons of cargo in 1700. By 1800 they could carry 1090 tons. After the middle of the 19th century when the steam ships were commercialised and the Suez Canal was opened in 1869, the Europeans were capable of transporting huge amounts of cargo cheaply and land routes were no longer considered.

Section 3 Roman Empire and Emergence of European Nations

The Indo-Europeans from east of the Adriatic Sea and the Hungarian plain migrated into northern Italy in about 900 BC. They brought the knowledge of iron making and settled in the Po valley and further south. One of the groups was the Romans. The Romans began to conquer their Latin neighbours, and had a territory of 800 square kilometres with a population of 40 000 by 500 BC. (Berg & Litvinoff 1992, p. 34)

The Etruscans (non Indo-Europeans) set up cities in Etruria (ancient geographical designation), stretching from the River Arno to the River Tiber by 800 BC. They founded Rome in 753 BC, and grew rich trading with the Phoenician city of Carthage and Greece, absorbing their cultures. Their dominance grew to north and south; however, they came into conflict with the Greeks in southern Italy over trade in 524 BC and 474 BC, the Greeks being victorious. The Romans expelled the Etruscan dynasty from Rome in 509 BC. The Etruscans were famous for their influence on the Romans who used the Etruscan alphabets, administrative frame work, century system in the army, gladiatorial games and military triumphs. The Romans further defeated the Etruscans over the city of Veii c. 396 BC, thus ending the 80 year old feud between the two peoples.

The Europeans have used Latin or Roman alphabets, the most widely used alphabetic writing system in the world. The Romans developed their alphabets before 600 BC from the Etruscan alphabets, which can be traced through Greek and Phoenician scripts to the North Semitic alphabets used in Syria and Palestine c. 1100 BC.

From the sixth century BC, the Celts, driven by the overpopulation in an agricultural society which had reached the limits of its productivity, began to expand south. North Italian Celts sacked Rome in 390 BC but the city recovered quickly. The Roman army forced its way into Western Europe over the Celtic peoples by AD 14 not including Britain, and established the dominance of not only the Roman culture but the Latin language. (Ostler 2006, p. 273) However, the two peoples lived together and gradually mixed. Only after the arrival of the Romans did Western Europe acquire writing and build cities. Roman citizens, made up mostly of the Italians, carried out the conquests.

We can trace the German peoples living in northern and central Europe to at least 1000 BC. However, it is unlikely that they migrated into this region but they most likely descended from the people who lived before 3000 BC. They made up of tribes, several large and many small, and the society was organised for war.

It is said that the Germanic migrations caused the collapse of the Roman Empire as they moved west; and the Slavs moved south. In fact the Germans invaded southern Europe late in the second century BC and pushed out the Celts in central Germany and the south-west after 100 BC. Further the Germans from AD 166 to 180 broke into the Roman provinces under the pressure of increased population and consequent need for fresh land. The Germans retained their language in Germany, and many people in Britain came to speak Germanic superimposed on Celtic and Latin languages; however, the peoples in Gauls and Iberia retained Latin even after the Germanic migrations. The Slav language spread to Eastern Europe and the Balkans.

The middle and upper basin of the river Vistula in Poland and western Russia are thought to be the original habitat of the Slavic people with the other groups coming from the Dniester and Dnieper valleys of the Ukraine.

The main focus of attention in this section is Western Europe. Many of the characteristics of Western European nations originated in the history of the Roman Empire. The following historical facts of Western Europe are particularly relevant to the developments of this book. The relations of the church and the government of Rome had deep implications for further history of Western Europe. Also Western Europe strongly resisted political unification after the collapse of the Western Roman Empire unlike China which strongly favoured a unified nation under one native emperor. Christianity unified Western Europe religiously, and Western Europe in the historical past formed the united military fronts against the Muslims and the Mongolian army. Though the Roman Empire and China, these two currents of civilisation, showed similar traits as huge empires, some political views were diametrically opposed.

The formative era of Rome is called the regal period (753 to 509 BC) with a king. The Senate was an advisory council to the monarchy. The republic was founded in 509 BC and ended in 27 BC. In the republican period, the Senate became the chief governing body, and fixed the level of taxes and controlled finance and advised the magistrates on various policies. The Senate was a council of elders, about 300 strong, who mostly had the experience in public office. Two magistrates or consuls having the functions of the replaced king were annually elected.

Agriculture remained the most important source of wealth in the Roman Empire, and commercial and industrial activities were completely subordinated to the needs of agriculture. Generally in any pre-industrial society, 90% of the working population (free, serfs and slaves) were tied to cultivating soil and tending animal stocks to feed the entire population. The Roman society may have been an exception. Rome as a republic and a subsequent empire was geared to the preparation and execution of wars and mobilised a high percentage of its male population for war over sustained periods. The Roman army contained between 9 and 16 per cent of male citizens in normal times and 25 per cent at times of crises. (Freeman 1996, pp. 169, 317) The above observations justified the existence of slaves and serfs in the Roman Empire.

It is estimated that the Roman Empire had between 2 and 3 million slaves by the end of the first century, over a third of the population. Slave labour was all the more attractive to the landowners as slaves could not be called up for military service. (p. 335)

After acquiring control over the whole of Italy, Rome came into direct conflict with the Carthaginians based on the North African coast. The fierce Punic Wars (264-146 BC)--the Romans called the Carthaginians Punic--ended in Roman victory razing Carthage to the ground. These wars gave Rome control over Sicily, Spain and North Africa. The victories over the Hellenistic kingdoms resulted in the conquest of Macedon (168 BC), Greece (146 BC) and western part of Asia Minor (133 BC). Further campaigns by the generals led to the conquest of Asia Minor and Syria (67-64 BC) by Pompey; and Gaul (58-51 BC) by Caesar. The rivalries among the generals led to the civil wars (49-45 BC) and Caesar came out a victor. However, the republican conspirators assassinated Caesar one month after he declared himself dictator for life in 44 BC.

Octavian was born in Rome, and was the great-nephew of Julius Caesar. On the death of Caesar, Octavian, who was 18 at the time, learned that Caesar had adopted him and made him his heir in his will. Subsequently he manoeuvred to win over his opponents. He became a triumvir together with Mark Anthony and Lepidus. He forced Lepidus to retire. The naval battle of Actium under the command of Agrippa (deputy of Octavian) in 31 BC sealed the fate of Mark Anthony and Cleopatra, and Octavian became the undisputed master of the Greco-Roman world.

Traditionally the Roman Senate was the power behind the Roman Republic. Octavian ruled as consul from 31 to 23 BC, preserving the republican form of government. The Senate gave Octavian the title Augustus in 27 BC, and also gave him Rome's religious, civil and military authority with the Senate as an advisory body. Under this arrangement the real power rested with him controlling the state finances and membership in the Senate. As a matter of fact, he was an absolute ruler and held the power of life and death over his subjects. As for later stage of the empire an emperor's order overruled any act of the Senate. However, in his political shrewdness he valued, and avoided disputes with, the Senate as the repository of the true Roman spirit and traditions as well as the body representing public opinions. Augustus preferred to be called Princeps, meaning first citizen, rather than Emperor. A princeps heads the principate, and an emperor, an empire. In the early Roman Empire some republican features, that is, of principate, in the government survived. By the time of his reign, the empire incorporated so many provinces and it looked natural that Italy would become one with Rome. He promoted this cause by such measure as the elite of the municipal towns entered the Senate.

The Roman Empire started in 27 BC by the person of Augustus, and from then on the emperor was set to rule for life. The huge empire was split into two parts in 395. The West Roman Empire ended in 476; however, the East Roman Empire kept going, though feebly, through the Middle Ages, in fact another millennium.

The Mediterranean Sea is the inland sea, and usually calm and easy to navigate. The weather during summers is hot and dry and free from storms; it during winters is mild and wet but has travelling cyclones. When Augustus founded the Roman Empire, the Mediterranean Sea became free of piracy and the Romans began to call it 'Our Sea'.

The Mediterranean Sea was the superhighway of trade and cultural exchange. As a matter of fact the sea was the focal point of the empire and gave it cohesion and strength. By AD 44 Rome controlled the entire Mediterranean coastline. At this time the Roman territories included the western fringes of the Middle East which was the western pole of the Silk Road. The eastern goods were further transported through the Mediterranean Sea and the Roman roads. Trajan conquered in 115-17 Armenia and Mesopotamia, further east of the fringes but these territories were soon lost.

Though Italy was assimilated with Rome by the reign of Augustus, the provinces were sharply distinguished from Italy. There were two types of provinces from 27 BC onwards. The Senate supervised the long-established provinces, so-called public provinces. Their governors were chosen by lot. The rest of the provinces called imperial provinces came under direct control of the emperor. He appointed the governors. The Senate gradually acquired non-Italian elements and the western provinces were already supplying senators under Augustus. The western provinces were the provinces in western part of the empire and most were the imperial provinces at the early stages of the empire.

When Augustus died in AD 14 he left the enduring legacies to be followed by the subsequent Roman emperors. His style of principate set the tone for the next century and three quarters with modifications. He expanded the empire farther than ever before and avoided to antagonise, and proceeded with Romanisation of, the provinces, and maintained the law and order within the empire.

Claudius I (ruled 41-54) further expanded the empire. He annexed southern Britain. He promoted Romanisation especially in the western provinces, granting Roman citizenship liberally and inducing provincials into the Roman Senate.

There was further evidence of Romanisation in the western provinces. Nerva (ruled 96-8) adopted Trajan, an outstanding soldier but not related by blood; in fact he was a Spaniard. Trajan became an emperor upon the death of Nerva. The fact that a Spaniard became an emperor was not unexpected because a large number of provincials were Roman senators by this time. Trajan (ruled 98-117) on his death bed adopted Hadrian, also a Spaniard. Upon the death of Trajan, Hadrian (ruled 117-38) was recognised as an emperor by the Senate and soldiers. Though Trajan aspired to expand the Roman territories Hadrian opposed the expansion.

The empire in the second century still carried on the policies of Augustus and peace and stability prevailed. This is clearly seen by the army strength which had been kept at about the same size as during Augustus' reign in spite of the fact the empire controlled a much larger area. In fact the expansion of territory was no longer the focal policy. Voluntary Romanisation was the general rule in the existing provinces. The Roman ways of life such as city planning, having baths and gladiatorial combats prevailed in the conquered cities but the rural way of life everywhere was untouched. The Roman government strictly enforced political control and tribute collections, which the cities responsible for the rural areas achieved as well. The Roman laws were enforced in the provinces everywhere. One chief characteristic of all these was the uniformity throughout the empire. However, this feature was particularly pronounced in the western provinces where the Iberian Peninsula and Gaul had been the provincial soil ever since the Second Punic War.

It is said that Britain was the main economic beneficiary under the Roman rule. Though Latin was the language of officialdom and literacy in Britain for four hundred years, rather surprisingly it did not become the language of the common people, who spoke Celtic. After the German migrations into Britain people in the occupied territories spoke Germanic language. Latin remained the language of learning in Britain as elsewhere in the western Roman dominions to be unchallenged until the Renaissance when the vernacular languages took over for serious factual writings.

In contrast the Gauls and the Celtiberians (Celtic people who inhabited the Iberian Peninsula) adopted Latin language, and people in France, Spain and Portugal have spoken Romance (or Latin) languages to this day, though they have made independent developments over the centuries and are mutually incommunicable today.

The modern consensus holds that the Roman civilisation peaked around the year AD 160. As a matter of fact the political stability and economic success went hand in hand. A strong and stable monarchy backed by a strong army made these successes possible.

From the beginning of the principate the princeps had the authority to legislate though no legal documents authorising this power existed. By the 2nd century, the emperor had the authority to promulgate the laws overriding any other sources of legislations.

There was strong resistance to taxation among the provinces and the tax was naturally fixed at the enforceable maximum: higher taxes would have resulted in frequent revolts. It may be surprising but the fact of the matter was the tax thus raised fell far short of the official expectations and this was one fundamental reason why the empire stopped expanding. The government could not maintain a large army because of lack of revenues. The net result was peace and stability prevailed within the Roman Empire with more or less fixed frontiers.

Diocletian (284-305) became an emperor after near anarchy in the 3rd century, and multiplied the number of provinces in order to create more efficient administration. By this time Rome ceased to be the effective capital of the empire, and each emperor nominated his residence city as his administrative capital. Also the empire was too large to be administered by one person. He divided the empire into two for easier administration, and nominated Maximian as Augustus (emperor or co-ruler) of the half empire in 286. He subsequently established the tetrarchy (four-men rule) by appointing Caesar (deputy) to two emperors in 293. This system lasted till the year 305. The western half was ruled from Rome, whereas the eastern half from Nicomedia. Later, Emperor Constantine was to rule the eastern part from another city Byzantium to be renamed Constantinople. Diocletian's reforms temporarily halted the decline of the empire.

In the course of the fourth century, the vast differences between the Western and the Eastern empires were consolidated. The focal attention moved to the east, as evidenced by the military recruitment and expenditures. None of the tetrarchs chose Rome as their capital; in fact its days as imperial capital were over. Constantius I, the emperor of the Western Empire, died in 306, and the army proclaimed Constantine (his son born of a Christian concubine) as emperor, to become Constantine I or the Great. The tetrarchy set by Diocletian broke down completely and seven claimants struggled for power.

Constantine became the emperor of the West and a Christian after victory at the Milvian Bridge outside Rome in 312. Constantine with Licinius (the emperor of the Eastern Empire) issued the Edict of Milan in 313, granting tolerance to Christians and restoring church properties. Constantine gave large gifts of land and money to the church and offered tax exemption together with special status to the church property. After defeating and executing Licinius he gained the control of the East and became the sole emperor in 324. He chose Byzantium as his permanent residence in the same year. He convened the ecumenical council at Nicaea in 325, and henceforth the Nicene Council outlawed Arianism. His stated vision before the battle at the Milvian Bridge, his policies favouring the church and the fact that he ascribed his success to Christianity among others, all indicate that he genuinely believed in Christianity. He further gave land and special privileges to the church, which started to grow into the world religion. The Orthodox Church regarded Constantine as a saint. Most of the Roman emperors that came after him were Christians.

At the end of the 4th century and the early fifth century, the West Roman Empire was in disarray. Corruptions set into the government, and bribery and extortion were the order of the day. Soldiers were often undisciplined and unpaid. They in their turn resorted to extorting their civilian hosts. Corrective measures could not be carried out because the enlightened men at the centre were screened from the truth by the corrupt officers who plotted to remove any men intent on reforming the system.

At the early 5th century the division of the two empires became permanent. The church, further accumulating land, became the largest land owner in the West by the 6th century when the Western Roman Empire was no more.

Outside the eastern borders, many different Germanic tribes lived in villages, farming land and breeding sheep and cattle. They despised peaceful life and participated in a war whenever they had a chance. The Romans regarded the peoples outside the empire as barbarians no matter how they were civilised or educated. The barbarians in their turn regarded the life in the empire with some envy and wanted to enter and enjoy, not to destroy, the good life within the empire. To the Romans a large number of these barbarians was a menace and they were determined not to let them into the empire. (Richards & English 1985, p. 2) Contrary to the above observations, the Roman army had long drawn its recruits from the barbarians and was under command of barbarian generals. In fact in the 5th century the generals had more power than the Western emperors.

Under these sorry circumstances of the Roman Empire, the barbarian invasions took place against the Roman frontiers. The Chinese empire made the strong fortification against the Huns in order not to let the Huns into their territory in the same token the Romans did against the barbarians. The Huns were nomadic herdsmen and highly skilled in horse and bow, but tolerant in religion and easy going with their subject peoples as long as they paid the tributes. The Huns, several hundred thousand strong, in short of pasture for their herds made sudden appearance on the eastern fringe of Europe in 370. Subsequently the Huns moved westward. Panic stricken by the savage Huns, the great invasion of the Germanic barbarians started in 407 and lasted roughly for ten years. The migrations of the Slavic peoples also took place 450 onwards following the German migrations westwards, and settled in eastern Europe, the Balkans and western shores of the Black Sea. The Germanic peoples set up kingdoms all over western parts of Europe, causing turmoil for the next 150 years.

Britain was abandoned in 407 and fell to the Angles, Saxons and Jutes. The Visigoths under their King Alaric captured and looted the city of Rome in the year 410. Alaric's successors led their people into Gaul and Spain. The Franks drove them out of Gaul. Clovis established the Frankish domination in Gaul, and was baptised with all his people. The Visigoths established a Suebi kingdom in Spain after the departure of the Vandals to North Africa. Gaiseric, a ruthless ruler of the Vandals, brought 80 000 people including 15 000 warriors out of Spain, and invaded North Africa in 429 and conquered a number of Roman provinces and established a kingdom. His conversion to Catholicism assured him the support of the bishops.

The situation in England was quite different. The Anglo-Saxons were pagans and drove out the Britons, the original inhabitants, together with Christianity from England. These people with the faith of Christianity fled to Wales, south-west England, and later to Ireland. The Celtic Church of the fled Britons sent missionaries to England and converted the Anglo-Saxons to their faith by 664 after long struggles. Also the Roman Church spread its version of faith in England. Thus belatedly the Anglo-Saxons were converted to Christianity.

The Anglo-Saxons were farmers and unlike the Romans they understood and practised the mechanism of the three field system. The Anglo-Saxons were the first English people--the term 'England' being derived from Angle-land.

These barbarians (Germanic peoples) were a minority, except in England, and existed uneasily with the Romans in the conquered territories. Some of the barbarians had been converted to Arianism and these converted Christians did not wreck the local church. The Vandals, though they were Arian Christians, were exceptions and ravaged Gaul, Spain, Rome (455) and North Africa in the 4th-5th centuries. The name 'Vandals' has been associated with wanton destruction ever since.

Odoacer, Germanic or possibly Hunnish, was the band leader of foederati (federates) in Italy in the Western Roman Empire. Orestes was the leader of the Germanic foederati and incited Odoacer and his soldiers to revolt. Foederati was non-Roman but an ally of Rome. Subsequently Odoacer defeated Emperor Nepos. Orestes elevated his son Romulus to an emperor. However, Orestes rescinded on his promise of land distributions, and Odoacer attacked Orestes. When Odoacer defeated the Roman general Orestes in Italy and deposed the Roman Emperor Romulus Augustulus in 476, the empire ceased to exist. Odoacer became the king of Italy. However, non-existence of the empire made little difference to the church of the former Western Roman Empire. Theodoric, king of the Ostrogoths, reigned in Italy after defeating Odoacer in battles and assassinating him in 493. The Eastern Roman Empire was not subjected as severe a pounding as in the west and managed to survive the barbarian migrations.

The German speakers thoroughly overran the Western Roman Empire in the fifth century. These conquests laid the foundations of modern Western Europe.

Arian missionaries converted the German tribes in northern Europe to their faith in the 300s and 400s. They kept their faith until the 600s when the last German tribes converted to approved Christianity.

The church survived largely intact through the two cataclysms of history. The German invaders did not wreck the church establishments wholesale because not only some were Arian Christians but they wanted to enjoy life in the empire and recognised that Christianity was the essence of the good life. The church also survived the collapse of the Roman government because they not only were independent from the government administratively but financially, and relied on the gifts of land and money from the benefactors and not on the imperial handouts.

Thus the church organisation, the church buildings, bishops, priests survived the German migrations intact as a living organism. Not only the original inhabitants but the Germanic invaders looked up to the church for guidance. The administrators of the Roman Empire in local governments, justice, public works, and law and order ran away, and the church organisation undertook some of the functions of the government.

From 529 onwards, only Christians were allowed to live in the Byzantine Empire with the exception of the Jewish faithfuls. The vast majority of the people in the defunct Western Empire were converted to Christianity at the end of the 6th century. (Boulnois 2005, p. 223)

The illiterate people of Gaul and Iberia embraced Latin discarding Celtic languages; however, the sophisticates of the eastern Mediterranean spoke Greek and Aramaic even after they came under the Roman Empire. At the end of the fourth century, the Greeks, Syrians and Egyptians were still speaking in Greek after 500 years of Roman rule. (Ostler 2006, pp. xx, 20)

Latin was the language used by the Indo-European people in Latium which was located near Rome. Rome defeated the Latins in the war of 340-338 BC, and subsequently dominated the region.

The earliest Italian language dates from the 10th century. Standard Italian, developed in the 14th and 15th centuries, is based on a Florentine dialect.

We have the impression that the Roman Empire extended only to Western Europe but it is noteworthy that Romanisation extended even outside Roman frontiers. For example, Romance (derived from Roman) speech marks Romania (also derived from Roman) today though it was a briefly occupied outpost of the empire and was called Dacia during the Roman era. The Roman Empire was such a potent force for many centuries that practically the entire Europe was deeply influenced by its presence. (Fernandez-Armesto 1994, pp. 11, 12)

Today we find in Romania, at such a distance from Rome, a tongue closest to the parent language Latin. People in France, Spain, Portugal and Italy spoke Latin under the Roman Empire, and speak variants of Latin to this day; however, as the empire collapsed and time passed these nations and languages made independent developments, though their languages are classed as Romance.

The fertile productivity of the Po valley was outstanding, and its heavy soils were now able to benefit from a wheeled plough introduced from the upper Danube. As the Italian peninsula gradually faded from the forefront after AD 200, north Italy, closer to the critical frontier zones, became ever more important. (Grant 1969, p. 302)

The displacement of Italy's focal point from Rome to the Po valley was due to a general diminution of the Mediterranean's significance in favour of more northern lands; and both phenomena resulted, in part, from the campaigns when Caesar had advanced the frontier to the Rhine, and Augustus, following up various explorations during the previous century, moved forward from the Alps along the whole length of the Danube.

But the full consequences of the enlargements only became apparent under Marcus Aurelius (161-180), when the population pressures from the European interior impelled unprecedented hordes of Germans against the river boundary.

The great Mediterranean civilisation of Greece and Rome started to end in the AD third century and was completed in the fifth, thus inaugurating the end of antiquity. Nobody seems to know why this civilisation ended. (Eliade 1985, p. 38)

The campaigns by Caesar, Tiberius and Claudius took place in central and northern Europe. It was only in the fourth century that the economic and cultural focus gradually moved from the Mediterranean world to the Atlantic seaboard of Europe.

Both the dominance of Christianity and the low cultural web marked the Middle Ages in Europe. St Augustine (354-430) gave the concrete expression of the world government of the church in his book *The City of God*. The European church struggled to realise this divine world government from the fifth century onwards to the fifteenth century with only partial success. (Wells 1925, p. 341)

In Western Europe no single nation was strong enough to dominate for long after the end of the Western Roman Empire. Also strong monarchy was a serious threat to the popes and the church; so they did their best to prevent the formation of a powerful nation and often played politics. This was particularly true during the Middle Ages when the papal power was at its zenith. See Chapter 3 European Middle Ages (600-1492) for examples. Western Europe established the church under the Roman Empire but kept its administration after the collapse of the empire. Its income came from the gifts of land and money from a large number of faithful people at all levels of society, and did not depend on the finances of the empire or the states. The Western Church enforced tithes obligation from the sixth century onwards. Tithing is a biblical idea (Deuteronomy 14:22-7): the early church in some districts collected voluntary tithes.

The emergence at the early 7th century of Islam and the repeated crusades (1096-1291) indicate that the Middle East and the Silk Road were still important economically and culturally in these centuries. The ushering in of the modern era by the discovery of the American continent and the African sea route to the orient critically reduced this importance. In the modern era the countries on the Atlantic seaboard such as Spain, Portugal, the Dutch Maritime Empire, France and England came to play the major role in trade, politics and culture. The development of steam ships and the opening of the Suez Canal in the 19th century accelerated the process, and the Middle East and the Silk Road lost their economic significance.

The Eastern Roman Empire was not really a continuation of the Roman tradition but a resumption of Alexander's empire. This empire maintained the Greek tradition but its cultural centre was not in Greece but in Alexandria, and it did not have the vitality of the ancient Greek culture and in fact was as good as dead. (Wells 1925, p. 318)

Chapter 2 Development of China

Section 1 Before Establishment of Empire

The Chinese have a history (with a system of writing) of nearly 4000 years, that is, from the Shang era to the present, without any fundamental break in their culture, though there have been many upheavals.

Chinese culture spread from the middle Yellow River valley to all directions but the southward movement was most important in many ways. The dry, cold plains in the north where wheat and millet were cultivated were sharply contrasted with the warmer, wetter uplands in the south where the staple diet was rice. As the proverb says 'south boat, north horse' the terrains were quite different, and it was easier to travel by boat in the south. (Ostler 2006, pp. 136-7)

The Yellow River is called the cradle of Chinese civilisation. Its basin is the birth place of ancient Chinese culture and was the most prosperous region in the early Chinese history. It is the second longest river in China next to the Yangtze River. The general flow of both these rivers is from west to east since the land layout in China predominantly slopes down to the east. The Yellow River flows from the eastern Plateau of Tibet to the Yellow Sea, making a grand detour to the north at the first bend, to the east at the second, to the south at the third, and to the east at the fourth, and then traversing the North China Plain on the way.

The river is also called 'Sorrow or Scourge of the Sons of Han' because of repeated floods. It was said that whoever controlled the Yellow River controlled China. The river carries a large amount of sediment, which build up the river bed until it is above the surrounding plains in the North China Plain, water breaking the banks and flooding the plain. This resulted in the changes to the river course catastrophically, sometimes by hundreds of kilometres. It is said that the river had 26 major changes of course in the past 2000 years. The tireless and repeated efforts by succeeding generations using huge manpower with primitive techniques were often futile.

Why then did the Yellow River regions attract a large number of people from ancient times in spite of numerous floods and consequent human sufferings, with the population pressure being assumed?

The answer lies in the yellow loess, which gave the name to the Yellow River. The yellow loess is mostly responsible for the flooding. The Nile River used to flood annually not carrying loess but simply silt: water carried black silt down the Nile River from the highlands of the mid to south African continent for millenniums. By definition air carries loess (meaning loose in original German) which is naturally very fine particles of soil. Loess is also found in western Iowa and western Nebraska, USA and central Belgium. However China's loess deposits are the world's thickest and most ancient. The loess strata have the thicknesses of 50 to 60 metres and in some places as much as 150 metres. The thick Chinese loess deposits have blown in from the vast arid regions and deserts in northern China and Mongolia encompassing the Gobi Desert. The sun heats up the dried earth with little or no vegetation, and minute particles of soil are sucked up by the wind and carried to all directions, the finest particles reaching the furthest; but the bulk went south. The prevailing winds blew the dusts south over the past 2.5 million years. The prevailing wind direction changed a few times due to the changes of both the rotating axis of the globe and the orbit of the globe around the sun.

The following are today's data. The prevailing wind direction in northern China and Mongolia is south due to the comparatively high pressure in Siberia during summer when suction by air of yellow loess is greatest. It is both north and south during winter when the suction by air is weak.

The loess in question is non-glacial and was formed during the Paleognene or Neogene age (65.5 million to 2.6 million years ago) in northern China and Mongolia by weathering. One serious problem for researchers is that the loess formation lasted so many millions of years that physical and chemical changes occurred and today's analyses do not provide consistent answers.

The loess deposits extend from the Plateau of Tibet all the way to the North China Plain. The Loess Plateau, also known as Huangto Plateau, is a plateau that covers an area of 640 000 square kilometres in the upper and middle regions of the Yellow River. The Loess Plateau and its dusty soil cover almost all of Shanx, Shaanxi and Gansu provinces, the Ningxia Hui Autonomous Region; and parts of others. The river cut deep valleys through the loess region and the easily eroded loess accounts for the instability of riverbed. The Yellow River carries the silt (carried by water by definition though it was the aforementioned loess) downstream, and it, spread also by floods in the past millenniums, covers the North China Plain.

Yellow loess, whose colour is ochre (yellow to orange), is extremely nutrient rich and can produce phenomenal yields provided farmers practise erosion control. It was said that fertile loess was especially suited for growing millet, though rice is extensively cultivated in the region today. Loess is the accumulation of wind-blown soil, homogeneous and highly porous. Its layer is traversed by vertical capillaries that permit the sediment to fracture and form vertical bluffs. Loess ground is said to be 'the most highly erodible soil on earth'. Erosion in this context means wearing away of the soil by such agents as water and wind. Famers had to devise various erosion controls.

Yellow loess has also been used extensively as material for ceramics, tiles, bricks; and the building material together with woods. It was used to make terracotta figures protecting the First Emperor. It has been also used as material for high-quality moulds for metal casting. It seems that ceramists mixed different grades--clay to sand--of loess to achieve desirable qualities such as cohesion and plasticity at the manufacturing stage; and strength as products.

The Chinese made well-fitting ceramic moulds of yellow loess that carried extraordinarily elaborate decorations. Moulds made of yellow loess exhibited minimum shrinkage while being fired and cooled. The moulds were porous to let gas escape from the molten metal. Both of these qualities made yellow loess an excellent material for moulds.

From the middle Yellow River valley to the North China Plain was the birthplace of ancient China, though the river was liable to flooding and not navigable along its length. Peking Man lived in northern China between 500 000 and 250 000 years ago. Peking Man was at the Old Stone Age and identified as extinct hominids, *Homo erectus*. The remains of Peking Man were found at Zhoukoudian cave near Beijing (Peking) in the 1920s. *Homo sapiens sapiens*, whose bones were found with Middle Palaeolithic artefacts, developed a number of New Stone Age cultures in this area by 10 000 BC. Neolithic settlements in China date back to about 7000 BC and became widespread to the lower Yangtze River, the middle Yellow River and the south-east coast by about 5000 BC. The Yangshao (Yang-shao) culture emerged as a distinctive culture from one of them and reached its peak of development around 3000 BC. The Longshan (Lung-shan) culture gradually displaced the Yangshao and spread over the eastern third of the country. During the 1700s BC, the Shang dynasty, a local dynasty, arose from this culture, centring in the Huang He Valley. The Shang culture was a highly developed society governed by hereditary aristocrats. This society was noted for making bronze vessels, the use of horse-drawn chariots and the creation of a system of writing. It seems that the highly advanced culture of the Shang derived from sheer survival struggles among the neighbouring peoples, which the Shang fought against incessantly and obtained the various ideas from.

The earliest Shang sites were in much the same era as the Yangshao villages but more to the east of the big bend of the Yellow River where the Wei River meets. It is also evidenced that the Shang culture was based on the earlier Yangshao rather than the Longshan. The Shang culture displayed many of the characteristics of Sinitic culture, and can be termed 'Chinese' in many ways.

The Shang cultural influence encompassed the Middle Kingdom and Beijing (Peking), and stretched further to the south. The Middle Kingdom meant that the Chinese were surrounded by barbarians. High culture of the Shang era amid no notable cultures around--in fact no high cultures at all in contact--generated the Sino-centric notion which defined superior Chinese, primarily culturally and secondarily racially. The Sino-centric notion perpetuated the Chinese society through the ages and is still clearly in evidence today, and is one distinguishing feature of the Chinese view of the world. The Chou tribes of western China conquered the ruling Shang dynasty and started the Chou dynasty.

The meeting area of the Wei River and the Yellow River and just its east is the nuclear area of Chinese civilisation. The dominance of Shang and Chou seems to be based on geography more than any other factors. This region and the area further east of later development along the Yellow River to the Yellow Sea had the advantage in communication and trade in East Asia and the Eurasian continent, and the Chinese historians traditionally regarded this whole stretch as the Central States or the Middle Kingdom to be the original bearers of their culture. Today the Chinese use the Central States or the Middle Kingdom commonly and loosely to denote China, mainland and Taiwan.

Though China's literature goes back to the Shang era, what we think typically Chinese cultures is evident by 2000 BC, that is, at the formative era of the Xia (Hsia) (2000-1750 BC) dynasty. This is the first known dynasty on the North China Plain in the middle Yellow River valley. However, this dynasty appears in legends and is historically undetermined.

Chinese speaking people occupy only one-third of so-called China today but they comprise 95% of China's population. The remaining 5% of the population are Mongolian, Uighur, Tibetan, Tai, Miao, Yao and Mon-Khmer, and spread over two-third of the land mass.

China is a vast country with a huge population and long history and it is hard to make generalised statements about China and the Chinese with regard to their interests. It seems that the bulk of the Chinese being practical-minded were more interested in material objects rather than spiritual matters, which manifests in China's greater contribution of the former to the world. Nevertheless the following observations which may sound contradictory to the above statement are true beyond any doubt. Through the course of Chinese history, the Chinese believed that the essence of civilisation was in the form of written language and exceptionally prized the records of classical thinkers. They regarded scholars more highly than anywhere else in the world. The elite were scholar officials rather than soldiers or merchants. People looked at calligraphy which expressed words on paper as the most highly regarded art form, even more than paintings which people adored. The literati in China spent a few hours daily to improve their calligraphy and expressions, since people poor in these skills did not have much hope of advancement: in a similar way people poor in these fields anywhere in the world today cannot expect to make much advancement in any professional capacity.

The Semitics and then the Europeans adopted alphabetic scripts to express language in writing. They based written language on a limited number of sounds because human beings have the capacity for a limited number of articulations. However, they could create practically unlimited number of words by combining alphabets. The Chinese adopted scripts based on meaning. They can create an infinite number of scripts as the need arises.

Chinese scripts proved to be superb as people with different dialects could communicate with each other on paper without much difficulty beyond the time frame. I believe that the fantastic flowering of Chinese material culture during the classical and medieval eras of European classifications had much to do with this written communication through the ages. Western scripts proved their worth at the printing stage and again at the computer age in the modern setting. These correspondences between the cause (writing) and effect (culture) may be coincidental.

People of different dialects in China made use of the same scripts because the scripts as a whole represented meanings rather than sounds. Peoples understood the meanings of characters but pronounced them differently in a similar manner different nationalities understand Arabic numerals but pronounce them differently today. In Europe, in spite of the common language origin, the scripts adopted, as a rule, represented sounds rather than meanings. Hence the uniform written words across the various European languages were not possible, as long as they spoke mutually unintelligible tongues. However, they used Latin as an international language from the Roman era to the beginning of the modern era.

Many peoples of different ethnic backgrounds in China proper of later concept who spoke mutually unintelligible languages did not have a sense that they belonged to China before the unification by Shih huang-ti (Murowchick 1994, p. 103).

There have been several attempts in Chinese history to simplify Chinese writing and to adopt an alphabetical system. In the early days of Buddhism in China, when there was a considerable amount of translation from Sanskrit, Indian influence came near to achieving this end. (Wells 1971, p. 493)

Some scholars stress the importance of the ideographic (that is, non-phonetic) script as the key unifying force of the various Chinese peoples: the Chinese peoples felt that they belonged to the same culture. The adoption of the uniform scripts came just after the unification. There have been many organised campaigns to adopt various Romanised (alphabetic) systems of writing under the communist rule but they all failed the test of mass acceptance. (Murowchick 1994, p. 178)

> ... and the nomadic herdsmen of the steppes, the Hsiung Nu [Hsiung-nu], who encroached southwards. At the same time the Chinese themselves were moving southwards into different climates. Rice had penetrated from India by about 3000 BC but until the Chinese had moved south of the Chin Ling mountains they did not encounter it. (Cotterell & Morgan 1975, p. 43)
>
> The Tai came from the flatter lands of the Yangtze valley and later spread throughout South East Asia, particularly in Thailand and Burma. They had a sophisticated agricultural system based on rice and it was through contact with these people that the Chinese improved their own agriculture, adopting many new crops and animals like water buffaloes. (p. 63)

By the Shang period, the Chinese cultivated wheat and barley, though they were not native in China (Loewe 1990, p. 251).

God-kings, ritual bronze, human sacrifices, gigantic building projects and military prowess marked the Shang period (c. 1750-1027 BC). The king was the intermediary between heaven and earth. Large scale human sacrifices were excavated from the foundations of buildings and also from a dozen or so grand royal tombs at Anyang. Bronze, lacquer and silk made their appearance. In the great royal tomb near Anyang, explorations reveal human skeletons as well as animal skeletons, which are presumably to accompany the sovereign into the other world.

The use of bronze spread to China much later than to the West, from its Middle Eastern origin. During the Shang period China entered the Bronze Age and developed written ideographic scripts which the Chinese further developed into the uniform scripts and the modern scripts. The earliest written records of religious practice in China are the 'oracle texts' or 'oracle bone inscriptions'. They date from the Shang dynasty.

> The abrupt appearance of the light, spoked-wheeled war chariot in about 1200 BC suggests contact with the bearers of Indo-European culture: similar chariots with large, many spoked wheels had been in use in the Caucasus for several centuries (Ebrey 1996, p. 22).

Though bronze reached China as late as 1500 BC, the Chinese reached a far higher level of technique than other bronze users. Bronze remained a very expensive alloy.

There is evidence that the Shang metallurgists knew how to make cast iron. Since bronze was expensive they made agricultural implements made of cast iron.

The Zhou (Chou) kings were feudal monarchs rather than unquestionable chieftains as the Shang kings had been, and handed out territories in exchange for military and other services. The feudal vassals recorded on bronze vessels the kings' words and gifts, and as the result we can construct what was happening in that era. In this new era the extravagant rituals as practised by the Shang were curtailed, large-scale animal sacrifice disappeared, and human sacrifice became rare. (Milston 1978, pp. 69, 72)

The capital of the Western Chou (1027-771 BC) was Hao.

Chou literature indicates that the Shang king lost the Mandate of Heaven because of inferior government, that is, their moral level was not satisfactory in the eyes of Heaven, thus justifying the conquest of the Shang family by virtue of higher moral standard of the Chou family. This is the beginning of the idea of Mandate of Heaven. The literature stresses the religious and political continuity from Shang to Chou; the Shang dynasty was known as vigorous and was highly regarded even in the Chou era in spite of the failing of the last king. It also used Di (God), Shang Di (God on High) and Tian (Heaven) interchangeably. The Chou king is the sole link between Heaven and his subjects and he alone, as Son of Heaven, had the right to sacrifice to Heaven. This reinforces the importance of family and ancestor worship in the Chinese society. Vassals made sacrifices to their ancestors and to the gods of land and grain in their own territory. (p. 71)

Shang Di was probably the original ancestor of the Shang family. Tian (Heaven) was the ancestral deity of the Chou dynasty and the kings called themselves Son of Heaven as the later emperors in China did. Heaven was meant to embrace the entire world. Thus officially Son of Heaven was supposed to rule all under Heaven, the Chinese and the barbarians. But factually its rule did not extend even to many known barbarians.

As time went on the religious and political hold of the Chou king weakened, feudal states became virtually independent and the Chou king ruled only a tiny area by about 700 BC.

From about 700 BC, there was a revolution not only in the increased number of cities but in their configurations. They changed from the villages to the cities as we understand today. In fact these changes were induced by increased productivity of farming in surrounding areas which supplied food to city dwellers. Farmers used agricultural implements made of cast iron, used cattle and plough, large-scale irrigation works, accompanied by the institution of taxation on agricultural lands. (p. 72)

The capital of the Eastern Chou (771-256 BC) was Lo-yang. This was a period of bloodshed and misery but also an age of creativity. The Chinese made use of iron tools and iron weapons. They constructed canals and irrigation systems, came to use the first money, had flourishing cities and trades, and effected technical improvements such as efficient ploughs and horse harnesses. (Harris 1999, p. 10)

> The second half of the first millennium BC was the golden age of classical Chinese philosophy. Due to the increasing social and political change and instability in the Spring and Autumn [770-476 BC] and Warring States periods, many educated Chinese tried to come up with solutions to political, social and ethical problems. This was a period of intellectual ferment when a 'hundred schools' of thought blossomed. From Confucius and Mencius, to Lao-tzu and Han-fei-tzu, great thinkers of the well-known school of Chinese philosophy such as Confucianism, Taoism and Legalism transmitted their teachings which were often recorded by followers. (Murowchick 1994, p. 84)
>
> The Warring States period [475-221 BC] was an age when all social norms were collapsing and the search was on for new system of thoughts existed. This was an era of the 'Hundred Schools' .... (McGreal 1995, p. 62)

During this period of incessant fighting a tradition was born to venerate the early Chou era, particularly the reign of the Duke of Chou, and the concept perpetuated until the intellectual revolution of the twentieth century in China. Also feudal society was collapsing and the army composition changed from feudal levies to professional soldiers.

All the states tried to control and tax trades. Rulers of the states tried to make all profitable enterprises state monopolies. The Ch'in state was most successful in making money out of iron, salt and alcohol. It was in fact state capitalism. This was one of the reasons why Ch'in pushed aside the other states and became dominant.

The rulers and subjects in the Middle Kingdom were supposed to observe the *li* or the correct customs in peace time or even during war time. People had to wear correct clothes for occasions, give appropriate gifts, use correct address and not attack till the enemy is ready for battle, and so on. Those people who do not follow the right conducts are treated as barbarians. People from the Middle Kingdom should not be made slaves while barbarians could be.

The Chinese people had been traditionally centred on families; a person was defined by the status of the family and also within the family. Warfare shattered the old kinship structures and annihilated many aristocratic families. This resulted in some people making their own contractual relations to improve their status in society and looked up to the law rather than the *li.*

Section 2 Shih huang-ti (First Sovereign Emperor) of Ch'in Dynasty

> What has been revealed in the last 20 years or so is an extraordinarily sophisticated and complex state whose cultural level was every bit as advanced as Rome's when it founded its own empire in the Mediterranean two centuries later (Murowchick 1994, p. 102).

The historians generally agree that when China as we know was unified for the first time in 221 BC, it exceeded the Mediterranean world in almost every measure of material civilisation (Guisso & Pagani 1989, p. 30). Qin (Ch'in) ruled China proper where the people speaking Chinese were the dominant ethnic group. China proper progressively extended to the south as the Chinese migrated south under population pressure through its history. Shih huang-ti of the Ch'in state unified all other competing states and assumed the title of Emperor. Subsequently China became known to the world by the state name of Ch'in. This emperor who wanted to be known as the First Emperor predicting a myriad of the emperors of his lineage had such an extraordinary character and instituted the matching policies that even Mao Zedong (Tse-Tung) admired him (Fryer 1975, p. 39). Prior to the unification the Chinese states were going through the troubled times called the Warring Period, noted by the intense competition among the warring states, which resulted in astonishingly rapid technical as well as ideological progress. The nature of the struggles for sheer existence forced the combatant states to pay their major attention to material culture, though idealism by scholars also made a quantum leap. The Ch'in regime adopted Legalism, which strongly centred on defence, materialism and law, as their guiding ideology. Subsequent Chinese policy makers adopted the fruits of materialism eagerly and some aspect of Legalism, and also set up idealist culture as their guiding principle through Chinese history.

One major task after unifying China as we know was to break the aristocracy of the states Shih huang-ti conquered. Since the power base of the aristocrats was land, he made sure that they did not accumulate land. Land was broken up to be distributed among the sons when an aristocrat died. He imposed heavy tax, up to two-thirds of crops, on the farmers, and he used the tax collected for his projects. Many peasants thus ruined sold their lands to people with money such as merchants, officials and wealthy farmers. Landless peasants became serfs or were drafted into building projects as labourers.

The Ch'in dynasty unified China in 221 BC. Since then the Chinese people thought it norm that one emperor of Chinese stock ruled the entire Chinese territory, though in reality this normalcy prevailed for only half of slightly over two millenniums of Chinese history since the first unification. Aliens governed or one central government did not exist during the other half of the history.

In the fierce struggle for survival during the Warring Period, the states were eager to adopt new techniques; among them were iron swords, transport canals and efficiently harnessed horses. By the time of Shih huang-ti, the artisans in his state had developed the skill to cast iron swords up to 3 feet (1 metre) long, a factor in the military superiority of the Ch'in state.

Shih huang-ti's harsh and impersonal methods aroused criticism, and he must have been uneasy and even threatened. Grand Councillor, Li Si (Li Ssu), advised him to stifle the criticism. The emperor, following further advice, burned non-Legalist literature such as Confucian and Daoist, and killed hundreds of non-Legalist scholars who dared to defy the order to burn the prohibited books. His edict allowed members of Academy of the Learned Scholars to retain their books, and also some scholars successfully hid the books. One of the aims of burning the books was to unify Chinese scripts according to the standard he set out, as part of the general policy to introduce the standard laws, weights and measures. He further wanted to carry out thought control which is a familiar feature of a modern totalitarian state: He was more interested in the welfare of the state as a whole rather than that of the individuals. He could have been afraid that the other ideologies may have pushed away the

Legalist doctrines if he permitted the natural course of events to run, which prompted his harsh measures.

The prohibition of private doctrines led to the Burning of Books, and subsequently the ruling dynasty periodically banned personal doctrines through Chinese history.

This emperor merits some description so far as they are relevant to our discussion. He adopted Legalism as his guiding principle. The Legalists preached that the world or life consisted of material objects and placed their emphasis on agriculture, industry and defence. This facet of the doctrine is materialism. The Legalist doctrines further declared that the practice of literature, arts and philosophy would be the ruin of any kingdom. The law must rule everything, and its objective was to make the country strong for war; nothing else mattered, and it must suppress any doctrine which detracted from this purpose. Though Shih huang-ti had seventy court scholars, he solely relied on the law officers. (Chien 1979, p. 180) They outlawed philosophy and wanted to confine literature to the narrow field of law and administration. Though Shih huang-ti instituted vigorous law enforcement, strangely he himself was beyond all the laws and behaved as such. He defined what were right, oppressing his subjects and delivering harsh punishments on people who broke the laws. He took away half of his subjects' income as taxes and conscripted even those who should have been exempt. He employed scribes who tried to outdo each other in harshness and severity, enforcing the letter of the law. (pp. 329, 340)

We can see this emphasis on law in the teaching of Helvetius in the West who preached that education and law were the best means to procure the happiness of people. Claude-Adrien Helvetius (1715-71), a French philosopher, was a patron of philosophes, philosophers of the 18th century French Enlightenment. He claimed that all men were equally capable of learning and attacked all forms of morality-based religion.

Many of the Legalist policies the emperor adopted were in fact initiated earlier by Lord Shang who served Duke Hsiao of Ch'in. Lord Shang (d. 338 BC), chief minister of the state of Ch'in, wrote the lengthy Legalist measures intended to strengthen the power of the ruler.

The northern state of Chao, occupying the modern province of Shansi bordering on the Inner Mongolian steppes, was exposed to the raids from the nomadic tribes of that region. Chao began the practice of building defensive walls to cover exposed passes and other points of easy access from the steppes--walls which Emperor Shih huang-ti linked up and incorporated into the later Great Wall.

Moreover the purpose of the great majority of nomad tribal attacks was not to invade and try to conquer the Chinese empire, but to conduct a limited raid on the districts nearest at hand and to escape with the booty back to the Mongolian steppes.

'In 214 BC the First Emperor sent his general Meng T'ien to the empire's northern frontier with an army of 300 000 workmen and an unaccounted number of political prisoners in order to build the chains of fortifications.' The safety of his empire and the love of grandiose schemes obsessed him. He sent the soldiers he no longer needed and many trouble makers away from his capital. (Davison 1993, pp. 50, 52)

When the First Emperor died in 210/209 BC, the minister Li Si and the eunuch Zhao Gao conspired and the general was forced to commit suicide in prison. The two conspirators quarrelled about the succession issue, and Zhao had Li executed.

This phase of wall construction--there were many phases in later dynasties--ended in 207 BC and tens of thousands of labourers were known to have died under the harsh working conditions.

The emperor understood that in spite of his army, huge and well organised, he could not suppress the nomads in the north, particularly the Huns or the Hunni people, or possibly the same people called the Hsiung-nu (Wells 1925, p. 308). Thus he ordered the construction of the Great Wall: this was a defensive move and an admission that the Chinese army was not capable of permanently holding in check the marauding nomads whose distinguishing features were mobility and superb horsemanship. When the Chinese assembled a large and strong army, the nomads who could move faster than the Chinese army scattered and disappeared into the vast steppes and the Chinese army simply did not have the target to attack, hence there was no gain in organising an expeditionary force. The steppes were the natural habitat of the nomads who could live off the lands. The wall snakes across mountains and valleys over 3200 kilometres with watch towers at every few hundred metres and military encampments at intervals. It was also expected to prevent limited raids by neighbouring people who wanted booty to carry home. The succeeding emperors restored the wall whenever the part was crumbled with almost a religious fervour.

> Defending against the raids of non-Chinese peoples had been a problem since Shang times, but with a rise of nomadism in the arid steppe, north of China proper in mid-Zhou [Chou], the severity of the problem was greatly exacerbated (Ebrey 1996, p. 68).
>
> There the Wall traversed the fertile loess country, land whose earth is made of yellow silt, highly porous and so fine that when rolled between the fingers it disappears into the skin (Fryer 1975, p. 53).

A similar story unfolds regarding the construction of the Maginot Line in the early 20th century by the French against the superior German army. Hitler's army poured into France through Belgium where this defence system simply did not cover. France was in no position to close the gap due to the cost, though it was acutely aware of its vulnerability. Only after the German armies were well inside the French soil, the German troops attacked and penetrated the Maginot Line which had lost any military significance. Therefore, seeing that the huge costs to build these defence fixtures were a total waste, we can see how stupid and obsolete the French defence thinking was after the French dominance of Europe which lasted till the early nineteenth century.

However, the Great Wall was partially successful as a bulwark against the nomads, The nomads did not have a strong logistics and they relied on quick victory to feed their soldiers from the conquered territory. Fabian tactics by the Chinese defence force behind the fortified wall proved to be a formidable strategy. The emperor must also have known that the nomads' way of life was fundamentally incompatible with the Chinese way of life which was sedentary. The Sino-geographer, Owen Lattimore, concluded that the Great Wall was the outward limit of desirable expansion of the Chinese people. (p. 50) The Great Wall, a manifestation of materialist defence thinking, became the cornerstone of defence by successive Chinese empires against the incursions of the northern barbarians.

Some walls were constructed mainly of rammed earth, some mainly of sun-dried or burned bricks. In the west earth walls were predominant and in the east, close to the capital, brick walls were predominant. Naturally earth walls decayed and crumbled easily and we see many traces of earth walls built in the west; some are running nearby and some, even parallel to the older walls.

The Great Wall and the script reform fostered the national identity of the Chinese people. National identity has been an important feeling as for any other societies through human history, giving security and bonds to people and helping make policies.

In the early 13th century, during the Sung dynasty, the wall proved strong enough to hold Mongol invader Genghis Khan for two years (Davison 1993, p. 53). The Sung court had moved to southern China and the Mongols fought against the Jurchens who occupied the region as a part of their empire and defended the wall.

The Great Wall as it stands now is primarily a Ming (1368-1644) creation, 'being faced with brick and stone and averaging 25 feet high and wide, extending about 1500 miles' (Ebrey 1996, p. 208). The inside walls were filled with earth. The Ming government began repairing and building major walls in fear of the Mongol invasions in the late 1400s. It is said that construction of the walls fatally weakened the Ming dynasty because of the huge cost. Later dynasties repaired the crumbled walls, and the communist government repaired them to attract tourists.

By a twist of history the above broad argument concerning the construction and preservation of the Great Wall was to break down from the setup itself as well as the fact it was built on the wrong side. Some vigorous Chinese empires such as T'ang controlled the area beyond the wall. The territory of the Manchu (Ch'ing) dynasty (1644-1912) extended far beyond the Great Wall, to Manchuria and further north, hence the Wall did not have any military significance at the time. Manchuria was the homeland of the Manchus. Also the Chinese built it in anticipation that foreign incursions would be from the northwest and from the land. In the nineteenth century, foreign incursions took place from the east and from the sea.

Shih huang-ti did not foresee that his works on the northern defence line contributed to the downfall of the Western Roman Empire. Many centuries later, Huns, unable to penetrate the Chinese setup of defence, migrated westwards and subsequently pushed the Germanic tribes to cross the frontier line into Roman territory. Thus the German tribes routed the Western Roman Empire already weakened by preceding internal decay, and it ceased to exist in 476.

There is another interesting feature about this defence line. Shih huang-ti achieved the unification, and thus peace prevailed within China proper. Land shortage was not to be felt in China for another two centuries; however, there is some evidence to suggest that the emperor was aware land shortage would eventuate and topple his empire unless many of its inhabitants perished. With this thinking superimposed on other reasons, he initiated the huge construction works such as the Great Wall to kill off a large number of people so that the surviving people could live comfortably. This is in fact the kind of policy which a modern totalitarian nation would advocate and adopt.

I believe that the welfare of people within his empire genuinely concerned the emperor. People under his control did not, in fact could not, raise serious grievances in spite of heavy taxes and large drainage of manpower while he was alive. His subjects might have looked at him as the father who was harsh on his children for their sake. After his death in 210/209 BC, serious revolts broke out and the Han dynasty replaced the Ch'in dynasty in 206 BC.

In spite of these successful measures, though harsh, adopted by Shih huang-ti, in an effort to develop China under the Legalist doctrines, the subsequent Han dynasty nominated Confucianism as its state philosophy. As a matter of fact Confucianism became the state philosophy of almost all the succeeding Chinese dynasties. A few emperors were Confucians by belief. Inclination of Chinese people was such that they favoured the peace loving doctrine of Confucianism rather than Legalism which laid stress on defence. However, the fact that its teaching was pro-establishment and hence favourable to the governing class was the fundamental reason for the triumph of Confucianism in the Chinese civil service examinations over the few other doctrines. The Han dynasty introduced the examination system by which they graded rather than selected bureaucrats; gearing the pass on Confucian classics most prestigious.

Shih huang-ti had one fatal weakness; he was very much afraid of death though he did not regard the other peoples' lives with the same respect as his own. Ssu-ma Ch'ien vividly narrates in his memorable book *Shih-chi* how the emperor narrowly escaped an assassination attempt. He was even more worried about death after this event and subsequently tended to avoid contact with people. Adolf Hitler also became distrustful of his subordinates after an assassination attempt on him nearly succeeded. Probably the state of mind of both these figures were in after going through near death under hostile atmospheres came naturally to them as it would to us.

The emperor was so afraid of death that he sent out emissaries to find an elixir of life with which he hoped to prolong human life indefinitely. Readers may scoff at the idea; however, let me remind them that people of the classical world were unfamiliar with science of today's standard and were quite superstitious. For example, it was believed that Greek gods fed on ambrosia and drank nectar, both of which were said to bestow immortality. It is not hard to conclude that no emissaries returned with the wanted substance.

As was mentioned earlier the emperor was extraordinary in many ways--his character, his determination, his foresight, his authority, and as an originator of many concepts which succeeding Chinese emperors emulated. Yet he was no different from any other person when it came to death. He had to die as had slaves, soldiers and peasants. He unified all the civilised worlds known to him. He was above the laws he set up and had virtually unlimited authority, that is, he could have done anything he wanted to do. These facts must have made him feel more acutely that he could not escape from one fate--death. He was no better than any other person as far as the mortality was concerned. See Section 6 Fear of Death, Chapter 1, Book Four for brief accounts of his search for immortality.

What Worries Did Shih huang-ti Have?

I am going to speculate what he was mainly worried about after unification. I have to emphasise that the following presentations are only speculations and not based on historical records. The emperor attained virtually everything he set his mind to. People who get to the top of their profession such as a president or a prime minister of a nation or a managing director of a large corporation or an multi-billionaire are in a similar mental state as far as the fulfilment of their ambitions are concerned, though they have very much limited authority compared with that of Shih huang-ti. The above comparison makes the inquiry more relevant to us.

It is most likely that these top people do not reveal their innermost feelings. When they are asked what they are most afraid of, I imagine, on many occasions they may evade the answer or jocularly tell a story which does not reflect their true thoughts. Under these circumstances, biographers of prominent individuals have to work out what these characters are most dreaded of from the available evidence.

I am going to guess what Shih huang-ti was fearful about, not from the evidence since I am not here to write his biography. My aim is to highlight if the emperor was any happier than the average person of classical times or even today. However, happiness is very much a subjective quality. I am to guess what his main worries were, and make some statements about his happiness, assuming that happiness is directly related to absence of worries:

- I noted earlier that death terrified the emperor. The probability of his being assassinated was a lot higher than an average person of today even in a violent city such as Washington, DC, USA or Johannesburg, South Africa. He had good cause for alarm of being killed by an assassin but his fear was in fact in death itself, not the high probability of assassination. He could have conquered any other problems but he was utterly powerless in the face of mortality.
- He was concerned with managing his various projects, particularly about money and manpower. He tried to solve the money problem by simply raising taxes. Higher taxes must have made the taxed worried, but he could have ignored them as the politicians of the present world tend to ignore the sufferings of people under heavy taxes. The large number of labourers who were recruited and died also alarmed people. However, I am sure that the emperor was confident he could enforce his will to obtain the necessary money and labour.

He himself and his subjects were well aware that the imperial army under his command could suppress any revolt.

- He did not have to be worried about how to acquire food, clothes and shelter for his consumption. However, every time he took food or a drink, he might have been apprehensive that fatal poison might have laced them. Today an ordinary person even in the most violent cities aforementioned does not have a concern of this kind.
- Noise sensitive people may try to block the sounds surrounding them; however hard they may try a small noise can irritate them. They have to get used to noise in the same way they have to get used to criticism and abuse. Average people of any era are hurt and brood over what other people say--abuse, insults; and denigrating remarks, sometimes intentional and sometimes unintentional. I know that not even members of royal family of various countries were not immune from these verbal assaults. These attackers were well aware that a king or queen was reluctant to act on such verbal crimes even for his or her relatives and oftentimes he or she could not punish the abusers from various reasons. Today even the pope and the president of the United States have to put up with criticism and abuse. Was Shih huang-ti worried about other people's remarks? I am inclined to say 'Yes'. It is obvious that nobody dared to abuse him to his face since he could have delivered an instant punishment. However, some people could have criticised his policies, his projects and his character. He might have overheard such criticisms or they could have been reported to him or they may have been within a report. In the absence of abuse, he might have taken these criticisms to heart and brooded over them as any other person would do. Also he could have been worried that some subjects did not bow deeply or long enough, causing him to suspect that they wanted to show him disrespect.

<u>Concluding Remarks about Happiness of Shih huang-ti</u>

The vast majority of human beings are worried about one thing or another. Most think that when a distressing event at hand is over, they don't have anything to fret over. However, they normally get another worry after that. Apart from minor apprehensiveness, a sudden and serious problem they cannot overcome for years if they can at all can strike people. It is not an exaggeration that all human beings are worried about something all the time, irrespective of whether it is serious or minor per se.

Without any doubt the emperor was worried about one thing or another like any ordinary person of classical era or even today. However, since he had enormous, virtually unlimited, power within his empire, the nature of his anxieties was considerably different. He was free from some common worries but he suffered from some disturbing thoughts which the average person did not experience. Since every ordinary person would have anxieties which are common, say money problems or verbal assaults, as well as some particular, the emperor was no different from any average person of classical time or today as far as the process of worrying was concerned.

I can make a similar statement about happiness. Without any doubt, he had happy times as well as unhappy times as any average person would. If the last assessment is true, what is the sense of being an emperor? The question can be raised to the people in today's organisations: What is the sense in being on top? The answer to the question is, I believe as follows: power is an independent desire of human beings from happiness. People want power provided they are in a position to obtain it whether they are happy or not though the driving force may be the thought that they will be happier if they obtain power. The same thing can be said about food, clothes, shelter, wealth, sex, honour and so forth. After acquiring the necessities of life, everyone has different priorities: some are fond of fine food and some want honour more than anything else and so forth.

Not only do people prefer one desire to another, some show definite preference for one aspect of desire to another aspect of the same desire. For instance, some people want their favourite food cooked in a certain way and in no other way. Socrates wondered why some men wanted honour of an office even though they sacrificed their personal honour. He was referring to the occurrences where some men, wanting the position of honour so much, used underhand means in an effort to obtain the official position, thus dishonouring themselves. He stated that he could not understand why people behaved in such a manner. Probably he did not know that one kind of honour was independent of another kind of honour, though both honours were the same in that they were how the public look at them. There are two issues intertwined here: the personal preference of the seeker and moral codes. In the above example, some people prefer the honour of the office to their personal integrity. Some philosophers insist that personal preference is the sole criterion of judgement and others place stress on ethical judgement. Confucius said, 'Wealth and honour are what people want; however, wealth and honour falsely acquired are like a floating cloud to me'. Obviously both Socrates and Confucius believed in morals and could not accommodate that there could be other values as well. The Buddha would have argued that everything, honour of every persuasion, wealth, morals, life and the world, is an illusion.

These two philosophers were married and had children. I am quite sure that when they saw young and pretty girls, they felt sexual desire towards them, though I have some reservation about the Buddha after the enlightenment and Jesus Christ during the ministry. Every girl was an independent experience for them in a similar manner that one desire is independent of another and also one aspect of desire is independent of another. Such logic explains why a divorced man with a bitter memory of marriage often remarries and some people try to obtain a high office using unethical methods.

Section 3 After Ch'in Dynasty till Yuan Dynasty

Major Empires in China

221-206 BC Ch'in dynasty
206 BC-AD 220 Han dynasty
581-618 Sui dynasty
618-907 T'ang dynasty
960-1279 Sung dynasty
1279-1368 Yuan dynasty
1368-1644 Ming dynasty
1644-1912 Ch'ing dynasty

Chinese creativity peaked in the last few centuries BC: during the turbulent Eastern Chou, the Ch'in era, and the stable, prosperous Han period. It is noteworthy that these creative periods did not have any political or dynastic order or disorder in common. (Harris 1999, p. 175) In other words Chinese creativity did not have anything to do with the dynastic cycles.

Today the Chinese people use the term *Han jen* (men of Han) meaning Chinese distinguishing themselves from minority nationalities, while they use the term *Chung-kuo jen* (men of the Middle Kingdom) designating the people of China as a whole.

The Han Empire made advances in iron manufacture, hydraulics, paper making and international trade. Iron production during the Han state was on an immense scale, far surpassing the output of the Roman Empire, with tens of thousands of tons of cast iron manufactured each year. (Murowchick 1994, p. 76) The later Chinese regarded the Han Empire as a model to measure many things. Though the Ch'in dynasty was also a creative era generating many new ideas which later dynasties followed, the Ch'in's state cult was Legalism which centred on organising the state according to the laws in anticipation of war. The Chinese people in subsequent history shunned Legalism dominant during the regimented Ch'in Empire and preferred peace-loving Confucianism advocated by the Han Empire as its model. The Han drew revenues from both a poll tax and a tax on agricultural production which was only one-thirtieth of the autumn harvest during most of the Han period. The government taxed heavily on commercial and manufacturing sectors, which set back seriously the private business sectors. (Ebrey 1996, p. 75)

Liu Pang, founder of the Han dynasty, and his successors had to curb the power of feudal lords. The central government suppressed the revolt of seven kings led by the king of Wu in 154 BC. The powers of feudal lords were subsequently curtailed and the imperial government appointed civilian and military officials but the Han dynasty was not secure.

Theoretically emperors had unlimited power as Shih huang-ti had previously. However, seeing the unpopularity of Shih huang-ti and Legalism in subsequent China, Han emperors accommodated the theory that the emperors' power had to be tempered by advisers and the acceptance of the emperors by the people made the throne possible.

The first Han emperor, Kao-Tsu (Liu Pang was his personal name), did not appreciate scholarship and did not withdraw the Ch'in decree to burn non-Legalist books, though Confucian scholars at times gave him useful advice. The second emperor favoured the Daoist school and made the Confucians retire. The third emperor, Wen, preferred Legalist-trained advisers but employed scholars of all schools. The next Han emperor, Ch'ing, selected advisers who knew all schools of thoughts. The fifth emperor, Wudi (Wu-ti) (reigned 141-87 BC), established the system by which the government officials were trained, tested and graded on their scholarship of Confucian classics.

A Confucian scholar educated Emperor Wudi, and learning and literature genuinely interested the emperor. However, his governing style was autocratic and his policies were Legalist.

In the Han era, the tradition of recording and compiling dynastic history began; however, only from the T'ang era, did the government set up the formal History Department. Confucian scholars became the historians in this light, and I am sure that they adjusted historical records when uncertain to suit their interpretations of Confucianism in much the same way Jewish scholars adjusted their records when uncertain to suit their belief in compiling the Old Testament.

The Han Empire was not secure along several border regions, and the chief threat came from the Hsiung-nu, a Turkic people.

The Hsiung-nu was nomadic people and bred a large number of horses. Horses were invaluable for transport of goods and people during war and peace, and the nomads ate their flesh and drank their milk. Sheep were also important as food and material for clothes. Their way of life was incompatible with that of the Chinese who were sedentary and lived on farming and industry. However, the Chinese had the commodities the Hsiung-nu could not live without, that is, they needed salt and iron products and coveted luxury items such as silk. The Hsiung-nu raided Chinese territories to obtain the above items and even slaves, or at times traded with the Chinese goods for horses.

There were many attempts to contain the Hsiung-nu during the Han times. In 139 BC during Emperor Wudi's reign, Chang Ch'ien, a general, was dispatched to make friends with the Yueh-chih, an Indo-European people, on the far side of the Hsiung-nu. The mission failed. In the first century, Pan Ch'ao marched with the army of 70 000 men as far as the Caspian Sea. He sent an ambassador to the west, receiving the reports of the Roman Empire. (Milston 1978, p. 127)

In AD 5 Wang Mang usurped the throne. He tried to curb the power of large landowners, by such measures as declaring that all land was the property of the state, prohibiting the sale of land; and freeing peasants from the bondage of serf and slave and restoring them the land. He met fierce opposition. At this time the Yellow River flooded and changed its course from north to south in Shandong (Shantung) Province, resulting in devastation, shortage of food and rebellions. The opposition saw an opportunity and a member of the Han family successfully challenged and killed Wang Mang and set up his court in Loyang in AD 25, thus starting Eastern or Later Han.

The Chinese felt and behaved superior to all their neighbours since the Shang dynasty (the first verifiable Chinese dynasty) through the centuries; however, it seems this superiority and often resulting arrogance did not come from physical and biological concepts but rather stemmed from the cultural pride (Ebrey 1996, p. 179) and the sense that China was a civilised centre, that is, the Sino-centric notion. Accordingly when the foreigners showed good attitude the Chinese recognised them as their equals. This sense of superiority had further developed by the Eastern Han period, and as the centuries passed was more and more ingrained in the minds of the Chinese. The custom of recording all foreign visitors and vassals bringing tributes to the Chinese court was firmly established by the Eastern Han period. The Chinese authority took the attitude that what was happening beyond the borders did not interest them. However, the Chinese had to face some awkward facts that contradict the above assumption. For example, they could not quite defeat the Hsiung-nu and had to receive their ambassadors as equals. Also new ideas or inventions from the foreign countries came to their attention and they adopted them pretending that they were their own.

The Sino-centric notion ingrained in the Chinese people above mentioned is one fundamental distinguishing feature of Chinese culture together with its cultural continuity through the ages. The Sino-centric concept is different from the aggression that the Russians exhibited during the communist rule and the aggression that the Germans exhibited during the Nazi rule. The belligerence of these peoples stemmed from their desperate urge to achieve hegemony on the foundation of communism for the former and Nazism for the latter.

The Chinese bureaucracy which Confucianism fostered disdained armed forces and traders. Though they were certainly necessary, the mandarins disliked them intensely; and placed all kinds of restrictions on traders. The toiling masses also disliked traders who made profits by selling and buying. (Kennedy 1987, p. 8)

The Yellow Turbans, a messianic Daoist sect, staged a rebellion in 184. They and contending generals fought until the Han Empire became ineffectual and the last Han emperor survived until 220.

By 567 Northern Chou controlled all north China with its capital at Ch'ang-an. Emperor Yuwen fell ill and died before he could pay attention to the south. Yang Chien usurped the throne, starting Sui dynasty in 581. By 589 he united north and south China for the first time in 360 years. Yang Chien, as Emperor Wen, was Buddhist and thrifty, and kept a small court at Ch'ang-an and demanded soldiery obedience from his officers. These officers being deprived of their sinecures plotted with one of the emperor's sons and murdered the emperor. They made this unfilial son the emperor with the title of Yang Di (Yang Ti). (Milston 1978, p. 146)

Yang Di came to the Sui throne in 604, and set to work on the Grand Canal system between Beijing and Hang-chou, linking the North China Plain and the Yangtze valley with waterways 40 metres or more wide. He improved and extended the ancient canal connecting the Yangtze with the old capital cities of Loyang and Kaifeng, and these canals aimed at connecting the well-watered Yangtze valley with the drier north China, thus fulfilling economic combinations. His immediate aim was the logistic support to attack the powerful kingdom of Koguryo in Korea. As soon as he completed the canal system in 610, he launched attacks on Koguryo, all of which ended in disasters. The lasting role of the canal was to become commercial, prominently to transport rice from the south to the north. (The Editors of Time-Life Books 1988, p. 101)

The Mongol conquerors of China further extended the Grand Canal to their new capital Ta-tu (meaning great capital) (Beijing) in the 13th and 14th centuries.

The first Sui emperor and the first two T'ang emperors achieved the reunification and centralisation of the Chinese empire after four centuries of northern invasions and divided rule.

During the T'ang dynasty, China maintained diplomatic relations with Byzantium and Sassanid Persia. China exchanged people, ideas and goods with these countries through the Silk Road and sea routes.

During the early T'ang era the Chinese were in contact with a large variety of peoples and were more willing to absorb foreign ideas than any other period. The followers of Zoroastrianism, Manichaeism and Nestorian Christianity all practised in China. Judaism and Islam made their way into China for the first time in this era. The foreign tributary system with China was somewhat modified and the emperor was encouraged to treat all peoples under heaven equally--the Chinese and foreigners. By the end of T'ang all but the Buddhists and Muslims were purged out of existence from China. Trade by sea and land was an important source of revenues, and many Chinese officials in coastal and frontier regions actively encouraged it. However, the central authority persistently made light of the trade relations with foreign countries—in fact until the 19th century, which led to serious difficulties as time went on as the text discloses.

The T'ang period was the golden age of Chinese literature, though the first Chinese novels were written later during the Ming period. The four greatest poets in Chinese history lived during the T'ang dynasty: Wang Wei, Li Bo, Du Fu and Bo Juyi. Du Fu is considered to be the greatest among them, though he failed the civil service examinations twice, expressing in his poem the deep hurt of failure and ill behaviours of his friends. Some say that he failed because his prose style was too dense and obscure. Some say that he failed because he did not have any connection in the capital. Li Bo liked drinking alcohol and travelling, and did not sit for the civil service examinations. Folk literature went through the evolution for popular acceptance. Han Yu carried out the major reform of prose literature freeing the genre from cumbersome restrictions.

In the eighth century, during the T'ang dynasty, the Chinese began to make much finer wares known as porcelain. During the Sung era the manufacture of porcelain took the mature form and the art of making porcelain reached its apogee. From the early 14th century, porcelain began to find its way via the Silk Road to the West, where the people highly prized for its elegance and delicacy. Not until the early 18th century, however, was the porcelain produced in Europe matched to that of China. (Williams 1987, p. 148)

Though the rebellion (755-63) led by An Lu-shan was eventually suppressed, the prestige of the T'ang dynasty was broken and the emperors found it necessary to appoint military governors to protect the northern boundaries. These governors as the head of the military became powerful and virtually independent from the central government, and appointed their sons as their successors.

General Chao K'uang-yin usurped the throne of the child emperor and established the Sung (Song) dynasty. The fact that he became an emperor using political skills without warfare indicates that the economic pattern required unified China at the time.

The Sung court started the custom of foot binding around the 10th century, which became widespread by the 14th century, originally among the upper class women. The result was exquisitely tiny feet, indicating they do not have to do the manual labour and thus the social status. (Harris 1999, p. 80)

As the result of the spread of printing since the ninth century, new farming knowledge spread fast in China, and China's agricultural techniques were the best in the world during the Sung period.

In this era the road transport was maintained in the traditional manner. Local officials were responsible for building and maintaining roads using the corvèe labour. More spectacular than road transport was water transport; rivers, and canals for inland. Water transport was cheaper undoubtedly and suitable for heavy goods such as grain or salt. In fact the amount of traffic carried by inland waterways far exceeded that carried by road.

Steel production made huge advances. China made coke from coal and produced steel according to what may be the predecessors of Bessemer steel process and Siemens-Martin process. In the later decades of the 11th century, northern China had an enormous steel industry mainly for military and government use, producing around 125 000 tons per annum. This was far larger than the British steel output at the early stages of the Industrial Revolution, 7 centuries later. (Kennedy 1987, p. 6)

Between the eighth and twelfth centuries in China the use of paper money together with the institutions handling money and credit was widespread. Regional and international trade increased tremendously.

The great wealth of Sung cities allowed many people the leisure to pursue arts or to patronise them. In this period the visual and plastic arts reached a level which has never been surpassed.

For centuries, the government officials selected by the civil service examinations formed a minority. Even under the Sung dynasty, the officials tended to place their sons in the service.

There were three levels of examinations, that is, the local level, the provincial level and the national level. (Harris 1999, p. 90)

The Khitan incursions into Chinese territories remained problematic. The Khitan settled inside the Great Wall during the Five Dynasties and established the Liao kingdom. The Sung government initially tried to fight the Khitan off. However, they resorted to buy them off with silk and silver and also they buttressed their defences with Khitan horses and fortifications. The Five Dynasties quickly succeeded one another in the Central Plain in the 10th century before the Sung imperial dynasty was firmly established.

The Sung invited the Jurchen to help them against the Khitan Liao. The Jurchen were the ancestors of the Manchus. The Jurchen conquered Liao, Xi Xia (Hsi Hsia) and further northern China, establishing their capital at Yen-ching (Peking). They gradually extended their control southwards and in 1126 captured the Sung capital Kaifeng and the leaders of the imperial family. The remainder of the imperial family fled south and settled at Hangchow, making it their capital. The capital city of the Chinese empire was always the hub of the empire. Officials, civil and military, all congregated there, and the tax tributes and the foreign luxuries all went there. The Jurchen took the name of their dynasty as Chin (meaning gold). After 1141 the Southern Sung paid tribute to Chin. As the Sung court moved south the economic life of China moved south too. In Chin the Chinese lived according to their customs, and the Jurchens, few in number, soon became sinicised. The Jurchen (or Chin or Jin) Empire, which at one stage extended to the Yangtze River, lasted from 1122 to 1234, when the Mongols overcame them.

The Chinese had moved from the north to the south in the preceding centuries under the thrust from the Jurchens but the loss of the north did not cripple the Sung dynasty. The Southern Sung had the majority of Chinese population and wealth and was strong enough to resist further incursions by the Jurchens. As a matter of fact it is said that the Southern Sung came to be wealthier than the entire Sung Empire in the past had been.

The Southern Sung government, being unable to obtain tax in the north, encouraged sea trade and shipbuilding to raise revenue. The government also built a navy to protect merchant ships and to guard against any possible foreign incursions and at the same time to supervise the tax and licence on trade shipping. A large number of the Arabs and Persians lived in Canton, Ch'uan-chou and Yangchow. Overseas trade was for luxury items only and as the matter of fact the Emperor Kao-tsung, the first emperor of the Southern Sung (1127-1279), decreed overseas trade as luxury and tried to stop it in 1127. However, one fifth of the government income came from overseas trade at the time and his decree was effectively ignored. Kao-tsung's hold on power was tenuous until he chose Hangchow as his new capital and began peace negotiations with the Jurchens.

The Chinese economy of the twelfth to thirteen centuries was by far the most advanced in the world.

Through the course of Chinese history, the Chinese assigned merchants to a low social status and ranked them below officials, farmers and artisans. Confucian scholar officials looked down on the merchant class who engaged in non-productive activities and promoted the use of superfluous luxury items. (p. 92)

During the Southern Sung period, the Chinese constructed big seagoing ships and expanded international commerce dramatically. The technical innovations of the period together with the use of the compass invented earlier made possible the expedition of Zheng He (Cheng Ho) in the Ming era.

The Mongols extended their territories in east Asia. They captured Beijing in 1215. They completed the conquest of Xi Xia in 1226. They occupied the Jin capital Kaifeng in 1234.

They commenced the conquest of the Sung Empire in 1252, and Kublai Khan completed it in 1279.

The pattern of Mongol administration was the same in all of China. The elite of the Mongols occupied the top government posts and held the largest estates. All the Mongols were soldiers and did not regard Chinese scholar officials as reliable. Hence foreign administrators--the Arabs, Persians, Uighurs and even Europeans--held the next level positions by virtue of their special abilities. Tax farmers collected taxes, making profits above the amount the central government required. Local people were employed at the lower levels of government. For the rest life continued much the same as before. The Mongols classified families according to occupation and did not allow people to move from fixed occupations; this was another means to subjugate the Chinese people. Also the Mongols enforced a strict racial policy. The removal of the Confucian scholar officials, who hated military and merchants, from the administration resulted in the resurgence of merchants and an influx of foreign traders.

Since the administration did not employ many scholars, and the Mongol court did not attract Chinese talents; scholars wrote stories and musical plays for a general audience.

As a result of the secure passage in the Eurasian continent by the Mongol dominion, various Chinese inventions such as the compass, paper, paper-money, playing cards, printing, porcelain and firearms appeared in the Middle East and Europe.

The Mongol garrison armies weakened considerably under the influence of a good and peaceful life. Sensing this fact coupled with poor administration and heavy taxation provoked the Chinese to rebel.

A warlord, the leader of the rebellion, captured Nanjing (Nanking) in 1356 and declared himself an emperor and called his new dynasty the Ming. This new dynasty was formally established when this warlord Emperor Hung-wu took the Mongol capital Ta-tu, and the Mongol Emperor Togan Timur and the Mongols fled in 1368. The name of this new capital was changed to Peking; however, the emperor kept Nanking as the southern capital.

Beijing (Peking)

Beijing is in Pinyin; Peking is in Wade Giles: both mean northern capital. The Pinyin Romanisation system developed in the 1950s largely supplanted the older Wade Giles system.

Beijing was nominated as the capital of the People's Republic of China in 1949, and is the second most populous city in China today after Shanghai. The city was the centre of government for more than 2000 years with some interruptions. Beijing and its surrounding area are on the northern boundary of the North China Plain and covered by yellow silt (originally loess) due to repeated flooding of the Yellow River. I noted earlier that *Homo erectus* lived in caves near Beijing and also *Homo sapiens sapiens* lived around Beijing. Though Beijing and its surrounds were not within the Longshan Neolithic cultures, the Yangshao Neolithic cultures extended to the Beijing area, which began to take shape as a city in the later period of the Shang dynasty. It is rather strange that the city played such a prominent role in spite of the fact it is 160 km from the nearest sea. It was in the extreme north of China if we do not take into account Manchuria which became a part of China only in the modern context.

The answer lies in geography. Beijing is situated at the apex of the North China Plain hence naturally people and traffic converged into the area around the city. The Chinese were sedentary and farmed the plain intensely resulting in dense population, and it was so even before the Shang era. Also the Beijing embayment (the apex of the plain) borders on the Mongolian Plateau and the Yen Mountains. Though these mountainous regions posed formidable barriers, there were a few passes cut through. Hence the Beijing embayment was an important terminus for trade between the North China Plain (the Chinese) and the vast Asian hinterland (the nomads) and even further west. Hence Beijing developed as an important trading centre from the earliest times. Further the nomads from the north invaded and occupied part of the plain repeatedly through history. For example, the nomads occupied the northern territory including Beijing for nearly 300 years until the T'ang ruler recovered. Hence Beijing and the surrounding territory were strategically important: the densely populated region with important government buildings and the emperor's palaces worked as a check against the invading barbarians. The Great Wall runs just north of Beijing.

Beijing was founded as a trading centre around 2000 BC, and has been the focus of Chinese (Han), culturally and militarily, since.

During the Warring States, the kingdom of Yen, one of the powerful feudal states under the Western Chou, established its capital near Beijing, making it a virtual capital for the first time. The Mongols under the leadership of Genghis Khan repeatedly attacked and eventually conquered the city, the capital of the Jurchen Jin dynasty at the time. They razed the city to the ground and in the process even burned the palaces. Kublai Khan made Beijing a winter capital building it in its present form and named it Ta-tu (meaning great capital), thus it became the capital of the entire China for the first time. Marco Polo visited Ta-tu in the 1280s and was astounded by the setup such as the imperial palaces, the lakes, and a canal connecting the lakes to the Grand Canal.

The third Ming emperor moved the capital from Nanjing (meaning southern capital) to Beijing in 1420, and built palaces and temples.

The Ch'ing rulers made Beijing their capital and enlarged, and added palaces and temples.

Beijing lost its trading and military significance in the way I have described here but is the political and cultural centre of China today because of its historical role and infrastructures. I may also add that historically emperors and courts made light of the contact with overseas nations and concentrated their policies on lands (within and outside China) before the middle of the 19th century with the exception of the Southern Sung.

Section 4 Topics Indicating Rise of China

When doctors diagnose a sickness they look for a few symptoms rather than continuous indications of the sickness. Also in finger-printing identification, experts look for a few identical features to conclude that two finger prints are the same or different. Using the same logic I present in this section a few key indications to demonstrate that China was superior to Europe in material culture before the modern era. In this approach the probability of making a mistake is small in the absence of the contrary evidence in these fields of study: besides we do not have a better method to proceed with diagnostic analyses.

A Three Greatest Inventions in History

Roger Bacon (?1214-1292)--a monk, scholar and scientist--made a proposition that paper, gunpowder and magnetic compass were the three greatest inventions in human history. He in fact chose four inventions including printing; however, the historians are normally in agreement on three inventions, and I followed the convention. He, being a part scientist and a major proponent of experimental science, reached the above conclusion after exhaustive research on inventions, of the tangible objects rather than the concepts. Though these creations are quite modest by today's standards, they left indelible marks on world history. He measured the greatness of these inventions by the size of the changes to be brought to Europe and subsequently to the world rather than by their inherent inventiveness. The full effects in Europe of these inventions were to be realised in a few centuries after his proposition. Strangely, however, it seems that Bacon did not know the Chinese invented all three items. He regarded the origins of these inventions as 'obscure and inglorious', and died not ever knowing the fact. He urged his contemporary Europeans to study Arabic and Greek scientific knowledge which was far advanced of that of contemporary Europe.

As a matter of fact, these three inventions were only a tiny part of a vast number of creations that the Chinese had made, and propagated to Europe through the subsequent course of history. We don't have to revert to religion to postulate that decisive events, good or bad, tend to happen as a result of preceding minor happenings. We often hear that such-and-such a company went bankrupt because of a series of incorrect decisions made by managers. We also can expect to find good management and well-directed efforts behind victories in such events as sports and armed conflicts. I present the three inventions aforementioned in this section because they not only are major events in history but by no means are isolated incidents in the material zest of the Chinese people.

Paper

Before the invention of paper, the Chinese wrote on wood, silk, bamboo strips or stones. The situation was no better in other parts of the world. The Egyptians wrote on papyrus reeds (the origin of the word paper) and slabs of stone. The Europeans used sheep skins and stones for preserving documents.

> This [paper as we know] was undoubtedly a purely Chinese invention, later exported to the West. Tradition asserts that it was first made in AD 105 by Cai Lun [Ts'ai Lun], a eunuch at the imperial court, ... However, it appears that Cai Lun must have improved an existing product, rather than made a new invention, for paper made of hemp and ramie (another Asian fibre plant) has been found in Shangsi province which can be firmly dated at 49 BC. (Williams 1987, p. 97)

Archaeologists found another piece of paper made from hemp in a tomb near Sian, Shensi Province in 1957. The investigation dated the manufacturing date of this paper between 140 BC and 87 BC, making it the oldest surviving paper. (Temple 1986, p. 81)

Paper was not used as a writing material until the early 2nd century. It had been used for clothing, wrapping, lacquer ware and personal hygiene. It had been widely used even for armour, though paper armour was made quite differently from what we imagine today. (p. 82) By the 5th century paper was the standard writing material in China, and also used for kites and toilet paper. Seven centuries after the invention of paper, the Chinese introduced the printing technique. (Harris 1999, p. 176)

> At the same time when printing was introduced as a means to reproduce texts in the 9th century, it also began to be used to decorate textiles (Ebrey 1996, p. 130).

The Chinese attacked the Arab Muslims of Samarkand in 751 and were repulsed. However, among the Chinese taken captive were paper-makers, who passed their skills to the Arabs.

> The Chinese art of paper making found its way to Arabia. By the eighth century paper making workshops were established there. The art was further conveyed to Europe through Moorish Spain in the 12th century. (Williams 1987, pp. 97-8)
>
> The first paper-mill in Europe was established in 1270 at Fabriano in Italy (Harris 1999, p. 176).

Printing using a movable type, credited to Johannes Gutenberg (?1398-1468), was introduced into Europe in the 1450s and widely available by 1500.

It does not take a wild imagination to conclude that paper made education widely available to the general public everywhere, and specifically ended the monopoly of church education in Europe. Until the rise of the universities in the twelfth century, monasteries were almost the sole seats of education in Europe.

Gunpowder

The Chinese knew how to make gunpowder as early as the 7th century. Gunpowder was not developed as explosives but the alchemists seeking the elixir of life discovered it more or less by chance. The Chinese knew saltpetre (potassium nitrate), the crucial element of gunpowder, to liquefy or dissolve metals and minerals at least from the second century BC, and to prolong life if people ingested it. Saltpetre formed natural deposits in hot climates and it burned violently, a fact used to detect deposits on the ground. China had an ample supply of it but it was scarce in Europe. The Europeans could not develop fully the gunpowder industry until the 18th century when the British opened up India for the supply of saltpetre. (Temple 1986, pp. 224-6)

By the AD third century the alchemists in China put together saltpetre and sulphur to try to create gold from lead. Carbon of charcoal had to be added to make gunpowder to the mix of saltpetre and sulphur. The weight proportion of saltpetre was gradually increased in the mix to the point of 75% of the gunpowder, which is the same in modern gunpowder, and explosion and even detonation was obtained. Saltpetre contained enough oxygen to ignite without additional oxygen, and in later centuries this made possible bombs and rockets. The Daoist classic dated around AD 850 recorded the formula of making gunpowder for the first time as we can trace. (pp. 226-8)

As the Sung government moved south in the wake of the Jurchen invasion in the early 12th century, the government soldiers were starved off horses from the north and west. Under this difficulty the Chinese used the firearms for the first time in battles.

> The first description of gunpowder as an explosive dates from the first quarter of the 12th century, when iron fragmentation bombs were used with devastating effect (Williams 1987, p. 134).

In the 11th century the Chinese used explosives to make bombs and grenades; in the 12th century they fired explosive projectiles from bamboo tubes. The Chinese used firearms in 1232 against the Mongols, who captured the artisans skilled in the use and manufacture and employed them. The Mongols utilised firearms in subsequent battles.

Cannon and handgun seem to have originated in China too; the cannon by 1290.

Knowledge of how to make gunpowder made its way to Europe at the end of the 13th century possibly via the Arab world. Rodger Bacon was the first person in the West to write the instructions on how to make gun powder (1242). It is conjectured that he got the idea from an Arab source since he read Arabic. Muslim armies used these weapons against the crusaders in the thirteenth century.

The fact that gunpowder remained the only explosive in use until the end of the 19th century underscores its importance. Western powers developed high-effect explosives which were many times more destructive than gunpowder. They also developed slow burning and smokeless propellant designed to propel the projectiles. (p. 213) It is noteworthy that gunpowder is still widely used today in sophisticated weaponry though high-effect explosives and propellant completely replaced gunpowder in the above applications.

Gunpowder revolutionised warfare in Europe and heralded the end of the Middle Ages by eliminating the usefulness of knights.

Introduction of gunpowder and guns into the European battlefields brought:

- Mounted troops using carbines and horse pistols preceded the end of knights in armour.
- The new defensive siege wall of a circuit of low, thick walls punctuated by square bastions replaced the high thin walls of the Middle Ages.
- Naval guns changed the scene of naval vessels and battles completely.

> [In Europe], this period of quiet evolution came to a dramatic end in the 14th century with the introduction of gunpowder. This quite literally revolutionised warfare: in a very short span of time new kinds of weapons had to be made and men trained to use them. Almost overnight, fortifications which had seemed impregnable became highly vulnerable. Military engineers, after a period of strengthening existing fortresses as best they could, responded by introducing new designs. (p. 131)

As a matter of fact the transformation of battles in Europe wrought by gunpowder was not as dramatic as the foregoing paragraphs indicate.

Montaigne (1533-1592) wrote concerning printing, pistols and artilleries; the use of gunpowder made the last two items possible. He wrote the following passage:

> We claim at the miracle of the invention of our artillery, of our printing; other men in another corner of the world, in China, enjoyed them a thousand years earlier (Montaigne 1965, p. 693).

He also wrote the following passage:

> But as for the pistol, I shall speak of it more amply when I make a comparison of ancient arms with ours; and except for the shock to the ear, with which by now everyone had become familiar I think it is a weapon of very little effect, and hope that someday we shall abandon the use of it (p. 211).

He further wrote:

> In China--a kingdom whose government and arts, without dealings with and knowledge of ours, surpass our examples in many branches of excellence, and whose history teaches me

> how much and more varied the world is than either the ancients or we ourselves understand ... (p. 820).

Guns and gunpowder had little influence on the outcome of battles for a few centuries after the introduction in the European theatre. Firearms and artillery did not decide the outcome of battles until the late 15th century. (Harris 1999, p. 178) However, Montaigne's observations in the battlefields cited earlier about pistols were made in the middle of the 16th century and are different from today's overall assessment of pistol use.

Compass

> As early as the fifth century BC a lodestone carved into the shape of a spoon, and known as *sinan*, was used for direction finding (Williams 1987, p. 111).

Thereafter there's constant reference to *sinan* in Chinese literature, but no major development took place until the utilisation in the 11th century of magnetism induced steel. A very thin sheet of steel was cut in the form of a fish, magnetised by rubbing with a lodestone and floated on water.

The Chinese widely used compasses for direction finding; and particularly geomancy, the technique of aligning houses and cities in accordance with the earth's forces. The navigational use of the compass came in much later centuries and they had to alter the design of compasses for this purpose.

The Chinese used rudders to guide ships by the AD 1st century. During the Sung era, when long distance commerce was flourishing, Chinese ships began to carry compasses. During the same era, before abandoning Cheng Ho's journeys, the Chinese rounded the Cape of Good Hope and sighted Australia. (Harris 1999, p. 182)

Joseph Needham established that the Europeans acquired the compass from China. The first recorded mention of a compass in Europe was in 1190. (Temple 1986, p. 149)

Magnetic compasses made sea voyages a lot easier and thus led to the discoveries of the lands unknown to the Europeans. It is well known that Columbus used compasses in the voyage which eventually led to the discovery of the American continent in 1492.

Magnetic compass was the most useful among the various navigational aids such as astrolabe (to measure the altitudes of stars, the sun and the moon), sextant (to determine the angular differentiation of the two objects), together with maps. The following inventory which Magellan carried on the first circumnavigation of the globe in 1519 shows the importance of the magnetic compass. The inventory was probably typical for the long sea voyages of the day:

> 21 quadrants (to measure altitudes of stars)
> 7 marine astrolabes
> 18 sand glasses (to measure time)
> 23 charts
> 37 compass needles
> note: For centuries seamen calculated latitude by measuring the height of the sun at noon above the horizon by using a sextant or quadrant or astrolabe.
> (Williams 1987, pp. 108-10)

When we focus attention to European history, all three inventions facilitated to end the Middles Ages and heralded the arrival of modern Europe.

A similar story unfolds for other notable inventions made by the Chinese; cast iron (the Shang period), printed books (ninth century), water driven clocks (eleventh century), and circulation of paper money (eleventh century). 'Between 605 and 617 Emperor Yang Ti [Yang Di] extended the Grand Canal (parts of which had begun centuries before) to such an extent that he may be regarded as its prime architect. With tree-shaded roads, posting stations and imperial pavilions along its banks, this immense trunk system linked the Yangtze, Huai and Yellow Rivers to give China the world's most extensive inland waterway network until modern times.' (p. 123) 'The early Sung authorities awarded a small set of shops a monopoly on the issuing of the certificates of deposits, and in the 1120's took over the system, issuing the world's first government paper money.' (Ebrey 1996, p. 142) 'Another genre--land scape--is generally recognised as the greatest glory of Sung painting. Centuries before Western artists began to see natural scenery as anything more than background, Chinese artists had developed it into a great art.' (Murowchick 1994, p. 141) Inquiries reveal that the Chinese people, during the classical and middle ages of European history, were quite innovative and credited with a large number of discoveries and inventions. Roger Bacon picked only three (in fact four) which he thought were most important to human history, out of perhaps hundreds and called them 'The Three (Four) Greatest Inventions in World History'.

> Only with the breaching of China's isolation by the Mongols did a flow of technical information actually influence the technical development of the West .... Mongol Empire helped to transfer Chinese knowledge to the West by its tolerant policy. (Cotterell & Morgan 1975, p. 192)
> ... the Chinese of whose achievement the West had become increasingly aware since the Jesuits established themselves in China in the 17th century ... (Williams 1987, p. 172).

B Mongol Empire

The Mongols (or Tartars) are ethnically different from the Chinese; still the Mongol expansion into Russia and Eastern Europe indicates the general superiority of the East over the West. The Mongols also utilised the various Chinese inventions, particularly gunpowder, in the process of conquests. Tartar is the European designation of Mongols meaning a sunless abyss below Hades.

In the pre-modern era the East was generally stronger militarily than the West, corresponding to the general superiority of the East. We can see the above assertion in the expansion of the Huns. People often refer to Attila the Hun, king of the Huns, as Scourge of God. His army devastated much of the Roman Empire in the middle of the AD fifth century. The Roman Empire seemed at Attila's mercy, when Leo I, bishop of Rome, meeting him in person, dissuaded him from attacking Rome, by his resolute stand and not by any show of force. Attila died in 453 and his empire subsequently collapsed.

The Mongol occupation of much of the Eurasian continent may be another example. The Mongols were a nomadic people since their first emergence in the AD early centuries, and a large proportion of them were illiterate and the society was an oral culture. It seems that they were related to the Huns. The Mongols came suddenly into prominence towards the close of the twelfth century, prior to which they were in obscurity in historical terms. The man behind the Mongol rise to power was Genghis (Chingis) Khan. Born in 1162, Temujin (the original name of Genghis) started his empire from Karakorum. In his 40s he was proclaimed Khan (ruler) of the Mongols in 1206, and set about creating a war-machine of unprecedented power. He exploited a traditional military system in conscription--all men between 15 and 60 were liable for military service. War became the life of the Mongols. Non-military tasks were carried out by slaves and women, the latter of whom often worked as business managers. He set forth the laws governing this society in the codes written in the Uighur scripts (phonetic) since the Mongol language did not have a written form. The codes, partly traditional and partly his own, covered moral, civil, criminal, commercial and international laws. He demanded absolute obedience to one's superior under the penalty of death. He reportedly said, 'Men's greatest delight is to chase and defeat their enemy, seize his total possessions and use the bodies of his women'. (Davison 1993, p. 92)

In less than ten years after becoming Khan he invaded and occupied north-eastern China including Beijing, the capital of the Jurchen (or Chin or Jin) Empire at the time. In 1218 he broke off further campaigns into China and turned west. He conquered Central Asia as far as the Caspian Sea by 1220. Further his army went north of the Caspian Sea and conquered the Kipchaks by 1223, and defeated the Russians in Russia in 1223. Kipchak was a region corresponding to present-day South Russia and Ukraine. He turned east again and conquered Xi Xia (Hsi Hsia), which had allied with the Jurchen Empire, in 1227 just before he died. His grandson Kublai Khan conquered the entire China by 1279.

It seems that Genghis and his army had a considerable difficulty in subjugating China, in part because of China's dense population. The Mongolian army took 5 years (1210 to1215) to capture the Jurchen capital Beijing. Also the Mongols had to wait until Genghis' grandson Kublai to conquer all China by 1279. These observations confirm that China, though a non-militaristic empire, was in advance in material culture than Europe. We also have to take into account the vast distance the Mongolian army had to travel to subjugate western Russia and subsequently eastern Europe; China was adjacent to Mongolia.

Jochi (Juchi) was the eldest of Genghis Khan's four sons and ruled over the domain of the western section of the Mongol Empire. Though Jochi participated in his father's campaigns, antagonism developed between the two after 1221. Jochi died six months before Genghis died. When Jochi died in 1227, Batu, his second son, took over the above domain. In 1235 Batu was elected to be commander-in-chief of the western part of the Mongol Empire. He conquered all of Russia by 1240 and eastern Europe. He founded the Khanate of Kipchak or the Golden Horde.

When the Mongol hordes invaded Russia and Eastern Europe in the 13th century, the Russian and East European armies were no match against the Mongolian army, though we are comparing only military might. Western Europe was, we are certain, saved from total defeat when Batu, the Mongol commander of the European campaign, had to return to the capital Karakorum hastily at the news that Ogodei Khan, son of Genghis Khan, died in 1241. A death of a khan created a crisis due to the Mongol tradition of succession by election rather than descent. He had to attend the general council which was to decide on Ogodei's successor. Consequently western Europe did not suffer devastation but its population reduced radically as pestilence spread.

> Ogodei died suddenly, and in 1242 there was trouble about the succession, and, recalled by this, the undefeated hosts of Mongols began to pour back across Hungary and Romania towards the east. To the great relief of Europe the dynastic troubles at Karakorum lasted for some years, and this vast empire showed signs of splitting up. Mangu [Mongke] Khan became the Great Khan in 1251, and he nominated his brother Kublai Khan as Governor-General of China. (Wells 1925, p. 441)

Batu failed to obtain the title of Great Khan, and settled in the city of Sarai on the lower Volga, and attended the administration of the domain of the Golden Horde. When Mongke, his ally, became Great Khan in 1251, Batu received complete autonomy. Though Batu planned to invade western Europe he died in 1255. His empire survived until the end of the 15th century.

> The Mongol dominion over the Russians lasted from 1240 to 1380 or even to 1480 depending on whether we include the period of a more or less nominal Mongol rule (Riasanovsky 1977, p. 72).
>
> Two centuries of Tartar dominion over the small Russian state of Muscovy were broken in 1480 when Ivan the Great, Grand Duke of Muscovy, refused to pay further tribute to his

> Mongol suzerain, and toppled the Khanate of the Golden Horde. Ivan swept the Tartars out of Muscovy. Thus began 300 years of expansion which was to spread the Russian Empire into three continents covering one-sixth of the world's land mass. (*Early Civilization* 1984, p. 237)

Since the Tartars ruled their dominion by sheer military strength, as soon as the vassal states (in this case Muscovy) felt the Tartars' reign weaken they mobilised their army to shake off the burdensome yoke.

The Mongol Empire reached the widest extent in the late 1200s; however, already in 1234 there were clear signs that it was too large for one central administration to govern. In the process with the struggles with the Jurchen Empire the Mongols learned much of the military science of the Chinese, among which was the use of guns and gunpowder. Incredibly the Mongols could not have numbered more than 1.5 million. The fundamental reason for the Mongol expansion may have been, seemingly betraying the last statement, overpopulation: the steppes could support only a limited number of people. Their success in expansion was due in large part to their willingness to incorporate other ethnic groups into their armies and government. They also owed success to discipline, organisation, strategy, and above all to the warlike way of life they adopted. They also practised the complete religious toleration. The Mongol Empire was nothing but the taxing government for the conquered, and left them alone, careless how they lived. However, the Mongols treated conquered China differently and set up a local government to govern as I explain briefly in Section 3 of this chapter.

Mongke, Kublai's older brother, died in 1259 after reigning for only eight years as Great Khan leaving no firm direction for the empire, which essentially marked the end of the unified Mongol Empire. Kublai, grandson of Genghis, received the news that Arig Boke, his younger brother was elected Great Khan in Karakorum in 1260. Karakorum, the favourite campsite of Genghis, had become the capital of the Mongol Empire in 1235. Kublai's relatives vigorously opposed Kublai settling in China, and also Arig Boke had the advantage of reigning the heartland of the tribes (the Mongol Khanate). The Mongke's old officials and Mongke's army supported Arig Boke. Kublai subsequently claimed the title of Great Khan at Shang-tu, Kublai's summer capital in present day Inner Mongolia.

A civil war ensued. Kublai's authority was strong in Ilkhanate and the Golden Horde as well as western parts of the Mongol Empire. The war ended with the capture of Arig Boke in 1264. However, the civil wars, which raged in Karakorum too, destroyed the internal solidarity of the empire, and the unity never returned since. Though the Mongol Khanate came under his control, Kublai's claim to Great Khan was not recognised among the other khanates including Ilkhanate and the Golden Horde. Kublai proclaimed the creation of the Yuan dynasty in China with the capital at Ta-tu (Beijing) in 1271, and subsequently annihilated the last resistance of the Southern Sung dynasty. Kublai twice attempted to conquer Japan--in 1274 and 1281--but failed when monsoons, called Divine Wind (kamikaze) by the Japanese ever since, scattered his ships. His maritime expedition to Java (1292) was also unsuccessful. He died in 1294. Disputes over succession weakened the central government from 1300 onwards and the Yuan dynasty was overthrown in 1368.

The Mongol Empire broke up into four separate parts: the Empire of the Great Khan, the Golden Horde, Ilkhanate, and the Jagatai Empire. The Mongols also settled in India and ruled the Mughal (Mongol) Empire in later centuries.

Genghis Khan started the building of post roads to facilitate the transport of armies, trade goods and people. His successors extended these roads. Under Kublai the long disused trade routes across Asia reopened, and caravans journeyed between East and West. With one such, the Polo brothers travelled east. (Roberts 1973, pp. 30-1) The Mongol conquests expanded contacts across Eurasia, which led to not only the transfer of technical and scientific knowledge from East to West but also possibly the spread of deadly plagues.

In 1279 for the first time in Chinese history the entire China came under the foreign rule of Mongols. During the Mongol occupation, China was tied into a Eurasian empire, and foreigners from West Asia and Europe visited in unprecedented numbers. These cross-cultural contacts whetted the appetite of Europeans for increased contact with distant lands but had the opposite effect on the Chinese. Chinese inventions--such as printing and gunpowder--spread westward, and the demand for Asian goods eventually culminated in the great age of European exploration and expansion.

> In this sense, Western culture, as Hegel himself had said, was a higher stage, perhaps the ultimate synthesis of its forerunners, the Oriental and Greco-Roman civilisations (Carmichael 1968, p. 34).

The Mongol army did not even complete the conquest of the Eurasian continent, and they were defeated when they ventured to conquer beyond the continent. Hulegu, Genghis' grandson, had to stop further advance into Africa, when the Egyptian army defeated his army in 1260.

> An army under Sultan of Egypt completely defeated Ketboga, Hulegu's general, in Palestine in 1260, and stopped them entering Africa. From this time on Mongol army lost its vigour and became defensive of its conquered territories. (Wells 1925, p. 442)

Paper money was widely used in the Mongol Empire. In Europe the currency in the form of banknotes was not introduced until the late 18th century.

Though the Mongol army utilised firearms, these did not decide the outcome of battles until the 15th century. The Mongols could not develop sophisticated firearms being illiterate and preferring to live in the steppes. When conquered nations such as China and Russia in the fourteenth and fifteenth centuries revolted with advanced firearms, the Mongols were spent force.

C Marco Polo

There are many written accounts of the journeys in the thirteenth and fourteenth centuries by the Europeans as well as by the Chinese. In 1245 Pope Innocent IV sent two Franciscan and two Dominican friars to establish diplomatic relations with the Mongols and introduce them to the Catholic faith. Catholic here denotes the Latin or Western Church after the Great Schism of 1054. One of these, Friar John, wrote *History of the Mongols*, which is one of the most important information sources on China. Giovanni de Piano Carpini travelled into the Mongol Empire with missionary zeal from 1245 to 1247. William of Rubrouck went to Karakorum, from 1252 to 1255, with the similar intent but was equally unsuccessful. William wrote *Itinerary*. Another Franciscan, Friar Odoric of Pordenone, reached Canton by sea in 1324 and wrote his *Travels,* which was widely read. Some Chinese travellers went in the opposite direction and brought back their stories to China: they were aware that the Chinese were on a higher cultural ground than the Europeans. For all these tales and stories, we wonder why Marco Polo's story has fascinated people most all these centuries.

Many Europeans at the time read Marco Polo's book and were fascinated by the beautiful Chinese cities, huge and prosperous at the same time and their riches, an orderly society and so much inter-regional trade, and their interests were aroused to trade with China which he called Cathay. Columbus studied his book with close attention. It is said that Marco's story concerning the abundant gold on the island of Cipangu or Cipango (Japan) spurred Columbus to set off on his trip to discover the American continent by accident. (Boulnois 2005, p. 342)

Niccolo and Maffeo Polo, merchants from Venice, travelled from 1255 to 1269, deep inside the Mongol Empire for a trading trip. Marco Polo accompanied his father Niccolo and his uncle Maffeo on the next trip, 1271-95. It was Marco's journey accounts which gave Europe the accurate picture of the empire and literally changed the course of history. (Roberts 1973, p. 30)

The Mongols ruled a large part of Eurasia, and a safe land passage between East and West was more or less assured. Venice and Genoa reigned over European trade with the East at the end of the 13th century. Marco returned to Venice a rich man. The Genoese captured Marco in 1296 or 1298 during a naval battle between the Venetians and Genoese in the Mediterranean. He was imprisoned in Genoa until 1299. In prison he found another Italian, a writer, Rustichello of Pisa. During their long stay together the writer wrote down what Marco dictated, in French, the language of prestige, in prison, since Marco was illiterate. The original manuscripts were lost but copies survived and they were eventually known as *The Travels of Marco Polo*.

Everyone agrees that he exaggerated his stories. He did not mention the Great Wall of China, the foot-binding custom for the Chinese ladies and the widespread custom of drinking tea. Some of his stories do not match the facts. The Chinese annals do not have a record of Marco Polo in an official capacity though the book says he worked for the Chinese government. Is it possible that he did not go to China and contrived so ingeniously all his stories as to be believable and accurate? Many people have raised a serious question if he really went to China and the debate is still continuing today. (Boulnois 2005, pp. 353-5) Some speculated that he travelled as far as the Black Sea, and collected stories from Persian merchants. I proceed this article on the assumption that he wrote the book.

Marco arrived at the magnificent summer palace of Kublai Khan at Shang-tu (meaning upper capital) in Inner Mongolia together with his father and uncle in 1265. They presented themselves to the khan bearing the gifts from the pope. The pope was wishing the conversion of the Mongols to Christianity and a military alliance against the Muslims: on both counts the mission was a failure. The crusades lasted from 1096 to 1291.

Marco Polo narrated in his book *The Travels* that China, though under Mongol rule when he visited after the middle of the 13th century, far surpassed Italy, his native country, in wealth and technical expertise. He was a merchant and not a scholarly person. He wrote only what he saw and heard hence he limited the scope of his concern to material culture. He often did not make a distinction between what he saw and what he heard, that is to say, we cannot tell whether his narration was first hand or second hand. Also he did not interpret what he observed from philosophical or broader viewpoint. For example, the daily use of coal in China amazed him. Obviously the Italians did not make use of coal as a heat source in his days of the 13th century. He did not know that in the ancient Greece and Italy people used coal domestically for cooking and warming. The Greeks and Romans made some use of coal, but only where they encountered it as outcrops (Williams 1987, p. 193). Though he wrote that Hangchow was without doubt the finest and most splendid city in the world, he could not appreciate the literary and artistic heritage of the city: As noted earlier he could not read or write in any language.

Marco was young and clever in the affairs of the world and had a full mastery of the Tartar language which did not have a written form, but he did not speak Chinese. Kublai's command of Chinese language was also poor. The Polos had taken about three and a half years to get to China and stayed there upwards of sixteen. (Wells 1925, p. 444)

> In his dominions no fewer than two hundred thousand horses are thus employed in the department of the post, and ten thousand buildings, with suitable furniture, are kept up (Polo 1959, p. 158).
>
> Throughout this province [Cathy] there is found a sort of black stone, which they dig out of the mountains, where it runs in veins. When lighted, it burns like charcoal, and retain the heat much better than wood, ... (p. 164)

> In the eleventh, twelfth and thirteenth centuries China was the leading society in the world. By the eleventh century, Europe was certainly out of the shadows of the Dark Ages, but improvements in its economy were not occurring at anywhere near the rate they were in China. At the end of the thirteenth century, when Marco Polo crossed Asia, neither Venice where he came from nor any of the countries of Europe or Asia that he passed through could compare to China in agricultural productivity, industrial technology, sophistication of commercial organisation, urbanisation or standard of living. (Ebrey 1996, p. 161)

> Marco became the favourite of the emperor, travelling through China on special missions and finally being appointed governor of Yang-chou. In 1292, after the Polos' spending seventeen years in Kublai's service, he allowed them to return to their native country. Kublai's death in 1295 ended the *Mongol Peace* (Pax Mongolica) and closed the Silk Road. (Harris 1999, pp. 183-4)

Chapter 3 European Middle Ages (600-1492)

Introductory Remarks

In 'Introduction to Series' I stress the importance of idealism represented by Christianity, Greek and Latin cultures in Europe, and also represented by Confucianism, Daoism (Taoism) and Buddhism in China. Idealism played a crucial role as the basis of the general education in both Europe and China, and became instrumental in setting up the church in Europe and the civil service examinations in China. The Chinese civil service examinations integrated idealism through the course of Chinese history overriding dynastic changes. The European Middle Ages is said to be in cultural decline; however, it is more in accord by the deep study that this era was in fact the formation period for later development. Without the diffusion of idealism in this era among the Europeans, Europe would not have made the growth in modern era possible and consequently would not have surpassed China. I am to advance a chapter of the European Middle Ages corresponding to the Chinese civil service examinations in 'Introduction to Series'. It looks into how Christianity permeated the European society; though the way the church tried to dominate the society was often not honourable as readers will see, as the examination system was often not in China,

One fundamental difference between Europe and China was the organisational strengths of the state(s) and idealism. The European church had an ordered administration with its own hierarchy, though, with the absence of the army, it had to rely on the states to resolve any armed conflicts. The church gradually acquired lands since Constantine the Great recognised the Christian Church and delivered favourable policies. The church in the West became the most powerful feudal lord and held a quarter to one-third of the land in Christian Europe during the medieval era. Gifts of properties including land together with tithes made the church rich. Also in the medieval times the Roman Catholic Church was exempt from paying taxes.

Further it collected service charges from everyone from a serf to a king on occasions of baptism, marriage and burial. Opposition to the church could have resulted in excommunication: Excommunicated persons could not attend church services and would go to hell when they died, they were told. The church flaunted its wealth in its buildings such as churches, cathedrals and monasteries.

In the Middle Ages the scattered independent states simply did not have both the effective bureaucracies and the regular armies to resist the pope and the church with the sophisticated and unified administration backed by authority, land ownership and wealth. Only in the modern era did European states--towards the end of the Hundred Years' War for England and France--acquire revenues and as the result effective bureaucracies and standing armies; they still did not have the preponderance over the church with its own revenues and spiritual persuasiveness. In China idealism did not have the organisation since its inception to withstand the powerful state with its army. The elite of idealism were in the state bureaucracy which was under the strict control of the emperor. Consequently idealism in China was at the mercy of the emperor who decided which idealism (Confucianism, Daoism or Buddhism) should be the examination topic and how it should be interpreted and conducted.

Section 1 European Dark Ages (600-900)

In Section 3 Roman Empire and Emergence of European Nations, Chapter 1, I outline how the Germanic peoples overran the West Roman Empire. The administration in the empire collapsed and the officials ran away. The migrating Germans established their kingdoms in Western Europe as we roughly recognise them as such today. The Christian Church being independent of the empire administratively and financially survived largely intact though certainly some churches (buildings and organisations) were damaged or destroyed through the chaos.

In the eighth century Europe was beginning to settle down and to give some semblance of order to society following the turmoil of the barbarian migrations and the collapse of the Western Roman Empire. Anglo-Saxon society was established in England, and the Frankish Empire in western continental Europe inspired new learning and culture. However, beginning just before 800 for about three hundred years, the Vikings raided and settled in the coastal regions of northern and western Europe with such a fury that they caused the utmost fear among the inhabitants: This was the Viking Age.

Vikings

People lived in Scandinavia as hunters-gatherers as early as 12 000 years ago. Gradually they developed farming and fishing. At around 500 BC the Bronze Age gave way to the Iron Age.

The Vikings, meaning sea-raiders, had a society divided into classes and their scattered kingdoms merged into three of Norway, Sweden and Denmark at the Viking era. They spoke the same language with different dialects, they had common cultures and they relied on each other for trade and mutual defence. Norse or Norsemen or Northmen refer to Norwegians, Rus to Swedish, and Danes to Danish. Contrary to these designations, Norse or Norsemen or Northmen can mean the Vikings generally. Subsequent history shows that their rivalries were quite strong at times as evidenced by Danish-Norwegian rivalries in England and Ireland. These Vikings lived in Scandinavia, and are classed to be north Germans today.

Although backward compared with the rest of Europe Scandinavia had a strong economy based on agriculture and trade at the beginning of the Viking era. The Vikings thought it natural they plunder what they wanted from other peoples as long as they could get away. Once the custom was born and became a way of life it was hard to change the way in the same token that it is hard for drinkers, gamblers and criminals to stop the habits. The booty including slaves was sold at markets, benefiting also traders and craftsmen, and Scandinavian kings controlled trading settlements and levied taxes on transactions.

At first the Vikings raided and pillaged the shores of northern and western Europe but in the course of the ninth century they became eager to migrate and settle. It seems that there was a population explosion and the surplus people had to emigrate from Scandinavia. Kings had to organise large-scale raids involving hundreds of ships and thousands of Vikings, hence the large-scale raids coincided with the emergence of powerful kings in Scandinavia. The Vikings were no longer the sea rovers of an earlier age but formed a disciplined standing army. There were always attractions of wealth of the southern lands in the minds of the Scandinavians, which had prompted trade and exploration in the first place. Kings' organising the raids was a two-edged sword in that kings exercised the authority and got a portion of booty, which prompted further explorations by the rank and file Vikings for the purpose of settlements. It is conjectured that the explorations by the Vikings to the American continent was to get away from the king's dominance and confiscations of the booty; these Vikings were Norse, that is, they were Norwegians.

The Vikings wrote in runes, rudimentary alphabets, on weapons, jewels and stones and left few written records except for the Skaldic legacy of the 13th century sagas. The runic alphabets are believed to have developed from Greek or Latin, and their inscriptions were found throughout Europe dating from the AD 1st century. With the introduction of Christianity, Latin came into use in Scandinavia and the old runes were marginalised.

The Scandinavians developed their famous longships in the 7th century from their earlier versions to navigate the oceans and narrow rivers in Norway and Sweden. In the early 8th century they fitted masts to their longships for sailing. They were designed for speed, and had shallow draft for shallow water, allowing landing close to the shore and a quick getaway. They were the first raiding arrivals.

The Vikings also built knorrs with sails for bulk carrying capacity; one of them was capable of carrying up to 20 tons of cargo. They used these knorrs for trading and also carrying their booty from raids: cargoes such as animals, treasures and humans.

The Vikings had to build both longships and knorrs sturdy enough to withstand the North Sea where weather was known to change suddenly and endanger shipping. The North Sea was their vital trading route. When they failed to control these avenues of transport, the Viking Age came to an end. It is said that the death of Harald Hardrada in 1066 marks the end of the Viking era.

In the course of raids and colonisation, both the Vikings and the inhabitants of Scandinavia came into contact with the civilised cultures of the Mediterranean and the Middle East, and became Christians. By the end of the Viking Age the Scandinavians were no longer backward in their culture and in the process facilitated the creation of trade routes crisscrossing Europe and Russia. Thus they lost the culture of raiding, plundering and colonising and came to settle peacefully in the lands where they lived towards the end of the 11th century. The base of Scandinavian society remained economic rather than ecclesiastic or political and relied on farming and trade. To ensure its survival and prosperity, kings introduced fiefdom modelled on the rest of Europe and the people had to support the church and state which continually squabbled.

King Canute the Great (Canute I or II) (d. 1035) ruled the kingdoms of Denmark, the Anglo-Danish realm of England, and Norway. This was the greatest extent of the North Sea Empire which the Vikings dreamed.

As the Scandinavian (Viking or North Germanic) trade declined, the Hanseatic League (Germanic) came into existence in the mid-12th century and eventually dominated trade in the North Sea. Danish kings vigorously opposed the League resorting to military force well into the 14th century. By this time the Dutch emerged as a maritime economic power pushing away the League as a dominant trading group. Without the trading networks the Vikings developed, the above mentioned Germanic and Dutch maritime trading blocs would not have developed. It is not an exaggeration to say that they owed their existence to a great extent to the earlier explorations by the Vikings.

Section 2 Basic Structure of Society

The Renaissance scholars called the Middle Ages for the first time the era between the classical age and the revival of classical learning in Europe. The Middle Ages for them was the period of ignorance and barbarism. This series of books marks the Middle Ages from 600 to 1492. However, there are other classifications. Maurice Keen, for instance, sets the limits: as beginning at 800 when Pope Leo III crowned Charlemagne the king of the Franks and closing at 1449 when the Council of Basle was finally dissolved after 20 years of sessions (Keen 1991, p. 11).

Europe, as geographically defined, has today, more or less, uniform racial and religious characteristics. The Roman (initially non-Christians and then converted to Christians), Germanic (some, Christians and some, non-Christians before migrations, and then they all converted to approved Christianity), and Slavs (converted to Christianity around the 10th century) overran Europe in the classical to medieval eras, which resulted in permanent residence. However, in the Middle Ages the Moors (Muslims since the 8th century), the Turks (Muslims since c. 970) invaded Europe; and the Mongols (pagans, and converted to Muslims in the process of conquering the Middle East) invaded the Middle East, though their occupations were not permanent. These data show that Europe since converting to Christianity resisted the incursions of non-Christians strongly, and non-Caucasians absolutely. The contact with the barbarism of the Mongols made the Europeans realise that the difference between Christianity and Islam was comparatively small.

In the modern era, Europe, particularly Western Europe, was largely united racially and religiously. Rather strangely Western Europe went through fierce religious conflicts in the name of the Reformation in the 16th and 17th centuries.

Latin (Western) Christendom in the 13th century was reminiscent of the Roman Empire. The Romans under the banner of the empire controlled the entire coast lines of the Mediterranean Sea and their prosperity depended on its commerce. Latin Christians controlled a large part of the Mediterranean coastal areas, and the merchants of the Italian towns who controlled its trade were the richest people in Europe. Although the trade along the Mediterranean coast remained important until sometime after the American discovery, the towns of Flanders and the Baltic emerged as commercial rivals of the Italians in the fourteenth century. (p. 14)

Soon after the year 400, the Huns, a savage nomad people from the steppes of Asia, pressed on into the whole Teutonic world, and subsequently the Goths, the Vandals, the Burgundians and later the Franks fled for their lives and crossed the frontiers of the Roman Empire (p. 15).

The feudal system emerged from the mid-11th century and lasted for about 400 years in Europe. Its central motif was land which provided the necessities of life and was the centre of life of society in the absence of significant industry.

Village Life in Feudal Society

A local lord owned a village in which the peasants cultivated the land and tended cattle. The entire village including the lands was called a manor. A local lord was usually a knight and lived in a manor house. There were two types of peasants. Churls were free men and rented the land from the lord for a fee. Villeins tilled the big fields around the village to feed their families, and had an obligation to perform extra works for the lord for three days a week. Life for the villeins was harsh and many tried to run away. To prevent them from running away the lord placed various restrictions as well as severe penalties when they were caught. The lord administered justice within his jurisdiction mainly relying on precedent; most of the laws were not written down. All the people had to pay a tithe, one-tenth of all income--produce for the peasants--to the Western Church. The payment of tithes was enforced by Roman Catholic Church as well as Protestant churches after the Reformation, from the 6th century to 1789 (France), 1871 (Ireland), 1887 (Italy) and 1936 (England). There was no tithe obligation to the Eastern Orthodox Church.

Town Life in Feudal Society

During the Dark Ages towns were not common. In the High Middle Ages the stable society prompted trade, and towns developed apace. As towns, still under the king's estate, grew prosperous people demanded independence from the king and obtained freedom, individually or as a town, for a set of fees. As towns became independent of the king, citizens had to manage the day-to-day running of affairs in addition to the defence obligation. Towns organised borough courts and formed councils presided over by a mayor. Merchants and trade craftsmen organised guilds to protect their interests, and formed merchant guilds and craft guilds; they further subdivided into specialised trade groups such as the Guild of Wool Merchants or Butchers or Carpenters.

People in the Middle Ages believed that the Roman Empire, though only the Eastern Empire remained at the time, gave peace and unity to the world and a fitting field for spreading Christianity. This concept was also backed by the biblical scripture (Daniel chs 2-8): Daniel, a 6th century Hebrew prophet, prophesised in his few visions concerning five kingdoms. Babylon, Persia, Alexander's Macedon and Rome will become history, and the fifth kingdom of God is to endure forever. Noting an improbability of his visions with the future history—he lived at around the time of the Neo-Babylonian Empire--, a note in my Bible said that later authors added or altered the relevant verses. Another note said that his visions were prophetic: Still this does not explain from the modern viewpoint why the kingdom of God did not succeed the Roman Empire.

The Middle Ages saw the steady and progressive decay of the Roman world as had been shown in such events as the Viking invasions of the ninth, tenth and eleventh centuries and the break-up of the Carolingian Empire of the tenth century. The Carolingian Empire originated in the Frankish dynasty and reigned in Germany till 911 and France till 987. In the upheaval of the ninth and tenth centuries, little people such as small farmers or descendants of slaves sought protection from lords who wanted people to till their lands. Thus the little people became serfs of the lords, surrendering their freedom and that of their children. Lordship could be transferred, bought or sold. Most lordships were hereditary tenures and passed from father to son according to the custom. Lords looked for every opportunity to increase their dominion. They at times obtained estates as a reward from their king who was really a great lord. They at times obtained estates by alliance or marriage. Lords with a large domain gave a fief (property or fee; called benefice before the 11th century) to create another lord. In this sense the European Medieval Ages was a feudal society. Feudalism was of Germanic origin in the European context. The lord lived in his castle protected by his soldiers and held his court and judged his subjects. The most essential obligation of the vassal was his service in war and vendetta, and his estate was valued by the number of soldiers it could maintain. (Keen 1991, pp. 47, 51, 57, 262)

The principle of primogeniture was not necessarily enforced among the royal house though royal blood was of prime importance in inheritance. Since the right to rule over lands and men was thought to be inheritable, dynastic consideration as well as the assent of the vassals was the prime factor in building the empire. The royal house was eager to secure favourable marriages rather than to rely on the sword to increase its property. The ruler had the right to take over the lands of a vassal who died without heirs or without legal protection.

In Europe around Charlemagne's time, that is, the ninth century, the society fragmented into small rural communities, ignorant of other communities and the world. People's attitudes were formed by the Roman (laws), Germanic (feudalism) and Christian (religion) traditions. Rural communities were self-reliant for the necessities of life, towns were too few and too small to register as consumer markets, and trade was limited to luxury items. Poor harvests and enemies imperilled the precarious subsistence of people. The great domain, the typical economic unit of the Carolingian period (751-887 in western Europe), came into common existence with the ability to respond to these dangers.

The English kingdom which Henry III ruled in the thirteenth century was no more advanced than the Holy Roman Empire of Charlemagne (800-814). It had no capital, no official bureaucracy and its chief revenues came from the private estates of the king himself. Kings were not universal rulers unlike the pope who was the unified authority in Christendom. Hence the unifying force of kingdoms was religious and ideal and not political. However, power in the last resort rested with the lords who could build castles and maintain enough fighting men. (pp. 45-6, 58)

Kinship was the most important of all social bonds, and vendetta for the kinsman was the prime social duty in society.

Christian practice permeated many social customs. The vassal's oath of fealty was sworn on the Bible. Serfdom was ordained by God. However, the strongest religious force in this era was in the monasteries. Monasteries had to have land endowments and labouring men to cultivate them. Their influence was in the moral field only and they had to look up to the secular authority in political and legal contexts. Land endowments in the first place most likely came from the generosity of the lay noblemen.

Popes, being deficient of material resources and army, had to manoeuvre even more desperately than kings. This became particularly obvious when the western and northern kingdoms grew their secular public authority as the Medieval Ages progressed challenging the universal authority of the papacy. (pp. 172, 206)

Towards the end of the medieval era, that is, in the course of the fifteenth century, the Europeans discarded the beliefs in Christendom as well as in Europe as a kind of superstate. They no longer believed that princes and priests or state and church work side by side in compliment to achieve political and religious ideals.

Section 3 End of Viking Era, and Norman Conquests

A major part of England became a Viking state from the end of the 9th century for two centuries. There were the Norse (Norwegian) enclaves on the west coast of England, but the Danes controlled the northern and eastern England and this rule was known as the Danelaw indicating that Danish laws prevailed. To control this Anglo-Danish kingdom, Danish kings used sheer military might to subjugate the Anglo-Saxons who fought back the invaders. However, both parties signed the Treaty of Wedmore in 878 and general peace, though uneasy, prevailed. The Danes and the Anglo-Saxons did not have much problem in communicating in their respective languages; the Anglo-Saxons had migrated from the south of Denmark to England during the earlier German migrations.

King Canute the Great was a king of Denmark, a king of England and nominally a king of Norway. He made Norway a province of his Danish kingdom with successful campaigns in 1030. When he died in 1035, Norway became independent and a Norwegian king ruled. One of Canute's sons, Harold, succeeded England and another, Hardecanute, Denmark. Harold died in 1040 and Hardecanute succeeded the English throne. When Hardecanute died two years later, the English crown passed to Edward the Confessor, the old royal line of Anglo-Saxon.

The Vikings made raids on the Frankish kingdom in the early 9th century, Viking enclaves on the coast providing bases. Louis I, son of Emperor Charlemagne, split his kingdom among his three sons, and from 829 onwards there were constant wars among his siblings. This gave an opportunity for the Vikings to exploit, and they had almost free rein on raids for a quarter of a century. Danish-Norwegian rivalries in England and Ireland forced the Vikings to slacken their attacks on the Frankish Empire for a while. When they returned in greater numbers their aim was to conquer not to plunder. The Vikings rowed up the rivers, Seine, Elbe and Rhine, attacking the major cities; however, these attacks were repulsed by the end of the 10th century and the Vikings made only confined raids on the coastal regions from then on.

Normandy--French royal accounts first described this term in the mid-tenth century--was the land ceded in 911 to Rollo, a leader of the Vikings, by Charles III, the Frankish King, on condition that Rollo, as Duke of Normandy, swore allegiance to the king. The Norsemen had raided and settled in the northern part of the kingdom and the king could not dislodge them and so came up with this arrangement. The Vikings in Normandy were called the Normans, became Christians and adopted French language and customs. Though the Vikings administered Normandy, most of their subjects were Franks. In time they became the mixed blood of Vikings and Franks. Historically the Normans are not classed as Vikings.

When Edward the Confessor died in 1066, the succession problem to the English throne arose. The Witan (the King's advisory council) elected Harold Godwinson as a successor to the throne and he became king. Harold was an Anglo-Danish and possibly the only man capable of uniting the kingdom, the Saxons supporting him. Harald Hardraadi, king of Norway, claimed the succession right. William of Normandy also claimed that he was the legitimate successor to the English throne since Edward had designated him as successor in 1051.

Harald Hardraadi was the first to land on the coast of Northumberland and attack in 1066. However, he was killed in the battle and his army was defeated.

William of Normandy landed his army of 5000 knights near Pevensey, and won over the English army in the Battle of Hastings on 14 October 1066. During the following weeks, the Norman army made its way to London and subdued southern England. Hence William was crowned King William I of England. The outcome radically changed the course of English history. The struggle for control of England which had lasted for centuries was at an end. The future of Europe lay in the axis of England and France, pushing aside the dream of the Viking North Sea Empire. English rebellions lasted till 1071. To secure England's frontiers he invaded Scotland (1072) and Wales (1081). William was thus called William the Conqueror.

The Vikings always looked at warfare as a noble pursuit with the rewards of booty, land and status. Even after settlement in a new colony the spirit of adventure lived on in the minds of former Vikings in the same way wild animals long for a free and wild life for many years after humans capture them. It seems that this restlessness among the Normans was one reason why William ventured his knights into Britain; he could not control their wild passions by peaceful means.

The Domesday Book, the results of a survey by the order of William in 1086, says that the king kept one-seventh of the land of England, the church controlled about a quarter, and about 180 barons kept the rest.

The bourgeoning military might of the Normans further extended. They conquered southern Italy by the end of the 11th century and took the island of Sicily from the Muslims. The Normans conquered about three quarters of Ireland by 1250.

Vikings from Norway and Denmark pillaged and colonised the shores of western Europe and the Mediterranean Sea, whereas mainly Vikings from Sweden ventured out into what we now call Russia. The Vikings explored the extensive river networks of Russia in order to reach the wealthy trading centres of Byzantium and the Middle East through the Black Sea and Caspian Sea. These trading centres were the terminal points of the Silk Road connected to Asia. From about 850 the Swedish Vikings started to settle along the river routes among the native inhabitants of the Slavic people. These Swedish Vikings were known as Rus (red-haired). By the 11th century the lands of the Rus were called Russia, a series of semi-autonomous city-states dominated by Kiev and Novgorod. In time these city-states developed into what we call the Russian state, the Vikings being absorbed into the Slavic people. When the Viking Age came to an end, the trade link between Scandinavia and the Middle East or the Byzantine Empire ended. (Konstam 2004, pp. 162-65)

Section 4 Papal Supremacy

Constantine the Great, the emperor of the Western Empire, and Licinius, the emperor of the Eastern Empire, granted toleration to Christianity in the Roman Empire with the Edict of Milan in 313. Further, Theodosius I in 392 made his edict of 391 more stringent by completely prohibiting the worship of pagan gods. This was actually an attempt to avert a crisis arising from the pagan usurper. He retained the emperorship after defeating his opponents and his edicts remained in force though he died shortly after. From the late era of the Western Roman Empire, Eastern Orthodoxy and Western Catholicism stood on opposing camps. Five sees in Jerusalem, Alexandria, Antioch, Constantinople and Rome were recognised as having patriarchal status. Pope (the Roman patriarch) claimed but failed to establish primacy over the others: Rome was an imperial capital (political) for many centuries with a high prestige. Paul had fully exploited the prestige of Rome, and the New Testament enshrined his character and his works, which further added importance (religious) to Rome. However, in the 7th century, Antioch, Jerusalem and Alexandria came under Muslim rule and declined in importance. Animosity between the two churches of Rome and Constantinople continued and culminated in the Schism of 1054. The relations between local Greeks and Latin crusaders were always strained. (*The Cassell Atlas of World History* 2001, 3.09)

Gregory VII was elected pope of the Roman Catholic Church in 1073, to be one of the greatest leaders of the medieval church. Gregory made no distinction between spiritual and secular and thought that he was the highest authority in Europe overriding that of the kings and emperors. In 1075 he promulgated a decree forbidding the investiture of ecclesiastics with spiritual office by laymen. When Henry IV, German king at the time, opposed the decree, the pope excommunicated him, who then submitted in humiliation to revoke the papal sentence. Thus Gregory asserted the superiority of papacy over the monarchy. However, Henry did not recognise that the pope was the highest authority and his soldiers stormed Rome in 1084 and deposed Gregory.

Though pope, pontiff and papacy can refer to the other Christian patriarchs of the Pentarchy mentioned earlier in conjunction with five sees, I refer exclusively to the Roman patriarch, that is, head of the Roman Catholic Church, in this series of books which focuses its attention to Western Europe and China proper.

The papacy had the professional administration no secular government could match in the efficiency at the time. Papal authority was universal in Europe, not limited by the bounds of any kingdom or the customs of any locality. Certainly the church did not have an army to enforce its will and had to rely on its prestige and sometimes on the secular authority which expected advantages in return for their assistance. Especially the papal judicial system was most effectively organised. It had practical working codes, travelling legates, even appointing local churchmen for the occasion. (Keen 1991, pp. 112-3)

In the twelfth century, a powerful monarchy was beginning to appear in England and France; however, the same conditions in Italy and Germany made the local authority powerful rather than the central authority.

When Innocent III became pope in 1198, he had to deal with the pressing affairs of secular kingdoms and empires. He studied theology and canon laws and was an able administrator. Henry VI, German king and Holy Roman emperor, was the most formidable secular force he had to contend with. When Henry VI died, two groups of backers appealed for their candidates, Philip and Otto, to be approved by the pope. There was also Frederick (later Frederick II), a 3 year old son of Henry, to be considered. Philip was murdered by a personal enemy in 1208. The pope recognised the crowning of Otto as emperor elect. Otto, fearing the future prospect of Frederick, embarked on an armed attack but was defeated by the army of

Philip of France. Thence the pope announced the claims of all rivals in favour of Frederick in 1215. In all these manoeuvrings, the pope's main concern was the preservation of papacy and his personal well-being, and his decisions did not have much to do with the fitness of the candidates or the future well-being of Europe. (pp. 136-8)

The decades which followed the Fourth Crusade of 1202-4 brought the papal supremacy to the highest level that had never achieved before and would not exceed ever since. Papal power did not make any distinction between temporal and spiritual, and extended to both spheres. The church's ability to contain and control new forces brought about its supremacy. This was primarily due to the genius of Innocent III. During his reign (1198-1216) the Roman Church was united on the powerful religious faith, buttressed by the near monopoly of learning.

After the death of Innocent III in 1216, the Roman Church maintained its leadership in Western Christendom. There emerged two institutions of the universities and the mendicant religious orders both of whose vitality closely interwove with the life of the church. The universities were formal recognition of learning in the tradition of learning such as Paris, Oxford, Bologna and Salerno. The qualifications obtained in the universities were recognised anywhere in Christendom reflecting the church authority. The two most important religious orders were the Dominicans and the Franciscans. The mendicant orders were subject directly to the pope. The friars, members of the mendicant orders, had good grounds for looking on themselves as the elite. (pp. 149-51)

Frederick II of Hohenstaufen was the most powerful emperor the West had seen since the end of the Western Roman Empire. His sheer territorial authority was daunting extending over Germany, Lombardy, the Arelate and Sicily. He made the most formidable political adversary for the medieval papacy. The popes did not have allies strong enough to outdo the hereditary power of Hohenstaufen. In the process of desperate manoeuvring by the popes it became apparent that they had to rely on the northern kingdoms which were coming out strongly economically and politically around this time. (pp. 162, 192)

> In the late eighth century, the pope first brandished a document known as the Donation of Constantine, in which Emperor Constantine in 313 supposedly gave political control of the western parts of the Roman Empire to the bishop of Rome. The document was not frequently cited, but its appearance in the eighth century demonstrates that the popes were already interested in boosting their claims to temporal power. Although the document was a forgery, the fact was known to few people, and the Donation of Constantine was periodically cited by popes throughout the Middle Ages, boosting papal power. (Spielvogel 1991, p. 238)

In the Medieval Ages in Europe, the divine right of both pope and emperor prevailed. Both were vice-regent of God on earth, the one supreme in matters spiritual, the other supreme in the temporal affairs of the world. They were responsible for God alone and unchallengeable on earth. (Davison 1993, p. 164)

> In the thirteenth and fourteenth centuries, the general population of Europe was religious and only vaguely patriotic; by the nineteenth century it had become wholly patriotic (Wells 1925, p. 527).

The separation of religion and politics is a division of power. We can see its development in the Bible in conjunction with the formation of the Jewish state. Europe in the Middle Ages showed the dominance of religion, but political power was vying for supremacy which the latter attained in the modern era.

It is interesting to note that in historical China the division of labour between religion (church) and politics (state) as it existed in the West did not appear. Chinese emperors were both rulers and high-priests. The function of the latter was chiefly sacrificial. One emperor may have ceased to rule as a result of disorder and continued only sacrificial duties. In the civil service examination system which lasted until the early 20th century, the candidates with high pass marks in the Confucian Classics obtained high posts in the government bureaucracy (secular).

Section 5 Crusades (1096-1291)

Crusade derives from the Latin word for 'cross', the symbol of Christianity.

Refer to 'Introduction to Series' for the births of Judaism, Christianity and Islam; and also Section 1, Chapter 2 Judaism-Christianity-Islam, Book Two *Religion.*

Muhammad (570-632), an Arab, founded the first community of Muslims in Medina, which grew into a state that controlled much of the Arabian Peninsula. After his death the army under the banner of Islam seized the rest of Arabia and the area stretching from Egypt to Iran. The Arab Muslims dominated the vast empire thus created, and made Arabic the official language and Islam the official religion, both of which were strong unifying forces assisted by the cultural pride the empire promoted. Many conquered people adopted the Arabic language and Islam.

The Umayyads, the Abbasids and the Alids, three families from Muhammad's tribe of Quraysh, dictated the political life of the empire for several hundred years. The Umayyads ruled from 661 to 750 from the capital of Damascus. They extended the empire to Spain and India. The Abbasids took control of the empire in 750 except Spain and made Baghdad the capital of the empire. After the middle of the ninth century the Abbasids increasingly lost control of the empire, and distant parts of the empire became independent. The Alid family established the Fatimid dynasty in northern Africa in 909, which lasted until 1171.

The Turks from Central Asia converted to Islam faith c. 970. They made inroads into the Middle East and northern India from 990 onwards. They also made themselves useful as mercenaries for the Arab armies and some achieved positions of power and influence. Among the various groups the Seljuk Turks which the Seljuk clan led made a firm territorial hold in the Middle East by 1037. They took Baghdad, the capital of the Abbasid family, in 1055, and conquered Syria and Palestine. The Seljuk Turks' hold on the Middle East increased until the Mongol invasion of 1219. The Mongols conquered Baghdad in 1258 and remained the dominant power in the Middle East until Tamerlane's death in 1405.

While the Arabs (Muslims) occupied the Holy Land the Europeans did not have much problem in way of pilgrims provided they paid a safe-conduct pass tax. The Arabs came to terms with the Christians. However, when the Turks (also Muslims at the time) overthrew the Arabs and took control of the Holy Land around the year 1065 ending the Arab's political domination in the Middle East, the situation radically altered. Pilgrims who returned to Europe reported that there were numerous incidents of beatings and robberies, and some were sold as slaves and some, even killed, by the Turks. (Richards & English 1985, p. 124)

The nomadic Seljuk Turks made advances into Anatolia from the east and won a tremendous victory at Manzikert over the Byzantine armies and captured Emperor Romanus Diogenes in 1071. The Turks even threatened to capture Constantinople in the ensuing years. In desperation Alexius I Comnenus, Byzantine emperor since 1081 and one of the strongest Eastern emperors, requested help from Latin Pope Urban II in 1095. The pope responded by calling the First Crusade at the Council of Clermont. His primary purposes might have been to unite the Eastern and Western churches and to recover the Holy Land from the infidels. (Keen 1991, p. 117) At that time the pope in Rome ruled the Western Church; and the patriarch in Constantinople, the Eastern Church, though the Byzantine emperor appointed the patriarch.

Strangely, Emperor Alexius did not look at the First Crusade once launched as his own cause and his subsequent uncooperative actions shocked the crusaders.

The crusades fostered the fusion of Christian faith and martial ideals; and the new military orders, the Templars, the Hospitallers and the Teutonic Knights, clearly showed this fusion. The Templars were the most effective soldiers. The crusaders were recruited from all over Christendom and could not have been launched without the papal organisation. The church helped the ventures in various ways such as to collect the alms to finance, or even to protect the property of all who left for the Holy Land.

The crusades became increasingly temporal affairs rather than spiritual in the subsequent ventures. The Christian knights fought the Muslims in Italy, Sicily, Spain and in the Levant in the course of the crusades. They glorified in battles and looked at them as opportunities to obtain land and wealth.

The other deciding factor was the Italian quest for new markets in Palestine. The Italians sought quarters in conquered territories and trading privileges. Italian cities such as Genoa, Pisa and Venice with their squadrons and ships helped the crusades on many occasions. Italian merchants often made ready finance to pay for the soldiers and others to save the ventures from collapsing. (pp. 123-4)

The Fourth Crusade, presided by Innocent III, is a good example of the quest of gains by Italian merchants. When the crusade was being planned, the ruler of Venice offered free transport to the crusaders if they captured Constantinople, which was the capital of the East Roman Empire and the resident city of the patriarch of the Eastern Orthodox Church. This arrangement suited everyone concerned. The Western Church would damage the Eastern Church, and the crusaders would gain treasures, and the rival cities of Venice would suffer. Thus Constantinople was sacked in 1204, and the Greek emperor was expelled until 1261. (Richards & English 1985, p. 69) In all these events we must remember that the enmity between both two empires and two churches was quite strong.

The Kingdom of Jerusalem which the crusaders established in 1099 during the First Crusade was internally weak and beset with diplomatic problems; however it lasted till 1291.

During the years leading up to the 13th century, new prospects emerged in conjunction with the crusading zeal. Since the Latin empire stood on different political environments now that it might be possible to unite the Eastern and Western churches diplomatically. It also looked that Greece was a better place than Palestine for those wanting new lands. For the Italians Palestine ceased to be very attractive as a trading interest because many other opportunities opened up for them such as Cyprus, Constantinople and the Aegean. The crusade was still looked as a common political ideal welding together the otherwise divided Christendom. (Keen 1991, pp. 133, 177)

The characters of crusades in the 13th century were quite different from those of the earlier ones. People lost interest in the Frankish Kingdom of Jerusalem--the Franks were dominant--because it ceased to function as a political unit. The ambitions and adventures of the European powers came to dominate. Holy Roman Emperor Frederick II, King Louis IX of France, Richard and Edward of England and Charles of Anjou (formerly a small province in western France) all led expeditions to the east, though they all had the reasons of their own. (p. 178)

The popes hopefully looked at Charles of Anjou, the most powerful Latin prince of southern Europe, as the great crusading leader; however, his dream was to found a Latin empire in the Mediterranean for his house in the same way Frederick II's was for his house. It seemed that Louis IX of France, brother of Charles, was genuinely concerned with the fate of the Holy Places of Jerusalem. Charles and Philip III of France fought a crusade against Sicily and Aragon respectively for purely political reasons with the blessing of Pope Martin IV. (pp. 186, 188-9)

The above Charles of Anjou was Charles I, the initiator of Angevin (meaning 'of Anjou'), a great but short-lived Mediterranean empire. He conquered Naples and Sicily in the 1200s.

His son Charles II, an extremely pious man, was called Charles the Lame, sometimes also called Charles of Anjou.

> The church in the thirteenth century was extending its legal power in the world, and losing its grip upon people's consciousness. It was becoming less persuasive and more violent. (Wells 1925, p. 430)

The crusades were a part of a thousand year struggle between Christianity and Islam (Davison 1993, p. 88).

> Europe's first great adventure of expansion in the crusades brought many into contact with the much higher civilisation of the Saracens and Moors, and the conquest of Constantinople in 1204 brought a firsthand experience of Greece (Randall 1976, p. 15).
> Note: The term Saracens means for us rather loosely the Muslims of Arabs, Turks and even the Arab Moors who set up the Spanish kingdom in the 700's.

The crusading knights found that the local people were better educated than themselves; as a matter of fact, most of the knights were illiterate. The Europeans came to know paper, glass-mirrors, slippers, carpets, carrier pigeons and the use of Arabic (in fact, Indian) numerals. (Davison 1993, p. 89)

Osman, a Muslim prince, conquered neighbouring territories of the Seljuk dynasty and founded his own dynasty (the Ottoman Empire) c. 1300, making himself Osman I (r. 1280-1324). The Ottoman Turks made the most of the weakened Christian and Turkish states and occupied most of north-west Anatolia and captured Gallipoli in 1354. Though the Mongol army checked its power, it recovered quickly and conquered Constantinople and the Byzantine Empire in 1453. Constantinople was to become the Ottoman capital as Istanbul. Under Selim I and his son Suleyman I the Magnificent the Ottoman Empire took control of Persia, Arabia, Hungary and the Balkans. By the mid-1500s the Ottoman Empire controlled nearly all the Arab lands. By the early 16th century the Ottomans defeated the Mamluks in Syria and Egypt. The Ottoman sultans were Turkish but the generals, admirals and administrators of the empire came from throughout the Mediterranean world. Many Ottoman officials were of Arab origin, and regarded themselves as Ottomans, rather than Arabs or Muslims.

The Ottoman fortune went into decline in the late 16th century. It was attributed to storms and disease that the Turkish army under Suleyman I, the sultan, could not take Vienna and retreated from the city in 1529. The imperial Muslim fleet was destroyed during the reign of Selim II, the son of Suleyman I, at the Battle of Lepanto in 1571: the numerically superior Turkish galleys clashed with the combined Christian galleys of such navies as Spain, Venice, Genoa, Savoy, which Pope Pius V promoted. In 1683 the Christian army routed the Muslim army which had encamped around Vienna. Further the imperial troops led by Charles, the duke of Lorraine, drove out the retreating Ottomans from Hungary with a series of victories in 1685. The Turks were not suffering from the military defeats: morale in their ranks was low, the soldiers were unpaid, government corruption was rampant, and decadence was set in their minds. With a series of defeats and setbacks for the next few centuries the Turkish Sultanate was dissolved to be replaced with a republic in 1922 and their territories were to be confined to Turkey.

The shifting powers of the Muslims from Arabs to Seljuk Turks to Ottoman Turks to Mongols in the Middle East showed a remarkable unity among themselves being united under Islam as well as general tolerance even towards the non-Muslims excepting the Seljuk

Turks in certain situations. The Mughal Empire in India may also be an exception. The Muslims collected trade taxes from East-West trade while they held political dominance in the Middle East. They used different official languages which were often not the same languages of the population: Arabic for Arabs; Persian for Seljuk Turks; Arabic, Persian and Turkish for Ottoman Turks; Persian for Mongols in India. We also note that the Seljuk Turks passed not only their Islamic faith but their eastern traditions to the Ottomans. However, we occasionally see fierce rivalry among Muslim dynasties such as witnessed by that between the Ottomans and the Safavid dynasty in Iran. The Safavids were originally Sufis (a Muslim mystical order) from the north-western Iran. They fought devastating wars throughout the 1600s, ending in a stalemate. Safavid kings ruled Iran until 1722.

The Turkish Muslims controlled much of the overland trade routes between Asia and Europe since the 11th century, and travel and trade became uncertain. Europe's response to the blocked trade was the crusades. The Mongol Empire began to break up into smaller states towards the end of the 13th century, and as a result overland trade between China and Europe became increasingly difficult and expensive though we cannot quantify these facets of trade. The Italians did not see much opportunity since to make money in the Middle East, and paid attention to the other regions for trade and subsequently brought the flowering of the Renaissance. When economic reasons for the crusades became insignificant, even the popes could not organise the ventures though religious and political reasons still existed. The Europeans thenceforward became hell-bent on exploring sea routes to the East driven by the same desire to make money.

In general terms, the superiority of Islamic culture over Christian culture lasted until the fourteenth century. For centuries, Islam and Christianity interacted. At first Islam overshadowed Christian culture and then entered Christian societies and enriched their culture. Then Christendom discarded the fetters of medievalism and developed its own strength. As this happened, Islam began to stagnate, weighed down by an orthodoxy that had become cumbersome. (*Early Civilization* 1984, p. 132)

Section 6 Rise of Regional Powers

Since 1215 the English government has increased the scope of its activities, directed by an efficient bureaucracy. However, the government administration costs money. By the time of Edward I (1272-1307), the precedent had been set that the assent of all the baronage was needed for new taxation to be lawful. The king had to call a meeting of barons and commoners and explain why he had to raise tax; these meetings were the forerunner of the later parliaments. England was a rich country and was the chief supplier of wool to the continental market; woollen cloths were the most important European export. Local communities supplied knights and archers. For these reasons the English king needed the cooperation of his subjects to be an effective ruler. (Keen 1991, pp. 193, 195-6)

France made the similar progress along the line of England with one notable exception. The English king's authority was limited with the reasons mentioned in the last paragraph; whereas the French king's power ever increased to later become absolutism and a sense of national interest developed in pace. A French king was similar to an emperor in the defunct Western Roman Empire. Also Aragon and Castile in the Spanish Peninsula set up a representative body called the Cortes and began to play important roles in European affairs from the 13th century onwards. (pp. 197, 203-5)

Feudal noblemen, vassals of the king, owned estates and they often experienced troubles with their subjects and tenants. They looked to the king for arbitration and protection. Thus the feudal kings had to promote justice in this respect and expanded the bureaucracy--their administrative tools--to function properly under their guidance. (pp. 198, 200)

The papacy emerged triumphant from its struggles with the Hohenstaufen with money and arms supplied by England and France. The church had promised the crowns of Sicily and Aragon to English and French princes. Further Gregory IX had to pay cash for the assistance the papacy received. He began the practice of charging the whole clerical body throughout Europe to support the crusades; the struggles with the Hohenstaufen were deemed as a crusade. (p. 208)

The conflict between Boniface VIII, pope, and Philip IV, French king, clearly indicated the papacy did not hold the authority it once enjoyed. Threatened with excommunication Philip's supporters captured the pope, who died shortly after in 1303. Indicating further victory for Philip, a Frenchman was elected as pope in 1305. Even after these events the papacy remained immensely powerful in Europe exerting authority beyond national boundaries. The day of the universal empire in Europe died when Frederick II, Holy Roman Emperor, died in 1250. By the 14th century people no longer believed that the Roman Church as the upholder of Christian universalism was capable of holding both secular and spiritual worlds in Europe. (pp. 217-8, 221)

It was noted earlier that during the Middle Ages Europe's most important export was finished cloths and the most important import, silks and spices from the Orient mostly through Italian merchants. Furs, waxes and honey were also imported from the Baltic region. The cities around the Baltic Sea formed the Hanseatic League to protect their trade. Its member cities virtually monopolised the trade of the Baltic and the North Sea. By the year 1347 the membership amounted to 160 cities, and their power was at its height in the 1360s. The League was a union of independent cities; however, it could organise an army, navy and the governing body to wage war against any opposition though none of them was permanent.

In the late Middle Ages tremendous changes in European society were taking place. Chief among them were development of banking, large scale finance, advances in the techniques of war and the use of the three greatest inventions. They were not independent phenomena, interacting within society. The use of gunpowder was by far the most important in the art of war. I referred to this matter together with the use of paper and compass earlier in A Three Greatest Inventions in History, Section 4, Chapter 2.

I might add here that the use and production of gunpowder and guns were very expensive. The fortifications and ships had to be built strongly to withstand bombardments, thus incurring more expenses. National governments had to raise taxes to pay for these large expenses and taxed both people and products. England introduced customs duties on wool and hides export in 1275; France heavily taxed salt mined in 1341. Edward I, king of England, borrowed money from Italian bankers using customs duties as security. The government looked commerce and industry as the money raising source and hence thought that it had to look after them for their own benefit.

Black Death

The merchants from Genoa set up a trading station and a fort at a city Tana near the Black Sea. In 1346 a brawl broke out between the Tartars, the local people, and the Genoese, triggering an act of war. The Black Death disease broke out among the Tartars, which spread to the garrisoned Genoese and later the general population of Europe. No one could have predicted that this disease would wipe out 20 million of the total European population of 60 million within 3 years and further contribute to the end of the feudal system current in Europe.

Since a large number of peasants died as the result of the Black Death prompting shortages of labour, the surviving peasants demanded better working conditions and more pay. They often got what they demanded but the produce of their farms fetched drastically lower prices; the prices for the farm animals dropped between 30% and 50%.

In England unhappy peasants demanded improved working conditions. However, the government was determined not to let things change and the parliament passed an act to freeze wages and costs to keep peasants in their place. What brought the boiling point was the poll tax introduced in 1379 to pay for the war with France. This tax was not heavy but was imposed on every man, woman and child. When collection time came people refused to pay and revolted openly. A large number of rebels entered London and made furious rounds of burnings and destructions. The rebel leaders were captured or executed and the revolts ended in failure. However, the poll tax was not reimposed and more lords released villeins to work on pay. It is interesting to note that the peasants opposed high-ranking priests, and the rebels attacked these priests during the rioting in London.

John Wycliffe made the first translation of the Bible into English in 1382 but the church was very much against him. Before this the Bible in England was written in Latin and the church services were conducted in Latin. (Richards & English 1985, pp. 219-23)

Hundred Years' War (1337-1453)

As regional powers grew in reverse proportion to the decline of papal power in the fourteenth and fifteenth centuries, the rivalry between England and France came to open conflict called the Hundred Years' War. King Philip VI's disputes with Edward III of England led to the outbreak of the war: Edward III had the succession right to the French throne and invaded Flanders in 1337.

The popes through the conflict, except during the Great Schism, did their best to restore peace and revive the crusades without any success. Also King Philip VI (1328-1350) of France and Henry V (1413-1422) of England dreamed of sending troops to the Holy Land; however, the crusade did not eventuate.

Edward brought Philip to his knees after 20 years of fighting on French soil. However he won the war through expedient means to continue the expensive battles. Hence the victory was as a matter of fact not complete at it looked. Bands of soldiers nominally on the side of

England and normally unpaid terrorised the countryside to obtain the tributes, capturing people for ransom and attacking cities for loot. These bands came from all over Europe; Italy, England, Spain, Germany and Languedoc. These men were after profits and had a sense of chivalry and thought fighting was a noble occupation. (Keen 1991, pp. 247, 249)

Henry IV of Lancaster, who deposed Richard II, Edward III's successor, was a grandson of Edward III, so the English claim for the French crown did not lapse. Only after Henry V, a successor to Henry IV, was England strong enough to resume the fighting in France.

Charles VII was roused by his mistress from the lethargy and began to show that he was worthy of a good ruler. He laid down an ordinance in 1439 to organise a standing army, and made arrangements to pay by annual taxation. This still left a substantial number of the unruly bands, normally unpaid, in the country: they had hitherto passed as an army. (p. 257)

England and France emerged as self-conscious independent nations through the prosecution of war.

In almost all large scale wars in Europe in the fourteenth and fifteenth centuries, the free companies not only played significant role in deciding the outcome of war but were the social menace the society had to suffer. England and France did not have sufficient financial resources to carry on struggles for long hence they had to rely on the services of the free companies who were prepared to serve on any side. However, England and France eventually brought on a standing army during the course of the war. It was proven that the free soldiers were no match for the regular army. (pp. 260-1, 269)

Great Schism (1378-1417)

We must keep in mind that the Hundred Years' War between England and France was in progress from 1337 to 1453, covering the entire duration of the Schism.

This schism is sometimes called the Western Schism, to make a distinction from the East-West Schism of 1054. The Great Schism as well as the Hundred Years' War was an indication that papal authority was in decline and the emergence of national interests came to the forefront in European politics and religion.

Clement V was appointed pope through the machinations of Philip IV of France, and four years later moved the papal capital to Avignon, France, for political reasons. By creating a majority of French cardinals he ensured the election of French popes. During this Avignon papacy (1309-77) all seven popes were French as were most of the cardinals. Fearing further decline of the papal authority Pope Gregory XI returned to Rome in 1377. Urban VI (an Italian) was elected pope amid the local demands for a local pope, but the French sympathisers elected an antipope, Clement VII (born a Swiss), who took up residence in Avignon. France, Scotland and Castile backed Clement; England, Flanders and most Italian states supported Urban (Keen 1991, p. 287). Both sides appointed a third pope without any resolution. The problem was resolved when the Council of Constance vacated all three seats and elected Martin V (born a Roman) as pope in 1417. As German king from 1411, Sigismund had urged the unwilling pope to call the Council of Constance and brought the schism to an end by his tireless effort during a lull in the Anglo-French war.

The Schism exposed what lay deeply in the concept of the universal church of the past. It turned out to be really a confederation of national churches. The authority of the popes did not hold the church together but their diplomatic skills dealing with the secular powers were the keys.

Two kingdoms, Castile and Aragon, emerged as the reconquest from the Moors proceeded in Spain. The marriage of Isabella of Castile and Ferdinand of Aragon in 1469 fused the two kingdoms into one, and the offensive against the Moors was pressed and subsequently completed.

As I pointed out earlier, in the fourteenth and fifteenth century in Italy as in any other states in Europe, the free companies of soldiers played a crucial role in deciding the outcome of conflicts. The key to despotic power in Italian cities was the ability to pay and control troops rather than legal sanctions, taking the various forms depending on social settings. At the end of the fifteenth century, five great cities emerged, sitting on equilibrium: Venice, Milan, Florence, the Papal City and the Kingdom of Naples.

Eugenius IV (1431-47) and Pius II (1458-64) tried strenuously to organise crusades but their efforts proved futile even under the threat of the Turkish menace. Holy war took second place to diplomacy and political and economic conveniences of the secular powers. In the fifteenth century the universal authority of pope in Christendom failed miserably. (pp. 310, 312)

In the middle of the fifteenth century, the events to signal a break with the past happened at about the same time. The Council of Basel abandoned the attempt to bring an end to the East-West Schism of 1054, in 1449. The Ottoman Turks seized Constantinople in 1453, ending the Byzantine Empire. The French won the great victory at Castillon in 1453 to mark the end of the long struggle with the English.

The Roman Empire encircled the Mediterranean basin for centuries of dominance: the basin was the focal centre of commerce and culture. France became involved in the active politics of Christian Europe from the end of the 12th century under the Capetian dynasty. Particularly noteworthy was Philip II Augustus (1180-1223), who greatly strengthened the French monarchy. He descended from Charlemagne through his mother. The French asserted their dominance in the Mediterranean world since religious and popular St Louis (Louis IX) (1226-70), the French king of the Capetian family. It was to manifest as French leadership of crusades, the power of Frankish states in Greece and French succession in the house of Anjou in Italy. Louis XIV (1643-1715), the Sun King, who ruled France during its dominant era in Europe, was of later century and of the Bourbon dynasty which began to reign France in 1589.

As the medieval era was drawing to a close, the influence of the church diminished and the growth of a lay spirit prevailed. As lay literacy spread, local vernaculars came into general use and Latin, once the lingua franca of all educated men in Europe, began to lose its influence. What people knew about religion and the meaning of life came from the church before but they began to learn many other things in life from books. Efficient regional governments brought security for all within the national boundaries. Secular princes no longer had to live in their castles but built houses for beauty and convenience. (pp. 317-21)

Chapter 4 Rise of Europe and Decline of China in Modern Setting

Section 1 Cultural Movements in Europe: Renaissance and Enlightenment

The Swiss historian and art critic, Jacob Burckhardt, created the modern concept of the Renaissance in his celebrated work *The Civilization of Renaissance in Italy* published in 1860. He portrayed Italy of the fourteenth and fifteenth centuries as the birth place of the modern world--the Italians were 'the first born' among the sons of modern Europe--and saw the revival of antiquity, the 'perfecting of the individual', and secularism (worldliness of the Italians) as its distinguishing features. The essence of the Renaissance was not classicism but release.

> Renaissance is a huge pouring out of creativity in fields as diverse as architecture, poetry, painting, science, sculpture and political theory (Davison 1993, p. 106).
>
> Renaissance originated in Northern Italy and flowered there during two centuries between 1275 and 1475. It spread out north of the Alps from about 1475 onwards. (Toynbee 1962, p. 2)

Even after the fall of the Western Roman Empire, Latin remained the lingua franca of Western Christendom for one millennium. The literati and the church used Latin as a vehicle of communication, spoken and written.

In the 12th and 13th centuries poetry began to be written down in the vernacular languages in Western Europe. Dante Alighieri wrote *The Divine Comedy* (c. 1313-4), a monumental epic poem, in Italian not in Latin, and made Italian a literary language almost singlehandedly. It is often said that the Renaissance started with him, giving him the credit though the movement existed in northern Italy before his publication.

Johannes Gutenberg published his edition of the Bible printed using movable type in Mainz in 1450. Soon publishing houses sprang up all over Europe. Referring to the movable type, 'Thus by 1500 all the chief countries of Europe were provided with the means for the rapid multiplication of books' (Randall 1976, p. 120).

> … the Alps are not so impregnable as they seem. Although Petrarch said they warded off the cold, the wind and the barbarians, a long tale of pre-historic penetrations had shown that the range is not an impassable, isolating obstacle. Easy gradients in the northern flanks encouraged invaders such as Hannibal; 'There is no need,' said Polybius, 'for gods, or heroes to help someone cross the Alps'. The lowest landward pass, the Brenner, had been in use since remotest antiquity, the others were gradually occupied by the Romans to pacify the highland peoples, and there were practicable passages where the mountains came down to the sea on either side. (Grant 1969, p. 268)
>
> By the end of the 15th century the most important centre for this manufacture [mechanical instrument, especially those for astronomical observations and navigations at sea] was the Bavarian city of Nuremburg, already noted for skilled metal-work. One reason was its strategic position astride the important trade route from Italy to the Lower countries and Britain. (Williams 1987, p. 114)

In a broad historical perspective the Renaissance was in force from the mid-fourteenth century to mid-sixteenth century in Europe.

Though papal Rome was transformed during the Renaissance, Florence became the hub of the Renaissance in the 15th century. This burgeoning of Florence as an artistic centre owed much to the patronage of the Medici family who dominated the city for three centuries.

During the course of the two centuries of the Renaissance Europe experienced the waning of the Middle Ages and established itself as modern nations. Europe woke up from the slumber of the Middle Ages and had to go through the waking process of the Renaissance before it became fully grown up. The European nations went through religious reformation before they started large-scale expansions into the world but many historians mark the year 1492 as the beginning of the modern ages. Needless to say that 1492 is a mere convenient year identifying the European discovery of the American continent and this convention is from the European viewpoint.

The Inquisition (1232-1820) by the Roman Catholic Church carried out witch hunts as much as the Reformed churches did in the sixteenth and seventeenth centuries. One of the most creative centuries in Europe was at the period preceding the intensification of witch hunts. (Eliade 1985, pp. 228, 236)

One important characteristic of the European Medieval Ages is the dual power between church and state. During the Middle Ages, philosophy, politics and jurisprudence became subdivisions of theology. The Renaissance made state power predominate within society and as time went on this trend accelerated.

Before the Renaissance the lettered class in Europe communicated in Latin beyond national boundaries. After the Renaissance the Europeans became conscious of their nationalities and communicated in their national languages.

It is hard for us to comprehend why the Europeans discarded Latin as an international language of Europe. Montaigne (1533-92), a French essayist, wrote that though Latin was his mother tongue, he lost its command in speech and writing through lack of its use (Montaigne 1965, pp. 484, 615, 667). He wrote his *Essays* in French and is said to have completed the Renaissance which Dante started earlier. Also it is well known that Queen Elizabeth I (1533-1603) spoke fluent Latin. The Chinese used the same written scripts beyond the various dialects through their history since the script reform by Shih huang-ti of Ch'in. Latin gave a similar advantage to the Europeans; however, the national consciousness must have been really strong to discard Latin in favour of national languages.

Italic languages were spoken in Italy during the 1st millennium BC; Latin was one of the three Italic languages. Latin emerged as the predominant language by the 3rd century BC, and replaced all the Italic languages in Italy by AD 100, though the Greek language was still widely used in Italy. Romance languages began as dialects of Vulgar Latin and developed into separate languages in the 5th-9th centuries. Italian, one of Romance languages, established itself in Italy about AD 1000 and almost completely replaced Latin by the middle of the 16th century.

As the nations emerged as sovereign within national boundaries, the kings, as heads of states, had to administer the nations; to collect taxes, establish the bureaucracy and the army and navy, and carry out wars as needed.

The Renaissance at the initial stage, with its centre in the city-states of Italy which had grown rich in trade with both East and West, was essentially a product of the towns and hence the burghers, and was in part a cultural movement. Wealthy patrons could encourage writers, painters, architects, sculptors and craftsmen skilled in working in such material as silver and leather. Yet it was based upon a great increase in commercial, rather than industrial, activity. (Williams 1987, p. 142)

In the early sixteenth century, four regions of the world were roughly at the similar stages of development, and way ahead of the rest: The Ottoman Empire, China under the Ming dynasty, the northern India under the Mongols, and Western Europe with scattered states with the offshoot of the Muscovite. There was no indication that one of these regions would come out on top in the future. (Kennedy 1987, p. 4)

In the fifteenth century China under the Ming dynasty with a population of 100-130 million looked more advanced than Europe of 50-55 million. The Mandarins under the Ming dynasty banned foreign trade and fishing, though the Portuguese and Dutch conducted limited trade in luxury items. The Mandarins also disliked commerce and private enterprise, though they permitted state enterprises to flourish. The overall effect was that Ming China became a much less vigorous and enterprising land than it had been under the Sung dynasty four centuries earlier. (p. 8)

The Ottoman Turks, too, were to falter, to turn inward, and to lose the chance of world domination by the second half of the sixteenth century, after the strikingly similar Ming decline (p. 11).

Babur was of the Mongol blood from Central Asia, the descendant of Timur and Genghis Khan, though he was of Muslim faith and was Persian culturally. His army was a diverse ethnic mix made up mainly of Persians, Arabs and Mongols. He became the first Mughal Emperor (1526-30) in India after defeating the local Hindus. Akbar (r. 1556-1605), his grandson, created a powerful state in northern India. Yet the vast Mughal Empire fragmented at the death of the last great emperor Aurangzeb (r. 1658-1707). The Portuguese, the Dutch and the English established trading posts along the Indian coast. Incompetent emperors, wars of succession and corrupt governments followed. Also religious intolerance grew strong and Hindu revolts became widespread.

Kievan Russia, whose peak was in the 10th-11th centuries, imported Christianity, Greek and Latin cultures from Byzantium. In the 13th century the Tartars devastated Russia, until 1480 when Ivan the Great threw off the Tartar yoke except for the south. The Renaissance did not spread to Russia. Russia, after acquiring muskets and cannon from the West, could subdue the horsemen of the Asian plains. The gunpowder empire since then ever pushed the frontiers to the east, and Russian troops reached the Caspian Sea by 1556, and the Pacific coast by 1638. (p. 15)

In the fifteenth century Europe recovered the population lost due to the Black Death and the Italian Renaissance blossomed. Europe also established itself as a gunpowder empire. In the broad period from 1450 to 1600, other gunpowder empires such as Muscovy, Tokugawa Japan and Mogul (Mughal) India were established. (p. 20)

Historians today are in unison that by the end of the Renaissance of the European scene, that is, the mid-16th century, Europe was decidedly superior to China in virtually all aspects of human culture. It seems that the contemporary general public in Western Europe as well as in China proper did not realise this sense of Western superiority until well into the 19th century. After the Mongol expansion which did not reach Western Europe and before the 19th century, the contact between Western Europe and China proper was limited to trade and various knowledge, hence the comparison was merely speculation, and superior and inferior criteria did not mean much. When the contact became massive and especially military as it did after the middle of the 19th century, the comparison became real and meaningful.

Scientific Revolution

The Renaissance gave an impetus to scientific revolution. Classical Greece laid the foundation of scientific thought. In its investigations Western Europe took up once again the long road of scientific discovery where the Alexandrian Greeks had left it a thousand years before. It was not humanism, and it was not the Reformation, which was destined to work the greatest revolution in the beliefs of men, however triumphant they seemed centuries ago; it was science. (Randall 1976, p. 203)

The Scientific Revolution represented a major turning point in modern Western civilisation. In the Scientific Revolution, the Western world overthrew the medieval, Ptolemaic-Aristotelian world view and arrived at a new conception of the universe; the sun at the centre, the planets as material bodies revolving around the sun in elliptical orbits and an infinite rather than finite world. (Spielvogel 1991, p. 590)

> Aristotle's influence was profound not only in the Western world but also in the Islamic world. Between the twelfth and fifteenth centuries his scientific work dominated medieval Europe. (Freeman 1996, p. 238)

Aristotle argued that the highest aim of human beings is happiness backed by moral excellence. He despised manual labour and trade and did not have any interest in the rights of women, and defended slavery. (p. 237) He regarded slavery as a natural thing and women unfit for freedom and political rights (Wells 1925, p. 177). For modern people these ideas are hardly acceptable.

Ptolemy, a 2nd century Greek astronomer, mathematician and geographer in Alexandria, expounded Ptolemaic earth-centred or geocentric system in *Almagest*. He argued that the earth is the centre of the universe with the planets revolving around the earth. The Christian Church adopted this system, and it remained undisputed until the Copernican sun-centred or heliocentric system became predominant.

The Bible makes a few references to the movement of the sun. Martin Luther quoted the following verse to support the notion that the earth does not move (Spielvogel 1991, p. 568); Joshua spoke to the Lord: Sun, stand still at Gibeon, and Moon, in the valley of Aijalon (Joshua 10:12-3). The sun and the moon stood still and the Israelites' victory over the Amorites became complete. Also the church authorities used the following verse in defence of their view: The sun rises and the sun goes down and hurries to the place where it rises (Ecclesiastes 1:5).

Copernicus, a Polish astronomer, published *On the Revolution of the Heavenly Spheres* (1543) in which he advanced the solar system to be known as the Copernican system. Galileo confirmed this with the use of telescopes he built. Galileo's telescope gave a convincing evidence of a heliocentric system and he made it clear in his book *Starry Messengers* (1610). The telescope was an important tool to delve into the heavenly study in the same way the microscope aided the biological study. Copernican theory, though it was a guess work when he proposed and he wrongly assumed that the orbits of the solar planets were circular, triggered the Copernican revolution, the turning point for how we look at the universe and human's place in it. It appears to us that the sun moves around the earth. To casual observers the solar planets and stars rise in the east and set in the west every night. However, the ancient scientists could not explain why the planets and stars moved at slightly different speeds, which are termed prograde and retrograde.

The Copernican revolution in the 16th century was for the natural science, as the Cartesian revolution started by Descartes was for philosophy in the 17th century (Randall 1976, p. 235); Descartes is regarded as the founder of modern philosophy. We still use the expressions in our daily life: The sun rises and goes down. Copernicus's heliocentric theory, though it may be unimportant in itself for our daily life, emancipated natural science from theology and the former became independent of the latter and made giant strides from then on (Whitehouse & Wilkins 1986, p. 43). If the earth is not the centre of the universe, then humans are not as important as we may think and there is some doubt as to the correctness of the creation theory of the Bible. Further we must explain why the weighty objects fall on the ground. Copernicus did not answer the above queries but left them for later generations to answer.

The ancient Babylonian and Chinese astronomers observing the heavenly bodies believed that the earth was flat (Wells 1925, p. 7).

The ancient Greek world knew well that the earth was spherical at an early date but still thought it to be the centre of the universe. In the third century BC, Eratosthenes (c. 275-194 BC), geographer and astronomer and at the same time director of the Alexandrian Library, made further discoveries. He estimated earth's circumference to be about 46 000 kilometres, which is not very different from the best modern value of 40 000 kilometres, by measuring the angles of the sun's rays at different places at the same time. He further attempted to determine, though less successfully, the sizes and distances of the sun and the moon. After Pytheas of Massalia discovered that the moon and not the sun caused tides, Eratosthenes concluded that a ship sailing west from Spain would eventually reach India. (Grant 1969, p. 219)

Plutarch (c. 46-c. 120), a classical Greek biographer, refers to a man called Philolaus and a number of others who believed that it was the earth and not the sun that moved (Spielvogel 1991, p. 563).

And though science as a serious factor in either men's beliefs or actions did not make its appearance until the eighteenth century, its birth in the minds of the few and the greatest new ideas on which it is based entered the world in the humanistic sixteenth century (Randall 1976, p. 203).

Machiavelli was among the first to abandon morality as the basis for the analysis of political activity. He expanded his theories in the book *The Prince* (1513) concerning political power. His book takes the form of advice to a prince. He taught how to win and maintain political power, belittling Christian morality. He preached that the foundations of all states are good laws and good arms. A prince ought to study war and its rules and disciplines and nothing else. Since the state is corrupt and evil, a prince wishing to maintain it should appear to be good and upright but he should not carry out good works which have as much chance as acquiring hatred from evil works. (Hutchins 1952, pp. 18-28) He is regarded as Europe's first modern political theorist. He elaborated the rules of the governing body, later known as Machiavellianism, to his contemporary people. The Italian states of his day already practised these principles though abhorred in public. All over Europe towards the end of the sixteenth century, monarchs were consolidating their power and tending to absolutism. In every court there were groups of ministers and secretaries who played Machiavellian games. Lenin wrote in 1917, just before the Communist Revolution, that there is not a country in the world that conducted foreign policy in the open. The general public, not to mention politicians and diplomats, still widely practise Machiavellianism today. Machiavelli's theory came about from his fundamental belief in power. (Randall 1976, pp. 195-6)

Enlightenment was a European intellectual movement of the 17th and 18th centuries and emphasised a reasoned approach to life rather than tradition. The Enlightenment period is often referred to as the Age of Reason or the Age of Rationalism. Though the movement was started by 17th century philosophers it came to encompass diverse fields such as philosophy, arts, education, politics and science. Idealism became the foundation of the Enlightenment. Its leaders were the French philosophers; Descartes, Diderot, Rousseau and Voltaire: and also the English philosopher; John Lock.

Gerald Malynes in the seventeenth century advocated an economic approach based on an ethical foundation of the medieval mind (Roll 1961, p. 71).

Some monarchs were called enlightened rulers though these rulers were in fact materialists and realists at heart. Hence they did not, perhaps could not by circumstances, institute the serious reforms proposed by the philosophers. They also carried out wars which the philosophers opposed.

Voltaire (1694-1778) and the other philosophers of the Enlightenment portrayed China as a model for Europe, seeing that it practised religious tolerance and scholars became government officials in China (Roberts 1998, p. 20). The Enlightenment movement stressed religious toleration among other creeds.

While true, the partition of Poland at the end of the eighteenth century also serves to remind us that the cynical politics associated with the name of Machiavelli were becoming Europe's norm (Spielvogel 1991, p. 640).

Material civilisation distinguishes modern nations among other features. In the classical era and the Middle Ages, civilisation was more idealistic rather than materialistic. Many people in the modern age find the pursuit of idealism rather boring and some merely study what people discovered in this field in the distant past. I believe that all idealist doctrines were fully explored in the late ancient to the early classical times and there is nothing much to add, however enthusiastic a small number of people may have been.

In the broad measure, the interest of the bulk of the Europeans was in idealism before the Renaissance and it turned its attention to materialism after the Renaissance.

> We have seen how the chief political struggle of the Middle Ages was waged between a religious and lay control of society, the contest between the Papacy and the temporal monarchs (Randall 1976, p. 162).

People express the decline of religious faith of the modern era as God is dead. I have come to believe that people took this idea from the following biblical verses:

> As I live forever,
> When I whet my flashing sword,
> And my hand takes hold of judgement;
> I will take my vengeance on my adversaries,
> And will repay those who hate me.
>
> (Deuteronomy 32: 40-1)

> Western people were attempting to gain salvation through the construction of a materialistic paradise built only by human reason and will. Dostoyevsky (1821-81) feared that the failure to incorporate spirit [idealism] would result in total tyranny. (Spielvogel 1991, p. 881)
>
> The only substantial state in the Middle Ages was the church. Since the Protestant revolt, these powers have all been transferred to the national states, and the theory of omnipotence, which the pope held on the plea that any action might come under his cognizance if it concerns morality, has been taken over by the national states on the theory that any action, if it involves money or contract, must be a matter for courts. (Randall 1976, p. 179)
>
> Development in Europe between 1500 and 1700 (including foreign trade and agriculture) were, in many ways, the crucial differentiating themes when considering the mysteries of why industrialisation should spring from the British or European context in the eighteenth century, and not from the Asian (Mathias 1969, p. 16).

Section 2 Discovery of New World

The Europeans forgot the new lands the Vikings had discovered. Trade with the Orient since the days of the Roman Empire went into lapse. The narrations by Marco Polo who travelled through the Mongol Empire reminded the Europeans that there lay in the East splendid countries whose wealth and splendour surpassed those of Europe. However, the situation radically changed since then. By 1400s, Europe imported many of the necessities and most of the luxuries of European life from the East.

All Eastern goods reached Europe through the ports and markets of the Middle East, and from the early 7th century onwards till 1500s these vital commercial centres were in Muslim hands, though the political dominance of the region passed from Arabs to Seljuk Turks to Ottoman Turks to Mongols; they were all Muslims. Though the Muslims were still dominant in the Middle East, the importance of trade there was very much reduced after 1500s.

The Arabs under the protection of the Saracen Empire came to control the main arteries of international trade during the medieval era. After conquering Syria, Mesopotamia, Persia and the territories across the Oxus, the Arabs diverted trade through the northern route to their domain of north Africa and Spain, ultimately to reach the markets of Western Europe. It is not an exaggeration that the Arabs conducted the entire trade between the East and the West from the eighth to the eleventh centuries.

The Muslim Arabs traded solely with the Italian city states of such as Venice and Genoa, and the other European countries had to buy through them (Roberts 1973, p. 32).

<u>Reasons Why Muslim Arabs Traded Only with Italians among Western Europeans</u>

The Arabs deeply resented the intrusion of the Europeans into their trade routes: still they needed the traders who carried the goods between their ports and Europe. The Christian kingdoms abstained from selling swords to their Muslim customers but the Republic of Venice did not have any scruples and did the business willingly. The Italians had the largest fleet and controlled the sea; many of them spoke local languages. Genoa, for example, had the control of the Euxine and Crimea, thus enabled a monopoly of trade from Central Asia along the northern route for some time. More fundamentally the Italians were wealthy and excelled in trade. The wealth meant a large producing and consuming population enabling them to take and pay for the costly products from the East.

The Turks overran the Middle East in the 11th century and subsequently made difficult the land route trade by which silk in China and spices in the East Indies (or the Spice Islands) reached the West. The Europeans needed spices to preserve meat. Further the 14th century onwards East-West trade became uncertain because of the breakup of the Mongol Empire. All over Europe in the fifteenth century merchants and sailors were speculating about new sea routes to the East. The Spanish looked to the west route, while the Portuguese to the African routes.

The 1400s and early 1500s were the age of great explorations and discoveries for the Europeans. In 50 years, European sailors crossed the Atlantic to the Americas, rounded the Cape of Good Hope and sailed to India, and sailed all the way around the world. Once into the Indian Ocean the Europeans could rely on the local pilots to navigate and did not have to know the way around. After 1500, the Europeans extensively used long-ranged gunned sailing ships and the Atlantic trade rose.

When the Great Age of Discovery drew to a close, the Portuguese and Spaniards who took the initiative in exploration held sway in the eastern hemisphere and the western hemisphere of the globe respectively, though both countries at first had shown little interest in the New

World which offered little compared with the spice trades of the East which had been in fact their goal of exploration.

Since the discovery of the sea route to the Indies by Vasco Da Gama in 1498, the importance of the land routes ever diminished over the passage of time. Subsequently the Arabs, the Turks, the Mongols and the Italians lost their commanding positions in trade, and the Portuguese and the Spanish increasingly became dominant in the trade between the East and the West.

We are just beginning to realise how important was this rapid enlargement of the horizon of Europe through its swift discovery of the rest of the world in the changes that followed so swiftly after 1500. Directly, of course, the new importance of commercial relations with the Orient and the empires built up by the conquistadores in America were outstanding factors in the great Commercial Revolution from which we date modern times.

The year 1500 was chosen by numerous scholars to mark the divide between pre-modern and modern times in European societies. Around this time, the Europeans had the view that the empires of the East possessed fabulous wealth and vast armies.

After the discovery of America by Columbus in 1492, the Europeans were still anxious to reach the Orient by other routes. Vasco da Gama discovered the sea route from Portugal to India around the Cape of Good Hope in 1498. Some tried to reach the Orient navigating the north of Canada, the so-called Northwest Passage, since the 16th century. Some dreamed of the south of South America, the so-called Southwest Passage. In the latter view Ferdinand Magellan set sail in 1519, obtaining assistance from the Spanish king. His fleet sailed south of South America through the so-named Strait of Magellan. They reached the Philippine islands in 1521 and the fleet without him--the local rulers killed him--continued west and reached a harbour in Spain in 1522, thus providing conclusive proof that the earth was a sphere.

The English East India Company and the Dutch United East India Company were established by 1600 with royal charters granting a monopoly of trade in the East. Macao [Macau] grew rapidly as a trading centre from the sixteenth century because the Chinese were forbidden to go abroad under a penalty of death. (Milston 1978, p. 228) Macau became a Portuguese territory in the 16th century, and subsequently became the principal entrepot (a warehouse for commercial goods) for international trade. Though the Chinese government centralised trade in Canton towards the end of the 18th century, merchants congregated in Macau because of the restrictive trading season of Canton. The Canton regulations forced the Westerners to live in Macau and come to Canton only in summer when the monsoons were favourable. By the mid-19th century Hong Kong eclipsed Macau in trade and the merchants deserted Macau.

The saying ‘Light comes from the East’ had a double meaning as is normally the case for the proverbs of this kind. It denoted the everyday observation that the sun rises in the east and also expressed the Occidentals' experience that new ideas came from the East. Strangely the proverb repeats itself even today in many fields. For example, if we look into the history of American gangsters, the Chinese dominated the American crime scene first. The Irish mobs made headway after the decline of the Chinese, and eventually the Italian mafias came to dominate the organised criminal activities in America. To cite another example, it is a popular belief that Mussolini (an Italian) started the modern fascist state before Adolf Hitler dominated Germany with the totalitarian ideology. However, we can see some semblance of the state in Ch’in, the ancient to classical Chinese state.

The following historical records highlight the backwardness of the Europeans of the pre-modern era who were ignorant that people in other parts of the world had discovered and taken for granted centuries earlier what they thought they were pioneering.

Backwardness of Europeans before Renaissance

Teachers say that Christopher Columbus discovered America in 1492 as the head of the royal Spanish expedition. However, archaeological evidence shows that the so-called Vikings inhabited the east coast of North America extensively long before that year. They geared some settlements for permanent habitation and some for temporary accommodation.

According to the Icelandic sagas, a storm blew Bjarni Herjulfsson, a Viking fisherman from Greenland off course, and drove him south until eventually he reached a point off the coast of Labrador, or perhaps Newfoundland. When he returned he related his adventures and described the forested shore he had seen. Lief the Lucky sailed off in search of these new lands. He and his companions reached the coast of what is now New England in about 1003. There they landed, and called the territory Vinland after the wild vines that grew there. Other Viking expeditions to the North American continent followed. Life in America seems to have become more and more difficult, and the Vikings eventually abandoned Vinland, probably in the early twelfth century. (*Early Civilization* 1984, p. 140)

Also in search of knowledge and tribute, a massive Chinese fleet—made up of junks, each with a crew of 1000 and five times larger than Columbus's tiny ships—discovered the American continent in 1421, not only North America but South America.

Similarly, teachers say that Vasco da Gama, funded by King Manuel of Portugal, discovered the sea route from Portugal to India around the Cape of Good Hope in 1498. However, Pharaoh Necho the Second of Egypt, during the 26th dynasty (663-525 BC), sent a Phoenician fleet to explore the route around the same cape. Though the expedition was successful returning in 595 BC, it took 3 years to complete. As a consequence they did not use the route at the time for trading purposes. (Casson 1978, p. 161; Grant 1969, p. 129; Mercer 1996, p. 84) Herodotus wrote that the sea surrounded Africa and cited the above Phoenician voyage as definite proof (Roberts 1973, p. 16).

So you can see the accepted statements concerning Columbus and Gama are not correct. Are they teaching lies at school? Both of these explorers and their sponsors (Spanish and Portuguese monarchs respectively) may or may not have been aware that these routes had been explored before. In the absence of the accurate knowledge of prior explorations, these adventurers most likely believed they were going through unknown territories.

How can we interpret these strange observations? The best way to understand them may be to think in terms of importance. Prior explorations were done in isolation from other political and economic considerations and independently of other nations, and historians dismissed them as unimportant. Though this view may be taken as the modern or European standpoint, we have to recognise that the modern or European inspired cultures mainly decide the world affairs today.

The fact that there were earlier visits to the American continent possibly does not diminish the significance of Columbus' reaching the West Indies in 1492, if we think of the subsequent world history resulting from this discovery.

The discovery of the New World in 1492 has shifted the centre of world affairs to Western Europe and opened the world market for the West Europeans. Before this the Muslims controlled the lucrative routes to the East.

Section 3 Reformation (1517-1648)

Martin Luther (1483-1546) posted his Ninety-five Theses on the church door in Wittenberg, Germany, in 1517, thus triggering what we call the Reformation, though John Hus in Bohemia and John Wycliffe in England had attacked the abuses of the church in the late medieval period. The church sold indulgences and important positions to raise money and interfered in politics whenever they could. Originally indulgence meant forgiveness of sins by penance but after the 12th century it was put up for sale. Though Luther's 95 theses centred on indulgences, they released pent-up anger towards the institution and corruption of the church and led to the establishment of the Protestant Church in defiance of the Roman Catholic Church. He wrote his notes in Latin and the sale of indulgences was immediate cause of his stand.

The Reformation movement when it started was a part of the Renaissance in Europe. Also regional nations in Europe, particularly England, France and Spain, were increasing their power as manifested in finances and armies and tried to be independent of the pope. It was an attack on the church to tell how the Christian faith should be.

Luther effectively challenged the papal claim to be the sole authority on the Bible and affirmed Christians' personal right to faith. He insisted that only the Scriptures should be the source of authority, and justification was by faith alone and not by works. This creed became the central theme of Protestantism since its inception through its history. He did not intend to break with the church; however, the Imperial Diet of Worms tried him in 1521 and Pope Leo X excommunicated him. Luther's stance touched a popular chord, particularly in Germany; he called for German control of the German church. He translated the Bible from Latin to German; and thanks to the printing press, many German people could read the Bible at first hand. Rather strangely Luther turned against the peasants' rebellion (1524-6) in Germany by 1525 contributing to its defeat; his teaching had been one of the causes of the revolts. He further called for the brutal suppression of the rebellions.

The Reformation movement within Germany diversified quickly, and other movements in Europe arose independently of Luther and spread in the course of the 16th century. By the mid-century Lutheranism took root in northern Europe. Calvin (a French theologian) led the Reformation movement in France and Switzerland and established the first Presbyterian government in Geneva by 1555. Presbyterianism is the form of governing body by elders or presbyters. Eastern Europe offered more radical varieties of Protestantism.

Ulrich Zwingli (1484-1531) practised a simple service replacing the Roman Mass and operated in Zurich, Switzerland, independently from Rome. His teaching acquired huge followings appealing to the mountain spirit of the Swiss. He was a rebel preacher, though his inspiration came from Luther. He rejected the notion of transubstantiation of Lutheranism. Transubstantiation states that the bread and wine changes into the substance of the body and blood of Christ when consecrated in the Eucharist. Zwingli was killed in a battle between Protestants and Catholics while serving as an army chaplain.

Sweden and Denmark also broke with the pope.

Gregory IX established the Papal Inquisition c. 1231 to last to 1820. A papal bull of 1478 by Pope Sixtus IV established the Spanish Inquisition; though it was set up by the order of the pope it was answerable to the Spanish crown. The Catholic monarchs of Aragon and Castile demanded establishment of the Spanish Inquisition when they almost completed the expulsion of the Muslims. It persecuted deviants, religious (Catholics, Protestants and Jews) or otherwise, and burned some thousands at the stake. However towards the end of the 16th century the practice was no longer prevalent and the inquisition condemned only a few people for execution. The Spanish Inquisition came into being before the start of the Reformation. Refer to the next section for further reasons for establishing the inquisition.

Pope Paul III set up the Roman Inquisition to combat Protestantism in 1542. It was introduced to counterbalance the severe Spanish Inquisition, particularly in Italy though it had general authority. He appointed six cardinals as Inquisitors-General with the powers to imprison on suspicion, to confiscate property and even to execute the guilty.

The nation-state was a novelty in the 16th century Europe, and was quite different from today's concept of nation. Material conditions, slow communications, local customs, economies and laws limited the royal power.

In the early part of the 16th century guns and gunpowder were widely used in Europe and they were going to change the warfare on land and sea, and the conventional thinking about wars had to change or face inevitable defeat.

The Reformation which began as a religious revolt involved also widespread economic and political conflicts. It entered a new phase in the 1560s when Calvinism spread with its more radical and uncompromising attitude than Lutheranism. Scotland adopted the former faith as Presbyterianism in 1560. The growth of Calvinism in the Netherlands underlay the Dutch revolt beginning in 1566 against the Spanish rule.

It is said the Reformation ended in 1648 at the Peace of Westphalia which concluded the Thirty Years' of War. Both sides (Catholics and Protestants) realised that they could not win over the other side and the peace treaty brought a compromise solution. As it turned out eventually the war was political and social struggles among the competing national princes, having little to do with religion. Spain was the greatest casualty of the war, and also Germany, the scene of so many battles, suffered a lasting setback as the result.

Northern Europe became Protestant and southern Europe remained Catholic. This rough rule showed that papal authority diminished with distance from the papal administration obviously because of the difficulties of both communications and transport. Though the Roman Catholic Church was under the unified rule by the pope, many Protestant denominations appeared forming a variety of organisations. Lutheran regions tended to be conservative and supported strong central government. Calvinists supported democracy and tended to oppose the tyranny of the monarchs. Lutherans and Calvinists together with Catholics existed side by side in Germany and the enmity between the first two was quite strong.

The Catholic Church, realising its past mistakes, conducted the Counter Reformation from the middle of the 16th century to the 17th and gained new vitality and strength. Spain and Italy did not have the foothold of Protestantism and were the centres of this movement.

Erasmus was the great representative of the Renaissance in Holland as Luther was in Germany, but the former wrote not in Dutch but in Latin. Erasmus as a humanist criticised the rigidity of the Roman Church and proposed reform but he remained a Catholic. He died in 1536 after being exiled from Protestant Basle. His major work was the first printed edition (1516) of the New Testament in Greek joined by Latin translation. Luther came into contact with the reformist ideas then circulating European academic circles. He became a friend of Erasmus of Rotterdam.

King Philip II of Spain became the champion of Catholicism since he was able and willing to take military actions against its opposition. However, Spain became the greatest casualty of the Reformation. By 1596 Spain was bankrupt though not for the first time. Philip II admitted that the royal treasury was empty and the economy was in ruins; he cited the series of wars as the major reason, apart from poor weather, poor administration and heavy domestic spending. The Dutch alone gained from the long religious struggles. Spain and the Netherlands finally reached a truce in 1609 after 40 years of rebellion and repression. The

Netherlands became independent of Spain, set about commercial expansion, and by 1650 Amsterdam's financiers dominated the entire European economy.

William Tyndale translated the New Testament in Greek to English while he was in Germany. His English version began appearing in England in 1526. The Reformation in England took the form of the break with Rome and setting up the national church with the monarch as the supreme governor. The pope's refusal to grant Henry VIII a dispensation to allow him to divorce Catherine of Aragon in 1529 touched off the move. I expound in some depth how Henry VIII set up the Church of England in way of divorce with his wife in Section 15 Sex as Basis of Civilisation, Chapter 1, Book Five.

Henry VIII was in fact a devout Catholic. The religious wars were going in Europe at the time, and he like many other princes and kings saw the opportunity to confiscate the Catholic Church properties in England in conjunction with the divorce with Catherine of Aragon. Pope Clement VII excommunicated Henry VIII in 1533 shortly after Anne Boleyn was crowned queen. Henry founded the Church of England in 1534, in effect a state church independent of the Roman Catholic Church. The Dissolution of Monasteries started in 1536 and completed in 1540; 550 properties with their treasures of plates and jewels passing into the king's possession. The monasteries had also been an obstacle to the consolidation of his power over the church. King Henry VIII became the head of the Anglican Church, and thus assumed the supreme authority both spiritual and temporal. This is another indication of the growth of nationalism. England was dangerously isolated and had to build a powerful navy in preparation for possible attacks from Spain and France, both Catholic states.

Edward VI succeeded to the throne of England and Ireland at the age of nine at the death of Henry VIII. Edward died of tuberculosis at the age of fifteen hence he did not govern as a king. Before his death he nominated his Protestant cousin Lady Jane Grey as the successor instead of his half-sister Mary who was next in line to the throne but a devout Roman Catholic. Lady Jane reigned only for 9 days to be dethroned in favour of Mary.

During the reigns of King Edward VI (1547-53) and Queen Mary I (1553-58) the dispute took place whether the Church of England was Protestant or Roman Catholic. Mary was the daughter of King Henry and Catherine of Aragon and became illegitimate when Henry divorced Catherine with papal condemnation. Mary was determined to restore Catholicism in England, thinking that if she had restored papal authority over the English Church her birth would have become legitimate. After becoming queen in 1553--her illegitimacy did not prevent her becoming a queen--she married Prince Philip (the future King Philip II) of Spain the following year. However, the marriage was extremely unpopular with the English, and the English Parliament refused to crown him jointly with Mary so he had little power in England. She persuaded the parliament to abandon the independence of the English Church and submit to papal authority. Accordingly Pope Julius III appointed Reginald Pole as Archbishop of Canterbury, who restored Catholic services and sacked the priests who had been allowed to marry under the previous monarchs. The marriage between Mary and Philip was without love and children and he stayed in England only for short periods. In fact the marriage, combining Catholicism and Spanish arrogance, had triggered a rebellion in 1554 which almost overthrew the Tudor throne. She earned the nickname of Bloody Mary persecuting Protestants and executing 300 heretics.

When she died in 1558 after 5 years of reign the English crown passed to her sister Elizabeth, Philip's sister-in-law, with enthusiastic support from the English. Henry VIII's will designated Elizabeth as the successor. It is on record that King Philip, who became king of Spain in 1556, tried to persuade Elizabeth to marry him without success. Queen Elizabeth I established a compromise between the two positions and brought peace in England with so much rejoicing of English people to usher in the flowering of the Elizabethan age in literature, and further laid the foundations of the British Empire. She also repelled the

Spanish Invincible Armada: Philip II sent the armada in 1588 with the intent to punish England for supporting the Dutch cause of independence from Spain and plundering Spanish possessions in Mexico and South America.

John Knox had established the Presbyterian Church of Scotland in 1560, which made possible the eventual union of Scotland and England, when Elizabeth passed away in 1603.

Religious war started in France when Francis, duke of Guise, son of Catherine de Medici, ordered the massacre at an illegal Huguenot congregation at Vassy in 1562. The Huguenots, followers of Calvin, retaliated by attacking Catholic establishments. A terrible massacre of the Huguenots took place in Paris on St Bartholomew's Day 1572. Catherine de Medici, the king's mother, was the instigator. She feared that Gaspard de Coligy, using his influence over young King Charles IX, also a son of Catherine, might push the king into war with Spain, and conspired with the Catholic leader, Henry of Guise, to have Coligy removed. Once the killing started, a general massacre followed, and hundreds of men, women and children were killed

Henry IV (1589-1610), first Bourbon king of France, signed the Edict of Nantes in 1598, at last bringing peace from the religious war. Though the king had fought hard on the side of Protestantism, he accepted the Catholic faith, which was his masterstroke in ending the agony in France. He granted religious freedom and equal rights to Huguenots as Protestants were called in France. Many Catholics were reluctant to accept the terms but they were so war weary that they submitted, and the army of King Philip II of Spain marched home after signing a treaty with Henry IV. Thus peace prevailed in France.

The Reformation in Europe came to a close with the signing (1648) of the Treaty of Westphalia which marked the end of the Thirty Years' War. The next section gives a brief account of the Thirty Years' War. In signing the above treaty whose negotiations lasted for four years, the Catholics in southern Europe and the Protestants in northern Europe realised that neither side could win over the other and both sides were forced to respect the existence and the rights of the other party. This solution was a compromise reached by Queen Elizabeth I in her dominion a century earlier. Compromise is a manifestation of middle path.

The underlying reason why Britain became the eventual winner on the European rivalry may have been:

- England overcame her religious conflicts one century earlier than the continental Europe--half a century earlier than France--and devoted her efforts to develop literature, empire, parliamentary democracy, and industrial revolution among others.
- England lost her foothold in Europe as the result of the Hundred Years' War and she was aware of strong resistance among continental Europeans if she tried to dominate them, and skilfully played European and global politics being aware of her strengths and weaknesses.
- Hence England built her large yet efficient navy as well as her huge commercial shipping not only to defend her country and to expand trade but to direct her expansion zeal outside Europe.
- England eventually outperformed Spain, Portugal, Dutch and France and became the winner in Europe and the world.

Section 4 European Expansion

Europe went through commercial revolution since the 16th century. Britain ushered in the agricultural revolution closely followed by the industrial revolution in the middle of the 18th century. Book Three *Communism* deals with these topics.

As the consequence of European turmoils (the Hundred Years' War, the Black Death and the Great Schism) and the union of Castile and Aragon by marriage, four national states of Spain, Portugal, France and England emerged as powerful in Europe by 1500.

In the sixteenth century, the economic activities in Europe began to shift from the Mediterranean to the Atlantic seaboard. Thus Spain and Portugal came to prominence as commercial empires. In the seventeenth century, as Spain and Portugal declined the Dutch, the French and the English expanded. High taxation pressed Holland hard, without industrial strength, to maintain a huge mercantile and shipping empire and Dutch power waned by the 18th century. France dominated Europe in the 17th and 18th centuries; however, she faced serious financial problems, went through the French Revolution, and was defeated by the Russians. Britain initiated the Industrial Revolution in the middle of the 18th century and completed in the middle of the following century, and established supremacy over France by the naval and land victories in the early 19th century. The Seven Years' War confirmed the rising power of Prussia. Prussia seized north Germany and west Poland in the 18th-19th centuries and established united Germany in 1871 under its leadership.

<u>Thirty Years' War (1618-48)</u>

This war was a series of conflicts in central Europe. The fundamental cause may have been religious hostility between Catholics and Protestants but the political issues exasperated and sometimes became the main cause of conflicts. Main player was the Holy Roman Empire controlled by the Habsburg family (Catholic).

The archbishop of Prague, capital of Bohemia, ordered a Protestant church to be destroyed. The Protestants appealed to the Holy Roman Emperor, who ignored their appeal, and subsequently civil war broke out in 1618. The Bohemian Protestants removed Ferdinand, the Catholic king of Bohemia, and installed a Protestant king instead. Subsequently Ferdinand became Holy Roman Emperor with sovereign authority. The Catholic forces decisively defeated the Bohemian rebels and restored Catholicism as the state religion in 1624.

The Protestant king of Denmark opposed Ferdinand's forces but was defeated. Gustavus Adolphus, the Swedish king, was devoted to the cause of Protestantism and also afraid of Ferdinand becoming too powerful. He joined forces against Ferdinand. Though he was killed in the battle, the conflict continued.

The Bourbon family of France (Catholic country) was determined to block the growth of Habsburg power and joined the war on the side of Sweden. Their combined forces won a long series of battles in Germany. Eventually Ferdinand agreed to the Treaty of Westphalia.

The Treaty of Westphalia which ended the Thirty Years' War in 1648 had far-reaching effects in Europe:

- France, the richest and most populous state, emerged as Europe's dominant power.
- The Holy Roman Empire was to decay and to become the future Austro-Hungary.
- The Habsburgs no longer controlled the central German states. The war severely weakened Spain which had posed as the Catholic champion of Europe.
- Religion was the major cause of war before the Thirty Years' War. However, even in the Thirty Years' War religion was not an overriding factor of conflict, though the

> uncompromising stances of Calvinism and Counter-Reformation Catholicism generated religious tension in Europe. After the treaty the prime cause of war became nationalism.
> (Davison 1993, p. 153)

The treaty confirmed religious toleration—at least for private worship of minority religions within national boundaries. However, tolerance did not extend to non-Catholics in the hereditary lands of the House of Habsburg.

Habsburg Dynasty

The power struggles among European nations pushed these nations above the other regions of the world, economically and militarily. For about a century and a half after 1500, the Habsburg family--Spain and Austria together with scattered kingdoms, duchies and provinces--aspired to dominate Europe politically and religiously, but eventually the coalition of the other European powers defeated them. (Kennedy 1987, p. 31)

Stemming originally from Austria, Habsburg rulers managed to get themselves regularly elected to the position of Holy Roman emperor. The Habsburgs were without equal in augmenting their territories through marriage and inheritance. Maximilian of Austria brought in Burgundy and the Netherlands with his marriage to Mary of Burgundy. Another marriage compact of 1515 added the territories of Hungary and Bohemia. But the most far reaching of Maximilian's dynastic linkup was the marriage of his son Philip to Joan, daughter of Ferdinand and Isabella of Spain, in 1496. (p. 32)

In early modern Europe, roughly one-quarter of the entire Europeans lived in Habsburg-ruled territory (p. 43).

The spiralling costs of wars exposed the real weakness of the Hapsburg system. General inflation, which saw food prices rise fivefold and industrial prices three fold between 1500 and 1630, was in itself a heavy blow. The Hapsburgs further had to cope with the doubling and redoubling of their armies and navies. (p. 46)

The Hapsburg monarchies, to meet the rising costs of wars, had to raise money in the most precarious manners:

- hurting commerce, industry and ordinary citizens by imposing steadily increasing taxes,
- selling various privileges, monopolies and honours,
- selling interest-bearing government bonds. In 1543, 65% of ordinary revenues had to be spent paying interests on bonds: this came about by the late stage of reign of Charles V (1516-56)
- borrowing heavily from bankers on the credit of future Castilian taxes or American treasure.

(p. 54)

Spain and Portugal

Spanish towns, in decline under the Visigoths, revived under the Moors. Moorish Spain became one of the wealthiest and most thickly populated areas of Europe. The Christians in the peninsula acknowledged Islamic superiority and many of them even converted to Islam.

The Moors were called the Berbers during Roman times and lived in northwest Africa. In the early 8th century they converted to Islam and adopted the Arabic language. They joined the Arabs in conquering Spain and Portugal. They established the Moorish civilisation (756-1492) in Spain until Ferdinand and Isabella expelled them from Spain. Christian opposition to Muslim rule in the Iberian Peninsula was quite strong and persistent throughout. The Christians gained the upper hand in the 1000s, and forced out the Muslims by the 1200s from

Portugal and most from Spain. Portugal became an independent (from the Muslims and Spain) kingdom in 1143 and began the overseas expansion in 1419.

In the tenth century Spain, science ceased to be mere lore and was applied to the arts and crafts of the practical life (Randall 1976, p. 208).

There was order in the Moorish Spain with officials and regulations, and organisations with guilds and corporations. The Moors were better tradesmen, better architects, better engineers and better farmers than the Christians. They were better read and more cultured. Agriculture flourished with the Moors bringing to Spain new methods of irrigation as well as numerous crops and fruits such as rice, cotton, oranges, apricots and peaches. Industry thrived, Al-Andalus being particularly noted for its magnificent textiles, furs and pottery. Trade boomed as far afield as India and Central Asia. Scholarship and learning were stimulated by the Moors' access, through Muslim culture, to the best of Greek and Roman thoughts, and Byzantine and Persian arts. Standards in medicine and science were well advanced of other European states. Education was so widely spread that a high proportion of Spanish Muslims could read and write, a situation unknown in the rest of Europe. Spain, indeed all Europe, was greatly in debt to the Moors. It was through Moorish Spain that Europe's stagnating mind became acquainted not only with the advanced arts and scholarship of Arabic cultures absorbed through trade but with Greek philosophy.

European scholars made their way to the great Arab libraries, especially those of Moorish Spain. Many Europeans were astonished with the poor state of information in Latin compared with the great wealth of knowledge available in Arabic and many devoted their life to translating into their language.

> The greatness of the Arabs seems to have lain in their ability to assimilate the best in the intellectual heritage of the peoples with whom they came into contact, rather than in any striking originality. They took the mathematical and medical knowledge of the Hellenistic world, which the Roman had disclaimed and Christianity cast aside, ... They gained from India in Sanskrit language the indispensable 'Arabic notation', i.e., the decimal system of numbers in our everyday use, and algebraic form of thought .... (p. 208)

The Moors established Muslim states where Arabic was spoken, separate from the Christian kingdoms where Spanish was spoken. The Christian kingdoms coalesced into the larger states and came to dominate nearly all of Iberia by the 13th century. Many words in the Spanish language derived from Arabic words.

The marriage of Prince Ferdinand of Aragon and Princess Isabella of Castile in 1469 paved the way for the union of Spain. Isabella became queen of Castile in 1474; Ferdinand, king of Aragon in 1479. Both wanted to create strong kingdoms and thought that the Jews and Muslims were a threat to this goal. They furthered the Spanish Inquisition in 1483 under Pope Sixtus IV, which was to last 300 years. This institution came notoriously to try Catholics who did not follow Roman Catholic teachings. Isabella and Ferdinand were also bent on driving out the Jews and Muslims from their country.

The fall of Granada, the capital of the Moorish Kingdom of Granada, in January 1492, was only an end to the regional conflicts of Christendom and Islam. The Ottoman Turks were still in advance and had conquered Constantinople in 1453.

By the 1480s the Portuguese had invented the caravel, a sturdy ship that could sail against the wind. The caravel was smaller, lighter and easier to manoeuvre than the galleon which would appear on the sea later in the mid-1500s. The caravel made possible the exploration of the world by the Portuguese and Spaniards in later years.

Isabella took up the offer of Columbus, partly because she was seeking ventures after the expulsion of the Moors from Spain. In August 1492, with three small caravels and 90 men, Columbus set sail and reached Cuba in October the same year, and explored Cuba and Haiti looking for gold and returned to Spain. His navigation technique allowed him to repeat the second voyage to Cuba and Haiti, and reached the American continent on the third and fourth voyages. He made four voyages totally to the New World. However, he did not know he had discovered the American continent and died in Spain in 1506 at the age of 55 believing he had reached Asia. He and the Europeans did not realise at the time the significance of the American discovery. In fact those of the Portuguese explorers who had rounded the Cape of Good Hope in 1497 and opened the sea routes to India overshadowed his achievement.

In 1494, Pope Alexander VI promulgated the Treaty of Tordesillas. This treaty arbitrarily divided the lands and islands with a line drawn across the Atlantic at a point 370 miles west of the Cape Verde Islands. Everything east of this line went to Portugal as colonial possessions; everything west of it to Spain. The pope decreed his line of demarcation through the New World, believing that it would chiefly benefit his native Spain. (Davison 1993, p. 116) France, Holland and England all protested furiously; but Alexander, in his desire for peaceful development of the two huge empires, tried to force its obedience. However, the English, the Swedes, the Hollanders and the French, all flouted the pope and scrambled to share the good things of the New World. (Wells 1925, p. 530)

Long before Da Gama's voyage, Muslim mariners sailed the Indian Ocean coast for trade purpose. Even after the discovery of the sea route around the Cape of Good Hope, many of the important trade centres such as Hormuz and Aden, the trade's western centres, and the port of Malacca, the foremost trade centre of the East, as well as many of the lands where the Eastern goods originated were under Muslim control. The Portuguese set out to wrestle the rule from the Muslims. Almeida broke the Muslim grip on the Indian Ocean in 1509 with a naval victory. His successor, d'Albuquerque, captured Hormuz in 1507 but the assault on Aden was without success. He instead captured Goa in 1510. In 1511 Malacca itself fell to the Portuguese under his command. Under d'Albuquerque, for the first time a European power gained supremacy in the East. (Roberts 1973, p. 52)

Ferdinand seized the small kingdom of Navarre in 1512 to form what we know as Spain today.

Portugal was a sea empire, based on trade routes linking commercial ports. It was only made possible by the vast supply of men and arms which Portugal could not bear long particularly since the monarchs seized the riches for themselves instead of giving the necessary supplies. (p. 52)

Portugal could not colonise the captured territories because of its small population--probably not more than a million and a half. Hence this nation aspired to become the middle man in the trade between the East and Europe. It became an immensely rewarding operation: a trading profit of 800 per cent was reported in 1512. Portugal became Europe's richest state circa 1521, more or less suddenly. (Mercer 1996, pp. 400, 408)

Before the 16th century Spain remained a poor country; almost its only wealth lay in its mines. For a century after the discovery of America, through its monopoly of gold and silver, Spain dominated the world. Abundance of gold and silver reduced interest rates to a low level, two per cent per annum in Spain and Portugal in the 16th and 17th centuries. In Britain interest rates remained at six per cent in these centuries. (Robbins 1998, pp. 36, 67)

The bulk of Spanish people at the start of the modern era believed that acquisition of wealth was the aim of their life (Smith 1991, p. 326) rather than cultivation of their mind as the bulk of the ancient to classical Greek men did. The Spanish further thought that gold and silver were the fundamental form of wealth, which they wanted to acquire through trade and plunder. The Tartars thought before the establishment of their empire that cattle were the main form of wealth: When they achieved military superiority they proceeded with trade and plunder.

Between 1500 and 1700 European countries expended roughly one third of public revenues on wars and in the case of Spain this amounted to as much as 70 per cent (Galbraith 1987, p. 34).

In 1574, Spain was practically bankrupt. It had spent enormous amount of money on wars to maintain its power and prestige in Europe. Bankruptcy also resulted from paying too much attention to imperial interests and less on the economic matters with hard planning.

King Philip II of Spain invaded Portugal in 1580 and annexed Portugal which was also bankrupt as the result of a disastrous African crusade by King Sebastian, though the Portuguese colonies remained in Portuguese control.

It is said that the supremacy of Spain in Europe lasted until 1588, when England defeated the Armada. This event marked the rise of England to a great power status as much as it marked the decline of Spain.

The significance of the defeat of the Spanish Armada by the English was not clear for a while but it manifested as:

- The balance of power had shifted from the Catholic south to the Protestant north in European regional politics.
- Queen Elizabeth I had established Protestant rule in England, and after her death in 1603 King James VI united England and Scotland under Protestantism.
- The Dutch effectively became independent from Spain in 1609 and set out to build a huge empire in the East Indies.

(Davison 1993, p. 141)

In 1596, Spain admitted that it got into another financial difficulty as a result of wars with England (Mercer 1996, p. 487).

Although Spain remained a major European power after its Armada was defeated by England, its prestige had been severely damaged and its naval supremacy lost.

One of the crowning achievements of the Golden Age of Spanish literature was the work of Miguel de Cervantes (1547-1616); *Don Quixote* (1605) has been acclaimed as one of the greatest literary works of all time. The novel satirises chivalric adventure with the knight as a visionary and idealist and the squire as a realist. We are left with Cervantes's conviction that idealism and realism, visionary dreams and the hard work of reality, are both necessary to the human condition. (Spielvogel 1991, p. 518)

During the reign of Philip II, who ruled Spain from 1556 to 1598, the Spanish Empire reached its height and began to decline. Spain declined further under the weak rulers who followed him. The Spanish Empire began to crumble around 1629 under the strain of war in the Netherlands. (Mercer 1996, p. 525) In 1640 Portugal regained independence after driving out the Spaniards. Thereafter Spain and her allies tried to regain the control of Portugal; however, England frustrated the invasion of foreign troops. Napoleon I invaded in 1807 and occupied Portugal but England under the command of the Duke of Wellington drove the French out in 1811.

Portugal's status as an economic and world power showed signs of eroding in the late 1500s, and in the 1600s the European nations began to take over parts of the Portuguese Empire.

The flow of American gold and silver into Spain caused price inflation which no society at the time had the theory and experience to handle. The decline of Spanish power did not fully reveal itself until the 1640s; however, the causes had existed for decades before.

French forces continued to attack Spain in the late 1600s. King Charles II (the last ruler of the Habsburg family in Spain) named a French duke, Philip of Anjou, as heir to the Spanish throne in order to forestall the attack. He died in 1700 and Philip became the king of Spain as Philip V. Philip was the grandson of King Louis XIV and was the first of the series of the Bourbon family to rule Spain. This triggered the War of Spanish Succession (1701-14); European nations opposing the French control of the Spanish Empire. France lost the conflicts and consequently all Spanish possessions in Europe, though the Spanish crown remained in the Bourbon family. King Philip remained King of Spain but was removed from the French line of succession, thus averting the union of Spain and France. King Philip retained the Spanish overseas empire.

Why did Spain and Portugal rise as the two most powerful nations in Europe in the 16th century and declined in the 17th century? Though these two countries are geographically in Europe, they don't exhibit the industrial and vigorous characteristics of today's Europe. Many people are surprised to find what is in Spain as soon as they cross the Pyrenees from France: they wonder, standing on Spanish soil, if they are still in Europe.

Spain and Portugal came to the fore of European politics as their trade flourished. Still this explains only a part of the story. The exploration zeal by Spain and Portugal was mainly for trade purpose, though there were other elements such as religious missions, the spirits of discovery and adventure. Spain and Portugal looked at the New World as the source of gold and silver, and the pious purpose of converting the natives to Christianity was more a facade to cover up the above purpose and to satisfy the church. Without trade purpose, explorations would not have gone ahead in the same way that the core purpose of the crusades was temporal and without the temporal motive the initial and definitely later expeditions would not have gone ahead.

One fundamental problem for Spain and Portugal was the policy makers' premise that the national goal should be the acquisition of gold and silver through trade and colonisation. This proved to be an erroneous concept in the long run. One problem was the inflational effect caused by the great influx of gold and silver. Since the turn of the century to 1500, the cost of living in Spain increased as much as 1000 per cent in 50 to 60 years. Another problem may be the neglect of the home industries; England did not neglect her agriculture and home industries. The abundance of gold and silver in Spain and Portugal pushed the products of agriculture and manufacture dear, thus leading these countries to import most of those commodities and damaging the home agriculture and manufacture (Smith 1991, p. 399).

Gold and silver, imported, though they look huge, would not pay for the expenses of wars. The nations have to rely on the annual products of land and labour as the ultimate resources which enabled the country to carry on war. For example, the total gold and silver annually brought into Spain and Portugal would not have exceeded six million sterling, which hardly paid the expenses of 1761 which cost more than nineteen million for Spain. (p. 342) Spain was involved in Anglo-Spanish War as well as the war with Portugal at the time.

We can contrast the misconception of the policy makers in Spain and Portugal with the conception of those in Britain which certainly relied on trade with the backings of the home agriculture and manufacture. Britain eventually outperformed Spain and Portugal and became the Europe's and the world's dominant power in the few centuries to come.

The impetus for higher culture visited Italy first in the name of the Renaissance from 1275 to 1475. Then it went through France and Holland, and reached England. This impetus did not go through Spain and Portugal. This fact makes us doubly wonder where these two nations derived their imagination for higher civilisation. This question assumes that civilisations are not created from scratch but at least their seeds come from somewhere else. As far as I understand history this has been the norm from the ancient to the modern era. For example, people may think that the ancient Greeks originated their culture, but it has been established beyond doubt that the Greeks borrowed and imitated neighbouring high cultures—especially of Egypt and the east Mediterranean coastal areas--at the initial stage of their cultural ascendancy. Their unique social fabric made the civilisation flower into what the later generations of people admired and imitated. When the social fabric was destroyed the Greek culture lost all its gloss never to regain its impetus.

The Spaniards and Portuguese must have obtained their inspiration for high culture from the Moors and became dominant in Europe according to the conditions given. These Muslims with Arabic culture, in their zeal for religious expansion and plunder, conquered the Iberian Peninsula except for the north-west during the early part of the eighth century. These Muslim conquerors who came to be known as the Moors were of mixed Arab and Berber descent, and were to rule in the peninsula for more than seven centuries. I noted earlier that the Arabs and the Muslims were definitely on higher cultural levels than the Christian Europeans before the modern era.

Dutch Republic (1581-1795)

Beginning in the 1300s the French dukes of Burgundy won control of most of the Low Countries. The Low Countries consisted of the northern provinces--the Netherlands of the present day--and the southern provinces, now Belgium and Luxembourg. The Low Counties became a part of the Habsburg Empire when Mary of Burgundy married Maximilian (later Maximilian I) of the House of Habsburg in 1477. Charles, ruler of the Low Countries, inherited the kingdom of Spain in 1516 through his grandparents Ferdinand and Isabella. Charles became Holy Roman Emperor Charles V in 1519 by virtue of his grandfather Maximilian I.

Charles persecuted Protestant movements in the Low Countries, and Philip II, his son, becoming king of the Netherlands in 1555 (and king of Spain in 1556 as well), stepped up the struggles against Protestants. He was tyrannical and enforced strict Catholicism. In 1556 the people began to rebel. In 1579, the southern provinces, predominantly Catholic, returned to Spanish control.

In 1579, most of the northern provinces, favouring Calvinists, formed the Union of Utrecht and pledged to keep on fighting. The northern provinces had the tradition of shipbuilding and fishing, and trade as the nexuses of east-west and north-south in Europe, and were wealthy even at this time. In 1581, the northern provinces, later to become known as the Dutch Republic, declared independence from Spain and effectively war. The Dutch Republic boasted free expression and religious tolerance, and its cities especially Amsterdam were filled with the refugees from all over Europe. Spain lost its prestige when the English defeated the Spanish Armada sent by Philip II in 1588: England and Spain were locked in a fierce rivalry over religion and trade, and English help for the Dutch cause angered Philip II. The Spanish troops had the upper hand on land battles but the Dutch control of the sea eventually proved decisive. Except for 12 years of truce from 1609 to 1621, the conflicts went on: the Dutch threatened to break the stranglehold of Spanish colonial trade. Spain, during the reign of Philip IV, grandson of Philip II, formally recognised the Dutch independence at the Peace of Westphalia in 1648 which marked the end of the Thirty Years' War. Spain and the Dutch signed the treaty on 30th January, and the second separate treaty not involving the Dutch independence was signed in October the same year also in Westphalia.

The 1600s ushered in the Golden Age of the Netherlands, and the Dutch Maritime Empire became the leading sea power. Its merchant fleet tripled in size in the first half of the century, and its shipping controlled half of Europe's. Amsterdam became the great trading centre of Europe. Dutch banks, modernised banking institutions, and businesses thrived.

The Dutch developed an extensive colonial empire in many parts of the world. However, as a consequence, the Dutch Republic came into serious rivalry with the English and French over trade. The adoption of mercantilist policies by Cromwell's England and Colbert's France hurt Dutch commerce and shipping. The protracted wars with England and France exhausted the Dutch Republic which had a small population and an overextended empire. Its population is estimated to have been less than 2 million with a large number of immigrants included by the end of the 17th century. It was known that the Dutch had been reluctant to establish colonies. Dutch industry and trade began to falter and the republic entered economic decline in the 1700s. The English severely defeated the Dutch in the naval war in 1784. In 1795 French troops successfully invaded the weakened Netherlands. Britain seized most of the Dutch overseas possessions.

Prussia

Behind the sudden rise of Prussia to be a great power, were the organising and military geniuses of three leaders, the Great Elector (1640-88), Frederick William I (1713-40) and Frederick the Great (1740-86). The Prussian rise to power coincided with the collapse of Swedish power and with the disintegration of the Polish Kingdom.

Frederick II reigned Prussia from 1740 to 1786. He became a friend of French philosopher Voltaire. Though he ruled as an autocrat, he did so with progressive benevolence. He was indifferent to religion and allowed freedom of worship. Frederick II, sometimes called Frederick the Great, brought open the issue of conflicts between the popes and the secular rulers. He was the precursor of the age of doubt and declining faith. However, we have an earlier instance in the thirteenth century when Pope Gregory IX and Emperor Frederick II (1194-1250) engaged in a violent public controversy.

The Seven Years' War (1756-63) was fought when France, Russia, Austria, Sweden and Saxony, fearful over the rising power of Prussia, joined forces against Frederick the Great. Britain, allying with Prussia, wanted to settle the contest with France in North America and India. The various treaties brought the Seven Years' War to a close and:

- marked the rise of Prussia to be a great power,
- set Britain on the road to becoming the greatest colonial power of modern times.

(Davison 1993, p. 181)

Prussia had been the kingdom ruled by the Hohenzollern dynasty since 1701. It included Prussia and Brandenburg and its capital was Berlin. Prussia expanded to seize north Germany and west Poland in the 18-19th centuries, and united Germany under its leadership in 1871.

> Judged by English and French standards, Germany at the beginning of the nineteenth century was an economically backward country. Its economic basis was feudalist agriculture. It had only a primitive industry ruled by medieval guild regulations. Politically, the distinguishing characteristic was the multitude of small states ruled by absolute princes. (Roll 1961, p. 213)
>
> Under Bismarck's astonishing adroit handling, the Great Power system in Europe was going to be dominated by Germany for two whole decades after 1870. He was known as the Iron Chancellor and the driving force behind the unification of Germany. (Kennedy 1987, p. 187)

United Italy

The French army invaded Italy during the Napoleonic wars, and Napoleon crowned himself King of Italy in 1805. The Congress of Vienna of 1815 after the defeat of Napoleon left Italy completely fragmented. Austria occupied Lombardy and Venice in the north, the Papal States controlled the centre of the Italian peninsula and various independent states existed in the south.

A series of political and military events brought unified kingdom of Italy by 1861. Italy obtained Venice in 1866 and Napoleon III withdrew his troops from Rome in 1870. Rome was united with Italy in 1870 and became the capital of unified Italy.

France

> The seventeenth century in Europe was the century of Louis XIV; he and French ascendancy and Versailles are the central motif of the story. The eighteenth century was equally the century of the rise of Prussia as a great power, and the chief figure in the story is Frederick II or Frederick the Great. (Wells 1925, p. 528)

France became the dominant power of Europe in the 17th and 18th centuries, only to be eclipsed by Britain.

> England's dual for primacy with France was to last for more than a century, and was concluded only by the battles of Trafalgar (1805) and Waterloo (1815) (Rowse 1979, p. 87).
>
> From 1685 things began to swing against France. By the end of 1689 France stood alone against the United Provinces, England, the Habsburg Empire, Spain, Savoy and the major German states (Kennedy 1987, p. 102).

In the 1780s the French monarchy faced a mounting financial crisis with huge debts on the brink of bankruptcy after a century of foreign wars—Louis XIV's wars, the War of the Spanish Succession, the Seven Years' War, and wars with Britain in North America and India. Though the independent United States, a blow to Britain's power, well pleased France, France was in a dire financial difficulty. For decades, philosophers such as Jean Jacques Rousseau had been preaching against the tyranny of absolute monarchy and its great allies, the nobility and the clergy. Together with the failure to reform national finances the costs of the wars led France to economic distress, political discontent and social malaise. From 1787 onwards, as the internal crises worsened, France seemed even less capable of playing a decisive role in foreign affairs.

Agriculture remained the fundamental of British wealth throughout the eighteenth century, and exports (whose ratio to the total income was probably less than 10 percent until the 1780s) were often subject to strong foreign competition and tariffs. British trade with the Baltic, Germany and the Mediterranean lands were still substantial in the early 19th century. Hence the Continental System (1806-12) still dealt a dreadful blow to British manufacturing industry. British colonial trade was much less important than domestic production, as we might imagine otherwise.

The British economy certainly suffered as the result of the blockade; however, Britain was well under way in the Industrial Revolution and she switched her trade to non-compliant countries apart from smuggling into the continental eager customers at the vast profits. The overall trend was clear: total exports of British produce rose from 21.7 million pounds (1794-6) to 37.5 million pounds (1804-6) to 44.4 million pounds (1814-6). (p. 130)

The blockade had another undesirable effect on French industry. It effectively protected French products from superior British products, for example, in the cotton industry. Hence the blockade made French industry less competitive and less enthusiastic for technical improvements.

Plunders paid for Napoleonic imperialism to a large extent. Internally Napoleon declared the enemies of the revolution and confiscated and sold their properties. In the conquered territories the French army confiscated Crown and feudal properties, plundered the spoils, imposed war indemnities and quartered French regiments in the conquered territories requiring them to supply the regiments. France thus made considerable profits while winning the wars.

The revolution in Spain against French hegemony eased the 1808 economic crisis in Britain; the revolution began in 1808 lasting for six years as a war of independence against Napoleonic France, just as Russia's break with Napoleon brought relief to the 1811-2 slump; the Russians pulled out of the blockade in December 1810.

Prior to the outbreak of the Spanish revolution in 1808, Spain was on the side of France during most of the preceding Anglo-French conflicts. By 1811, there were some 353 000 French troops in Spain, and Napoleon could spare only a very small number of the troops to the Russian campaign. The defeat of the Grand Army in Russia in 1812 weakened the morale of the French army. The Russians did not have the enthusiasm nor capacity for pursuing the French across Germany. The Eastern-European and peninsular (Spanish) campaigns interacted from 1813 onwards to effect the eventual downfall of Napoleon. (p. 134)

Napoleon's Continental System against Britain and France's Maginot Line against Germany were similar in concept: both were defensive strategies, acknowledging the opponents' military superiority. Both of these schemes failed their purposes miserably.

Napoleon was psychologically defeated when he asked for help from his allies by imposing the trade embargo against Britain. Napoleon had defeated the Russians at Friedland in 1807 and won over Tsar Alexander I into his alliance. Though the two were hardly good friends, they did not have any serious rift so as to go to war before the imposition of the Continental System. 'The Continental System or Continental Blockage, proclaimed by Napoleon I in 1806, prohibited trade between the countries of the European continent and Great Britain. It was annulled after Napoleon's defeat in Russia.' Its theoretical creator was the Frenchman Ferrier. (Marx & Engels 1989, p. 526) When Russia breached the embargo, Napoleon had to send troops to punish her which had been a friendly nation before the imposition of the trade sanctions. Tactical defeat at the hands of the Russians led Napoleon to the eventual collapse of his empire.

Napoleon was a great reader of Plutarch's *Parallel Lives* and of Roman history (Wells 1925, p. 584). Learning the ancient history made him a supreme general but did not prepare him to foresee the problems of the Continental System. More fundamental problem may have been the supremacy of the British navy and shipping, as Hitler experienced over a century later.

British Empire

The British Empire (from Queen Elizabeth I to Queen Elizabeth II) showed strongly the following features since its inception:

- a low degree of government participation
- a small army and a huge navy
- an emphasis upon individual freedom and unfettered press
- the strength of parliament and of individual initiatives

(Kennedy 1987, p. 176)

At the conclusion (1453) of the Hundred Years' War England lost the power status in France and subsequently directed her expansion zeal to the overseas, not to the European continent.

There are a few indications that the modern England ushered in around the year 1500. By the end of the 14th century, it was no longer possible for the English kings to impose both direct and indirect taxes without breaking the law. By this time in England, the Parliament had the right to grant taxation and the power to pass statutes. (Blake 1982, p. 91) In England, serfdom had practically disappeared in the last part of the 14th century, and free peasant proprietors became predominant since the 15th century onwards. In England at the end of the fifteenth century the feudal system started to disintegrate and people around the manors lost their jobs to be absorbed into the manufacturing industries. The foundation of capitalist mode of agricultural production in England was laid in the last third of the 15th century and the first decade of the 16th century. This new production absorbed the labourers who lost their jobs in the feudal lands. From this time onwards money, not the loyalty of masters and servants of feudalism, became the prime bonds of people. (Marx 1954, pp. 671-2) In England, capitalist production began simultaneously in manufacture and in agriculture (Marx 1968, p. 56). However, it is in the nature of capitalist production that industry develops more rapidly than agriculture (Marx 1971, p. 300). 'To all economic intents and purposes villeinage had disappeared by the end of the fifteenth century. By the sixteenth century, England was politically unified and there were no internal customs barriers.' (Walker 1978, p. 7) Villeinage was the social system by which villeins were personally bound to the lord and paid dues and services in return for working and harvesting the crops in the land. Villeins were similar to serfs. By the middle of the sixteenth century feudalism practically disappeared from England.

The custom of resident ambassadors in Europe started around the end of the fifteenth century when commerce first began to extend to the greater part of the nations of Europe. Its initial interest was the protection of commerce.

The modern English language was firmly established by the end of the fifteenth century: the year 1500 is often used to demark the modern English from the Middle English. In the early sixteenth century English became respectable to replace French and Latin as England's institutional language.

The Separatists, one group of Puritans, totally rejected the Anglican Church and declared the need for a new and more austere church. This dissent was a threat to the crown since the king was the head of the church. A law passed in 1593, during the reign of Queen Elizabeth I, forbade the Separatists from holding their own services. The Pilgrims, one group of Separatists in Nottinghamshire, became convinced that their future was in America.

Patrick Henry, one of the prime movers of the American independence campaign, said, 'Give me liberty, or give me death'.

Elizabeth Tudor became Queen of England and Ireland as Elizabeth I in 1558. I outline how she came to power in Section 15, Chapter 1, Book Five *The Sexual Laws*. I also briefly mention what was her historical role as English queen in Section 2, Chapter 1, Book Two *Religion*. She remained unmarried, childless and the queen until her death in 1603, ending the Tudor rule in England and Ireland, though her hold on power was slipping away in her late years. King James VI of Scotland succeeded the English throne as James I in 1603, first Stuart king of England and Ireland.

Scotland adopted Presbyterianism in 1560, while Mary Queen of Scots (1542-67), a Catholic, resided in France. Her mother was French, and Mary was educated to be more a French than a Scot and her hold on power in Scotland was tenuous from the circumstances. Her feminine beauty was in sharp contrast with Queen Elisabeth. Her personal and political ineptitude was also in sharp contrast with the queen. Her actions provoked rebellions among the Scottish nobles. Her second marriage in 1565 to her cousin Henry Stuart, earl of Darnley, led to her destruction—loss of her Scottish crown in favour of her only son James, refuge in England and her eventual execution.

Elizabeth felt a threat from Scotland since her accession because Mary had a legitimate claim for the English throne: she had Tudor blood through her grandmother, a sister of Henry VIII, and was next in line to the English throne. Elizabeth even built a castle in anticipation of the armed invasion from Scotland. However, she had Mary in refuge tried and executed in

1587. On the following year Philip II sent his Invincible Armada in order to punish England for aiding the Dutch cause and to dethrone the Protestant queen, only to be defeated by the storms and the English navy.

King James VI of Scotland (1566-1625) was raised a Scottish Presbyterian. James was a cousin of Queen Elizabeth I and the great-grandson of Henry VII's eldest daughter. Elizabeth died in the early hours of 24th March 1603 without an issue, and James was proclaimed King James I of England and Ireland in London later that day.

James believed in the divine rights of kings answerable only to God, which went against the well-established parliament and ultimately led to the English Civil War during his son's reign. James dissolved parliament after parliament. He strongly supported the Church of England, which angered Catholics: the idea that he was the head of both state and church naturally suited him. Under his rule the freedom of worship for Catholics in England continued, which frustrated Puritans who, a faction in the Church of England, did not want Catholics in England. Guy Fawkes, a Catholic zealot, plotted to blow up the royal family and the parliament building in 1605, though the scheme was uncovered before the execution of the plot. Fearing for his life, King James enacted the laws enforcing the allegiance and conformity of Puritans and Catholics,

King James I was noted for his commissioning of the new translation of the Bible. It seems that he meant by the new Bible to confirm the divine rights of kings and to maintain the social hierarchy. The Anglican Church was given the task: all committee members of about 50 were members of the Church of England, and the Church of England was to use the text. Under James the golden age of Elizabethan literature continued. The translation thus compiled reflected this fact. King James, or Authorised, Version appeared in 1611 and its beauty and grace established it as authoritative among the multitudes of the Bible in English. By the first half of the 18th century, the King James Version was unchallenged in the Anglican and Protestant churches. Though the translation was revised many times since the publication, for instance, the Revised Standard Version, it, original and revised, is still dominant in all English speaking countries today. The Common Bible, a new edition of the Revised Standard Version, appeared in 1973 and this was the first English translation approved by Protestant, Roman Catholic and Greek Orthodox churches.

King James I had to recall the parliament in 1621 faced with the prospect of war in Europe. Charles I, son of James I, became king of Great Britain and Ireland in 1625. He also believed in the divine right of kings. His authoritarian rule and quarrels with the Parliament led to the English Civil Wars. The parliamentary soldiers, called the Roundheads, which were badly organised and undisciplined, opposed the Royalists. In February 1645 the Parliament formed from the Roundheads the 22 000 New Model Army, a highly efficient fighting force. Together with Cromwell's Ironsides, a superb cavalry regiment, they defeated the royalist army. Cromwell, a convinced Puritan, was an effective leader of the parliamentary army. After the defeat Charles I stood for trial, and was convicted and executed in 1649. Cromwell became Lord Protector of the Commonwealth (1653-8). He banned Christmas but did not ban music which was his favourite recreation. He smoked a pipe, drank ale and had a heavy love of plain English food.

After the death of Cromwell in 1658, his son, Richard Cromwell, was proclaimed Lord Protector but he was forced to abdicate in the following year being a weak ruler. Fundamentally the English people became averse to the Puritan rule. The newly elected Parliament abolished the Cromwell's Government and restored the monarchy by the process called the Restoration; Charles II (1660-85), the son of Charles I, was proclaimed king in 1660.

The Glorious Revolution of 1688 firmly established a constitutional monarchy in England and set the backdrop for the overseas conquests. The revolution ousted Catholic James II, brother of and successor to Charles II, to be replaced by the joint monarchs of Mary, James' daughter, and her Protestant husband William of Orange. The bloodless revolution greatly enhanced the powers of the parliament, with Mary and William acceding with the Bill of Rights. The British completed its dominance in the Indian Peninsula by 1761.

Britain became the ultimate victor of the European rivalries and its dominance lasted well into the 20th century. The British Empire's prestige peaked during the reign of Queen Victoria (1837-1901) and the year 1851, the year of the Great Exhibition which was held in Hyde Park, London, is said to be the pinnacle of the empire. Germany and Russia were late comers.

The decline of trade among other indications heralded the decline of the British Empire. Inglis Palgrave, the President of the Economic Section in the British Association for the Promotion of Scientific Development, expressed the opinion in 1883 that the days of great trade profits of England were over. Many other people shared the same view at that time. (Marx & Engels 1970, p. 449)

Section 5 China: Ming and Ch'ing Dynasties

Just after the establishment of the new empire the Ming dynasty was insecure, the Mongols being in the steppe nearby. Emperor Hongwu (Hung-wu) (1368-98) promptly banned foreign trade and closed the Superintendencies of Merchant Shipping and insisted that all foreigners come to China in the form of tributary relations. He was afraid of the conspiracy under the guise of trade. Tributary relations were cumbersome and expensive but better than wars. Despite the ban the foreign trade continued in illicit and the government missed out on the tax revenues. (Goethe 1985, p. 203)

The manufacture of pottery received the imperial patronage under the Ming dynasty to be developed with extraordinary energy and success. 'Painted decorations began to be used and it was in the fifteenth century that the finest blue and white porcelain was achieved.' (Wells 1971, p. 605)

> In a similar way the potters' art so outstripped painting that the European importers of Ming wares called all porcelain China, after the country that made the finest products (Cotterell & Morgan 1975, p. 225).

The Ming introduced paper money in 1374; however, they phased it out after 1450, not being able to rely upon. China reintroduced paper money in the 1850s after the Western influence.

Ming Hongwu, the first Ming emperor, set the basis of the Ming dynasty (1368-1644) which became increasingly inward looking, traditionalist and antiquarian. Yonglo (Yung-lo) became the emperor with the support of the palace eunuchs. Under Yung-lo (1402-24), China became once more the great and wealthy power.

He also directed to compile the encyclopaedia, which was completed as the world's largest known encyclopaedia in 1407, known as 'Great Canon of the Yung-lo Era'. Only 400 volumes of 11 095 original volumes have survived to this day.

Emperor Yung-lo dispatched Zheng He (Cheng Ho), the admiral, as maritime embassy to south and east of China. Cheng Ho conducted the official overseas expeditions between 1405 and 1433. He was a court eunuch but was suited being a Muslim to negotiate with Arab Muslim rulers. On occasion consisting of scores of ships and tens of thousands of men, the fleet visited ports from Malacca and Ceylon to the Red Sea entrances and East Africa. (Kennedy 1987, p. 6) He carried out seven expeditions with each the purpose of embassy, trade and scientific expeditions. The large ship was of 1250 tonnes and carried over 1000 men. Columbus' ships were of 100 tonnes. The first expedition consisted of 62 vessels and 28 000 men. The purpose of the expeditions was diplomatic and peaceful without any chance of forceful landing or occupation. (Milston 1978, pp. 204-11) Cheng Ho was a eunuch (the inside party) hence represented an emperor rather than the government. The bureaucrats (the outside party) were left out and jealous. The bureaucrats' rage together with other factors led to a series of events. After Yung-lo's death in 1424, the Chinese decisively reversed the policy, possibly by the influence of the Confucian officials who upheld anti-foreign and anti-mercantile attitudes.

In 1433 the expedition suddenly stopped. In 1436, an imperial edict banned to build the seagoing ships. The key element of the China's retreat was the conservatism of the Confucian bureaucracy. The official records of Cheng Ho's voyages were burnt in the 1470s. Between 1500 and 1550 a series of edicts made it an offence to build, retain, or sail in a ship with more than two masts. Similarly the ancient Egyptians neglected foreign commerce; however, the Chinese held it in the utmost contempt in the modern era of European designation (Smith 1991, p. 384). China became inward looking empire, rejecting the outside world. Sixty four years after the last expedition by Cheng Ho, Vasco da Gama rounded the tip of Africa.

> Contact with the Western countries, who were familiar with the crops of Americas, led to the introduction of groundnuts, the sweet potato and maize in the sixteenth century (Cotterell & Morgan 1975, p. 203).

The first years of Wanli's (Wan-li's) reign (1572-1620) of the Ming saw prosperous activity in many quarters. Agriculture thrived and the population expanded. Trade increased, and the Chinese enjoyed some European curiosities brought by the Portuguese, such as 20 foot cannons, superior in design to anything the Chinese had, which the Chinese placed with great reverence on the top of the Wall, defiantly overlooking nomad territory. (Fryer 1975, p. 147)

The Europeans reached China through the sea route in the 16th century. Most of the early arrivals were Portuguese traders who the Chinese allowed to establish a settlement in Macao [Macau] in the 1550s. Also the Jesuit missionaries, Alessandro Valignano and then Matteo Ricci, arrived in China. (Roberts 1998, p. 19)

From early times the Chinese referred to those people who did not recognise the superiority of Chinese culture as barbarians. The gentry were the main opponents of Christian missionaries. The activities of missionaries posed the challenge to the cultural hegemony of Confucian scholars, many of whom occupied the government posts. (p. 101)

The Jesuit Matteo Ricci mastered the Chinese language and the Confucian Classics. Though Emperor Wanli was delighted with Ricci' clock, the Chinese could not appreciate the scientific knowledge in casting cannons. The Chinese society went into a rapid decline. (Harris 1999, p. 55)

> Matteo Ricci's arrival in China in 1583 heralded a new departure in Chinese science. The ideas and inventions that he and his successor colleagues of the Jesuit Order introduced were quite new to the Chinese mind; once they had accepted that there was value in these concepts, the Chinese insisted that they should be described under the general term of the 'New Science' rather than that of 'Western Science'. (Loewe 1990, p. 245)
>
> They [Jesuits] showed their superiority in the all-important matter of predicting eclipses; they applied the principles of geometry to an understanding of the motions of the planets; they introduced a circle which was divided into 360 rather than 365.25 degrees; and they set about the manufacture of clocks, telescopes and instruments used in observing the heavens (p. 246).
>
> This was followed by *Complete Agricultural Management*, which was printed in 1639. Its author was a man who merits brief attention. A well-known figure in the world of politics, Xu Guangqi (Hsu Kuang-ch'i) (1562-1633) was a convert to Christianity; and it was doubtless from the Jesuit fathers that he had gained his acquaintance with the agricultural work of contemporary Europe, and with crops such as sweet potatoes.
>
> Comment: The fact that the author obtained the Western agricultural technique does not prove that the West was in advance of the East in this field; however, he must have at least some respect or worth in the management. (p. 255)

Since the arrival of the Jesuits in China in the 16th century, they were active in the scientific works, especially astronomy and mathematics, in the hope to impress the Chinese and to convert them to Christianity. With the advanced knowledge shown to them, the Chinese did not show any interest in them. It did little to alter the character of Ming intellectual life. They stopped learning from the various reasons such as conceit and figuratively speaking, old age. The Chinese traditionally were arrogant towards foreigners and had a wrong attitude to something foreign.

> Contact between China and the West from the late sixteenth century onward brought

> knowledge of these cataclysmic change to the Chinese, but they showed remarkably little interest in them until the late nineteenth century (Murowchick 1994, p. 155).
>
> Their results support the view that the Sung age (AD 960-1279) was a culmination of a period in which China's science and technology outstripped those of Europe; but by the middle of the Ming period (AD 1368-1644) the balance was changing beyond recognition (Loewe 1990, p. 110).
>
> A number of scholars have concluded that whereas up to perhaps 1500 China's understanding of nature, her appreciation of the heavens and her use of mechanical device, was considerably in advance of those of Europe, thereafter it was Europe which drew ahead (p. 239).

Among the reasons why the Chinese were reluctant to adopt Western technologies, we must include the following observations. The contact between China and Europe was limited to a small number of the Chinese and the Europeans before the 19th century. Thus the fact the Europeans had superior knowledge in many fields was only scholarly knowledge, and besides Europe was a faraway land removed from the everyday life of the bulk of the Chinese. After the contact was massive, especially military, from the middle of the 19th century the comparison became real and meaningful.

In the course of the 17th century, the Manchus in the north-east were threatening to invade China, taking advantage of the rebellions in northwest China arising from heavy taxes. Many gentries abhorred the rebellions and looked at the Manchus, the descendants of the Jurchen and being sinicised, as the lesser evil and threw their lot with them.

The Ming dynasty was about to fall. The cycle of dynastic rise and fall did not correspond with the economic rise and fall for the Ming as for the T'ang. The Ming court was certainly weakened but the economic development moved in a large cycle and economically the society was in a good shape.

Contrary to the policies of segregation, the Qing (Manchu, or Ch'ing or Ching) government imposed the hairdo of pigtails on the Chinese males beyond the age of puberty. As the Manchus were conquering China in the early 17th century, they issued the order for Chinese men to adopt this Manchu custom such that they could identify the Chinese who submitted to the Manchu rule. The Manchus could not enforce the order in some districts because of ferocious opposition from the Chinese, and killed many thousands of Chinese in some districts to uphold the order. Though the American Indians and the Indian Brahmins practised pigtails, the Manchu custom was quite unique in that the front of the head was shaved and the hair was braided into a single queue at the back of the head.

Once firmly in power, the Manchu government issued the edict on pigtails with the death penalty for non-compliance in 1644 and again in 1645 though Buddhist monks were exempt. It took the government 10 years to enforce compliance on the Chinese. The imposition of pigtails became an emotional issue through the Manchu era in China. The rebels to the Manchu government cut off their queues and let their hairs grow in front to show defiance. It is said that some rebellions erupted simply because of the deep resentment on this issue. The imposition order stayed till the end of the Manchu rule, and even after the collapse of the government some Chinese sported pigtails as a personal preference.

The Manchus were a land-minded people and conservative. The Manchu government spent their budget on the army rather than on the navy. They were serious about the landed threat such as posed by Russia in Sinkiang but made light of the overseas threats of Western nations. Traditionally the Chinese were prepared for the threats from the land but not from the sea, and they were not aware of the advanced Western military technology at this time.

The Manchus, though governed China as Confucian ruler, took the following measures to prevent assimilation into Chinese society:

- looking to Manchuria as their homeland
- retention of the Manchu military force as the Eight Banners
- use of Manchu as an official language
- prohibition of marriage between Manchu and Chinese
  note: The prohibition was rescinded in the early 1900's and since then many people intermarried.
- interdiction on Manchu women on foot binding (Chinese custom)

(Roberts 1998, p. 4)

The Han Chinese spoke several mutually unintelligible dialects yet have the same culture, the same traditions and the same written language. In later developments, the Manchus and the Hui (Chinese Muslims) also spoke Mandarin and utilised Chinese characters.

When European demand for Chinese goods and markets began to grow, Emperor Qian-long (Ch'ien-lung) issued an edict in 1757 restricting foreign trade to Canton. Thus the Canton System (1757-1840) came into being. Canton was designated as the only port open to foreign ships. A group of merchants (Co-hong) had sole dealings with groups of foreign traders and in effect a lucrative monopoly. A Manchu official appointed by the imperial government made sure that the custom duties went to the government as well as into his own pocket.

There was a large demand for Chinese tea, silk and porcelain in the West; however, the Chinese did not need any commodities from the West--except some after the Industrial Revolution in England--hence payment for the Chinese commodities had to be made in silver. This situation alarmed the Western nations, though unlike the Chinese imperial government many Chinese traders were eager to engage in commerce with the West. By the 1770s the East India Company realised that they could pay for Chinese commodities with opium made in India, thus exported a large amount of opium despite the imperial ban on the importation. (Harris 1999, p. 65)

Under Emperor Ch'ien-lung (r. 1736-95) the Chinese empire reached its greatest extent, and the prolonged peace and rising living standard were the most likely causes of the population growth during the 18th century (Roberts 1998, p. 2). The Manchu modelled their government on that of the Ming and set out to fill the role of Confucian ruler. In the three outer halls of the Forbidden City, the imperial palace, the emperor performed the public duties. In the inner palace, the emperor lived a segregated existence, accompanied only by the empress, the harem and the eunuchs. (pp. 3-4)

Until the end of the 18th century, the growth of agricultural outputs exceeded the growth of population in China. The opening up of new land for cultivation and in part the increase of yields accounted for the growth of production. (p. 8)

China has been a vast country splitting into many geographic and economic regions, and has been mostly self-sufficient economically by exchanging the products between regions. Naturally this arrangement led to unimportance of overseas trade and cultural pride and slight of the foreign goods and peoples. However, the Chinese were prepared to accept new inventions and new ideas depending on the circumstances, often with the pretence that they originated in China.

The Tungus-speaking Manchus conquered the entire China by 1644, yet within a century their own language died out in China. Though Manchu in the written form was the official language of the Manchu state till 1911, people even at court stopped speaking the tongue by the 18th century. (Ostler 2006, pp. 21, 144) A large number of the Chinese migrated into Manchuria after 1900, and in Manchuria today 90% of the population are Chinese and only

5% are Manchu who speak Chinese and follow Chinese customs. The Manchu language died out in Manchuria and is spoken only by the small number of people in Xinxiang in the Chinese Henan Province at present.

It was a common notion in China that the property, the chief of which was land, belonged to the family and not to the individual members. Hence upon the death of the male head of the family the wealth was divided equally among his sons.

At the end of the 18th century China looked at the outside world with a sense of superiority and a deep ignorance (Roberts 1998, p. 22).

When the Europeans approached China for trade in the modern context, neither side knew the strength of the other with certainty. The Europeans were possibly aware that their military organisation and equipment were superior to those of the Chinese: the Chinese were totally unaware of that.

There were enormous demands in England for Chinese silk and tea. Unlike tea there was a quota on the amount of silk a ship could load. There was no doubt that England would have imported more silk if the Chinese government had not imposed quotas. (Boulnois 2005, p. 379)

Chinese ideas influenced Western thinkers such as Voltaire, Leibniz, Quesnay, Adam Smith and Benjamin Franklin. The European missionaries' reports in the sixteenth century were full of admiration for China. In the nineteen century the missionary reports were not favourable at all. It is not that China went backwards or was static but Europe made cataclysmic progress in these centuries. Possibly the missionaries were not aware of these comparative changes in China and Europe.

The Chinese people had known the medicinal effects of opium for a long time. They did not adopt the custom of smoking opium until the Dutch introduced tobacco in the 17th century. In the reign of Yongzheng (Yung-cheng) (1723-35) the government recognised the danger of its use and made illegal of its sale and consumption. From 1773 onwards, the East India Company became involved in the growth of opium poppy and China became a lucrative market. In 1796 the Chinese court made the importation of opium illegal.

In the early 19th century, the trade imbalance between Britain and China became enormous; China exported a huge quantity of tea and imported only a third of the export, the balance being made up by silver. China was largely self-sufficient, and the bulk of its population lived at subsistence level and could not afford foreign goods. However, from the mid-1820s, China became a net exporter of silver through the importation of opium. In 1834 England ended the monopoly of the East India Company under the pressure of free trade. As the result the number of ships involved and the amount of opium traded rose rapidly. When Chinese officials seized opium chests from the British merchants in Guangzhou (Canton) in March 1839, a war broke out.

A sea-battle during the Opium War [1839-42], when the Chinese learned that their slow moving, cumbersome wooden junks were no match for European canon (Cotterell & Morgan 1975, p. 239).

The subsequent treaties (of Nanjing (Nanking) in 1842; of Bogue in 1843), which marked the end of the Opium War, were a complete success for the British and at the same time a total humiliation for the Chinese. The overwhelming British military superiority forced the treaties on China, which ceded Hong Kong to Britain, opened five coastal ports (Canton, Shanghai, Amoy, Foochow, Ningpo) and abolished the monopoly of the Co-hong. The colonial boundaries of Hong Kong were extended in stages and the Chinese Government agreed under duress to a 99-year lease to start in 1898. These treaties were a turning point in China's relations with the West. The opening of the five ports was extended to other Western powers. Unwillingness on the part of the Chinese Government and people to adhere to the treaties led to further campaigns by the British and French forces. Hong Kong was returned to Chinese sovereignty in 1997.

> Britain and France actually captured Peking in the Second Opium War (1856-60) and the Franco-Chinese War (1883-5) wrung suzerainty of Indo-China from a dynasty unwilling to face up to the desperate need for modernisation (p. 239).

As the result of the Second Opium War, China had to make further concessions to Great Britain, France, Russia and America. China legalised opium in 1858, and agreed for ambassadors of the signatory nations to reside in Peking. The smuggling trade immediately ceased, a small duty being charged on importation. Opium imports peaked in 1879. Opium came to be grown in China and the import from India fell off, still it remained a serious social menace. The Chinese government did not revive the edict forbidding its use until the anti-opium campaign of 1906.

The rivalry between England and Germany in Europe was played out in China as well, when Germany entered shipping and banking in China after 1870. German shipping in China was second only to England though the former was a long way behind the latter. The German banks set up the Deutsche-Asiatische Bank, the only financial institution in China which rivalled the British banks. The Germans strived to create a sphere of influence to match the other European powers.

By 1895 the customs duties and the revenues from the postal services made up one third of the total revenues of the Chinese government.

In the middle of the nineteenth century China realised the need for technological advance and industrialisation; it was the high-level officials who realised these needs, not private entrepreneurs as had happened in England a century earlier. The senior officials in the government put forward the slogan 'self-strengthening'; Chinese culture reinforced by Western technology.

After the Opium wars, a reform movement within the context of the Manchu (Ch'ing) Empire gathered strength from the 1870s. However, Dowager Cixi (Tz'u-hsi) who had been the real power behind the throne frustrated modernisation attempts, fearing modernisation would weaken her authority.

In the 19th century, Britain traded opium in exchange for Chinese tea, silk and porcelain. The opium came from Britain's colonial outposts of India and Afghanistan. The Chinese government had to submit to this trade after the defeats of the Opium wars of 1839-42 (China vs Britain) and 1856-60 (China vs Britain and France). Under these unequal treaties, China lost control of her customs revenues and sovereignty over her navigable rivers, and foreign companies built railways into the interior to transport the products of the mines to the coast.

The Treaty of Nanking opened China to English commerce. English manufacturing industry which had been sluggish since 1837 revived suddenly, and 1845 and 1846 marked a period of greatest prosperity especially in the cotton industry. (Marx 1959, p. 407)

The introduction of steamships from the mid-1800s by the European nations and the opening of the Suez Canal in 1869 greatly reduced the cost and the distance of transport between Europe and China. Europe still could not compete with the Chinese in silkworm breeding and had to import 50% of raw silk from China. At the end of the 19th century the biggest customer of trade with China was Britain followed by France, though as far as silk was concerned France was the largest buyer. (Boulnois 2005, p. 384)

Just before the Opium wars, China was inactive in the international arena and was known menacingly as a sleeping lion--a passive but formidable adversary. The Opium wars shattered that myth. China did not want anything from foreign countries except gold and silver through the centuries, cheap English textiles made by machines after the industrial revolution, and opium in the 19th century. 'Although China did not suffer outright colonisation or dismemberment after the Opium War, the Western nations posed more and more of a threat to China as a polity and a civilisation.' (Ebrey 1996, p. 220) The utter defeats in the Opium wars were the catalyst for Chinese thinkers to debate the value of traditional culture vs Western culture and the question of Westernisation in China. Japan defeated China convincingly in the war whose end the Treaty of Shimonoseki of 1895 marked, and got away with a brute aggression over the Chinese territories. The treaty allowed the Japanese to set up factories in China. Other nations followed suit under the terms 'the most favoured nations' of earlier treaties. From this time on foreign factories and mining enterprises developed making use of cheap local labour and the lack of health and safety legislations for workers. The Chinese thus revealed all the weaknesses and subsequently international powers lined up to carve up the Chinese territories.

After the humiliating defeat by Japan in the Sino-Japanese War (1894-5) and the subsequent demand for concessions by the great powers, serious reform movements arose in the form of a series of clubs and even within the Chinese government. Kang Youwei (K'ang Yu-wei), forming a club, had vigorously objected to the peace treaty with Japan and pushed for reform. Chinese Emperor Guangxu (Kuang-hsu) himself tried to enforce various reforms in 1898. Subsequently K'ang Yu-wei headed the Hundred Days of Reform and became a trusted imperial adviser. However the reform movements alarmed the conservative and privileged class in China, and Tz'u-hsi, Empress Dowager, tried to crush the reform. She, backed by the army, carried out a coup d'état; she imprisoned the emperor in his palace and executed six young reformers, but K'ang Yu-wei managed to escape to Japan. Thus the reform did not have a chance to materialise.

In the 19th century China experienced outbursts of rebellions. The White Lotus Rebellion (1796-1805) raged in the area between the Yellow and Yangtze rivers: The Taiping Rebellion (1851-64) in south China and two major Muslim rebellions (one in Yunnan from 1855 to 1873, the other in the north-west from 1862 to 1873). China was also afflicted by the Nien and Miao rebellions around this time. Scholars agree that the fundamental cause of the rebellions was increased population with a slight increase of cultivated lands. It was the period of dynastic decline, particularly from the 1840s, and neglect of public administration, both acting in ever worsening vicious circles. According to one estimate the population of China in 1779 was 275 million and in 1850, 430 million. Though large land owners became wealthy, the bulk of the peasants became impoverished and desperate for food, and any seemingly minor incident in a locality triggered a widespread rebellion. The land owners wealthy enough built granaries with walls and had also self-defence forces. It so happened that the very army who were sent to quell local disturbances often preyed on people more savagely than the bandits which had started a rebellion. Contemporary Chinese officials, contrary to the Western views, looked at these rebellions as the fundamental problem facing China, and at Western encroachment into the Chinese territories as doing business and a periphery problem. The Western impact was limited along the coast and the major rivers, and the vast interior was riddled with hunger, unemployment, rebellions and inadequate tax revenues. The rebellions suspended the printing of the classics and the civil service examinations both of which, many people thought, were the first duties of the state.

There were serious consequences from the rebellions. It is said that 20 to 30 million people died as the result of the Taiping Rebellion alone. Loss of military control on the affected areas meant loss of tax revenues, especially land tax. The government resorted to transit tax for goods transported and also to the sale of examination ranks. The latter resulted in unqualified people gaining official positions and the competence of the government ran down. Constant fighting also meant that military officials gained recognition and were promoted over qualified civilian officials.

It is also noteworthy what the Taipings aspired. They aimed for equality between men and women; the abolition of concubinage, domestic slavery, foot-binding, opium smoking; and the redistribution of land. They were the anti-establishment movements throughout Chinese history, and the communists and nationalists of the later era put up the similar slogans.

> The balance of world power slowly shifted in the eighteenth century without anyone in China taking much notice. Until 1700 China's material culture had been unrivalled; its standard of living was among the best in the world, and inventions flowed more commonly from East to West than vice versa. Yet by the nineteenth century, China found itself out matched in material and technological resources by Western nations. Europeans had been coming to trade at south Chinese ports since the late Ming. Spain and Portugal had been the main European traders in the sixteenth century; their place taken by the Dutch in the seventeenth century and the English in the eighteenth century. (p. 234)

It was at the end of the eighteenth century that the Ch'ing dynasty reached an irreversible stage in its decline. The decline manifested as the growth of bureaucratic corruption, the failure to achieve technological progress, and overpopulation. The population was estimated to have doubled in the 18th century. The revolt of the White Lotus sect in the 1790s spread in China. They preached the coming of the Buddha, promising an end to suffering and a new material and spiritual order. The White Lotus rebellion which started in 1796 was a symptom of the dynastic decline and the dynasty terminated in 1911.

Further Developments of China

Section 2 China's Dynastic Cycles, Chapter 2, Book Four *The Third Prophecy* gives out historical events in China; I present the later accounts of China under the heading of Modern China. Also readers should get a better insight into modern Chinese history from Section 3 Communism in China, Chapter 1, Book Three *Communism*.

Section 6 Overview of Further Developments till Early 20th Century, and Equilibrium Year of China-Europe Balance

> This was the era when Africa and South East Asia were being carved up by the powers, who each feared the others would get the best pickings. Seeing how easily China was defeated by Japan, the Western nations began scrambling for concessions in China. Germany seized Jiaozhou in Shandong [Shantung]; Russia got Liaodong [Liaotung]; Britain leased Weihai [Wei-hai] in Shandong [Shantung] and the New Territories next to Hong Kong; France leased Guangzhou [Canton] Bay near Hainan Island. Only the Italian demand for the territory was successfully refused. (Ebrey 1996, p. 254)

In the year 1800, the Europeans occupied or controlled 35% of the land surface of the world; by 1878 this figure had risen to 67%; and by 1914 to over 84% (Kennedy 1987, p. 150).

After the 1840s there was a spectacular growth of an integrated global economy, which drew ever more regions into a transoceanic and transcontinental trading and financial network centred upon Western Europe, and in particular upon Great Britain (p. 143).

Technology resulting from the Industrial Revolution began to realise in military and naval warfare only after the second half of the 19th century. Railways, telegraphs, quick-firing guns, steam propulsion and armoured warships became the decisive indications of military strength. (p. 144)

Since the publication of *On the Origin of Species* (1859) by Charles Darwin many people lost faith in the Bible. Darwin proposed the evolution theory--Darwinian explanation--in defiance with the biblical creation theory.

When *On the Origin of Species* was published, nobody, not even the author himself, expected it to sell well. In the event, it became an instant best-seller. Its central theme that God did not create the animal species, humans included, which were the result of evolution, became the controversy of the century. The creation story as narrated in the Old Testament was the prevailing notion in Europe up to the publication of the above book. However, a body of evidence challenging the creation theory was building up in the preceding century. Natural selection or the survival of the fittest is the process by which the most suited species come to be dominant in a particular environment. The major cause of anti-Darwinian view was that humans had evolved from lower animals; the Bible says that God created human in the image of God. (Davison 1993, pp. 25, 250)

The Great Powers of the world met in Berlin to reach an agreement over trade, navigation and boundaries in West Africa and Congo in the winter of 1884-5. This conference can be seen symbolically as the zenith of Old Europe's predominance in global affairs. Most Europeans at the time thought that Europe was the centre of the world. (Kennedy 1987, p. 194)

Towards the end of the 19th century, the great power struggles were no longer merely over European issues--as they had been in 1830 or even 1860--but over markets and territories that ranged across the globe (p. 195).

Italy, Germany and Japan were relative newcomers to international affairs at the beginning of the 20th century. The first two became established as unified nations in 1870-1; the third began to emerge from its self-imposed isolation after the Meiji Restoration of 1868.

When the Americans demanded that the Japanese open their ports to assist Chinese trade in the middle of the 19th century, at first the Japanese were determined to fight off the foreigners. There were two separate incidents; one in the fief of Satsuma in 1862 and the other in the fief of Chosu in 1863. The samurai warriors of these two fiefs were known as the most warlike of all Japan and were firm anti-Westerners. However, when these warriors learned that their obsolete weapons were no match to the Western powers during the battlements, they made about-face and supported to learn from the West, ceasing all hostilities against them. The Japanese combatants quickly changed their stance from a closed policy to an open policy. These people later formed the nucleus of the central government and upheld the basic foreign policy of the open door to the West.

Commodore Mathew Perry who was instrumental in opening the Japanese to the West made an interesting prophecy about Japan. He predicted that the feudal society of Samurais would become a world power. (Mercer 1996, p. 903)

Meiji Restoration of Imperial Government in 1868

The Meiji Restoration, the restoration of power to the emperor, followed demands for open ports by Commodore Perry and the American fleet in 1853 and 1854.

The 16-year-old Emperor and his advisers from the Satsuma and Chosu clans took the reign from the Tokugawa shogun, Yoshinobu, whose family had been shoguns for 200 years.

> But, unlike China, under Emperor Meiji (1868-1912) Japan became an industrial power soon capable of defending its sovereignty (Cotterell & Morgan 1975, p. 239).
>
> The Sino-Japanese War of 1894-5, after which Korea, Taiwan and parts of Manchuria were ceded to Japan, had shown the advantage of an oriental country could gain from Western technology. The modernised Japanese armies had inflicted a crushing defeat on Chinese forces. (p. 241)

The defeat of the Russian military by the Japanese in 1905 was the turning point in the history of Russia: the defeat dramatically weakened the hold of the autocratic Tsar and his ministers.

Port Arthur; January 1905
Bloody Sunday; January 1905
The battle of Tsushima; May 1905
The mutiny of the battleship Potemkin; June 1905
The peace of Portsmouth; September 1905

Bloody Sunday took place on 22nd January 1905 in the Russian capital of St Petersburg on the way to the Tsar's Winter Palace: Some 200 000 men, women and children marched to present a petition to Tsar Nicholas II. Police fired upon the peaceful demonstrators killing more than 100. War with Japan was going badly. The shattering defeat suffered when Port Arthur fell to the Japanese in the first week of 1905 brought affairs to a crisis point. The Mensheviks and Bolsheviks did not participate in the march. The Japanese navy inflicted another crushing defeat on the Russian navy and its reputation in the Battle of Tsushima.

After the Russo-Japanese War (1904-5), Russian influence in southern Manchuria and Korea was at an end. Russia's attention was again turned to the West, especially to the Balkans. These policy changes contributed to the outbreak of World War One.

The European powers had partitioned most of Africa and Asia by 1900. Around 1900 the European world empires reached their zenith and after that the United States, a non-European Western power, staked its first claim to power and influence in the Pacific regions. (Grenville 1994, pp. 6, 8)

In spite of the settled conflicts of 1776 (American independence) and 1812 (the US declaration of war on Britain concerning shipping), the only threat to American prosperity came from Britain before the 20th century. However, mutual trade and the inflow of British funds to develop America's vast economic potential minimised this threat.

The American Civil War of 1861-5 was:

- the first modern war and
- the victory of the north meant the end of the aristocratic age.

(Rowse 1979, p. 138)

Lincoln stood for the union. He was opposed to slavery but thought it as a secondary issue. Slavery was standing in the way of the union and the issue came to the forefront. Slavery had been abolished in British colonies in 1834.

The United States emerged as the world power backed by its industrial and military strength by the end of the First World War. The United States was by 1918 indisputably the strongest power in the world.

When Italy, Germany and Japan were fully industrialised at the beginning of the 20th century, they found that the Great Powers had already partitioned the globe for the supply of raw materials and the export of manufactured products, and demanded the re-division of the world. This led to the building up of international tensions in the decade or so after 1900.

Britain was imposing in 1900. It possessed the largest empire the world had ever seen; some twelve million square miles of land and perhaps a quarter of the globe's population. However, after 1870, the shifting balance of the world forces eroded British supremacy. The spread of industrialisation and consequent changes in the military strength weakened the relative position of Britain. It desperately wanted peace to maintain the status quo, fearing any disturbance would weaken the British hold on the globe.

Britain soon lost the early lead it possessed. Industrial production grew at an annual rate of about 4% in the period 1820-1840 and about 3% from 1840 to 1870, and became sluggish between 1875 and 1894 and it grew at just over 1.5% annually. Both the United States and Germany grew a lot faster and moved ahead of Britain. (Kennedy 1987, p. 228)

British share of the total manufacturing outputs:

22.9% in 1880
13.6% in 1913
(p. 228)

British share of the world trade:

23.2% in 1880
14.1% in 1911-3
(p. 228)

> From 1870 to 1970 the history of Britain was one of steady and almost unbroken decline, economically, militarily and politically, relative to other nations, from the peak of prosperity and power which her industrial revolution achieved for her in the middle of the nineteen century (p. 229).

By the turn to the 20th century, Britain was hard pressed in maintaining its empire. It was obliged to make concessions to the US on issues such as the isthmian canal, Alaska boundary, seal fisheries, thus securing peace in the western hemisphere.

Germany was possibly the most powerful state in Europe, exceeding Britain on the eve of the First World War.

The book *China: Land of Discovery and Invention* (1986) by RKG Temple describes in a quite interesting manner how the Chinese were far advanced than the Europeans in the various fields of technology before modern times. The Europeans adopted many of these innovations in much later centuries, often disguising the origins. It was stated earlier in this chapter that the European Renaissance was the turning period in the balance between the East and the West. After the Renaissance, European philosophers became interested in the phenomena of the material world.

In the process, the Renaissance Papacy (from the end of the Western Schism to the beginning of the Reformation in the sixteenth century) and the Catholic Church became noticeably secularised.

The Renaissance covers broadly 200 years in Western Europe, and there must have been a time, theoretically at least, when the two contenders' levels of material culture were equally matched and neither side, the East and the West, was better or worse than the other.

If I am to pinpoint the year when the two contenders might have attained that balance, I will tentatively give out the year 1492, when Christopher Columbus discovered the American continent by chance. Earlier that year, Granada, the last stronghold of the Moors, fell to Spanish forces, which completed the expulsion of the Moors from Spain thus consolidating the monarchy of Ferdinand and Isabella. Later that year Columbus obtained three ships and 88 men from the monarchy and set sail. The Atlantic crossing took them two months and nine days.

Some historians assume that the above year is the beginning of the modern era for the Europeans, recognising the fact that the discovery of the New World brought the Europeans enlarged horizons and allowed the subsequent colonisation of the huge American continent with all the economic and political consequences. Hence the year 1492 chosen is not as arbitrary as it may seem at first as the East and the West balance and the start of the modern era.

My history teacher taught me that Columbus discovered America in 1492. However, this statement is not true. I noted earlier that there is archaeological evidence to confirm, prior to 1492, Viking habitations and Chinese visitations in the North American coast. With their seaworthy long ships the Vikings probably reached North America about AD 1000. (Williams 1987, p. 95) It is true that the Vikings and Chinese explored North America before 1492; however, it is also true that Columbus discovered America in 1492, though not for the first time, and his repeatable voyage to the American continent opened the way for subsequent voyages by other Europeans. After the year 1492, the trade with the American continent and the Orient ushered in the Commercial Revolution in Europe with an emphasis on accumulating gold and silver bullion. Importation of gold and silver dealt a hard blow to feudal land owners in Europe. Accordingly the fact that Columbus, a Genoese, was not the first man who discovered America does not affect my proposition of the balancing year between the East and the West.

From the fourth century onwards, the so-called civilisation was moving from the Mediterranean basin to the northern part of Europe. The transition from the Mediterranean age to the European age was obvious at the eighth century and seems completed in 1492 when Columbus discovered America, and the Mediterranean era was at an end. (Grant 1969, p. xvii)

I am to propose the following two hypotheses:

Hypothesis One: China was superior to Europe in the aggregate of material culture until the year 1492 and the position reversed after that year.

Scientists widely use hypothesis in the scientific disciplines to presuppose the existence of a law. Scientists establish a hypothesis from what they know, without sufficient evidence, to see whether it contradicts any observations. This hypothesis becomes a law if there are no discrepancies between the hypothesis and observed phenomena. If somebody wants to overturn the hypothesis, that person must present enough evidence against it.

I compare material civilisation in aggregate terms and when we focus our attention to details, the foregoing hypothesis does not hold in some fields. For example, China is superior to Europe even in the 21st century in such pursuits as food, ceramics and artefacts.

Hypothesis Two: The Europeans were superior to the Chinese in the practice of idealism until the establishment of the People's Republic of China in 1949.

It is interesting to note that only after military confrontations the Chinese and the Japanese realised that their weapons and their material cultural levels were vastly inferior to those of the Europeans. Probably military equipment is a good measure of the standard of material civilisation since we know well that every nation uses all its skills to develop effective defence systems. The confrontations just described took place at the latter half of the nineteenth century. According to my hypothesis the West started overtaking the East around the year 1492. It is amazing that the East woke up to the change of relative balance after nearly 400 years since it actually took place. I suspect that some intellectuals of the West were aware of what was happening in the balance in those intervening centuries but those of the East were ignorant or unconcerned.

The evidence up to and to follow broadly supports the two hypotheses, though some evidence go against them. I would say they are more or less laws.

Chapter 5 Possible Causes for Rise of Europe and Decline of China

Section 1 Various Views Presented

Why was the reversal of fortune brought about in material culture between the two focal regions of the East and the West? Many historians posed this question. For example, HG Wells presented the inquiry in the following way:

> The urbanity, the culture and the power of China under the early T'ang rulers are in so vivid a contrast with the decay, disorder and divisions of the Western world, as at once to raise some of the most interesting questions in the history of civilisation. Why did not China keep this great lead she had won by her rapid return to unity and order? Why does she not to this day dominate the world culturally and politically? (Wells 1925, p. 361)

My history reference book of the secondary school, written by a prominent historian, noted that the East, though it entered a high degree of culture considerably earlier than the West, eventually lagged behind due to the stagnating nature of the Oriental society. However, this statement does not explain why the East was ahead of the West in materialism for the substantial length of the past. Besides it does not offer the Easterners any clue as to how they can rectify the problems or if this is even possible at all. He did not even elaborate the stagnating nature in a concrete form. For example, a doctor must diagnose a patient not only correctly but also specifically such that the doctor can treat the patient effectively.

HG Wells points out that the complexity of Chinese writing system hampered the development of China more than anything else. The following figures, though developed generally for scripts which represent whole words, are probably true for the Chinese characters:

- A person must master between 1000 and 10 000 Chinese characters for everyday use.
- A person must master between 30 000 and 50 000 Chinese characters for literary use.

(Whitehouse & Wilkins 1986, p. 132)

The Chinese have to spend an enormous amount of time and effort to master Chinese characters and thus have diminished energy for other activities. However, I have a serious doubt about this proposition. In the first place we have to take into account that while Chinese characters may look formidable to the Westerners they are not so bad for the Chinese who are brought up with them. In the second place, it may be true that English with 26 alphabets has a strong correspondence with spoken English, and the misspellings are often not fatal as far as the communications are concerned. The Chinese language has tens of thousands of characters which have virtually no connection with speech; however, the use of not so proper characters is not often fatal, again, as far as the communications are concerned. It is certainly hard to learn a large number of Chinese scripts; however, this corresponds to the difficulty of learning not only correct pronunciations and correct spellings of English words but also complicated English grammar such as placing the correct articles and using correct singular or plural nouns. Even intellectuals struggle with these subtle yet difficult problems. As a matter of fact Chinese grammar is surprisingly simple and has none of these problems. We also have to take into account that Chinese characters, essentially unaltered, were used beyond the dialects and through the millenniums in China proper. We may appreciate this enormous benefit if we think of the benefits for the Europeans if they had understood the same written language all over Europe through the ages.

Alphabetic representations of current English are not much different from the phonemic representations. However, the advantage of alphabetic symbols is not intuitively obvious and in fact the ancient Egyptians had alphabets but preferred to use other systems. (p. 136)

All people are born, grow, become old and eventually die but a few of them carry out remarkable feats at certain period of their life often from some unknown reasons. Many people try to ascribe the reasons for their prominence but their judgements can be wrong. We can say the same thing about civilisations. Civilisations are born, grow, become old and eventually die though people still live in the regions after the civilisations lose their entire lustre. Some civilisations show remarkable feats of creativity and vigour at certain era. In this respect, we can bring forward the argument that we don't have to know the reasons why the Chinese materialism surged ahead first and then the Europeans eclipsed it: we should accept history as it was and it simply happened. It is a universal law that everything generated must decay and civilisations are no exceptions.

Schopenhauer insisted that a sign of maturity in the early years of manhood be nothing but the inadequacy of that person; real maturity comes only with advanced age. His opinion matches with the Chinese popular saying: Large vessels take a long time to mould.

> The nobler and more perfect a thing is, the later and slower it is in arriving at maturity. A man matures of his reasoning powers and mental faculties hardly before the age of twenty eight; a woman, at eighteen. (Schopenhauer 1962, p. 103)
>
> It was not until the twelfth century that they [the Europeans] have reached a position where they could begin to comprehend the meaning of the ancient ideas, and it was not until the sixteenth century they stood upon the intellectual level of the men of Alexandria or Constantinople or Rome of over a thousand years before, and could rightfully claim to be civilised in the sense that the Hindus or the Chinese were civilised centuries before the Christian era. Perhaps it is with races as with individuals, and those whose infancy is most prolonged are for that very reason to continue learning when others reached the limits of their powers and their natural resources. (Randall 1976, p. 13)

Paul Kennedy proposes an interesting insight why the West surged ahead after 1500. Though Russia, China and the Ottoman Empire acquired modern technologies of gunpowder and muskets, they did not have much incentive to develop further since their empires were huge and stable. Europe was geographically divided into many small regions and people felt secure living in respective small nations. Europe was rich in natural resources in many regions and was easily accessible from Africa, the Middle East and Asia. Thus the Europeans were not unified and felt insecure against the other nations in Europe and the other peoples outside Europe, and were ever on competition among themselves and they had to develop technology rapidly for sheer survival after the collapse of the West Roman Empire. As the result Western Europeans had to develop not only military technology but any other technology such as shipbuilding and navigation. (Kennedy 1987, pp. 16-30)

Deep and long cultural divides marked European nations of distinct micro-cultures. People spoke Greek, Romance, Germanic or Slavonic languages. And also people adhered to the distinct faiths of Catholic, Protestant or Orthodox churches.

We can see this even today. If we travel to Europe, it is obvious that the neighbouring nations will take advantage of any weakness of a nation. Hence all the peoples stick to their nations and talk as if their country is the best in Europe. They cannot behave otherwise.

Apart from these ingrained divisions that characterised historical Europe, Europe has had another distinctly different concept acquired particularly in the modern era. That was the sense that they were Europeans and in the Old World and superior to the other peoples. The sense was nurtured by the Indo-European heritage, Christianisation, Greek and Roman cultural heritage, industrialisation and democratisation. (Fernandez-Armesto 1994, p. 17) As a consequence the European nations began to participate in the divisions of the world separately from the 15th century onwards. Even a Europe-wide network of exchange was complete and functioning and European nations were submerged in mercantilism and imperialism, each nation with the colonial markets set up protective barriers. It is surprising that the European nations did not want to unite economically and politically until after World War II when it became clear that European hegemony was at an end; though Europe had united religiously, and on some occasions militarily against the invasions from outside Europe.

Thus one reason why Europe surged ahead in the modern era may be competition among the small and scattered European nations. Each nation had to strive for sheer survival. When the Europeans set out to achieve world hegemony, European nations cooperated when it was advantageous and often they were at each other's throats. Spain and Portugal did not cooperate in the process of subjugating the New World and other territories. Also British and French rivalries in the American continent and India are parts of world history. Unified Europe did not materialise under Napoleon and Hitler, both of whom tried to dominate Europe. The fundamental reason why they failed may have been that each European nation wanted to be independent with strong sense of competition. This also makes sense if we think that Britain did not colonise Europe but her domains were overseas and outside Europe. England lost her foothold in France as the result of the Hundred Years' War and so directed her expansion efforts outside Europe since then. Germany aspired to expand after defeating France in 1870; however, Bismarck did not envisage expansion in Europe rather he wanted to establish a German sphere of influence in China, which led to the further rivalry with Britain. The development of the European Union may be the sign of European decay and an effort to survive in the world even though they have not lost the competitive spirit among the member nations.

Why Europe Has Not Been Unified Politically since End of Roman Empire.

The Chinese thought that a unified China with one native emperor was the ideal state. The Chinese have cherished this idea with fervour since the unification by the Ch'in state in 221 BC. They could not think any other forms of rules such as democracy or independent states within China or foreign occupation. These forms of governments were anomalies for them.

In contrast with the Chinese view the Europeans thought that independent and scattered nations in Europe were the norm and did not entertain any other model. It was the tradition of Western Europe that when one nation became strong and tried to dominate, the other nations united and fought against the domination. Why did the Europeans show such a strong resistance to political unification?

Is the resistance to unification in the blood of the Europeans who migrated from Central Asia? The steppe dwellers incessantly fought for grass and water rights. They worshipped military might unlike the bulk of the Chinese who detested the military. The Germans migrated en masse and settled into the regions defined by geography and weather towards the end of the classical era within the West Roman Empire, which collapsed as a consequence. The medieval to modern European attachment to their micro-cultures is inherent and incredibly strong and resists any logical explanation: we must locate the explanation in the instinct of self-preservation.

However after World War II the Europeans gradually headed for unification for their sheer survival. Western Europe exhibited a united defence when they agreed to set up NATO. They also agreed to unite economically in signing the Treaty of Rome in 1957, thus inaugurating the establishment of the European Economic Community and then the European Community in 1993. Western European nations had earlier united militarily when they launched the crusades, and got ready to put up a united front against the Mongolian army though the Mongolian invasion into Western Europe did not materialise.

Eastern Europe came under the communist rule after World War Two under the leadership of the Soviet Union. Still there are no political unification moves among these nations though they formed the Warsaw Pact in 1955 from a military necessity.

The cultural predecessors of Europe were in part Greece and Rome. The Greeks throughout their ancient cultural ascendancy did not have a national state but had independent city-states. This came about by geography: Greece was mountainous and narrow passages connected the city-states. The Greeks' pride for democracy and independence helped form 700 or so tiny states.

There is a strong parallel between ancient Greek city-states and modern European nations. Neither had unified political and economic institutions unlike China and the Roman Empire. The ancient Greeks had the same culture, language and race origins but the city-states fought incessantly for dominance in the similar way modern European nations with the common heritage and race origins ever fought for dominance. Competition helped achieve high levels of culture as well as warfare skills in both of these geographical regions though competition is not the only impetus for social development. The Chinese through history and the Romans from the ancient to classical eras developed their cultures under different (from above and each other) conditions.

The ancient Greeks, the ancient to classical Romans and the medieval to modern Europeans are all Indo-Europeans. The ancient Greeks aspired to have independent city-states; the ancient to classical Romans aspired to have an empire. The Europeans since the end of the Roman Empire have aspired for independent nations. Hence race does not seem to explain the desire of the late classical to modern Europeans to retain their independent nations with the micro-cultures.

While the Roman Empire extended to Western Europe, the divide and rule policy prevailed in Europe as in any other provinces outside Rome itself. The Romans under their policy implanted a desire for democracy and independence among the barbarians since unified barbarians posed a serious security risk for the maintenance of the empire. The empire had a strong (militarily and politically) hold on Western Europe which was underdeveloped culturally and militarily. Only after the German migration en masse into Western Europe in the late classical era, were the separate kingdoms set up and the strong desire for independence gripped the minds of the inhabitants of the kingdoms.

The West European nations spoke mutually unintelligible languages in spite of the fact that they had a common language origin. Latin was the international language in Europe through the Roman occupation to the Middle Ages; however, the separate nations discarded Latin as their international language in the modern era. The Europeans were unified under one Christian tradition of the patriarch and the church since the closing phase of the West Roman Empire until the Great Schism.

People in Italy, France, Spain, Portugal and Romania spoke Latin under the Roman Empire. However, as time passed their languages became unintelligible to each other in spite of the fact that these countries were geographically close except Romania: the Romanian language retained most of its original Latin. This is one strong indication that these peoples did not mix well and made independent developments.

The differences in cultures and nations among the Europeans were exaggerated and they fought incessantly over trade and national boundaries. They united during crusades against the Muslim Turks who were different racially and religiously. However, they realised that these differences were small when they came into contact with the Mongolians who were radically different racially and culturally.

These explanations do not account for such a strong feeling among the Europeans for separate states and there may be further reasons I don't know.

It is hard to compare the two currents of civilisation as superior or inferior. It is harder still to delve into the causes of the decline of the East in comparison with the West.
However, I am going to do my best in this chapter to present the possible causes and it is up to readers to judge their validity. My basic approach may be to postulate the causes in the first instance and try to justify them in the subsequent argument.

Historians justifiably cite the following factors as the underlying determinants of civilisations:

race; biological
environment;
  - physical (geography and climate)
  - human (culture of and interactions, friendly or hostile, with other peoples)
political and economic structures

Adolf Hitler laid a heavy emphasis on race, though he also claimed that physical environment played an important role in forming history. Karl Marx wrote that economic factor alone more or less decided the course of human history. Arnold Toynbee theorised based on his historical knowledge that the proposition that all the above factors interacted in a certain way gave the most satisfactory answer to explain the causes of a civilisation. (Toynbee 1962, p. 60) It is obviously not true that one individual factor alone accounted for the rise and fall of multitudes of civilisations through the course of human history, though some cultures may give the impression that one factor was the determining force.

As far as our point of inquiry goes, it is hard to believe that physical influences affected the balance between East and West to any appreciable extent. Geography and climate have not changed radically over the centuries of our concern to the extent they could alter the course of human development. Also many scholars note that racial characteristics have not changed much through the course of human history, provided that the race of focus does not intermingle with another race en masse. For example, Tacitus's descriptions about the Germans and the Italians of the first century roughly fit the image we have about these peoples today. The Romans, the founding tribes of the Roman Empire, were so different from the Italians that we think they were two distinct peoples. Marco Polo left a remark in *The Travels* (printed in 1477) of the thirteenth century Asia, though he did not go to Japan, that the Japanese were reputedly the fiercest people in East Asia. Many people today still believe this is the case.

Politics and economics--superstructures created by people based on racial and environmental determinants--may be a part of and a result from what we call civilisation. Certainly the high and low points of political and economic happenings mark the ebb and flow of the Eastern and Western civilisations.

I have come to the conclusion that the cause I am seeking lies in the setup of institutions in relation to idealism in China and in Europe. Confucianism and the civil service examinations characterised China through the successive Chinese empires, though Legalism was the guiding principle of the first empire Ch'in. Similarly Christianity and the church characterised Europe since the formation of the European nations. These fundamental differences of setup were beyond the political and economic institutions of China and Europe in the succeeding eras.

Some discernible causes (temporal) from history may be:

- No modern invasion by the non-Europeans took place in Western Europe: the West Europeans were militarily strong enough in some cases and lucky in some cases, and stuck with their micro-cultures.
- They synthesised what other peoples created and built upon them through the centuries. This came about as the results of the human environment.
- The West Europeans kept learning and growing but the Chinese looked to the glorious past and did not open the frontiers of learning. The underlying reasons behind these behaviours are hard to fathom from the temporal causes.

I am to expound after explaining two possible theories next that idealism is the fundamental cause (spiritual) conforming to and reinforcing the historical events (temporal).

Lottery Theory

Accident theory admits reality as it is and leaves everything to chance. It is a concept of pure luck or a lottery win. We attribute the decline of China and the upsurge of Europe in the modern era in respect to material culture to unadulterated chance, assuming that there are no human conscious efforts or interventions involved in the process as far as the progress of material culture was concerned. Certainly the peoples in the East and the West did their utmost in the survival struggles.

Many people would object to this proposition. This theory is non-scientific in that we don't have any logical explanation for the major events in the history of mankind. Historians would be most unhappy with this description since many of them want to see some reasons behind every historical event: that is the basis why the study of history is fascinating in the first place. This proposal is also unreligious in that it does not recognise any causal relationship between thinking and happening, between good conduct and reward, and between bad conduct and punishment. The communists would also reject this lottery-win theory outright: they don't believe in chance occurrences in history which, they believe, is determined by economic forces rather than any other influences, and by the masses rather than by eminent leaders. Lottery-win theory also flies in the face of the principle of sufficient reason which states that nothing happens by pure chance but that an explanation must always be available.

Certainly this lottery theory has many detractors; however, I have found that many happenings in life don't seem to have any scientific or religious or communistic foundations. Lottery is an obvious example. The rich and the poor don't seem to have any correlation to ethical levels: they have more to do with intelligence, diligence and luck. Some people seem to be famous, wealthy or powerful by sheer chance without discernable credit. By observing the upper society of his time, that is, 16th century France, Montaigne concluded that the least capable men commonly seized the chief places, and that he rarely found the greatness of fortune in combination with ability (Montaigne 1965, p. 114). Hence, it is not unreasonable to attribute the success or failure of a person, a nation or the occidental and oriental worlds to accident or chance.

When we assess a venture for an individual or a firm or a nation we have the following measures which come into play:

- theoretical background
- practical experience
- monetary backing
- environments (political, economic, etc.)
- right attitude and diligence

Apart from the above considerations we always have one element which we do not expect--accidents; luck or misfortune. Lottery theory enlarges this factor of accident and concludes that what really happens depends on it.

Polybius, a Greek historian (?205-?123 BC) who wrote a history of Rome from 264 to 146 BC, travelled widely through Italy, Africa, Spain and Gaul. He recognised that chance always played some part in victory or defeat in wars. (Freeman 1996, pp. 329, 330)

Sir Winston Churchill also noticed while he was Prime Minister of Britain during World War Two that the results of the battles between the allies and the axes depended on chance more than anything else.

Pestilence Theory

The Black Death struck Europe in the 14th century, decimating as much as one third of the European population and remained pandemic for the following three centuries, hitting Europe every 10-15 years (Mercer 1996, p. 526). Scholars of today, much less the contemporary Europeans, have not given us convincing, not even plausible, explanations as to why:

- The bubonic plague afflicted Europe severely and repeatedly. Though it is true that the Black Death was active in China and 13 million people perished as a result (Wells 1925, p. 469), there was no endemic problem there.
- The pestilence did not kill off all the people in Europe.
- The Black Death eventually left Europe.

We know for certain today that bacteria caused the Black Death but the above queries are quite puzzling to me and I assume that they are so to other inquisitive minds.

With the absence of reliable information, contemporary to present Europeans have put up their own theories about the spread of the pestilence. Some said that it was a divine punishment and some a biological freak. Some theorised that the Mongolian army brought in the bubonic plague. Whatever reasoning people may have proposed, the fact of the matter was that the plague came and left, killing a vast number of the Europeans and bringing dreadful fear to the surviving population.

We may liken the two civilisations of our attention to the visitation of pestilence: civilisation and plague had positive as well as negative effects on the Chinese and the Europeans. Generally speaking, the disease of civilisation comes and goes, sometimes not indicating where it comes from and why it comes in the first place; later scholars bequeath these queries to conjecture. First the inspiration for high material culture visited China and departed. Then it visited Europe and is about to go away in the early 21st century. Though this proposition may satisfy some aspects of what happened, it has a serious flaw in that the proposal attributes the queried causes to the unknown because scholars did not come up with convincing explanations, as they did not concerning the Black Death.

We can differentiate pestilence theory from lottery theory in that the former has the cause, though unknown, but the latter assumes no causes and only chance. For libido theory refer to Section 15 Sex as Basis of Civilisation, Chapter 1, Book Five *The Sexual Laws*.

I have come to believe that the real cause may lie in the different levels of adherence to idealism between the two sets of people. I formed this idea through studying history and also observing the Easterners and the Westerners not only in the media but in my daily contact. The next section explains this theory.

Section 2 Practice of Idealism; Most Plausible Cause

The bases of comparisons between the East and the West up to now were the planes of material culture. What sort of comparisons can we make in the field of idealism, another major sphere of human pursuit. I may briefly equate idealism for now to the teaching 'Love thy neighbour'. I have come to believe that this teaching is the central plank of idealism and its practical manifestation in our daily life.

It is hard enough to compare the material aspects of the two civilisations since we are dealing with entirely different sets of premises. For example, we may not be able to say that one instrument is superior to or in advance of another instrument of similar purpose from another part of the world because these instruments came from different backgrounds and people's attitudes to them are different. It is even harder to compare and contrast idealistic philosophies between the East and the West. Nonetheless I am going to delve into what may come out of idealism from the two currents of civilisations to see whether the results may have any bearing on the question of why China eventually lagged behind Europe in material culture in spite of the fact that the former went into a high state of material culture centuries earlier.

In the process of growing up, we have to learn some aspects of life at a certain age. If we miss that opportunity, we have to grow up without that advantage and we don't recover from the loss all our life in the normal course of events. For example, speech defects acquired during infancy remain with the persons all through their life unless treated properly by an expert who may not exist in the first place. Also while people are young--up to the age of 25, they must acquire the scientific approach. In the similar logic, a civilisation must master certain aspects of skills at some stages of development. The analogy between individual and state is old and well established. If we miss a skill for our survival, we must go through the growing-up process without that skill assisting us. China missed out on the proper diffusion of idealism in their society until the communist revolution.

The following observation can reinforce the analogy of individuals and states. Atoms and their bonding more or less explain the attributes and the behaviours of the matter made of atoms, for example, its physical and chemical nature. Similarly the characteristics of a nation are decided by those of individuals and the relationships among individuals in the nation.

I believe that the characters of a civilisation are similar to the personalities of an individual person; once set, the courses of both do not change easily. The young elite would choose their careers to be the most interesting and rewarding both within the society and the institution, for example, a university and a firm. The best of them will be successful in obtaining the positions they want because the society and the institution in their turn want the best people for their own prosperity and success. People (historians and philosophers) often say that Western civilisation is based on Hebraism (Judaism and Christianity) and Hellenism (ancient to classical Greek culture). The former originated in the Levant, part of Asia, and the latter in southern Europe. No leading nations of the modern world are in these regions and we can say that the main contribution of European nations may be in the field of materialism backed by science and technology. In the ancient to classical eras of the Mediterranean world, people admired Greek culture, which as a result dominated the region culturally. However, in the medieval times, Christianity held sway over the European continent. The Renaissance may have come into being by people's desire to revert back to Hellenism after so many centuries of Dark Ages under Hebraism.

I think that the essence of Western culture when viewed even in the 21st century is not materialism but idealism typified by Hebraism and Hellenism. Failure to observe this perspective may result in an unfortunate situation. For example, the introduction of Marxist rule into a nation without a sound understanding of idealist culture may cause an unhappy state of affairs for many of its citizens. Also, technological transfer to a non-European nation with no adequate base of idealism may produce a society where many intellectuals insist that their society was better before the implantation of the large-scale machine production. Because of this, many Europeans look at other peoples with advanced technology with some disdain though probably they are not aware of the reasons behind.

When we turn our attention to Chinese theatre, we see a similar trend to Europe except that the main inspirations for idealism came from the Chinese cultural regions.

The Chinese people were associated with Confucianism for so long that the general public, the Chinese and non-Chinese, justifiably think that the teachings of Confucius were the state cult of the historical Chinese empires. In fact the so-called 'Confucian Classics' formed the primary call of conduct in China from the second century BC to the early part of the 20th century. Daoism (Taoism) and Buddhism also had considerable followers in China through classical to modern times of the European classifications. Legalist doctrines reigned supreme in the Ch'in dynasty established in 221 BC but its influence has been minimal since the collapse of the dynasty, though some aspects of the doctrines survived through traditional China.

I may express the essence of Confucianism in the following paragraphs:

> According to Confucius, the right method of governing is not by legislation and law enforcement, but by supervising the moral education of people (McGreal 1995, p. 6).
>
> Ren [or jen: love of man] is a strictly natural and humanistic love, based upon spontaneous feelings cultivated through education (p. 3).
>
> In a word, virtue is the root. Everything else is the branch. And virtue is at the core of the Confucian ethics. (p. 54)

Confucianism had a few distinguishing features. The Confucians were against social revolution of any kind, whereas the Legalists advocated radical transformation of society. We can sharply contrast the realism and materialism of the Legalists with the idealism of the Confucians. Confucianism did not encourage creativity nor change. Confucius himself looked to the past for his inspirations and was an ardent admirer of the golden age of the Chou dynasty.

Buddhism viewed the material aspects of life as quite unimportant and many Buddhists lived a life of extreme asceticism doing away with even the necessities of life. Buddhism as a doctrine has no social message except in spreading their way of thinking, and especially the Hinayanists regarded the social reform as nonsense.

Emperor Asoka (c. 265-238 BC), last major emperor of the Mauryan Empire in India, may be considered to be the founder of political thought based on the principles of Buddhism. Asoka tried to build his kingdom with religious objectives. He endeavoured to build the welfare state, caring for the sick and the poor, and encouraging religious education among the people. (Kung et al. 1986, p. 336) Asoka, before being converted to Buddhism, had his brother murdered and seized power when his father's death was imminent (Eliade 1982, p. 213). However, I would say that there cannot be anything like a Buddhist form of government from the very outlook of Buddhism, that is, everything is an illusion.

Kongfuzi (Confucius), Laozi (Lao-tzu) and the Buddha lived in the sixth century BC.

Buddhism made its way to China through Central Asia, that is, Afghanistan and Turkistan. It reached China about AD 64, in the reign of Emperor Ming Di (Ming-Ti) of the Han dynasty. Bodhidharma (Indian) introduced the Ch'an school of Buddhism into China. This school further spread to Japan and was established as Zen.

Fazhao, a Buddhist visionary, is said to have received inspiration from the Buddhist divinities, Amitabha and Manjusri, which led to the establishment of Chinese Pure Land

Buddhism. 'Through the blend of ascetic rigour, sustained concentration and invocation of Amitabha's grace one sought to enter a state of meditative ecstasy, thereby achieving visions of the Buddha or insight into ultimate reality itself.' This school is to intone the name of Amitabha Buddha according to the five-tempo Buddha recitation. This is the technique of Buddha-mindfulness. "The sagely one, Manjusri, then spoke in verse, saying, 'Those of you who long for liberation should first eliminate all thoughts of selfish pride, envy, craving, desire for fame and profit--all such unwholesome motives you must cast away. Concentrate solely on invoking the name of Amitabha, and you will come to abide easefully in the realm of the Buddha'." (Lopez 1996, pp. 203-7)

The Daoists preached that spirit should prevail over matter, which is the basis for achieving immortality. I expound the teaching of Daoism together with the other religions in Section 2 Various Religions, Chapter 1, Book Two *Religion*. Daoism, as for Buddhism, does not have political and social messages and made only brief appearances in the Chinese political scene.

Can we put any value judgement on the Eastern and Western thoughts of idealism aforementioned so as to explain the decline of the East? Possibly we cannot answer the above question in any meaningful fashion. I can relate my personal preference from my experience. Daoism and Legalism do not have philosophical teachings as may apply to the present world. I have lost interest in Confucianism over the years. Hellenism is interesting to me as literature but does not appeal to the extent that I can make it my life-guiding principle.

I have found that only Buddhism and Judaism contain guiding principles which are relevant today and in the future. We find the teachings of Buddhism in the hundreds or even thousands of canons which do not seek any unification of doctrines. It is said that the main teachings of Judaism are in the Hebrew Bible, which is approximate to the Old Testament, though Judaism is also expressed in other written and oral traditions. Christianity's canons are the Old and New Testaments. Islam's canon is the Qur'an. However, the fundamental tenets of Christianity and Islam are in Judaism.

There is one twist of historical fact in conjunction with these two teachings. Non-Europeans formed and developed Christianity in a part of Asia but people now think it to be a part of Western culture. Whereas, the eastern group of the Indo-Europeans who invaded India and called themselves Aryans developed Buddhism in India but people now widely believe it to be an Asian culture practised largely by the Mongoloids.

Whatever the outcome of the comparative merits of the Eastern and Western idealism, the answer, one way or the other, does not alter the argument to be put forward in the following paragraphs. The discussion is on the levels of ethics among people and not on the inherent worth of idealism. We can assume that people's understandings in general, except for scholars, do not go beyond what they experience in their daily life, hence the inherent value of idealism is in fact irrelevant to the argument.

There is a Confucian dialogue which may pose an answer to our inquiry:

> Confucius was asked which of the three requirements--army, food and Jen--should be discarded if people are forced to give up. [Jen is the central theme of Confucianism and I rendered it as 'Love thy neighbour'.]
>
> He said, 'Army'.
>
> He was further asked which of the remaining two--food and Jen--should be discarded if people are forced to give up.
>
> He said, 'Food. There have been deaths from time immemorial, but no state can exist without the confidence of the people. Without Jen the human society does not stand'. (Chan 1963, p. 39)

The teaching of these exchanges is, in essence, similar to the biblical teaching spoken through Moses (Deuteronomy 8:3): One does not live by bread alone, but by every word that comes from the mouth of the Lord.

The foregoing assertion by Confucius is, of course, of a purely academic nature and has no probability of being put into practice. However, it tries to illustrate the importance of idealism represented by jen in contrast with materialism symbolically represented by food and army. Food in its simplest form is a necessity of life, and it together with clothes and shelter in basic forms, as I see, constitutes a prerequisite for idealism and materialism and all the other survival means humans have devised. Confucius taught that jen should be the central occupation of the human mind and activity. This teaching matches with the opinions of many scholars that virtue should be the foundation stone of all civilisations. Confucius often lamented his contemporary society and idealised the social order under the golden age of Chou rule when, he believed, jen was in full bloom. However, it is doubtful if we can justify his longing for olden times: his unbiased research might have revealed that the exalted society of his longing was just as harsh as any later society for common people to make a living. Possibly based on the romanticised society in the past he firmly believed that he could teach people to behave in a proper manner.

Jesus Christ preached with similar conviction (Matthew 13:31-2):

> The kingdom of heaven is like a mustard seed that someone took and sowed in his field; it is the smallest of all seeds, but when it has grown it is the greatest of shrubs and becomes a tree, so that the birds of the air come and make nests in its branches.

The Bible repeatedly urges people to choose the words of God rather than the callings of flesh and mammon. Christ said, 'Every plant that my heavenly Father has not planted will be uprooted' (Matthew 15:13). He also said, 'I am the way, and the truth, and the life. No one comes to the Father except through me' (John 14:6). Socrates also taught that we should devote ourselves to improving our minds: wealth, our bodies and personal reputation should not be our main concern. The Buddha's main concern was the mind and he taught his disciples to improve their way of thinking by constant vigilance. In all these teachings moral rectitude is assumed.

I may define practical phase of the idealistic culture in the following way. Idealism is a basis of civilisation. Without proper understanding and practice of idealistic doctrines among the general public, civilisation does not grow in a satisfactory fashion in the same way human bodies do not grow satisfactorily without the adequate, though small, quantities of vitamins and minerals. Idealism referred to here is not the metaphysical or philosophical concept but what the populace can understand and practise in everyday life. Idealism is simple and anybody can practise it under any social conditions. The central theme of idealism in practice may be 'Love thy neighbour'.

I am to explain using idealism theory how China declined in modern times though it showed superb material culture in the pre-modern era. The setup of the Chinese civil service examinations upholding Confucianism (idealism) had a fatal flaw in that Confucianism as a doctrine, and the examination system came under the total control of the reigning emperor as I explain in 'Introduction to Series'. The Christian churches in the medieval era had the different setup and operated independently of the scattered, political and economic, powers of nations. The Chinese eventually paid dearly by not making idealism properly integrated into society and lagged behind the Europeans in the field of materialism after the Renaissance of the European scene. We must take into account the time element in assessing the effect of idealism and materialism.

Another reason why China went down in the modern era is their belief that their culture was the best without question and without comparison, and they stopped learning from foreign countries. This happened prominently after the Sung period when the Confucians became dominant in the government bureaucracy pushing away the Daoists and Buddhists. The Chinese manifested this arrogance in their contempt for foreigners and foreign trade. During the early T'ang period the Chinese were in contact with a large variety of peoples and more willing to absorb foreign ideas than during any other periods. In the Sung era and also the succeeding Yuan era, foreign trade was conducted vigorously to make money. However, the Chinese became reluctant to absorb foreign ideas from then on till the 19th century.

From the 16th century onwards the Christian missionaries of the West showed the Chinese the advanced Western technologies but could not impress them. If the Chinese had known that their material cultures were very much inferior to the West's they would have put in place remedial policies; they were simply not interested in nor capable of understanding the true state of affairs for the reasons mentioned above. This is the attitude of the worst patients who are not aware that they have a serious problem compared with patients who are aware and prepared to seek remedial advice. The Chinese reached the latter position towards the end of the 19th century after going through tremendous sufferings at the hands of the Western powers.

The Bible narrates that God handed down the idealism represented by the Ten Commandments. The Westerners were careful to observe these commandments and hence eventually elevated to a commanding position in the affairs of the world. The West surged mightily since the commercial capitalism beginning in the 15th century. The industrial capitalism followed triggered by the Industrial Revolution that started in Britain in the middle of the 18th century. The European colonies necessitated the revolution, calling for the huge demands of industrial products. The Industrial Revolution, the historical culmination of materialism up to that time in the West, made Western material cultures superior to Eastern material cultures. The West could not have developed capitalism (commercial and industrial) in the way they did unless the Westerners were firm on idealism. In fact the Chinese got close to developing capitalism in the Sung period but could not follow up for the lack of various social settings, fundamentally originating in moral disciplines.

A natural corollary of the lack of idealism is low moral standards manifested in everyday dealings among the nominated people. It is widely reported in the Australian media that the main basis of complaints by the Australians against the Asians is that the latter (the Easterners) are unethical in their dealings compared with the former (the Westerners). It is true that everybody has some experience that all the peoples, whether the Easterners or Westerners, are cunning whenever some gain or loss is involved. It may also be true that everyone knows that the employers of whatever nationalities try to cheat and exploit them in some way or another. However, when we place the two groups of peoples on a comparison scale, most people say that the Easterners are generally inferior to the Westerners in the sphere of ethics, but the same people also express that the Easterners are smarter than the Westerners when it comes to intelligence and doing the job. This must be the historical result carried on through the centuries.

The foregoing argument may give the impression that the two currents of ideologies, that is, idealism and materialism, are in some way interlocked and are in a cause-and-effect relationship. We have to stress here that the pursuit of idealism is independent of that of materialism though low morality of people degenerates political and economic institutions. And that independence holds for individuals as well as for nations. An individual person or a nation can be both idealistic and materialistic; can be neither idealistic nor materialistic; can be either idealistic or materialistic. High morality does not necessarily lead to excellence in pursuits. Religion and capability to do a job are separate entities. For example, the Aboriginal people of Australia, as the British found, had extremely high morality but had only crude material culture and had to face the invading British with high--but lower than the Aboriginals--morality, and high material culture. Saint Edward the Confessor, king (1042-1066) of England, was a deeply religious man but was politically incompetent. Everybody can tell about a person with low morality yet placed in a high rank in the organisation and also an ethical person who is low in the organisational hierarchy.

Underlying Explanation of Idealism Theory: Evolution, God's Will and Cell Theory
I must stress that the three causes mentioned in the above heading are only for intellectual satisfaction and do not alter my presentation in this section. In fact all match with the conclusion I have reached. I am to give an example. Cell theory asserts that all the experiences of our ancestors and us as individuals are stored in our cells in coded form. Hence any decisions (good or bad) to act are made by the dictates of past experiences. However, if an individual radically alter his or her life attitude for good or bad, that individual makes the decision taking into account the change. This observation is in accord with religious teachings.

Even all three explanations are wrong, it does not make any difference to the argument I present in this section.

I explain the fundamental thoughts of the above heading in B Reward and Punishment for Thought and Conduct, Section 3, Chapter 7 to follow.

<u>Evolution and God's Will</u>
I know from my experiences that what I have thought and done has had a vital influence on my present self. I still remember the passages from a Buddhist text which the teacher taught in the language class at my secondary school. It may sound a bit odd that the normal educational institution taught Buddhism; however, the quoted paragraphs were referring to the daily life experience of ordinary people. We can see the parallel in Europe in teaching a part of the Bible for the sake of language development.

According to the text, what we are now has resulted from what we thought and conducted ourselves in the past. Also what we think and act at the present time will decide what we will be in the future. There are no accidents between the two time intervals on the same individual, as some people might assert otherwise. This Buddhist scripture further insists that by knowing the present state of a person, we can induce precisely the past as well as the future conditions of the person.

By learning what happened in the past, we are learning new lessons for us today. Unless history teaches us something new for us, there is not much point in learning history. History may be interesting as a narration but that would not be enough reason to become a school subject. There is a Chinese saying, ‘By warming up the past records we learn something new’. This saying emphasises the continuation of human thinking, and that people in the past had the similar problems possibly under different circumstances. Arnold Joseph Toynbee commented that people who lose sight of history lose sight of the future, when he heard that the Japanese government was going to abandon history lessons in the educational system under the militarism before the Pacific War. Later events clearly indicate that he was right on this matter.

In fact this is the plot of the Jewish prophets narrated in the Bible. By analysing the present thoughts and conduct of the Jewish people, the prophets can predict what will happen to the
Jewish people in the future, though the Bible emphasises that the predictions are revelations from God rather than from the prophets. If we use the same analytical technique, we can

construct a similar story told by the Bible for any human community or even for any individual, provided all the necessary data, historical or personal, are available. The importance of the Bible lies precisely in this, and if the biblical narrations apply only to the happenings among the Jews when the authors wrote, it would have no relevance for us today. We read the Bible searching for guidance and answers for our present problems apart from forming the basic attitude to life.

Confucius worked as a prophet, too. Living in a chaotic period, he made the following remark: Small though it is, Qin [or Ch'in] aspires to great things (Guisso and Pagani 1989, 94). Sure enough, Ch'in grew to become the efficient and strong state to unify China three centuries later. We can see in this episode that both the success of Ch'in and the shrewdness of Confucius observation were no accident.

Confucius spoke in reference to the historical interpretation of ethics:

> A society is not created simply by contractual relationship of interested parties. Society or culture comes into being through a very long and strenuous process of collective effort. Every human society has a collective memory. The ability to relate to that collective memory is also the ability to identify one's self. (Sharma 1993, p. 195)

According to this line of reasoning there are no such things as luck or accidents in our lives: we make every happening--intentionally or unintentionally. What happens to us results from our thinking and doing of the past, whether we intended it or not. Many people think that external happenings can have a vital influence on our lives; however, my life experience indicates strongly that external forces have minimal or helpful influence on our thinking. Our brain activities preceding every event decide every happening under our control, since we act according to our thinking. Sometimes we feel that what happened to us is unjust but this is because we made mistakes somewhere along the lines of thoughts--before the event, during the event or after the event at our assessment stage. We get what we deserve--good or bad: we feel it is unjust when we get a bad result though we worked for it unknowingly.

The conformity of thought and reward or punishment must have amazed many original thinkers as they were coming out of barbarism with not much information available for them, and they must have believed that the process involved something supernatural. Some must have said it was the act of nature and some concocted the concept of God (Truth) in an effort to explain this phenomenon. Thomas Hobbes wrote in *Leviathan* (1651) that nature is the art whereby God hath made and governs the world (Hutchins 1952, p. 47). Only God (Truth) does not make a mistake in handing down sentences and all the judgements on our thinking come from God (Truth). People in the first place do not know the intent of our thinking though they can observe some or all of our actions: Only God (Truth) knows what lay in our heart and prompted our actions.

The experiences of the forebears develop or inhibit the progress of a civilisation, in a similar way as past experiences of an individual person develop or inhibit the progress of personal growth.

The foregoing assertion matches well with my life experiences, and as I grow older the accuracy of the message amazes me ever more. Many people have noted this facet of life and expressed the idea in various ways in many parts of the world. The proverb 'As you sow so you must reap' is one example. One ancient Greek warned youths with the remark 'Rest assured you cannot carry lies to the old age'. The poet was referring to an individual's life span, but still it can refer to a civilisation. Many young people who go through life deceiving people will find, when they become old, to their bitter sadness that the above Greek warning is true and they feel a remorse, with nobody else to blame but themselves. In Christian theology, this is the punishment by God (Truth). The last verse of Ecclesiastes (12:14) goes; For God will bring every deed into judgement, including every hidden thing, whether it is good or evil. Also the ancient Greeks as for the ancient Chinese and Indians were not Christians but they all knew the retribution by the eternal and natural law.

It is comparatively easy to assume that the above line of causality exists for an individual by observations. The doctrine is possibly true even for a group of people; nation, race and the East and the West. When we apply the doctrine to a group, it may be termed collective unconsciousness. One possible explanation may lie in the brain cells. If the brain cells of an individual person account for the fate of the person, we can extend the hypothesis to a group of people. After all, the total cells of the group consist of the aggregates of the cells of individual persons. Group thinking and acting are only the sum total of individual thinking and acting. Hence it is not hard to assume that what happens to an individual can happen to a group as a consequence of brain activities: fortune and misfortune or reward and punishment follow the individual and the group according to what they think and act.

> The one most important conception in the system of Vijnanas is Vasana. What is this? Psychologically, as was stated before, Vasana is memory, for it is something left after a deed is done, mental or physical, and it is retained and stored up in the Alaya as a sort of latent energy ready to set in motion. This memory or habit-energy, or habitual perfuming is not necessarily individual; the Alaya being super-individual holds in it not only individual memory but all that has been experienced by sentient beings. When the [Buddhist] sutra says that in the Alaya is found, all that has been going on since beginning less time systematically stored up as a kind of seed, this does not refer to individual experiences, but to something general, beyond the individual, making up in a way the background on which all individual psychic activities are reflected. (Suzuki 1930, p. 184)

Buddhism also explains the above concept using the term karma. The idea refers not only to individuals but to nations and races but the Buddhists do not explain historical happenings with the idea of karma unlike the biblical authors who explain history in terms of faith in the Almighty. In fact history is nonsense for the Buddhists. Any actions, committed or even conceived, act like seeds to bear their fruition in the future. Good actions lead to good fruits and bad actions, bad fruits. Karma is not destroyed or lost after so many years and is sure to germinate precisely in the way conceived. Karma becomes the conservation of energy in the physical world, the evolution in the biological world and the immortality of deeds in the moral world. However, it does not apply to economic activities, which matches with our common notion that poverty and wealth have nothing to do with moral standards.

The value of a person is precisely a kind of interest they show in the process of growing up. We can say the same thing about a civilisation. When forming a society, the kind of interest its people have may decide its value. That interest may not alter for the life of the civilisation as for individual person, since young people with their sensitivity absorb from the society what their interest should be, what people value and what people strive for.

The Old and New Testaments take similar positions as outlined in the foregoing paragraphs. They address to individuals as well as to the Jewish people as a whole. Concerning the punishment delivered to the Jewish nation, I have never reconciled myself with one aspect. When a misfortune happened to the Jews as a nation as a result of disobedience to God (Truth), why some persons among them, possibly the prophets, had to suffer the same fate in spite of the fact that they were careful to observe the ordinances as prescribed in the Bible. The Old Testament delves into this problem in chapters 18 and 19, Genesis, and also in Noah and Ezekiel.

Hitler was an agent of God to punish the rebelliousness of the Jewish people. God sometimes uses an evil agent as a tool of his judgement. God subsequently punishes that agent for its rebelliousness.

We all know that if we mistreat our bodies by excessive use or non-use we will become ill in due course without fail. Hence it is a logical inference that if we misbehave in some way--misbehaviours come from our thinking--we will become deficient mentally in due course without fail. The prophets of the Bible warn people that they must adhere to justice, otherwise injustice will catch up with them sooner or later and they will pay a penalty in some way.

There is ample evidence to conclude that the punishments and rewards for a group of people are not accidents but depend on past thoughts and conduct of the people in the group. If we assume this logic to be correct, we can ascribe the decline of the East in material culture to the wrong thinking and acting of its people. Similarly we can ascribe the rise of the West in modern times to the right thinking and acting of its people. Right and wrong thinking here denotes presence and absence of idealism and nothing else: idealism is widely spread and quite simple once understood. The focus is people's thinking and acting according to idealism.

Cell Theory

I cite evolution, God's will and cell theory as possible underlying causes for the demise of China and the rise of Europe in the modern era, idealism forming the base. I am to expand the cell principle under the above heading.

I have to rely on cytology, the scientific study of cells, to further the argument of cell theory.

Many years ago when I was skimming through a book in a bookstore, a sentence caught my eyes and has stayed with me ever since. At first, the theory was so alien to me that I dismissed it as ridiculous. Over the years the notion has permeated my way of thinking and I now believe the proposition is in fact a truth. The theory went like this:

> All human consciousness whether of thought or of activity is stored in the cells and passed through generations.

Since the book was esoteric and non-scientific, it did not designate which cells carried consciousness--somatic cells or germ cells, and neither did it say how consciousness was transferred to the cells. The author conceived the theory by intuition without a doubt and subsequently the author must have found that it was in conformity with his or her life observations, though I have some reservation as to who originated the theory. The proposition matches with my findings in psychology and biology. It may also explain in part the phenomena of reincarnation and the process of evolution. I am to develop these aspects of cell theory in the following paragraphs.

Skin researchers reported that the damage done on the human skin due to overexposure to the sun's rays remained with the person for the rest of his or her life, though they could not even see the ill effects on the seemingly undamaged surface after the initial sunburn disappeared.

Skin colour (white, brown and black) of the humans is caused by the sun effect over the past millenniums without a doubt. I got a peculiar notion that the skin colour (yellow) of the East Asians and that (copper) of the American Indians were caused by the soil effect over the past millenniums, the effect being carried by the cells. The soil in focus is the loess and silt carried by the Yellow River, and the soil in the copper mines in the Rocky Mountains. The cells must know that the sun and soil effects have bearing only on the skin colour and not on the other part of the body. We must give satisfactory answers to a few challenging questions before the latter proposition can be established as true.

A few people who had visited northern China told me about the tremendous yellow-dust storms they had encountered.

Similarly, exercises, mental and physical, are carried by the cells. Proper exercises bring good results without fail; not enough, too much or improper exercises, bad results without fail.

When we talk about the memory of cells, we are not so much referring to physical and mental resemblances but rather to the remembrances of the specific physical and mental activities as our ancestors experienced.

Modern psychologists assert that once our brains register a thought or an action, they retain it somewhere until we die, though the memory may go out from our conscious minds. In fact all the experiences in my life support this assertion, which confines to the retention of information within our life span and does not refer to the passing of information from our ancestors to us nor from us to our descendants.

I have chosen the following examples from my experience in order to shed some light on how cells retain our daily experience.

In my childhood I ate vinegared mackerel for my evening meal and I liked it so much that I ate excessively. I woke up in the middle of that night and vomited fiercely. Since then every time I consumed vinegared mackerel I threw up without an exception. After about ten years of refraining from the food I did not think about the problem. One day I ate a few pieces of similarly treated mackerel and then threw up all the food from my stomach in the same night. I conclude that the cells must have been responsible for the vomit. I don't know which cells--brain or stomach--are responsible for the rejection but they certainly retained the memory. The brain cells are part of the nerve cells which do not regenerate and the same brain cells stay with us all our life, whereas the cells lining the inside of the digestive system incessantly renew themselves. From this fact we may draw the conclusion that nerve cells are responsible for the vomiting but we cannot disregard the possibility that stomach cells are responsible, each generation of cells passing the information to the next generation before they die. Another possibility may be that all the cells in my body retained the memory; cytology supports this view.

There is another illustration. I have made it a habit to go to toilet after breakfast every morning. I don't know how it works but by sheer habit I vacate my bowels thus with a few exceptions a year. Cells of either brain or digestive organs or all the body cells must be regulating this habit.

As I get older I realised that what I thought at my youth were recorded in my brain whether they were beneficial or harmful.

One of the fundamental principles of current biology is that all cells come from pre-existing cells. In the course of sexual reproduction of humans (multi-cellular organisms), the union of an egg cell (pre-existing germ or sex cell), and a sperm cell (pre-existing germ or sex cell), creates a zygote (one fertilised egg). This zygote (one single cell) develops into an embryo. This embryo grows into a full human being with a huge number of cells. 'Biologically, sex is a basic property of DNA; it is the ability of DNA molecules to exchange parts and to move from one cell to another. The sexual performance of complex organisms is the means of mixing their DNAs.' The basic acts of sex are the exchange of parts between DNAs. (Dulbecco 1987, pp. 168, 173)

Another fundamental principle is that all cells in a human body, 100 or so different kinds, carry essentially the same inheritance information, though it seems that the inheritance information is confined to a particular organ of the body such as skin colour or colour blindness. The entire DNA in a human cell contains as much information as several sets of encyclopaedia. (Pfeiffer 1976, p. 61) Each tiny cell respires, digests nutrients, excretes, becomes old and eventually dies, as if it were an independent creature, though nerve cells (neurones or neurons) can live as long as 100 years. Hence it is not illogical to assume that the cell receives more information from the brain which processes more experience, and passes them to the descendants, though we don't know how the imparting process takes place. We do know that memory in a cell is not stored in a language but in the form of coded DNA, and consequently the memory does not come out easily. Every cell in the body may store memories but only the brain cells are capable of recalling them.

> The hereditary information is contained in the chromosomes, strands of genetic material composed of DNA. The hereditary characteristics such as skin colour, hair colour, body type and height are determined by the precise combinations of DNA that we acquire from each parent and from subsequent environmental influence. (Westheimer 1994, p. 130)

> Cells can be self-sufficient generalists capable of carrying on an independent existence; single-cell creatures such as the amoeba and the paramecium are examples of these free-living cells (Pfeiffer 1976, p. 9).

> The first life forms on earth was one-celled creatures such as bacteria and algae (Balkwill & Rolph 1994, p. 12).

> Bacteria are very tiny, about one hundred times smaller than human cells, ... Bacteria cells do not have a nucleus and are called prokaryotic. Viruses are even smaller than bacteria. Viruses are tiny parasites and not cells. By themselves they are lifeless but inside a living cell, they become active and capable of reproduction. (p. 85)

> Biologists believe that when life first appeared in cellular form it did so in structures closely resembling present-day bacteria. These crude forms still get their energy from inorganic matter. They have fewer special parts than other cells. Such structures as true nuclei and mitochondria, found in other organs, were apparently products of later stages of evolution. (Pfeiffer 1976, pp. 88-9)

> At the heart of the cell is the nucleus, a control centre that bears within it the cell's hereditary material, ensuring the survival of its line (p. 10).

> Every cell contains all the genes of an organism, regardless of its size and complexity, but not all the genes are active at any given time (Dulbecco 1987, p. 147).

> Fats are stored within the cell (Pfeiffer 1976, p. 41), though the cell structures are mostly built of protein.

> All cells of an embryo carry exactly the same hereditary material; in reproducing they pass on to their daughter cells the same set of DNA molecules made up of the same set of genes-sections of a DNA molecule which dictate particular traits (pp. 101-2).

Chromatin contains all the hereditary information that the reproduction of new cells needs. Chromatin, the part of the nucleus that consists of DNA, RNA and proteins, forms the chromosomes, and stains with basic dyes. (p. 20)

The adult human body is estimated to contain 60 000 billion cells. Every second some 50 million of the body cells die. During the same period 50 million infant cells are born to take the place of the dying cells. (pp. 15-6)

Nerve cells and muscle cells are similar in some ways and these cells are less conventional among the aggregates of body cells. Both of these cells do not reproduce in the course of human life: the ones they are born with must serve all their lives. Both cells are electrical units, responding electrically to the stimuli. (p. 148)

The memories of the cells may be misconception. The pieces of the computer do not have the faculty of computing but the organisation of the pieces have the brain to compute. Also the activities of a large human organisation result from the joint efforts of many individuals of different functions. It may be that, in a similar way, the individual cells don't have memory but the system of the cells has the faculty of memorising.

The system of cells is infinitely more than the sum of its parts:

> Although the nervous system as a whole is the source of all thought, the individual nerve cell appears to engage in nothing which would pass as mental activity (p. 147).

An aggregate of cells forms tissue which in turn forms an organ, for example, a heart. The function of the cells mostly does not explain the function of the organ such as a heart. However, the nerve cell, a specialised cell, transmits nerve impulses, and nerve cells bundle together to make the nerves which transmit impulses.

One fundamental characteristic of all living things (insects, plants, animals, humans and even one-celled creatures) which are composed of cells is the desire for survival of the individual cell and the species. This matches the survival desire of human thinking. Humans want to preserve their identity. It is a logical statement that a cell wants to preserve its identity because the cell has a kind of thinking or memory function. The survival instinct of the cell manifests in various ways in its daily activities in the same way humans do. Will for survival presupposes thinking or memory faculty.

Cell theory thus outlined may also explain the phenomenon of reincarnation. The offspring may receive what the parents went through in their lives through a sperm cell or an egg cell. Thus all the cells of the offspring inherit information from the ancestors. For some reason or another the brain cells of the offspring activate their conscious mind. As a consequence the offspring think they had previous life experience.

> Recent surveys indicate that almost a quarter of the Europeans now believe in reincarnation (Sharma 1993, p. 10).
>
> Joan Grant believes that everyone has had similar past lives with deaths that are just as traumatic and horrifying. The difference is that most people can no longer remember their previous incarnations, whereas she had a 'far memory' since childhood. (Brookesmith 1984, p. 45)

Many believers of reincarnation rely on regressive hypnosis and corroborations with the known facts as proof for their case (p. 109).

Let me remind readers that a large number of people claim to have a previous life memory which may suggest reincarnation or may be cell memories as outlined above. I have some memories which I cannot trace to my present life but cannot dismiss them simply as dreams or fantasies.

The above explanation refers only to memory transference through blood relations. There are a good number of reincarnation experiences which did not have any blood connections. I can think of one way of imparting the cell information to a stranger. Suppose a person dies and an animal or a fish eats a part of it, some cells being intact from a quirk of nature. Another person eats that animal or fish, the same cells not being destroyed for some reason. Thus the body cells of an original person become a part of the stranger and activate, again by unknown process, the brain cells of the stranger, who thinks it had a previous life. This inference is certainly far-fetched for acceptance by reasonable people. We are talking about a tiny possibility among zillions of zillions of digestions.

A theory of preserved memory in cells may open another avenue of explanation in the cause of evolution as proposed by Charles Darwin.

Darwin seems to have believed in chance variations of animals and plants, which he called variants (Loewe 1990, p. 801); the evolution as an accident or freak. An animal or plant produces an offspring which is more favourable in the given environment by sheer chance. This offspring is more adapted for struggle for survival and hence likely to have more offspring of its own. In the centuries to come, only the descendants of this offspring are around and become the norm in that particular surroundings, the original 'normal' animals and plants having died out. The same process repeats endlessly through millenniums to produce the fittest species in the given surrounds and climate.

> How did this miracle of evolution happen? A large part of the answer is mutations: no organism can go on producing exact replicas of itself for eternity. Mistakes are made; a mutant is born; environmental conditions determine whether or not the mutant survives. (Pfeiffer 1976, p. 76)
>
> Perhaps a single mistake among the six billion steps, ..., is enough to cause an imperfect human being to develop. A mutant can be thought of an accident affecting one or more of the base-pair steps in the DNA strand. (p. 61)

However, it is more plausible to me to attribute the cause of evolution to the memory or will of the cells originally generated by the owner's desire to survive.

According to the Bible, whatever we want from our heart will be given to us. I cannot see why the same process should not apply to cells, provided the cells have memory or will.

Cells have life-threatening experiences which dictate that an animal or plant of which they form a small part should be bigger or faster, or more adapted to cold climate, or whatever quality is helpful for survival. The accumulation of this wish confirmed by subsequent generations may produce an offspring resembling the desired description. By the reasoning given in the previous paragraphs, this offspring comes out as a winner in the struggle for existence in the particular environment.

The main thrust of the argument here is that the descendants receive ancestral experiences on the basis that the cells of our body record all our thoughts and actions.

Cell theory states that the cells of the body store the experiences of the ancestors, and if stimulated by some unknown cause these experiences come into the conscious minds that possess the cells. Even if the experiences do not come into the conscious minds, what the ancestors thought and acted have some definite influence over our characters and also over our decision making process. We know that the similar process takes place through what we call culture. The culture of a society forms through various media such as race, language, custom, education and even material objects. The cell hypothesis proposes that our genes carry the information accumulated by our ancestors over the millenniums. The aggregate of the cells of a large number of people would form the collective memory. The cells would certainly contribute to the formation of culture; in fact the cells are the part of a race.

> Though the theory suggesting proteins as memory traces is still not fully confirmed, many investigators are convinced of the relationship between memory and the hereditary apparatus at the molecular level. DNA, RNA and proteins may play a role in our remembrance of things past as they do in evolution and the development of the embryo (p. 155).

The following quotation from Carl Jung, originally a follower of Freudian psychology, sheds some light on the proposition of the cell theory:

> Jung viewed the unconscious as two fold; a 'personal unconsciousness' and a 'collective unconsciousness', [the latter of] which existed at a deeper level of the unconscious. The collective unconsciousness was the repository of memories that all human beings share and consisted of archetypes, mental forms or images that appear in dreams. The archetypes are not derived from the individual's experience, however, but from the biological, prehistoric, and unconscious development of mind. (Spielvogel 1991, p. 965)

Children's language learning capacity so impressed the authors of *Psychology and Language* that they inferred that possibly babies are born with some background of universal language (Clark & Clark 1977). This opinion is in accord with the Jung theory above quoted. His collective unconscious memory perfectly supports the contention that babies are born with universal language which does not depend on the individual experience.

Cell theory also explains the evolutions of the East and the West. The East and the West have become what they are today by the process of gradual evolution, in the similar manner men and women have become what they are today as the result of slow evolution.

I fancied when I was young that the East had the characteristics of females and the West, males: the females were in many respects more advanced than the males before adolescence but the latter eventually overtakes the former in many capacities due to the inherent differences. Now I don't believe both the two cultures and the two sexes are inherently different but are the result of evolutions which are hard to quantify and visualise.

The term 'evolution' in this context often misleads us. The word implies that the new life form evolved is in some way superior or advanced, which I don't see. Humans are not superior to any other forms of life as far as existence goes. For example, bacteria and algae were the first living things on earth and they are not to evolve to humans, and probably will remain on earth after humans die out. Humans are not superior to bacteria and algae, nor are we more advanced than they; both deal with survival in different ways. Adaptation seems a more proper word than evolution.

Both the evolution of humans and cell theory match with the concept that God (Truth) is omniscient, and both point to the notion that God (Truth) is omniscient and omnipotent. All my experiences in life support the notion that everything external happens as the consequence of what we are. This is the only logical conclusion I can think of.

Chapter 6 New Developments in China

I give the outline of communism in China as well as that of Russia in Chapter 1, Book Three *Communism.*

I point out in Chapter 4 of this book that China lagged behind Europe in the material culture after the European Renaissance. Section 2, Chapter 5 says the low ethical level of the Chinese compared with that of the Europeans was the most plausible explanation for the decline of China. However, the communist revolution in China dramatically upgraded the moral standard of the Chinese. I think that the high ethical standard of its people in general marks the People's Republic of China since its foundation in 1949, more than any other features. Strangely the ethics adopted does not come from Confucianism, nor from the communist doctrines which in essence have nothing to do with moral behaviour.

Arnold Toynbee, a prominent British historian, made the following observation in his work *A Study of History*. The Chinese Communist government is attempting to combine a high ethical standard of people with industrialisation. He further commented that we need some more time before we know whether the above approach would be successful or not. *A Study of History* was his life work and he published it during the years 1934 to 1961. Though the book is voluminous, he made many fascinating commentaries regarding human history such as depicted in this paragraph. He made the foregoing remarks on the well-established premise that the industrialisation of a society brings alienation to the bulk of the population and also moral degradation to many people.

Bertrand Russell visited Russia in 1920 eager to support the Bolsheviks; however, the brutality fanned by their fanaticism, and lack of liberty bitterly disappointed him. He also visited China in 1920-1 before the Chinese communist revolution. Decades after the communist revolution he expressed an optimistic opinion about the prospect of success in what was happening there. He was talking about his gut feeling rather than the careful analyses.

Owen Lattimore, an American sinologist, formed a firm opinion many years before the reported rise of China as an industrial nation that the future course of Asia as a whole depended on what China would grow into, and even called China a future axis of the world, monitoring an enormous development taking place in China under the communist leadership.

I still remember Japanese correspondents for the newspapers referring to what was happening in China while Mao Zedong (Tse-Tung) was chairman. One reporter wrote that he felt enormous energy emanating from China and its people, seeing the way the Chinese were forging their country. Another journalist reported that China was becoming a moralist state. I also recall clearly an Australian professional woman's article in Sydney papers, which appeared many years later than the above articles, still while Mao was alive. This female contributor wrote that after living in China for a considerable time, she trusted the Chinese people better than any other people she had come into contact with in her life.

All my research indicates that the ethical standards of the Chinese after the revolution are higher than those of any other peoples in the industrialised societies and also that China has an enormous potential for industrial growth. However, seeing the collapse of East European and Russian communism in the early 1990s, China may not survive as a communist nation. Perceiving this threat, she is rapidly introducing capitalist elements into her society. She has shown willingness to learn from and to cooperate with the advanced capitalist countries. Probably, Toynbee is right even today, when he said that Chinese experiment to amalgamate developed industries with high morals had to go for some time before we can judge if it is a success or not.

Many readers may wonder why I made the lines of thoughts of the last paragraph: it may be contradicting my earlier proposition. Earlier I proposed that the reason China lagged behind Europe in the material culture was that the Chinese were ethically inferior to the Europeans. If the ethical levels of the Chinese and the Europeans are reversed after the communist revolution in China, is it not logical, many readers would argue, to predict confidently that China will sooner or later surpass Europe and possibly the USA in material aspect of civilisation. Obviously this is one possible inference; however, this is not the only logical conclusion. I made the earlier proposal in conjunction with history stretching millenniums and hence the correction of the moral standard at the later date may not necessarily correct the imbalance. The social changes today can take place much faster than in the past from the various reasons. The social changes in the modern settings can take place in a few generations, which would have taken in a few millenniums in the past as I wrote in the introduction. Readers should also appreciate that there are so many factors involved in history and all the settings are different at each epoch of historical development. India is also emerging as an industrial nation. Development of industries has nothing to do with ethics; it is the result of supply and demand. Industrial technology is widely available today, and any firm with capital can acquire it anywhere in the world. Earlier description of China's unethical attitude in conjunction with the development of the East and West was referring to the growth of the mind.

The apes and humans were separated at some point in the past and the separation was forgood. Apes are not going to become humans just as humans are not going to become apes. Humans will become more human-like and apes more ape-like as time goes on.

I refer to the psychological stages of development by Freud in 'Introduction to Series'. Correction of the arrested growth does not necessarily lead to proper growth. The stages are normal growth process. Similarly correction of the ethical level by the Chinese does not necessarily lead to industrial development. Ethics and industrial growth are two sets of unrelated human activities. Industrialisation originates in the profit motive, and demand and supply govern its growth. Hence it is possible to achieve a high level of materialism without exhibiting a high level of idealism. In fact many nations in modern settings achieved industrialisation without going through proper diffusion of idealism.

When I started writing this series of books in the year1989, China was insignificant economically and politically in the world affairs. However from the early 21th century we read in the mass media reports quite so often that China's industrial growth is enormous and many economic indicators of not only Australia but the world depend on Chinese economic indicators. Many politicians and economists talk about the rise of China as a nation, that is to say, the overall assessment of China is not restricted to economy. Though Western nations do not approve of China's political regime, they have no choice but to negotiate with her on various fields because of her importance. Still what would become of China in the future does not alter my theories in this history book, and I did not add any further analyses reflecting the emergence of China.

Chapter 7 Idealism and Materialism

Section 1 Causes of Culture

Religion bears on God, gods, Heaven and nirvana, and reaches to the ultimate as for Buddhism and Christianity denying even idealism. I treat religion in Book Two *Religion* separate from idealism in Book One *Idealism and Materialism.*

Religion, idealism and materialism are, together with various arts, parts of overt cultures. People talk about these subjects freely without inhibitions which the educators teach at school unlike the topics of sex, racism, nationalism and sexism that are also important currents of thoughts affecting the human race.

Spare Time: One Cause of Culture

I earlier proposed that the non-producing class was one condition for the meaningful existence of idealism and materialism. The non-producing class in a society has a parallel in an individual when that person has spare time: the person can do whatever he or she chooses since the person has basic needs. Spare time in a large number of individuals may be said to be equivalent in value to the existence of the non-producing class.

The class of people who were rich enough to be free from the daily labour cultivated and enlarged and diffused the human knowledge of the various fields, and gave the best education to their children to become the elite of the society. The literary and artistic expressions owed their existence to leisure. (Marx 1971, pp. 98, 261).

The above assertion in fact matches Lenin's belief that the theoretical background for the proletarian revolution must come from outside the proletariat. As a matter of fact, Karl Marx who provided the world with the theory of communism was not a member of the proletariat but was a member of the non-producing class in his life style.

One fundamental doctrine of communism was that the production and distribution of the necessities of life determined the characters of civil society, which in turn decided the form of the governing body and intellectual life.

I believe that one of the mistakes the communist countries made after the establishment of the communist regime was that the government tried to annihilate the non-producing class en masse. The capitalists, aristocrats and large land owners were either put to death, exiled or jailed, and the communists treated the remnants as outcasts just after the communist revolutions in Russia and China.

The communist revolutionaries believed that the non-producing people were the scum of society to be wiped out, and only the working people should lead a decent living. However, my analyses showed entirely different perspectives. I have come to believe that one reason for the demise of communism in the early 1990s may be scarcity or non-existence of the leisure class in their society.

In the ancient and classical Greece, the employment of domestic slaves created spare time for free citizens. In the 6th and 5th centuries BC, the majority of Athenian citizens owned slaves to do their chores. As a rule of thumb, in both the ancient to classical Athens and the classical Rome as much as one third of the population were slaves. These slaves did the household chores for the master citizens, who had, as a result, enough time to indulge in political, artistic and military activities. Thus people had spare time for politics, creative works and wars by sacrificing other human beings, not by high technical knowledge as in modern industrialised nations. In the various games in the ancient to classical Greece such as the Olympic Games, the participants were men who had the wealth to train and travel freely. Greek thinkers generally did not think this system was unjust or undemocratic as we modern people might suppose. In fact Plato in his *Republic* stressed that a few domestic slaves for a household were an essential element of democratic life of free citizens. He further stated that leisure was the prerogative of the philosophers and the troubles of the human race would cease only by the philosopher rulers. (Guthrie 1975, pp. 17, 90)

According to R Schlaifer, of all criticism of slavery as an institution (as distinct from errors and abuses in its application) there are only three surviving scraps: a sentence of Alcidamas, a reference in Aristotle and an echo in Philemon (Guthrie 1969, p. 157).

> The answer lies in the growth of the cosmopolitan idea, for, since the enslavement of Greek by Greek was generally unpopular, slavery could only be theoretically defended on the ground that barbarians [non-Greeks] were naturally inferior. This was the view of Plato, who would only admit the enslavement of barbarians. (p. 160)

Slaves were almost always non-Greeks without liberty, rights or property, and they were traded like any other commodities. There were as many as 100 000 slaves in Athens alone in Plato's contemporary society and they made up a third of the total population.

In the idealised *Republic*, Plato argued:

- rule by the philosophers
- abolish private property and family
- introduce eugenic matching
- an educational system to train young people

(Mercer 1996, p. 117)

Aristotle contended that some peoples, possibly he meant non-Greeks, were slaves by nature (p. 433).

The accumulation of wealth is without doubt one cause of culture. Wealth gives people the spare time and also the money to indulge in cultural activities. Wealth is one necessary requirement for culture but not sufficient reason.

The Roman Empire, the Renaissance and the British Empire all had a common origin in that they created wealth through trade at the initial stage of development. The Romans first showed their talent as a trading nation before they built the empire. The Italian city merchants made money through trade with the East and the West before they brought on the Renaissance. The English were more or less compelled to start the Industrial Revolution to make money because trade demands for their commodities from their colonies were immense.

Ninety per cent of people were in the agricultural sector the world over before the Industrial Revolution beginning in the middle of the 18th century. Before the Industrial Revolution the greatest wealth was made through agriculture, and large land owners accumulated wealth. However, by social structures such as taxes and rents, there was little money made through agriculture for the cultivators. Also mining and trade were important sources of wealth for governments and nations as a whole. Even after the Industrial Revolution, the gold rush for Australia and California indicated that gold mining created great wealth for the miners.

Probably it is wrong for us to pass a value judgement on the progress or otherwise of various cultures. Referring to the East and the West in chapters 2, 3 and 4 of this book, I passed the superior and inferior criteria on a particular field of the human endeavours, that is, idealism and materialism, assuming two cultures are more or less on the same track. In fact, the most underdeveloped peoples of today often have happier or even superior attitudes towards life.

In this light, the argument that one culture is better or worse is possibly nonsensical. We have to qualify the comparisons by the answer to the questions such as 'In what way?', 'On what basis?' or 'For whom?' to make some sense.

When we compare ourselves with other mammals we have to define in what way we are superior or inferior to them. Suppose, for argument's sake, we choose a criterion of the capability to wipe out the other party. In this standard we are definitely superior to other mammals: humans can destroy most mammals we select to obliterate from the face of the earth. Humans are capable of killing off all the large mammals but possibly not small mammals like mice. However, some mammals have distinguishing features which suggest that they are superior to us.

For example:

- Mammals are content and happy if they have food, sex and shelter. Many mammals don't even need shelter.
- Mammals seemingly live free from bad emotional traits of human adults such as anger, jealousy and greed except in a simple fashion as we see in human babies.

People have tried so hard over the millenniums to wipe out specific vermin insects such as grasshoppers, flies, mosquitoes and fleas without success: not even one species of insects has died out because people wished and tried. This fact does not mean that these insects are superior to us.

From the viewpoint of an individual, a person is born to a culture and makes a value judgement. The person may accept or reject the culture in which he or she lives. In turn, the society makes its separate judgement to accept or reject him or her.

<u>What Are Other Causes of Cultures?</u>

It is obvious that spare time, for an individual and a society as a whole, does not automatically lead to the creation of so-called culture. The ancient to classical Greeks thought it natural to devote their time to politics or various arts rather than pleasure seeking as dreamed by most people today, though we are not sure why in both cases people act in that way. Many primitive people of the present day have ample time to spare; however, they don't seem interested in promoting idealism and materialism. Enquiries show that they have been in that state many thousands or even tens of thousands of years without much progress.

We also need mental vigour, that is, libido, to develop any worthwhile cultural activities. Why is it that all those who have achieved distinction as philosophers, statesmen, poets or artists seem to be of a melancholic temperament [Aristotle]? (Harbottle 1897, p. 351)

I stress in 'Introduction to Series' that humans act consciously or subconsciously on the instinct of survival; and at times seek pleasure. Hence it is reasonable that when challenged for survival, the survival instinct plays the major role. I emphasise that the two motifs of development of China proper and Western Europe were idealism and materialism. When a nation had a joyous period they developed various arts.

I started this section by making a point that the non-productive class carried civilisations and it had to be that way with good reasons. I am going to qualify the proposition further.

Not many people would dispute that the history of humankind or civilisation has to be taught at school. Though historians may have varied opinions as to the purposes why all pupils before the tertiary level must learn history or as to how and what they must teach, historians would be unanimous that they must teach history at school. Since history covers vast topics in the varieties of the regions, eras and the range of human activities in the past, the writers of history text books have to make a vigorous selection of contents, in the same way as any other text book writers have to.

One selection criterion historians use may be how closely a piece of history has affected the lives of the students. The students may see the consequences of that history in their daily lives or a certain chain of events may be responsible for the environments in which the students live. The former event may be said to have influenced the students directly and the latter indirectly. Apart from the above rule that an event is important because it has affected the readers' lives, historians may select some topics because they are inherently important in understanding human history, irrespective of how these topics altered the course of human history.

Interest and pleasure may be another reason why people study history. People research topics that fascinate them and often publish what they learned and thought in the form of books, which a large number of people can share.

In summary, we can approach history in two ways. The textbook approach emphasises the importance of past events in affecting our present life directly or indirectly and understanding history. The leisure approach looks at history purely from the viewpoint of interest or pleasure. Many people are not bothered to make the above distinctions and may look at the argument with disdain. However, if readers go on reading, they will know the reasons behind the seemingly silly differentiations.

We must understand the proposition that mainly the non-productive class carried civilisation to the effect that civilisation means history looked at in terms of importance, not in terms of interest. I would like to explain this point using the ancient Egyptian civilisation cited earlier.

Strictly speaking, every person, every word uttered or written, every activity and every natural phenomenon in Egypt were all a part of Egyptian history without any doubt. However, if we apply the textbook approach to the selection criteria, we mention only the events or things that are important to human beings. For example, when authors refer to buildings, they would write about pyramids and palaces built for pharaohs rather than residential houses built for private citizens. According to my definition, the productive people built the private houses, whereas the non-productive people built the pyramids and palaces. They built the numerous residential houses in the course of Egyptian empires, though they were made with sun-baked bricks and most of them have not survived all these millenniums. In terms of money and labour expended, all the houses built through the millenniums would vastly outweigh all the pyramids and palaces constructed. Yet the historians hardly mention the houses in the history textbooks because they judge that they are not important historically. They think that the pyramids and palaces which were products of non-productive labour manifest the characters of the ancient Egyptian culture.

Why Idealism First Flowered in Both East and West

Materialism has always existed among humans since the dawn of civilisation. In fact, without adequate material culture no human society would have survived the harsh struggles for existence in the often adverse natural environment and among the competing societies. Material culture has increased supplies of the necessaries and secured the defence at each stage of human development, even in our present society. However, it did not become dominant concept in any society for many millenniums since the dawn of civilisation until modern times. As a general rule, people who were proficient in idealism as well as the aristocrats, the wealthy and the large landowners, or their sons became the elite of a society before the modern times.

I would say that the preconditions of idealistic culture were the necessities of life, that is, food, clothes and shelter. Before people have these necessities we do not expect them to behave in a civilised manner. Once people got their food, clothes and shelter, though in the simplest forms, they naturally wanted more. Some people must have wanted more and better of these commodities. Some devoted their attention to something more subliminal and looked into their minds and cultivated ideals of life. Idealism was the natural outgrowth of human craving in the absence of sophisticated forms of other knowledge in such as politics, economics and science.

Another requirement for opening up the frontier of idealism may be social disturbances and consequent sufferings of people. I detail how religion and idealism came forward as a serious human concern in 'Introduction to Series' and also in Chapter 1 Birth of Religion, Book Two *Religion*. These times were the troubled times or the times of troubles, sufferings or chaos. When humans suffer they naturally seek escape and comfort. They looked into their minds since the world around was the source of misery, and formulated what we call today religion and idealism. People pay attention to a situation when there is a problem, and with no problems they don't think much. The fact that Judaism was born among the Jews was not an accident. Since the emergence of the Jewish people they suffered by the evil conducts in the Jewish community which also prompted the attacks from the surrounding peoples. Hence the Jews had to develop a deep religious faith to combat the onslaught on their very existence.

The Qur'an (Koran) is sometimes called a healing because it is a remedy for the spiritual disease which damages the sufferers. 'Or do those in whose hearts is a disease think that Allah will not bring forth their spite?' (Qur'an 47.29)

If people's sufferings come from hunger, they want more food. If people's suffering is emotional, they want ideas which relieve their emotional pains. People cultivated idealism to answer the emotional cravings of people. For example, 'Buddhism was developed when the society was in a bad way and people were desperately seeking salvation with whatever method they could find.' (Toynbee 1962, p. 21) In summary, the development of idealism presupposes the following two requirements:

- People's requirements for food, clothes and shelter are more or less met.
- People are still unhappy because of lack of intellectual supports faced with fears and sufferings.

For the development of idealism, the main tool was speculation, and people needed a limited number of data in causes and effects of human experiences: whereas materialism required a large number of experimental data before people formulated the sophisticated scientific truism. The data required to develop and verify idealist doctrines were everyday experience and people did not have to experiment in the laboratory or in the field as they require for those in the technical theories. Hence the theorisation of idealism reached its peak at the early classical era in several parts of the world, and materialism had to wait till the modern era for its flowering.

People had to rely on idealism before the other branches of knowledge such as politics or economics or engineering were developed to be useful for decision makings. For example, in the ancient to classical Greece, people used oracles to decide the location for colonisation; however, once people had enough knowledge they decided such as where to migrate based on the information, and used oracles only for reference.

For the transfer of material culture in a crude form, people needed only the material objects which trade effected. Whereas the transfer of idealism depended on well written books which in turn the scholars proficient in the subject as well as in the two languages had to translate before people got impressed with the ideas. Besides, in any society before the modern era only a small to fair proportion of people were capable of reading and writing.

People fully investigated idealism in China, India, the Levant and Europe by the end of the ancient era or at the early classical era to such a level that later scholars felt that nobody could advance idealist culture any further. There is ample evidence to prove that idealism in China, India and the Levant enriched European wisdom long before the beginning of the Christian era (Hall 1984, p. v). People completed idealism and there was nothing more people of later era could do except to study and interpret and possibly modify what was discovered before to suit the new era. Confucius himself said in private that his philosophy was actually not of his own making but came from the ancient books.

In later commercialised societies, people gave the ethical system a different interpretation: people saw morals in the light of utilitarianism and self-interest. Political thoughts in these societies were also rooted in the concept of commerce--the social contract. (Walker 1978, p. 1)

The Bible says, 'You must diligently observe everything I command you; do not add to it or take away anything from it' (Deuteronomy 12.32), which meant that the Lord would give everything people needed as long as they adhered to the teachings to the letter. It also says that there is nothing new under the sun (Ecclesiastes 1:9): probably the author meant that all human endeavours including the concepts of idealism were out in the open by this time.

We should not expect the general public to have a serious interest in the pattern of thoughts unless they derive some usefulness or happiness out of them. Idealism came about because many people suffered in spite of the fact that they had the basic necessities of life. Some of them insisted that only idealism could help people who were suffering from mental agony. The ancient sages would not have expected that a time would come when materialism would displace idealism as the dominant ideology of the people.

Many people advocated that the adherence to idealism should be the ultimate defence strategy of an individual or a nation as the following verses exemplify:

> A king is not saved by his great army; a warrior is not delivered by his great strength (Psalms 33:16).
>
> But the eyes of the Lord are on those who fear him, on those whose hope is in his unfailing love, to deliver them from death and keep them alive in famine (Psalms 33:18-9).

The authors are saying that idealism is more important for the defence of an individual or a nation than materialism. In contrast with the above thinking many people advocated a strong army as a measure of strength or defence. For example, Shih huang-ti (259-210 BC) of Ch'in and Machiavelli (1469-1527) scoffed at idealism and did not think of anything else but heavy military spending for sheer survival of the nation. Thucydides wrote that the only sound basis of alliance is mutual fear (Harbottle 1897, p. 509).

Apart from the completion of idealism while the people greatly feared and suffered, population growth was another reason why idealism gave way to materialism. In order to feed more mouths people had to look for more necessities of life and hence had to rely on material culture as an aide: idealism simply did not help in this respect.

<u>Why Are Idealism and Materialism Presented?</u>

As I understand, the following factors more or less have decided conflicts among individuals within families, firms and nations, and among groups (families, firms and nations) throughout human history:

- might, physical for individuals and military for nations
- lying and cheating
- Machiavellianism

The outcomes of conflicts were dog eat dog, and eat or be eaten. Men tried to obtain by hook or by crook what they wanted such as money, position, fame and women. I believe the above assertions applied in any society or to any associations of nations at any era. I may even call it the universal rule of conflicts, though we sometimes witness some exceptions to the rule as we expect in any other rules.

If the above principles have marked the human struggles, why did I present this book exploring idealism and materialism and asserting that one of them prevailed in a society over the other survival means in a certain era. I am to answer the query in the following fashion:

- Idealism and materialism belong to the overt culture being taught at school, and people discussed these ideologies in the open. In contrast, the universal rules of conflicts are in the covert culture and people discussed only among the selected audience under certain conditions, and were not the school curriculum. Besides the conflicts are only a part of human activities and people spend their time in the other survival activities and pleasures.
- My personal experience showed clearly that the materialistic world view was inadequate to deal with certain kinds of misfortunes in life. When faced with a deep distress, I had to change my life view from materialism to idealism in a short time in an instinctive manner. I also believe that idealism governs the fate of not only individuals but also families, firms and nations or even races. This is precisely the reason why the prophets with high idealist outlook can predict the future with high degree of accuracy. Happiness and unhappiness largely depend on the idealistic thinking of persons and nations. The following ancient Greek verse well exemplifies the last statement: The good man is not always of necessity the happy man, but the happy man is also a good man [Archytas] (Harbottle 1897, p. 430). The Bible also says, 'There is no peace for the wicked' (Isaiah 48:22). The Tree of Knowledge in the Garden of Eden is a symbol of morality, the major manifestation of idealism. By profaning the tree Adam and Eve became imperfect.
- The distinction put up between idealism and materialism is a plausible basis to explain the demise of the East against the West as Chapter 5 of this book expounds.
- It is indisputable that some civilisations exhibited distinctly religious or economic ideologies. The dominance of Christianity characterised Western Europe during the Middle Ages. Communist countries in the past such as Russia and China had Marxism as their unifying force. These communist nations showed other features such as race and religion but the dominance of materialism in the governing body was undeniable.
- I look at religion as the crystallisation of idealism, and communism as the extreme form of materialism. I expound religion in Book Two *Religion*. Many people may object if I say that communism may be after all the terminal point of capitalism. It seems that at the early 21st century the Marxist theories have been thoroughly defeated. I would say that the decline of Marxism has come about from its doctrines many of which are useless or even erroneous. I present in Book Three *Communism* one version of communist theory called Partial Communism, which is the communism of non-Marxist orientation. I believe that once the Third Prophecy becomes the dominant thinking in a society, people will adopt an entirely different attitude towards life and society. At that time Partial Communism may become a successful economic doctrine.
- People formulated idealism in the early classical societies of the East, the West and the Middle East; and it subsequently became the dominant doctrine of China and Europe. Christianity dominated Europe during the Middle Ages and Confucianism was the state cult of the succeeding Chinese empires till the early part of the 20th century. In this sense I call idealism the First Prophecy, heralding the new society. Materialism became the guiding doctrines of the two regions--the Renaissance onwards for Europe and the 20th century

onwards for China, thus I call it the Second Prophecy. Idealism and materialism do not have
a complete hold on the human race and there is much to be desired in the economically advanced countries even today. I expound the new teaching in Book Four *The Third Prophecy*. This new philosophy does not displace the first two prophecies but explains why they were not really successful in converting the society as many people wished. This book explains further what this new philosophy is and how it will achieve what the two previous prophecies promised, and eventually will have to become the dominant teaching of the societies of the world in the next century on the assumption that the survival instinct will guide the human beings as they have all these millenniums.

Overt and Covert Cultures

Jean Jacques Rousseau lamented in his book *Confessions* (1782) that people did not express their innermost thoughts and talked about only the agreeable or disagreeable topics. In fact he himself did not state his true motives concerning his much criticised actions regarding his children: he sent all his babies, just after their birth, to orphanages. He made a few references in *Reverie of the Solitary Walker* (1779) that life in the orphanages would make his children one thousand times happier.

We cannot work out if the above statement reflected the true state of his mind. As a matter of fact there was an incident suggesting he did not tell the truth. According to his account in *Confessions*, a woman over a dinner table asked him about his children. Unprepared, he made a reply which obviously sounded untrue to her and even to himself. The woman seized an opportunity to say something unkind to his smarting ego. Rousseau went on to write that he later analysed the conversation and wished he had answered in a different way. He still did not disclose his true intent regarding his actions concerning his babies.

The book of Proverbs in the Bible has an abundance of teachings which tell youths to follow the sayings of their parents. Youngsters may go astray by following overt cultures, thinking that they can judge things by what they hear from other people. The Bible is teaching the young people only their parents will tell them what is really good for them. There is no doubt that in many cases the covert culture which the parents speak in the hiding is true and the overt culture people speak in the open is false.

When a person dies, the people associated and the mass media must say in the open that that was a good person and console the remaining members of the family though they may think otherwise in their minds.

It is obvious to anyone that different cultures of both overt and covert have existed in any community in any era. Time and place do not restrict the applicability of Proverbs in the Bible, which is supposed to be eternal truths as for any other books of the Bible. Consequently young people today the world over can benefit by following the instructions of Proverbs.

The above observation is generally correct, irrespective of location. However, when we contrast the East with the West, we notice that the differences between overt and covert cultures are greater in the East than in the West. In the Orient, the various authorities such as politicians, teachers and policemen say what appears to be correct but in fact does not reflect the true state of affairs. They are well aware what they are saying is not true. I call these false statements overt culture. These people sometimes mention their true positions in private, which we can call covert culture. I suspect that the greater chasm of the overt and covert cultures has existed in the Orient throughout history, compared with that in the Occident. After all the Jewish authors in the Levant, a part of Asia, wrote the Bible.

Section 2 Idealism and Materialism Defined and Contrasted; Theoretical Analyses

I am to disclose the theoretical foundations of idealism and materialism in this section. Section 3 to follow deals with the practical aspects of idealism. Subsequent Section 4 deals with the practice of materialism. Materialism in practice by the general public is the perennial desire for wealth; and also manifests in the modern era as strong military forces, sophisticated medical technology, high volume production of consumer goods, resulting in large population. Spurred by the desire for wealth the West Europeans expanded into the world in the modern era, later assisted by the industrial revolution.

Earlier in this book I used the terms idealism and materialism to describe two major currents of culture in conjunction with human history. I did not define both concepts in a scholarly manner but denoted loosely as people understand in everyday language. In this section I am to determine the boundaries of these ideas in a more acceptable way to the academics, hopefully giving deeper insight into the reasons why the distinction between the two has played a crucial role in the development of human race. Idealism and materialism are theories on the nature of reality.

Idealists believe that human problems lie in our defective way of thinking and try to improve their brain activities, and on a positive note pursue truth, justice and normally accepted moral principles. Whereas materialists believe that the physical world is the primary cause of life and the world, and try to advance the material environment.

The four great sages in the world history, Socrates, the Buddha, Confucius and Christ, all focused their minds on lofty concepts of idealist teachings and none of them stepped out of these boundaries. These sages summarised, modified and perfected the idealism that had been going on for centuries in their respective regions.

> The idealists, to whom nothing in the universe was real but the Spirit, which manifested itself in Ideas and in turn could be communicated by words, could construct a system that encompassed everything because the symbolic nature of language makes infinite abstraction possible (Carmichael 1968, p. 40).

Plato considered that there were three basic elements to human nature: material desire, spirit and wisdom (Roebuck 1966, p. 337).

Philosophy is the cognition of truth. One fundamental question of philosophy may be the relation of thinking (spirit) and being (the outside world). Nature was the predominant form of being for the ancients, and as humans progressed material objects became the focus of attention. Possibly, the gods appeared to humans as personifications of material forces which they held in wonder. These various gods by abstraction developed into one Supreme God. (Marx & Engels 1970, pp. 339, 345)

Schopenhauer believed that material objects had no value, though we can experience and investigate in them, compared with the timeless vision open to artists and saints (Janaway 1994, p. 15).

There are many faculties which we cannot class into either idealism or materialism. Acquisition of necessities of life, sex, religion, racism, nationalism, sexism and arts are obvious examples. Arts include literature, painting, sculpture, architecture and music. These classes may seem independent concepts in their abstraction and in the extreme situation some people want to live under only one concept. Practically they are all dependent in some way in the real world. For example, without adequate necessities of life, idealism and arts and all the other faculties have no place in human minds except in very crude forms. Also we can make buildings and household appliances purely from a materialistic or functional viewpoint, but without the arts incorporated they cannot attain public acceptance. We must express idealism artistically to receive ready acceptance. People often tie racialism and sexism to the attainments of idealism, materialism and arts. Idealism is a completed subject and embraces only a small number of topics, whereas materialism has ever expanding topics. Idealism is closed and materialism is open in terms of the number of the subject matters.

Some topics may belong to one realm in some situation and to the other in another situation, depending on how we look at the variables under consideration. The distinction in some cases does not come from the subjects but rather comes from the attitudes of the person involved. For instance, we should aptly call an individual who looks at religion purely as a means of making money a materialist and not an idealist. I recalled a Christian gathering I attended many years ago: I thought that 90 per cent of the organisers were there to pass time and make a living and only 10 per cent of them were serious about what they were preaching.

Another example may be sex. People may think that sex does not belong to either idealism or materialism. However, resistance characterises women as sex objects hence women are material and wealth. Men want to own as many women as possible and as much wealth as possible. Probably the desires for both are stored in the same part of the brain.

Idealism may be compared to leaven in the process of baking bread; without the leaven, though in a small amount, we cannot make full-blown bread. Without idealism, though simple and of the attitude rather than knowledge, a civilisation does not grow satisfactorily. The Buddha expressed this view when he said that unless our minds are clear we cannot see what is good or bad for us in the same way unless the water is clear we cannot see what is under the water. Montaigne wrote, 'Wisdom is the choice between good and evil' (Montaigne 1965, p. 369).

The necessities of life cater for sheer survival of the human physique. Idealism satisfies the spiritual cravings of humans and at the same time contributes to the survival of an individual and a society. People use idealism to try to solve the various problems of human life in the same way people use engineering theories to try to solve the technical problems. People keep the theories of both of these disciplines at the back of their head and it is rare that the theories offer solutions in a textbook fashion. Our bodies if undernourished do not have the strength to recover from various sicknesses. I have been convinced that in the same way, unless we live a moral life, we do not have the strength to recover from the various misfortunes of life.

We need material objects for the survival of the humans in the physical sense and it supports more population. One of the aims of the material may be to give people physical comfort. If people cannot find the necessities of life all the meaningful cultures will disappear from the society and so will idealism and materialism.

The classical Greeks read the following poems:

> Peerless is water [Pindar] (Harbottle 1897, p. 335).
> Virtue is a weapon which none can take from us [Antisthenes] (p. 324).

Water (physical substance) and virtues (spiritual quality) have parallel qualities in the poems though uttered by different poets.

With the foregoing remarks, we may be able to propose an inference in the following paragraphs with some degree of confidence.

An average person today may be preoccupied with idealism for and on less than one per cent of thinking in a normal course of a day. Also less than one per cent of people in a modern society are seriously concerned with idealism. A general library or a general bookstore reflects the above inference: we may find a rule of thumb proportions of books on idealism and on the rest including materialism are 1 to 99. We also find the rough proportions in Ecclesiastes which the author probably wrote around 250 BC: I found one upright man among a thousand, but not one upright woman among them all (Ecclesiastes 7:28). The Bible repeatedly asserts that people's attitude to idealism and God governs human fate.

Since idealism occupies only a small percentage of people's thinking and also it is a completed subject covering a small percentage of human knowledge, it may be easier to define idealism first. I also have come to the following conclusions. Idealism occupied probably roughly one per cent of human knowledge at the early classical era when it was completed, though its teachings have been repeated countless times over the centuries at home, at school, at church and by the government. Today with a vastly increased knowledge idealism comprises far less than one per cent of human knowledge.

Idealism Defined

The external world is viewed as illusion and people are urged to look into themselves. All human problems are said to stem from the deficiencies of the mind, and the corrections and developments of minds should be the chief concerns of the human beings. Idealism assumes that everything starts and finishes in the mind. Material objects, racism, nationalism, sexism and arts are secondary importance at most to humans.

Idealism Further Assessed

Any human activities require participation of the mind. We have to use our brains to indulge in such activities as sport, fighting, eating and lovemaking, though we often forget that. We can accomplish a high degree of performance in any human endeavour only through excellence of mind. However, we should not include these activities in what we call idealism. Though pursuits of fame and scholarship do not per se involve material as such, they should not come under idealism. We may find practical manifestations of idealism in ethics and philosophy. Some ethical scholars and some philosophers do not uphold idealistic views both in their hearts and in their daily life, and are not idealists in my book. No liar long escapes discovery; Falsehood is hateful to the good and wise [Menander] (Harbottle 1897, p. 535). A soul with good intent and purpose just discerns far more than a lecturer can teach [Sophocles] (p. 535). A soul that makes virtue its companion is like an ever-flowing well, for it is clean and pellucid, sweet and wholesome, open to all, rich, blameless and indestructible [Epictetus] (p. 535). He who with smallest means contentment finds will live the happiest life; so cries the sage, to whom whate'er he has suffices [Sextus Turpilius] (p. 219).

Most idealists do not deny the existence of the physical world, that is, realism, and their assertions are about the nature of the world. Realism asserts that the objective world revealed by experience is real and exists independently of being known (Koller 1985, pp. 83-4). Some metaphysical realists assert that the reality is objective, that is, its existence and nature are independent of our minds. Whereas, some metaphysical realists argue that we can only know the world in the form that appears to us, depending on our minds, senses and cultural tradition.

GE Moore (1873-1958), a British philosopher, asserts that since we cannot define the good and the bad, we can know the difference only by intuition.

Materialism Defined

Every individual perceives the external world differently and the materialists insist that these perceptions are illusions and only the concrete objects are real. Since the external world mostly conditions the human minds, our chief concern must be to improve the material environment and everything else will turn out to be right in so doing.

Materialism Further Assessed

The material environment has governed the human history, and idealism has played but a small part since the latter was in the main the product of the former. Some ideologies before the modern era emphasised material objects. For example, the Legalists in China advocated a strong national defence and also agriculture. The desires to possess both as many objects and as much money as possible governed the lives of the vast majority of people through the course of human history. However, materialism as scholarship of science and technology and also as economics came forward as the main concern of the human beings only in the modern times whose distinguishing feature is material civilisation. Materialism includes medical science. We live in a society where science and technology predominate over the other ideologies such as religion, ethics and philosophy. Materialism identifies mind with matter, that is, it postulates that the human soul is only matter and aggregates of cells.

Communists insist that history, religion and philosophy do not have the innate force to change but the changes come only as result of the changes of the production and distribution of the necessities of life (Marx & Engels 1989, p. 43). More generally, the material conception of history states that the ultimately determining factor in history is the production and exchange of the necessities of life (Marx & Engels 1970, p. 487). They maintain that the history of human kind has shown that intellectual production is the reflection, nothing more and nothing less, of material production (Marx & Engels 1989, p. 130). F Engels argued that religion was useless in explaining the world but the bourgeois thought religion was a useful tool to make their workers in submission and get the most out of them (Marx & Engels 1970, p. 106).

Idealism and Materialism Compared and Contrasted

Comparisons (similarities) and contrasts (differences) can be made in degrees or in kinds. We can express a difference in degree in terms of more or less, better or worse, stronger or weaker. Idealism and materialism are similar in that both try to achieve the survival and happiness of the human beings but different in their approach: both are only vehicles. Though some idealistic doctrines disregard the well-being of the followers in their hot pursuit of truth, the foregoing statement is correct for the general public. Idealism tries to attain its purpose by mental excellence and learning to live with as little material objects as possible. Whereas materialism tries to achieve its aim relying on the material objects by their possession and use. Idealists try to level down their desires rather than increasing the possessions; whereas materialists do the opposite. Idealists find happiness in cultivating their minds, whereas materialists find happiness in accumulating material (wealth). Idealists reflect in their daily life how they conducted according to the sacred books, whereas materialists reflect in their daily life how much wealth they made or lost.

The seers of the Upanishads discovered that Brahman is the ultimate external reality, the ultimate objects, the universe; and Atman is the ultimate internal reality, the ultimate subject, consciousness. They also discovered that the great power (Brahman) that energises the cosmos and the spiritual energy of the self (Atman) are ultimately the same. Hence they postulated that by looking within oneself or knowing self, they can know the entire outside world. (Koller 1985, pp. 11, 32) The above conclusion matches with Socrates' cardinal teaching 'Know thyself'. Indian thoughts also presuppose universal moral justice.

Idealism and materialism stand on an entirely different premise in their essence; however, in the real world which is compromise in many ways, some people are idealistic and at the same time materialistic. In the same logic, religion and communism stand on the different premises; however, some people are religious as well as communistic. The materialists argue that the material mode of existence is primary cause or agent but this does not preclude the ideological concepts act on the materialistic existence as secondary effect. (Marx & Engels 1970, p. 483)

The law of God as the Bible expounds refers to primarily the relationship between God and humans and secondarily the human affairs; however, many biblical scholars insist that nature and natural sciences are also in the domain of the law of God.

Materialists would argue that the concrete objects alone are real and true, and create substance on the human minds; human minds are unsubstantial without the material objects. Idealists, on the other hand, would argue that the material objects themselves are unsubstantial and illusory and have no power over the humans except the humans direct their minds to them. Materialism emphasises the influence of material (outside world) to the mind (inside world), whereas idealism emphasises the dominance of the mind over the material. In religion, the products of their own brain govern people. In capitalist production, the products of their own hands govern people. (Marx 1954, p. 582) Lenin, being a communist and hence materialist, wrote the following passage: Man's consciousness does not only reflect the objective world but also creates it (Dutt 1961, p. 113).

Idealism is general; materialism is particular. Idealism works as a guiding principle or attitude in all facets of life such as study and job, and seemingly tries to ignore the material aspects of human achievements. Whereas, materialism is the means by which we endeavour to obtain our specific purpose by objects and technical knowledge. One object useful in attaining one goal can be quite useless in another goal. For example, a heater is useful to warm us up in winter but quite useless in summer. An idealist tries to overcome the hot and cold weather by training themselves to face it.

Leo Tolstoy (1828-1910) wrote many short stories advocating the superiority of mind over matter and of action over speech, though some people commented that his presentations were naive.

Idealism is timeless and deals with eternal truth at all times. Time and space constrain materialism, which are apt to change as the environments change. Consequently happiness derived from idealism tends to be general and permanent; whereas happiness derived from materialism tends to be specific and temporal. For example, people who feel happy about their house are so only about it. These people normally find some defects around the house and are worried about damages by wear and tear, fire, malicious damage, earthquake or storm. The loss of the house deprives them of their happiness altogether.

During antiquity people posited Divinity and then constructed the universe: in the modern era people posit the universe and then look for God (Hall 1984, p. 40).

In the medieval Europe, the church representing idealism as Europe as a whole competed with the national states representing the multitudes of survival means and the national interests. The church swayed over the states but was not strong enough to override them. Sumer, the earliest civilisation, seems to have had a dual power of Temple, a symbolic representation of religion, and Palace, a symbolic representation of politics (Whitehouse & Wilkins 1986, p. 89).

The idealism which prominent religion universally advocates may be capable of running a community when the community is simple and undeveloped like the Jewish community at the time of the Exodus when Moses represented all authority. As the community becomes complicated the division of labour must exist in the first place. In the second place the temple or church with the simple ideology of idealism cannot cope with the complex dealings of the various people with the varying modes of survival techniques such as acquisition of necessities of life, sex, religion, idealism, materialism, racism, nationalism, sexism and arts. The palace or the government can handle politics competently with consistency only if the experienced specialists of various fields and their supervisors put their heart and mind into their jobs. It is often said that religion and politics do not mix. It has been proved to my satisfaction that many of the communism's doctrines are erroneous as I present in Book

Three *Communism*: the simple doctrines of communism with one survival guide of materialism cannot cope with the various problems of the society.

A small number of people completed the doctrines of idealism in several parts of the world in the early classical era. The teachings by the Four Sages, though Christ, one of them, appeared in the middle of the classical era, almost exhaust the entire topics of idealism, though these sages in turn based their learning on what the handful of predecessors cultivated. A fairly small number of scholars propelled quantum leaps in the field of materialism but a large number of people have contributed to this field in some way or another. We do not see any end today to the development of science and technology, a huge number of people making contributions.

Idealists' main concern is mind whose essential quality is thinking, and materialists' main concern is matter whose essential quality is resistance.

Idealists speculate on invisibles and materialists deal with visibles. Idealists look at life as an ideal of their conception and argue in the realm of 'ought to'. Materialists look at life as a reality and dwell in the realm of 'is'. Idealism often implies that its stated principles are ideal and removed from the reality and hence we cannot attain them fully in our life. The idealists teach people 'You ought to love your neighbour', the central theme of practical idealism; and people, while agreeing, find the teaching difficult in practice. The Christian theologians concluded, reading the Bible, that the earth ought to be stationary and flat but the scientists proved that it was a revolving globe. In this last example about the globe idealism and idealists are contrasted with realism and realists and not with materialism and materialists. Materialism is a form of realism but realism does not necessarily refer to materialism. Materialism is based on objects, and its principles must come from the actual phenomena. Materialism comes from the people's desire to solve human problems by the material objects and contains wealth acquisition, science, technical knowledge and communism.

F Engels wrote:

> People who insist on the primacy of spirit like Hegel did are called idealists. People who insist on the primacy of nature are called materialists. Matter is not the product of mind. Mind or brain is merely the product of matter, though it may be biological and intricate. (Marx & Engels 1970, pp. 346, 348)

Idealism looks internally and materialism externally for happiness and inspirations. Idealism is the domain of the good and the evil, the just and the unjust, the ethical and the unethical, the freedom and the bondage. Materialism is the domain of physical survival, comfort and luxury. The arts are the domain of beauty.

Islam seeks a balance between the outward and the inward and between the physical and the spiritual (Sharma 1993, p. 454).

The ancient Egyptians as a whole thought that material side of life was important, and speculated and acted on it; whereas the ancient Jews as a whole thought that spiritual side of life was important, and speculated and acted on it.

Idealists think that nothing is wrong with the external world, and people have a crooked way of thinking. Materialists think that nothing is wrong with their mind, and the external world is defective.

Idealists try to improve the way they think; materialists their environment. Idealists try to satisfy human needs by mental adjustments, while materialists try to do the same by supplying adequate objects. Idealism centres on soul (subject) and wisdom, and materialism on the world (object) and knowledge. Socrates said, 'He who has the fewest wants is nearest to the gods' (Harbottle 1897, p. 367).

Idealism teaches us how to think and behave and gives lessons even in defensive behaviour when other people misbehave. Many idealists insist that the cornerstone of national defence must be in the way people think. Many materialists insist that we must base defence on strong armed forces and in the modern age the nation must have strong economy and defence forces equipped with up-to-date weaponry.

There has been a strong tradition both in the East and the West that we should rely on idealism and not on material objects for the individual security as well as for the national defence. For example, in the ancient Greek world, Agesilaus wrote, 'The ramparts of our cities should be built not of stone and timber, but the brave hearts of our citizens' (p. 326). Similarly in ancient China Wu Chi, a military strategist, said, 'We must rely on our virtue, not on our strategic position'. However, this man, betraying the above statement, acted with such cruelty and ruthlessness that he brought about his own death. (Chien 1979, p. 33)

> Knowledge is no part of the saintly ideal (Randall 1976, p. 93).
>
> Should one recite a hundred verses, comprising useless words, better is one single word of the Dhamma, by hearing which one is pacified. Though one should conquer a million men in battle field, yet he, indeed, is the noblest victor who has conquered himself. (Narada 1993, p. 97)

How peoples in the pre-modern societies integrated idealism into their society gives some indication what positions the idealists and idealism occupied. In Europe, during the Middle Ages, the church and pope governed the spiritual life of the people beyond the national boundaries, and the kingdoms and empires had temporal power vested within the boundaries though they were not well delineated and the nations did not have the effective taxing power. In China there were four class distinctions in the pre-modern era:

- the literary class by merits
- the cultivators of land
- the artisans
- the merchant class

(Wells 1925, p. 145)

The Indo-Europeans, though dispersed over wide area over the length of 2 millenniums, showed a fundamental social structure of 3 classes; priests, warriors, stock-breeders and farmers (Eliade 1978, p. 192). The Indo-European people had the common language origin. The Indians (the Indo-Europeans) well preserved this class distinction as well as the race distinction in the caste system. However, the Romans (the Indo-Europeans) disrupted the social tripartition at quite early stage of their development.

In India, the priests formed the highest class in the society, and the four major castes and the outcaste are still in force:

- the Brahmans; the priests
- the Kshatriyas; the nobles and the warriors
- the Vaisyas; the farmers, money-lenders and merchants
- the Sudras; the subjugated people, still the largest stratum of society containing most of service-rendering people
- the Pariahs

The caste system is a Hindu tradition. Influenced by Hinduism, the Muslims, the Sikhs and the Christians in India also have their own castes though they are generally less strictly regulated. Though caste means race or colour, we may look at the first three castes as occupational division of labour.

During the feudal era in Japan, the warrior class was on the top social echelon suggesting the military society, and farmers, artisans and merchants formed the decreasing hierarchy in the society. The Buddhists were outside the social hierarchy.

Confucianism became dominant idealism in China through the examination system started by the Sui dynasty (AD 581-618) and ended in the year 1905. Legalism which preached vigorous legalism, regimentation and materialism became out of political favour after the fall of the Ch'in dynasty (221-206 BC). Confucianism, though vigorously promoted by the succeeding imperial governments, may not be after all conducive to the promotion of idealism in its best. Some scholars say Confucianism is the doctrine to teach the ruling class how to govern ethically, which may be the reason why the Chinese and other Asian governing bodies used them. Also the Chinese government did not represent the voice of the people as a whole, that is, the political system was not democratic. I studied Confucianism with fervour when young but lost an enthusiasm for it over the years. I do not think these observations alter the theories put forward in this series of books.

Section 3 Common Practice of Idealism World Over

I present five precepts (A to E) as the common practice of idealism in this section; however, 'Love your neighbour as yourself' far outweighs the other concepts in importance, being the kernel of idealism. Hence I almost always equate idealism to 'Love Thy Neighbour' in this series of books. The other doctrines not only exhibit their own correct way of life attitude but show the result of (as for B), how to apply (as for C, D and E) the precept of 'Love Thy Neighbour', which I relate in each article.

A Love Your Neighbour as Yourself and Resulting Moral Codes

The Ten Commandments in the Bible represent the moral codes which the ancients discovered in several parts of the world, though some commandments may not have direct bearings on ethics or morals. The Ten Commandments are:

- You shall have no other gods beside me.
- You shall not make for yourself an idol.
- You shall not make wrongful use of the name of the Lord your God.
- Remember the Sabbath day, and keep it holy.
- Honour your father and mother.
- You shall not murder.
- You shall not commit adultery.
- You shall not steal.
- You shall not bear false witness against your neighbour.
- You shall not covet your neighbour's possessions.

Some people insist that the moral codes are nothing but the convenience of the social order and have nothing valuable per se. Certainly it is hard for us to understand why the moral conducts are important to us and many people follow this argument and do not live the ethical life. However, the morals may be meaningful if we think that they come from non-hurting of the other people and the code of 'Love thy neighbour' as well as creating the stable society. In the Judaic tradition this concept comes from God, hence it defies all human scrutinies. We can express 'Love thy neighbour' also as 'Love one another', 'Honour one another', and 'Love each other'. If we love one another, God lives in us and his love is made complete in us (1 John 4:12). God is love. Whoever lives in love lives in God, and God in him. (1 John 4:16) Probably, the human beings are not capable of judging by the philosophical speculation alone why they must adhere to the command. If we look at the question from the opposite end, the Jews as for any other ancient peoples could not prove to their satisfaction why the rule was important, hence they had to rely on the higher notion of God and stopped any further inquiries.

> The instinctive judgements, primitive emotions, natural instincts and first impressions are more trustworthy as a basis for action than all the reflections, the caution, the experience that come from association with others (Randall 1976, p. 402).
>
> Morality and religion are not matters of reasoned thinking, but of natural feeling. Man's worth depends not on his intelligence, but on his moral nature, which consists essentially of feeling; the good will alone has absolute value. (p. 402)

Montaigne wrote in his *Essays* that lying, once born, grows like a child; we must keep battling against its birth and progress insistently (Montaigne 1965, p. 24). Justice is twofold; that which is written, and that which is according to law (that is, unwritten and the spirit of the law) [Aristotle] (Harbottle 1897, p. 510).

Anicius Boethius, once a Roman senator, finished writing *The Consolation of Philosophy* in prison just before being executed in 524. He emphasised the transience of earthly fortunes, and concluded that nothing except virtue has permanence. (Mercer 1996, p. 234)

Various institutions—governments, schools, religious establishments and families—teach ethics conforming to the moral life to help create the stable and harmonious society. However, as soon as these teachers as well as the recipients come to the situation that ethics is useless for their purpose, many of them discard it without any regret.

People generally behave nicely to the people who are important; their children, their supervisors, the rich and the powerful. The teaching of 'Love thy neighbour' says that you must treat the other people as if they are themselves even though they are not important for you.

Some people through history said that the moral codes were inherent in the humans and beyond any convenience; the codes distinguish the humans from the other mammals; high morals among humans are indispensable to maintain a civilised society. Socrates was insistent on this matter and 'He equated right conduct with knowledge; hence all wrong doing arose from ignorance, and would be cured by enlightenment' (Cotterell 1993, p. 38). He insisted that ethics be eternal and unchangeable truth and beyond human challenge. He believed that there is an objective distinction between right and wrong, and there are moral standards not dependent on the differing opinions of this or that individual. (Guthrie 1975, p. 88) According to Antisthenes, states are in process of dissolution, when they cannot distinguish the good from the bad among their citizens (Harbottle 1897, p. 501). I have the first-hand experience that injustice led to the dissolutions of the families and the firms, private and even governmental.

In contrast with Socrates, Wang Yangming (Yang-ming) (1472-1529), a Neo-Confucian, believed that moral knowledge was innate in the mind and hence the sagehood existed inside everyone and the learned had no special claims to it (Ebrey 1996, p. 206).

Seeing the difficulty of asserting any value to the moral codes, some ancient thinkers developed the idea by which gods gave the morals and they were not human creations. Thus, according to the Bible, God handed down the Ten Commandments to the prophet Moses who might not have understood why the Jews had to live by the moral codes except that God told them to.

Irrespective of how peoples interpreted the moral codes the world over, the following statements are true beyond any doubt. Without the moral restraints of the people the society could not carry on harmoniously. It is like the discovery that babies born from related blood tended to be inferior to the parents and even defective. Both are universal truths though people were sure of the latter truth but often did not understand the former and acted accordingly with dire consequences.

One fundamental reason for the existence of the moral codes lies in the concept of 'Love your neighbour as yourself'. We can interpret this precept to mean 'Love your neighbour as much as yourself' or 'Love your neighbour as if they were yourself', all of which effectively mean the same thing. When people put themselves in place of the victims, they realise for the first time what they had done on other people had been wrong. For example, the Jews learned the teaching 'You shall not oppress a resident alien; you know the heart of an alien, for you were aliens in the land of Egypt' (Exodus 23:9) while they lived in Egypt as aliens. According to the Bible, the Egyptians treated the Jews badly when their hospitalities worn out. The Jews developed the above teaching as kernel of the Bible under the general precept of 'Love thy neighbour' since then, though the Ten Commandments do not state the teaching expressly. Similarly, the teaching 'Do not lie' has a meaning when the person lied to has to suffer as a consequence. In the same logic, I did not know why the tradespeople were eager to protect their trade until I was put in the position to protect my professional qualifications.

Another substantive evidence for the moral codes being the universal truth is that they were formulated independently by the various peoples of the world as they came out of barbarism. The comparisons of the various ethical systems reveal that they are similar in spite of the vastly differing races and cultures. Thales (?624-?546 BC), a Greek philosopher living in Miletus, also taught the precept 'Love your neighbour' (Harbottle 1897, p. 310).

When Plato proposed the state rule by the philosophers in his *Republic,* the state and the philosophers meant different concepts to him as to us modern people. The state he meant consisted of a small number of people (some 5000 male adult citizens not including slaves, peasants, women, children and resident aliens), hence the state organisation would have been entirely different from what we think. The philosophers for him were a small number of the elite of highly trained men in morals and intelligence. He condemned democracy, arguing that the ordinary citizens did not have the moral and intellectual capacity to govern. In a similar fashion 'Love thy neighbour' meant different concept to the ancients as to the moderns.

For the people brought up in non-Judaeo-Christian-Islamic tradition, 'Love thy neighbour' sounds strange as it did to me at the first hearing. I wondered why people had to love their neighbour and not the other people. The neighbours meant to the ancient people a lot more than to us modern people because of their way of life and the undeveloped transport system. The neighbours for the ancients were really all the people they came into contact under the normal circumstances. They meant in fact everyone and every nation which people came to contact with in the course of everyday life.

The ancient Greeks preached justice among their fellow citizens; justice is also the manifestation of 'Love thy neighbour'. The Bible specifically states: The alien who resides with you shall be to you as the citizen among you; you shall love the alien as yourself, for you were aliens in the land of Egypt (Leviticus 19:34). The popular maxim 'Charity begins at home' has the same connotation. It is really referring to the large contact time of the people. Confucius also preached the concept of 'Love the fellow human beings'. The filial piety of Confucian teaching makes more sense since the people as a rule have got the largest contact time with their family: for most people the family members are lifelong associations, whereas the neighbours can change as the time goes on.

'Love thy neighbour' says 'Love the fellow human beings' with some restrictions or with moderation. The concept of middle path also applies to this teaching. This teaching is useless to some useless persons; we should not apply to them. The Bible and Confucius do not advocate unrestricted love but with two qualifications. Hence the concept expressed is not 100% correct. One qualification is contact time. There is another restriction implicit in the Bible and *Analects* (*Lun yu*) of Confucius and we should not practise the teaching to people who misbehave in a certain way. Christ's teachings 'Love your enemies and pray for those who persecute you' (Matthew 5:44) and 'If anyone strikes you on the right cheek, turn the other also' (Matthew 5:39) should not apply to some people. He said, 'Do not give what is holy to dogs; and do not throw your pearls before swine, or they will trample them under foot and turn and maul you' (Matthew 7:6). The same idea is expressed in the verse: Fly from the company of the wicked—fly and turn not back [Plato] (Harbottle 1897, p. 500). Confucius said, 'Women and small men are hard to associate with'. This effectively meant his teachings should not be applied to women, and men who misbehave in a certain way.

The sufferings of people in the distant countries did not mean anything to the ancient people, though the modern people may sympathise and try to help them. Today people in the distant countries are the neighbours. When the foreigners come to the neighbourhood to live, they are the neighbours of the teaching.

Ethics has a few attributes for the possessors. Happiness largely depends on the moral of the persons. Ethical persons can predict the future and see things precise as they are. Though ethics and capability to do the job may not correspond for the individual persons, the society with predominantly ethical persons makes good progress over the years. People with low moral standard degenerate the political and economic institutions.

B Reward and Punishment for Thought and Conduct
The practice and non-practice of 'Love Thy Neighbour' have reward and punishment. I present the conclusion in Chapter 5 that the reward and punishment emanating were the most likely cause of the rise of Europe and the decline of China in the modern era.

If we abuse our body excessively, we get sickness or physical impediment. Normally there are some warnings against physical excess, and we do not get the full punishment until years later. If we stop the abuse in time, we normally do not receive the full punishment. Once the impediment takes hold of us it is hard to recover fully and often we suffer the rest of our life. We can uphold the similar argument about the moral degradations with the bad results, and the sustained ethical conducts with the good results.

I know from my own experience that I have to pay for my mistakes. Not only the misconducts of ethical nature but also the misjudgements of any sort bring some punishments. In a firm, the mistakes made will show up somewhere in the future whether they may be managerial, accounting, clerical or whatever. In this sense also the notion propounded by Socrates that virtue is knowledge is quite right. Non-virtuous conducts emanating from ignorance give us some retribution sometime in the future without fail. I remember that I mocked at some topics the primary school teachers taught. As the consequence I did not develop some skills which average pupils mastered by a certain age. Even at my advanced age I lack those skills and the effort to overcome these deficiencies has not fully paid off. I am now resigned that I have to live the rest of my life without the useful skills which I ridiculed at class. These skills per se have nothing to do with virtuous life; however, the fact I despised some topics and possibly the teachers without cause were definitely against the ethical teachings. By ignoring them--virtues and some useful skills--at some stage of our life we have to eventually pay for the ignorance. We can ignore the irrelevant skills and useless persons without any punishment.

Wrong thought and wrong conduct sooner or later bring punishment on us in some way or another though we don't know when and how. Right thought and right conduct bring reward on us in some way or another though we don't know when and how. One of the reasons why we have to go to school is that teachers guide us not to go astray and try to put our thought and conduct on the right track.

The Buddhists call the above phenomenon dependent origination, that is, whatever is, dependent upon something else. *The Dhammapada* reads:

> Mind precedes all unwholesome states and is their chief; they are all mind wrought. If with an impure mind a person speaks or acts, misery follows him like the wheel that dogs the foot of the ox. Mind precedes all wholesome states and is their chief; they are all mind wrought. If with a pure mind a person speaks and acts, happiness follows him like his never-departing shadow. (Koller 1985, p. 142)

Also,

> From a pure heart proceedeth the fruit of a good life [*The Imitation of Christ*] (Thomas a Kempis 1980, p. 200).

Punishment and reward for thought and conduct are meted out without exceptions and also whether people believe in God or gods or whatever form of divinity. Jesus Christ said, 'And even the very hairs of your head are all numbered' (Matthew 10:30). 'And we have made everyone's actions cling to his neck.' (Qur'an 17.13) This makes the value of deity suspect. As far as my experience goes the above statement is true for the individual, and I was convinced it is true for the nation, for the race and for the East and the West. Plato had an opinion that punishment follows closely after sin; however, Hesiod could have said better when he said that punishment is born at the same instant with sin (Montaigne 1965, p. 264).

Sinners as for pleasure seekers cannot escape some form of punishment. Though some people may not be aware of the correspondence, the punishments are sure to follow sins and pleasures sooner or later because their brains like computer record what they did, or God matches them as some prefer to say.

There are some common things we all feel important such as ourselves (mind and body), family, job, study and human relationship. They all need constant care, without which they become burdensome and unbearable in the end. There is a strong correlation between care and the state of these and as far as my experience goes, there is no such thing as an accident. For example, many people attribute their family breakdown to accident but that is not so. The parents did not look after the family in a proper manner; hence the bad consequence of the breakdown ensued. The parents make all important decisions within the family hence we can say that the parents, especially the father, are responsible for what happens within the family.

Latin thinkers expressed the idea in various ways:

-Experience has shown that the truth of Appius' saying, that every man is the architect of his own fortunes [Sallust] (Harbottle 1897, p. 258).

-Every man's fortune is moulded by his character [Cornelius Nepos] (p. 258).

-Let it be first granted that we are given in charge of ourselves, and that the first thing we receive from nature is the instinct of self-preservation [Cicero] (p. 261).

-One path alone leads to a life of peace: the path of virtue [Juvenal] (p. 262).

-A well-behaved stomach is a great part of liberty [Seneca] (Montaigne 1965, p. 844).

-A wise palate should go with a wise heart [Cicero] (p. 851).

C Middle Paths

Life and human society are compromises in many ways. If we want to extract the rules from life and human society, they must be compromise and middle path.

The Buddha went through all kinds of asceticism in an effort for enlightenment. However, he realised the impossibility and abandoned the self-torture and then he reached the enlightenment.

The Buddha, just after the enlightenment, sought out his five former companions near Benares and delivered his first sermon: *Setting in Motion the Wheel of Truth*. In this sermon he preached the Four Noble Truth, and stressed the virtue of middle path. (Davison 1993, p. 39) These companions had deserted him earlier despising him, when he had abandoned asceticism and eaten ample food for nourishment.

This teaching was recognised to be important by the ancient to classical thinkers all over the world, and is still consequential to us today, as for the other idealistic ideas presented in this section.

This instruction was variously expressed, since peoples acknowledged its value under various circumstances throughout the human history. Solon taught 'Nothing in Excess' (Harbottle 1897, p. 414) and the phrase was inscribed on the columns of Apollo's Temple in Delphi. Hesiod expressed it in the verse, 'Preserve the mean; right season's best in all things' (p. 414). Euripides said it in 'God hateth overzeal' (p. 422). Martial wrote: Short life is theirs who know not self-restraint; pray not to love too much the things you love (p. 96). E'en virtue's self, if carried to excess, turns right to wrong, good sense to foolishness [Horace] (p. 107). Most safely shalt thou tread the middle path [Ovid] (p. 132). In everything the golden mean is the best [Plautus] (p. 138). The Four Books venerated in traditional China are *Analects* (*Lun yu*), *Mencius, Great Learning* and *Doctrine of the Mean*. The last book mentioned deals with the topic under discussion. Confucius interpreted the mean as the state of equilibrium (mean, centrality, harmony) of the exemplary man; moderating the emotions to reach psychic harmony. Confucianism took the middle path avoiding the political regimentation of Legalism and the political non-interference of Buddhism and Daoism, and incorporated some elements of Legalism in the government policies, and eventually triumphed over these doctrines and became the ruling ideology of the traditional China through the ages. I made a reference in another context that Confucianism was chosen as the ruling ideology of China because of its loyalty to the ruling class. It is interesting to note these two, that is, middle path and loyalty to the government, matched to prevail over the other doctrines. Aristotle, among his large number of books to his credit, has a treatise entitled *Nicomachean Ethics* which goes into detail the meaning of the middle paths. He also read a poem: A midpoint is in a sense a highest point (p. 415). The Bible reads: Do not be over righteous neither be over wise—why destroy yourself (Ecclesiastes 7:16); The man who fears God will avoid all extremes (Ecclesiastes 7:18).

Golden mean or a happy medium is a maxim in general circulation today, which extols the middle course avoiding the extremes in any matter, meaning in essence without excesses or inadequacies. The middle paths or the middle of the road, as expressed as the way to tread or to choose, are the universal truth, not confined to a particular place and era, applied to most thinking and action under virtually all circumstances. Hence people have expressed it in many other ways.

- Be not too zealous; moderation's best in all things [Theognis] (Harbottle 1897, p. 414).
- Best is moderation [Cleobulus] (p. 414).
- Cast all excess aside [Euripides] (p. 415).
- All excess is contrary to nature [Hippocrates] (p. 415).
- Whatever has passed the mean stands upon slippery ground [Seneca] (p. 239).
- That cannot last which knows not some repose [Ovid] (p. 244).
- Islam discourages vigorous practices and monastic life.

Moderation in food, clothes and shelter are the absolute virtue. We all have to eat to sustain our energy and health, but eating too much or too little is wrong. We must consume food moderately. Dieticians say that even the feeling of too hungry or too full is bad for the health and hence to be avoided. We should have the right weight for our height and age. We do not have to rely on Menander when he wrote, 'Keep ever tight rein on appetite' (p. 342). Though the ancient to classical sages did not elaborate the middle path prescriptions of the next paragraph they are also important for us. People at the time did not have the science of today's standard, and most of them died before we consider they were at the prime of life. That was their way of life and people took it as a matter of fact. For example in the ancient Egypt three to four children out of five did not grow into adulthood, and most men and women did not live beyond 30.

The human bodies absolutely need salt and fat for their proper function; however, the required quantities of these nutrients are small. They were proved by experiment under laboratory conditions. Therefore the dieticians ever urge us to restrict the intake of these nutrients. Also it is possible to do too much physical exercise; however, we rarely get to do too much. Hence we often hear that we should do more physical training. We must expose our body to the sun for limited durations only: I reckon half an hour exposure on a sunny or cloudy day is proper. The scientific researches time and time again have established that alcohol enhances the mental and physical health of the moderate drinkers: the problem starts when people take alcohol in excess.

Montaigne: The mean is possibly the most natural way too. Lucan: To keep the mean, hold our aim in view and follow nature (Montaigne 1965, p. 793). I have found in my life that even diligence, kindness and friendship if practised in excess do more harm than good to me, though these are important attributes for successful and happy life for ordinary people. Learning is certainly enjoyable to me but I know for a fact that learning carried to the excess in terms of time spent and subjects focused does not give me enjoyment. 'Slow and steady win the race' is my favourite axiom. I always remind myself of this teaching whatever I do--writing books, dealing with conflicts, accumulating wealth and so on.

We should apply the principle of moderation even to the matter of pleasure. Epictetus noted, 'If one oversteps the bounds of moderation, the greatest pleasures cease to please' (Harbottle 1897, p. 362).

The middle paths apply even to the selection of the production personnel in the explosive factory: I worked in the munitions factory. In dealing with initiating explosives which are extremely sensitive and likely to explode with a slight impact, the persons who are too cautious or too careless are not fit to work in the production line. Only the persons who are neither timid nor rough are suitable for handling the sensitive explosives.

We can say the same thing about nationalism, racism, religion, idealism, materialism and sex. Nothing is wrong in these things in themselves provided people take them in moderation. The problem arises when an individual or a nation indulges in one field of interest, excluding the others. For example, it is justified people should be worried about money, a practical manifestation of materialism, since money helps people in what they want to do. But they should avoid the excessive worrying. In this light, Islamic fundamentalism with the strict adherence to the Qur'an and Hadith (a basis of Islamic law) may have adverse consequences for the adopting nation.

If people are too artistic and absorbed too deeply in the matter of arts, as I had been for some time during my youth, they lose common touch with the reality, and tend to be misunderstood and may have a problem in getting a job. The interviewers want certain attitudes from the interviewees, and the good answers to the questions asked. The job seekers who are too deeply submerged in arts do not even try to conform to the job requirements. Also they may not be able to perform the functions of everyday life which the public take for granted.

Horace expressed people can practise even virtue in excess in the following passage:

> The fair man should be termed unfair, the wise unsound, if he seeks even virtue beyond the proper bound (Montaigne 1965, p. 146).

Montaigne wrote about his friend whom he loved dearly and esteemed as his second self. He expressed his pains losing him after four years of mutual enjoyment. He wished him on every action and thought and felt he was only half alive. (p. 143) He did not think his friendship had been in excess and a sin and did not realise where his pains came from.

Montaigne quoted the saying that the extremity of philosophy is harmful (p. 146). He further wrote the following witty comments:

> Some people kill themselves for trivial reasons because the reasons to keep them alive are not strong. We must have moderation on this matter as well and Diogenes Laertius called it a reasonable exit. (p. 255)
>
> To say less of yourself than is true is stupidity, not modesty; however, our experiences in our life teach us that we all have good reasons to be modest about our skills, means and ourselves (p. 274).

The middle path is a general rule and we should not practise under certain circumstances. Many people may think that the concept of 'Love thy neighbour' applies without restrictions. In fact the Bible and Confucianism did not intend it. We should practise the concept with the middle paths and we should not apply it to some people. Phocylides wrote, 'Seek not the bad to benefit; 'tis sowing seed in the ocean' (Harbottle 1897, p. 416). Also we should discard the middle path under certain circumstances such as artistic zeal, fighting or war for some duration.

D Conformance of Speech and Conduct

The Chinese proverb says, 'Doers are not always talkers, nor talkers doers'. In the other side of the world, Demosthenes uttered the following statement: All speech is vain and empty unless it is accompanied by action (Harbottle 1897, p. 332). Though he had a speech defect when young, he eventually became a fine orator through hard exercises. Also Euripides wrote, 'Speech ne'er prevails o'er action' (p. 410). 'Tis ne'er a tall talk when he who speaks matches his words with deeds [Antiphanes] (p. 465). It is disgraceful to say one thing and think another; how much more disgraceful to write one thing and think another! [Seneca] (p. 289) Let us mean what we say, and say what we mean: let our language and our life be in agreement [Seneca] (p. 245).

As a flower that is lovely and beautiful but is scentless, even so fruitless are the well-spoken words of one who does not practise them. As a flower that is lovely, beautiful and scent-laden, even so fruitful are the well-spoken words of one who practises them. [*The Dhammapada*: a Buddhist canon] (Narada 1993, p. 55)

If people teach ethics and morals, their way of thinking and life must conform to what they lecture. Socrates and Confucius were particularly insistent on this doctrine and both vehemently advocated that their actions must conform to their speech. In private life one differentiates between what a man thinks and says of himself and what he really is and does. (Marx & Engels 1989, p. 437) It is claimed that Socrates' teachings were indisolutely linked with his whole personality (Guthrie 1969, p. 326). He took alcohol only to comply with social custom. 'All his appetites and passions for sex as well as for food, he kept under strict control.' (p. 389) *The Imitation of Christ* stresses the conformity of life to the life of Christ (Thomas a Kempis 1980, p. 23). It says, 'Surely high words do not make a man holy and just; but a virtuous life makes him dear to God' (p. 24).

The following are a few other passages from the ancient to classical Greek world which expressed non-virtue of the non-conformity. Myson wrote, 'Seek not to learn a man's deeds from his words, but rather his words from his deeds' (Harbottle 1897, p. 415). Menander: I hate the wicked when their words are good (p. 422). Euripides: Him who professes wisdom I abhor, if for himself he be not wise (p. 422); yet words by words are overthrown (p. 435).

> Mao's most important philosophical work is probably his lecture delivered in 1937 entitled *On Practice.* In this lecture he shows how theory originates in practice and returns to practice for its justification and fulfilment. *On Practice*, Mao posited the theory and practice as two opposites and the dialectical process occurs between the two, knowing and doing. (Koller 1985, pp. 341, 343)

Confucius said:

> His [a superior person's] words correspond to his actions, and his actions correspond to his words. The superior man is ashamed his words exceed his deeds. (Murowchick 1994, p. 58)

To Confucius, a man's conduct and action are more important than his accomplishment in arts and letters. He said, 'Is it not pleasant to learn with a constant perseverance and application?' One measure of superior man for Confucius was to carry out in his conduct what he professed. He also said, 'The superior man wishes to be slow in his speech and quick in his conduct'. (Chen 1987, pp. 45-6)

Confucius asserts that every state has its name and actuality, and the two must conform. For example, a prince must behave like a prince. Hence Mencius' justification of a people's right to revolt against a tyrannical prince stems from the non-conformance on the part of the prince. (Ho 1976, p. 5)

Jesus Christ said concerning the scribes and the Pharisees (Matthew 23:3):

> ... therefore do whatever they teach you and follow it; but do not do as they do, for they do not practice what they teach.

The Muslims hold that belief is empty unless embodied in behaviour. The Qur'an covers every aspect of everyday life from dress code to divorce. (Davison 1993, p. 77)

The teachers of idealism whose central idea is 'Love Thy Neighbour' should learn to regulate their life so as to conform to what they teach. By constant discipline they should be able to achieve the conformity of their theory and practice. The mirror reflects the image of the bodily shape but the fashion of the soul is displayed in our converse and our speech [Photius] (Harbottle 1897, p. 404).

The good personal habits are hard to form but once formed hard to break as for the good social customs. It seems that any amount of reasoning has little effect in changing them unless something radically different events take place for the individual and the society. What fortune gives habit soon makes its own [Calpurnius] (p. 244).

Learning is one thing; teaching is another. Learning theory is one thing; learning in reality is another. The students normally excel in the formers but often neglect the latters. The school teaches mostly theories and some practices. It is thought that the school, including the university, has a limited duration and cannot accommodate the full practical lessons.

One of the problems associated with non-conformity of speech and conduct is that forgetting God (Truth) is about our life, and we deal with something remote, though lofty, from our daily life. Dianetics points out that metaphysics and mystics typify this wrong attitude, and do not contribute to the growth of our brain.

Like practically all ancient Chinese schools, the Legalists emphasised the theory of the correspondence of names [words] and actualities [deeds]. But while the Confucians stressed the ethical and social meaning of the theory and the Logicians stressed the logical aspect, the Legalists had an interest in it primarily for the purpose of political control. With them the theory is neither ethical nor logical but a technique for regimentation. (Chan 1963, p. 257)

Wang Yang-ming (1472-1529) tried different means of achieving Zhu Xi's (Chu Hsi's) objective of relating belief directly to action, and ensuring that practice did not diverge from ideas, and his emphasis was somewhat different. He believed that the intuitive knowledge from introspective or meditative methods formed a more certain way of attaining self-knowledge than concentration on a wide-scheme of learning. (Loewe 1990, p. 113; Mercer 1996, p. 418)

> Gandhi's philosophy cannot be divorced from his life, which was a continuing experiment of putting ideas into practice and developing ideas from practice (Koller 1985, p. 118).

Gandhi was a powerful symbol of influence standing apart from the power of wealth and army. He showed how the poor and non-military force can achieve so much in the twentieth century. (Grenville 1994, p. 142)

If one has faith in the Bible, one follows the ordinances of God hence one's life conforms with the ordinances. However, since every individual is different and they understand the Bible in different ways, their nature and degree of conformance would be naturally different.

In many subjects, typically science and social science, the teachers have no corresponding life. For example, mathematics teachers cannot lead their life mathematically: mathematics has nothing to do with the way of life except in the way to regulate things precisely. Also Malthus expounded his population theory in *An Essay on the Principle of Population* (1798). He wrote that the overpopulation eventually leads to the deaths of a large number of people through wars, diseases and starvation. He looked at the process as the folly of human beings and did not offer to solve the problem. Accordingly he did not have any obligation to limit the size of his family. He did not expect that any solutions would come out of his observations in the first place. As a matter of fact he was born to the second of eight children but raised only three children of his own. Whereas Karl Marx taught that the exploitation of workers by capitalists in the corporate environment was evil hence his life should have been free from the exploitation of his own making. However, he exploited people in his personal dealings.

If a person makes a statement, people around make the judgement of the utterance not so much on its own merits but rather on his or her conformance on the idea said. In other words, when a person makes a proposition, people tend to take it up only if it comes from the person whose daily conducts conform to the proposal. When the supervisors tell their subordinates what to do, if the instruction matches with the behaviours of the former the persuasive power is strong. The Bible mentions that people are saved by works at times and people are saved by faith at times. However, whichever way we interpret the Bible, there is no question that conducts (works) and faith must conform.

There is a correspondence between body and mind. Herodotus wrote, 'As the body grows, the mind grows with it; as it ages, the mind ages and becomes blunted to all things' (Harbottle 1897, p. 337). Menander wrote, 'It is better to be ill in body than in mind' (p. 339).

We all agree we should look after our body in any way possible, such as through good diet, proper exercise and cleanliness; however, we should care more about the health of our mind in any way possible; keep away from impure thoughts and foster good thinking at all times. The Buddha taught that as we use mirror to look at and improve our facial and bodily postures, even more we should look at our mind constantly to improve our thinking.

The ancient sages directed their teachings mainly to the individuals on the street and possibly not to the rulers: the sages were not political leaders but religious leaders. It is not hard for the individuals to achieve the conformity. In the political field it is extremely rare to find the society where the rulers, even if they achieved their power from the idealist doctrines, practised these teachings to the letter. One difficulty is without any doubt due to the fact that there are many pressure groups within the society which do not allow the soft policies put into practice, from various reasons such as their own interest and the prejudice against some group. The pressure groups in the society are incessantly colliding like colloidal phenomena in the tea cup. Thus before the modern times people wanted a king or an emperor who sorted out all the problems with the absolute power.

However, we still can find some examples of the conformity of the ideals and the ruling policies. The state policies of Periclean Greece were in accordance with the ideals of society, that is, the pursuit of justice, though only among the Greek men excluding women and foreigners. Another example may be Asoka's policies. He embraced Buddhism to heart and tried to create the welfare state of the Mauryan Empire in India. There is one problem in that Buddhism is not about creating the welfare state, though he genuinely believed what he did was in accord with the Buddhist doctrines.

My way of life must reflect the wish that I want to publish books before I die. Research and book writing control various, though not all, aspects of my life: my part time job, home arrangement and investment. Not doing so can mean that I may fall short of skills and time needed to complete the books.

E Indifference to External (Physical or Mental) Stimuli

The concept of 'Love thy neighbour' comes in part from making light the temporal gains. As soon as the people of the temporal mind see conflicts between the two they disregard the love without any regret. The indifference in question makes light of not only physical comfort and discomfort coming from heat and cold but likes and dislikes, praise and abuse, wealth and poverty, fame and disgrace, authority and nothingness, family and non-family, friend and friendlessness. They avoid the worldly matters and temporal gains. Particularly Socrates, the Buddha and the Daoists insisted on the above indifference.

> King Seleucus had an opinion that a man who knew the weight of a sceptre would not deign to pick it up if he found it on the ground. He said this because of the great and troublesome charges incumbent on a good king. (Harbottle 1897, p. 193)

Pythagoras wrote: Do what you believe to be right, though it be at the sacrifice of your reputation, for the mob is a bad judge of noble conduct (p. 481). As a solid rock is not shaken by the wind, even so the wise are not ruffled by praise or blame. The good give up (attachment for) everything; the saintly prattle not with sensual craving: whether affected by happiness or by pains, the wise show neither elation nor depression. [a Buddhist canon] (Narada 1993, pp. 77-8) The sword the body wounds, sharp words the mind [Menander] (Harbottle 1897, p. 427). As an elephant in the battlefield withstands the arrows shot from a bow, even so will I endure abuse; verily most people are undisciplined (Narada 1993, p. 251). He who has given up likes and dislikes, who has cooled and is without defilements, who has conquered the world of five aggregates, and is strenuous, --him I call a Brahmana (p. 314). Aggregates are the greatest ill and five aggregates are body, feeling, perception, mental states and consciousness (pp. 176-7). One basic aim of the yogins is to overcome desires for sex and hunger.

People who try to overcome the heat or the cold of the surrounding not relying on the cooler or heater are training themselves to get used to the adverse surroundings. The willpower developed can be applied to overcome the various problems in the similar way the physical exercises not only make the people fitter but make them overcome the various problems of life, provided they do not go to the extremes in the trainings of both fields.

Idealists the world over, especially the Buddhists, stressed that it is not right to satisfy five senses. Senses are the gates to the external stimuli. The Buddha based his objection on the idea that everything is an illusion and we cannot know the world by relying on the senses. The Christian Bible also urges the adherents to forego the indulgence in the senses. Both religions do not deny that people must satisfy the necessities of life, that is, eating and drinking, wearing clothes and living in houses. Both place strict prohibitions in deriving pleasures from the necessities. I detail the pleasures arising from the senses under the heading of 'Sex and Five Senses' in conjunction with sexual pleasure in Section 1 Sexual Desire, Chapter 1, Book Five *The Sexual Laws*. Also I reason the objection against pleasure seeking in Section 1, Chapter 2 Judaism-Christianity-Islam, Book Two *Religion.*

Section 4 Materialism in Practice

At first I wanted to write a history of discoveries and inventions in this section corresponding to the practical manifestations of idealism of the last section: I place an equal emphasis on idealism and materialism in this series of books. However, I decided not to on the belief that the presentation of that kind does not convey what I really wanted to say. Besides the books of that description are easily available in the book market.

Frederick Engels gives out the brief history of natural science in *Introduction to Dialectics of Nature*. The article is interesting showing how he looked at the subject from the communist viewpoint.

Section 1 of Chapter 1 explains how the Indo-Europeans bred horses in the Eurasian Steppes around 3000 BC, and invented spoked wheels to be used for wagons and chariots around 1700 BC, all of which gave them a decisive advantage in their subsequent migrations.

'Three Greatest Inventions in History' by the Chinese as expounded in Section 4, Chapter 2 gave the Europeans the material knowledge to head for the modern era leaving the feudal society behind.

I also expound the Industrial Revolution in conjunction with Communism in Section 1 Background of Communism, Chapter 1, Book Two *Communism*.

In the rest of this section I present the topical subjects in materialism rather than the overall picture.

China: Land of Discovery and Invention

Joseph Needham, the British historian of science, in the preface of *China: Land of Discovery and Invention*, makes a revelation that the Chinese made the vigorous inventions in the pre-modern era, and further writes that a similar pattern of advancement in science, technology and medicine will appear in the future if the scholars make the research in India or Sri Lanka. (Temple 1986) He wrote his multi-volume work *Science and Civilization in China*.

Robert GK Temple made the distillation of this book into *China: Land of Discovery and Invention* for the general readers with the detailed and documented explanations of each discovery and invention. He also gives the table of how long Europe took to catch up with China for each item. He writes that more than half of the discoveries and inventions upon which the modern world rests came from China. Anybody who disputes this statement has to do the years of research before he or she can make a contrary statement.

Temple claims how the Chinese discoveries and inventions made way to Europe, helping to create modern European supremacy, though he is not sure how some of them travelled to Europe. He explains each item in details under the divisions of agriculture, astronomy and cartography, engineering, domestic and industrial technology, medicine and health, mathematics, magnetism, physical sciences, transportation and exploration, sound and music, and warfare. He is adamant that these discoveries and inventions were made in China many centuries earlier than being utilised in Europe, and without transference of this knowledge Europe would not have gone through the industrial revolution. Only after the agricultural revolution in Europe was it possible to proceed with the industrial revolution. Growing of crops in rows, intensive hoeing of weeds, the seed drill, the iron plough, the mouldboard to turn the ploughed soil, and efficient harness on horse all reached from China to Europe. Without these the Europeans would not have gone through the agricultural revolution.

He continues. Johann Gutenberg did not invent movable type; the Chinese did. William Harvey did not discover the circulation of blood in the body; the Chinese did. Isaac Newton was not the first to discover the First Law of Motion; the Chinese were. (p. 9)

Materialism and Wealth Acquisition

These two desires are means for survival for humans and their essence may be different on scholarly enquiries; however, they come close on many points and may not be possible to separate the two. From the practical point of view it may not be advisable to make the distinction between the two. I am to note the differences of the two survival techniques in the next paragraph.

The stones left by humans who lived millions of years ago may be the first evidence of materialism, though these humans did not have an interest in the concept of materialism but needed these stones as tools of sheer survival. I conjecture that the desire for wealth came to the human mind only after they satisfied their bodily requirements of necessities of life. We all know that the acquisition of wealth and sex has been the major low desires of humans through the history and still they are paramount in the minds of men and women. Materialism may be in the higher plane of thinking and rooted in the desire to solve the various problems of life by the use of objects, and also manifested as science and technology. We can see the development of materialism in the inventions made by the peoples all over the world through the human history. Once they invented a new and useful object, it seems that they did not lose easily because of their strong attachment. People have made wealth through various means, such as lottery wins, frauds, inventions, speculations and hard works. Wealthy individuals and nations have full access to the latest fruits of materialism. However, even the wealthy individuals and nations don't get the advanced medical treatments or the sophisticated weapons unless the technology is available.

Origins of Materialism

The idea that humans try to solve the various problems of life by the material objects existed since they appeared on earth. Hominids left their footprints walking upright in Laetoli, Tanzania of East Africa. It is estimated that these footprints were made around 3.6 million years ago and were the evidence that the humans first appeared on earth.

The oldest known stone tools were found in Hadar, Ethiopia, estimated to be 2.4 million years old and this is thought to be the start of the Lower Palaeolithic age. Western Asia entered the Neolithic period at about 9 000 BC, prior to any other regions of the globe.

The ethical levels of these peoples are not known and only the material objects left give us some clues about their material life. These objects form the bases for studies about their spiritual life as well but they are only conjectures.

The upright posture of the Neanderthals (the Palaeolithic people), the subspecies of *Homo sapiens*, made quite difference from the prehominids (manlike primates). Another notable difference from the other mode of existence is the use and manufacture of tools. The other primates can walk upright, and sometimes can make and use tools. (Eliade 1978, p. 3) The Neanderthals appeared 100 000 years ago--some say 500 000 years ago--and died out 40 000 years ago. They lived by hunting, fishing and gathering; and lived in Europe, Asia and Africa.

The first technological discoveries—the use of stone and the mastery of fire—expanded the horizon of the survival of the human species; hence the instruments and their use became the objects of veneration and made the bases of the mythico-religious imagination. This is true to the primitive people still surviving today. (p. 6)

The Neanderthals developed elaborate burial rituals suggesting the wish for life after death. They suddenly disappeared to be supplanted by *Homo sapiens sapiens*. The first indications of the religious consciousness of Palaeolithic people go back only to Franco-Cantabrian rock art (30 000 BC) (p. 7).

We all need food, clothes and shelter to survive. Life revolves eating, drinking, clothing and housing before everything else. People who advocate an adequate supply of these material objects to themselves and the general public are hardly called materialists as long as they are necessities of life. The distinction between necessity and luxury of life is hard to draw in practice since it depends in the main on the personal assessment. Karl Marx defines luxury articles as all production that does not serve the reproduction of labour-power (Marx 1959, p. 106). The rich felt that the luxuries they wanted were their necessities (Whitehouse & Wilkins 1986, p. 108). Once people get to used to the comfort of any commodity it becomes indispensable for them in the same fashion idealism well digested becomes attribute of the possessors who feel it indispensable for them. The merchants do not care if the goods are necessities or luxuries as long as they can make profits on trading. If the rich want the luxuries, there must be a large amount of money to be made by buying and selling the luxury items. Some moralists may argue that a community should spend for the luxuries only after it meets all the necessities of life. However, the economic principle, that is, the profit motive, allows the inflow of the luxuries into the community before it fully satisfies the requirements of necessaries. We cannot define gold as necessity or luxury though majority of peoples the world over wanted gold for its beauty and exchange value. However, we know for a fact that the Aztecs valued quetzal feathers more than gold. The different assessments on gold are not important here in any case.

The savages who roamed the earth before any civilisation had to spend a part of their day for hunting, fishing and gathering in order to survive. The cave paintings and artefacts these savages left behind suggest that they had some leisure time as well and they satisfied their need for artistic and spiritual cravings. However, it is not hard to imagine that their daily life was sheer survival: they had to ward off enemies, humans as well as animals, and exert themselves in an effort to obtain the necessities of life. Failure in any of the chores could have resulted in their injury, sickness and even death. The savages acted according to their survival instinct and they did not have any other motives to do so. Though acquisition of material mostly occupied the minds of these primitive people, it was necessities of life and we can hardly call them materialists.

Hunting and gathering, contrary to the statements of the last paragraph, were easy way of life compared with the life of later stages of human developments, and hunters and gatherers rarely spent more than three to four hours a day to support them. The evidence also suggests that hunters and gatherers lived in egalitarian societies. Why then did they abandon this good way of life in several parts of the world (pp. 45, 90)? By 8000 BC, people in several parts of the world had discovered the secrets of cultivating crops and of domesticating animals.

Crude farming can support population density of 5-10 people per square kilometres; hunting and gathering, even in a favourable environment, can rarely support more than 0.1 people per square kilometres (p. 43). Hence, we can say that one major reason for starting agriculture must have been the population pressure.

There have been two major population explosions in the course of human social evolution. At the end of the Palaeolithic period the world's population was estimated to be between five and six million. Following the agricultural revolution in the Neolithic age, the world population exploded into around 150 million by the year 1000 BC. The two population estimates span 7000 years. The industrial revolution of the modern era is another cause of the population explosion.

There are two possible speculations concerning the population increase associated with introduction of farming. People wanted more population for whatever the reasons, hence they started farming. Another possibility is that they had to resort to farming to support increased population. Either speculation is possible as for the industrialisation in the modern era;

however, the speculation either way is not significant since the net result is the same, that is, the increased population.

Apart from the above reason, we can cite the security that came with the increased population and the division of labour that naturally people got to know for survival of the community as a whole. With the hunting and gathering as the population grew, the scarcity of food led people to starvation, forced abortion, infanticide, and even warfare though rare. With the arrival of farming, though it is a toiling regime, the population dramatically increased. (p. 48)

Cereal agriculture is about 22 times more productive than rearing domesticated animals for meat. Animal meat and fish were required to supply protein which was indispensable for human health. The rearing of animals for dairy products is about six times more efficient in terms of output per hectare than for meat. (pp. 103, 105)

> But probably most importantly, rice almost always yields more calories per unit of land than any other crops. In the most suitable climates, two or even three crops can be grown in the same field [in a year], or rice can be alternated with other crops. (Ebrey 1996, p. 156)

The discovery and practice of agriculture, that is, humans became the producer of food, had further profound effects on the course of human development:

- Humans had to predict the season in anticipation of sowing and harvesting.
- Division of labour had to develop between men and women: Women had to assume the important responsibility for subsistence. A nomadic stage is not really a predecessor of a settled stage. They are more diversifications and division of labour. (Wells 1925, p. 91) The division of labour, individually and regionally, necessitated the increase of trade (Smith 1991, p. 29).

There were further effects from the establishment of farming:

> Most obviously, there was sufficient food for many more people to be able to settle in one location for longer periods. This allowed, even demanded, the construction of more substantial and long-lasting buildings, while fragile but useful products such as pottery became practical. Social organisation became more elaborate as some people gained power and prestige by taking control of production. Thus farming itself resulted in massive increase of population density. (Burenhult 1994, pp. 9, 181)
>
> The large number of people was also an advantage when dealing with competing or even hostile groups. As a result, sedentariness is closely connected with a heavy increase of population growth. (p. 82)

As the barbarians acquired a certain level of intelligence which reflected how they lived, they entered an era of culture. The speed of human development is not uniform and some regions were far advanced than others. Even in the 21st century, some tribes of the remotest jungles of the world are left behind in the race for development. Some anthropologists claim that the way of life of these people is similar to that of our ancestors at the stage of barbarism. More specifically, the primitive peoples who are still at the stage of hunting, fishing and gathering today constitute a sort of living fossils, their development being arrested at the stage similar to the Upper Palaeolithic. (Eliade 1978, p. 24)

As people acquired culture and the division of labour developed in the community, many of them did not have to spend all that time to make a reasonable living. They may have owned some form of wealth, by succession or by acquisition. Some may have become aristocrats, large landowners or wealthy merchants, and as a consequence had considerable leisure time.

The wealthy people, though they did not perform any manual labour, consumed necessities of life which manual labourers had to produce. Hence, the farmers, merchants and artisans had to produce and merchandise the necessities of life over and beyond their consumption. In other words, non-labouring class came into existence only after the manual workers were capable of producing and merchandising the surplus food, clothes and shelter. The improved production methods would generate surplus products. Hence the existence of non-producing people is a telltail sign that the society was technically advanced. Hard work would produce more products; however, the hard work alone is hardly enough to explain the sustained large increase of surplus products in one large area.

Generally, through the course of human development all over the world, the existence of a sizable non-productive class has played an important role, whether the hard work or improved production techniques supported this class. In the modern setting with comparatively smaller percentage allocation of the resources for the production of the necessaries of life and also the complicated social system, the term non-productive class may be nonsensical. As a broad measure, the productive class consisted of people who were directly engaged in the production and distribution of basic material needs of the population and it included farmers, merchants and artisans whether they owned or did not own the land and the means of production or trades.

The emergence of the cities was a definite sign that there was surplus food available since the city dwellers did not engage in the crop production and the animal rearing.

Emergence of Cities

Until the late Neolithic age when the agriculture was widely practised, the dense human population as in cities was not possible.

One of the oldest known agricultural villages was Jericho in Palestine near the Dead Sea. Jericho existed by 8000 BC and covered several acres by 7000 BC. It had a wall several feet thick that enclosed houses made of sun-dried bricks. The Bible narrates the collapse of the Jericho wall at the shout of the Jews (Joshua 6:1-27): Joshua led the Jews around 1400 BC and the collapsed wall is most likely not the one above mentioned. Catal Huyuk, located in modern day Turkey, was an even larger community. Its walls enclosed thirty-two acres, and its population probably reached several thousand during its high point from 6700 BC to 5700 BC. (Spielvogel 1991, p. 2)

The concentration of the population clearly indicates that some people were not directly involved in producing and merchandising the necessities of life, thus suggesting a fair degree of culture. It is not hard to imagine that there must have been some form of law and order within the city. People in the city must have shown moral standard, though we cannot quantify its levels. People's life and properties were not in immediate danger within the city during the peace time as in contrast with the emergency situations such as civil unrest or enemy invasion.

Savages, at the stage of hunting, fishing and gathering, cannot form a city. They don't have enough people who are freed from obtaining the necessaries of life. They don't have technical skills to build one. They are not interested in building a city in the first place.

The non-productive class consists of people who are not directly engaged in the production and distribution of the necessaries of life and it includes large landowners, aristocrats, rich merchants, scholars, entertainers and soldiers.

The distinction made above, that is, the necessity and luxury of life; the productive and unproductive classes, are fairly arbitrary and are not based on inherent values. It does not signify the upper or lower classes; the owner of the means of production or not; rich or poor. Hence we make or reverse the differentiations depending on the circumstances. For example, we should class the huge number of the labourers, artisans, engineers and supervisors who participated in the constructions of the pyramids in the ancient Egypt as non-productive according to my definition. I introduce the concept to highlight the fact that the existence of a sizable unproductive people proves to me that the society had reached an advanced stage of civilisation. The size and nature of the non-productive class determined the prevailing characteristics and the future course of the society. I am to present the examples of Egypt and China to clear the points in the above question of materialism, not referring to the idealistic culture. Both of these peoples historically have excelled in material culture rather than idealistic culture, and left vast number of objects for later generations.

Egyptian and Chinese Examples

The Egyptians and the Chinese retained the same speech and traditions for thousands of years in the single territory defying all invaders, though the former markedly changed after the invasion by the Arab Muslims in AD 641. Both established since the dawn of their recorded history their unique way of writing their language based on pictograms. The status of universal language has never been challenged in China, and for three and a half millenniums in Egypt, yet their languages did not become lingua franca beyond their territories despite their immense cultural prestige.

Latin became the lingua franca of Europe since the dominance of the Roman Empire till the end of the medieval era; English became the international language since the spread of the British Empire into the world till present.

Egyptian language has survived as Coptic (written in the Greek alphabets) in the liturgy of what was the foreign religion, Christianity. Six per cent of the population of Egypt today is Coptic Christians, speaking Arabic: Most of the people in Egypt speak varieties of Arabic language. Chinese has dialects but 70% of the Chinese today speak a single variety, Mandarin, which spreads over 75% of the People's Republic of China. Egypt formed its civilisation along the valley of the Nile River, China, along the Yellow River, though the latter expanded to take the next great river the Yangtze. Both countries succumbed to foreign invasions but retained their language, possibly by the dense population and the cultural pride, though Egypt adopted foreign tongue as its official language when the Assyrians, the Persians, the Greeks and the Romans invaded Egypt; the official language of the first two peoples were Aramaic.

In the Hellenistic period (332-30 BC) a large number of the Greek speaking Jews came to live in Egypt. The Egyptian language belongs to the Hamitic family of Afro-Asiatic or Hamito-Semitic (Semito-Hamitic) but it is noteworthy that it has no close relatives. Though spoken Egyptian changed phonetically and syntactically over time, hieroglyphic writings used in religion and rituals were set in the early third millennium BC and did not change until the end of Egyptian civilisation. The ancient Egyptians in their eagerness to preserve their culture copied the writings so many times that several hundred rolls of papyrus papers have endured to this day. Popular literature, school text and administrative documents increasingly used variants: cursive hieratic and even simpler demotic. Spread of Christianity put an end to hieroglyphics and the ancient Egyptian culture at the end of the AD fourth century. (Ostler 2006, p. 133) The administration and cultural life were conducted in Greek, though the populace spoke Egyptian. The Arabic language dominated Egypt since the coming of the Muslims in 641.

The Chinese language and history have had 50 times of the adherents than the Egyptian language and history, and 150 times of the space to act (p. 152). Literacy was confined to the elite in Egypt, whereas it was widespread in China. Both cultures were built on the respect for tradition and were reluctant to change their traditional pictographic writing system.

Today some 98% of the Egyptian population live in the cultivated area of the Nile Valley and the delta which account only for 6% of the land mass of Egypt, and the Egyptians have relied heavily on agriculture for economic survival. The official language of Egypt today is Arabic. The classical Arabic language used in the books and media is quite different from the spoken Arabic on the streets.

I am to cite Egypt and China as an example of material culture. The ancient Egyptians and the classical to medieval Chinese showed talents and excelled in material aspect of civilisation. They are often referred to genius in this field with a good reason. They invented and left a huge number of material objects, whose ideas and later innovations we still use in our daily life.

When we think of ancient Egyptian civilisation which lasted three millenniums, many of us immediately picture the pyramids. We can see the evolution of the burial monuments from mastaba to stepped pyramid to true pyramid. Early tombs in the middle of the First Dynasty featured bench or mastaba on top of the grave. Many mastabas were built from the sun-dried mud bricks; however, some are still in good shape after 5 millenniums. The Egyptians knew how to fire bricks at that time but they used sun-dried bricks from economic reasons. The grave contained the funeral complex, though modest at this stage, with chambers, boats and jewellery, which were meant to support the pharaohs in the afterlife.

Later pharaohs made their tombs with additional steps to make them higher and grander. Djoser, the Third Dynasty pharaoh, built the grand--60 metres high--step pyramid at Saqqara, fit for a pharaoh. Sneferu, the Fourth Dynasty pharaoh, constructed three major pyramids, and a small pyramid at Seila. He built an eight-stepped pyramid—his first—at Meidum. He also built two pyramids at Dahshur; the Bent Pyramid and the Red (or North) Pyramid. The Red Pyramid with smooth slopes and the apex pointing to the sky was supposed to be a true pyramid. It seems that the architects started to build straight sloped pyramid in the Bent Pyramid but they had to change the angle of slopes in the midway, because cracks appeared and bent as a result. It is noteworthy also that Sneferu towards the end of his reign tried to convert the step pyramid he built at Meidum to a true pyramid: we do not know how far he progressed because the layers of stones were stolen over the ages and the outer layers collapsed. (Smith 2004, pp. 44, 55) Khufu, the Fourth Dynasty pharaoh, commissioned to build the Great Pyramid at Giza, the largest ever built, though Sneferu was the greatest pyramid builder in terms of the volume of material and the manpower used. Sneferu was Khufu's father. Khafre, son of Khufu, and Menkaure, son of Khafre, both the Fourth Dynasty pharaohs, are also credited as the great pyramid builders. Without these four pharaohs pyramids have not been credited with anything approaching greatness.

There are about 100 pyramids still standing on the west bank of the Nile, over the distance of roughly 100 kilometres, almost all lying in the thin strip on the edge of the desert from Meidum in the south to Abu Roash in the north, within easy reach from Memphis, the ancient capital and royal residence. Though the pyramids look similar to us, in fact they were designed and built differently and it is apt to say that each pyramid is unique. The building of pyramid proceeded only while a pharaoh was in power, that is, the planning started after a pharaoh assumed authority; and the construction, at whatever stage, stopped when the pharaoh died or deposed. That was the nature of the society over which the pharaoh had an absolute power. The treasures the pharaohs stored inside pyramids were all robbed in spite of the elaborate antitheft measures. To combat this problem Tuthmosis I (1524-1518 BC), pharaoh of the New Kingdom, sought and built his tomb in the Valley of the Kings, a desolate spot across the Nile from Thebes; the Valley of Kings is in the heart of the Theban Necropolis. A custom came into being after a while to bury pharaohs in this location. 62 tombs have been identified so far but the research suggests that there must be as many as 150 tombs altogether. The robbers detected the burial grounds except the tomb of Tutankhamun, the pharaoh of the Eighteenth Dynasty, who died at the age of nineteen under highly suspicious circumstances. He was an insignificant pharaoh in the era and we can guess how rich the pharaohs and Egypt might have been at that time judging from the immense treasures this boy king bequeathed to us.

The Book of the Dead is the collective name given to the writings wishing the well-being of the deceased. It could be on the wall of the pyramid's burial chambers, on the coffins or on the papyrus placed inside the coffins.

When the builders could not obtain the material they needed—stones, timber, food and even people—they transported along the Nile estimating the water level of the river for loading and unloading of the heavy material. Many ships sailed out of the Nile into the Mediterranean Sea. Donkeys made land transport of light material. Pyramids were built from the Third Dynasty of the Early Dynastic period to the Sixth Dynasty of the Old Kingdom. The majority of the pyramids were built during the Fourth Dynasty (c. 2613-c. 2498 BC), the first dynasty of the Old Kingdom (2686-2181 BC). The Egyptians at the time did not have pulleys, wheels, iron tools and compasses: they built the pyramids using only chisels, saws, hammers and drills made of copper, wood and stone with remarkable ingenuity. Ample use of copper and ornamental gold was made in Egypt through its history. The Egyptians knew how to make copper tools before the First Dynasty. Alloys of copper and accidental inclusion of tin were widespread; however, bronze as such did not come into use until the Middle Kingdom.

Limestone is not hard and yield to chisels and wedges made of copper. There have been considerable speculations as to how the Egyptians cut hard granite. We know that copper tools cannot do the job. Most likely the stone cutters used abrasion operations: a paste of water, gypsum and quartz—quartz being the hardest component of granite—was spread on the granite, and the cutters applied over it a saw or drill to cause abrasions to effect cut or drill.

Wealth, prosperity, splendour and stability marked the Fourth Dynasty with power overwhelmingly vested with the king (Freeman 1996, p. 22). Pyramid buildings placed an enormous strain in the economy, consuming a large amount of resources; manpower, material and administration. Stated in reverse, these pyramid-builder kings were strong enough to withstand the economic and personal pressures imposed on them. Obviously as a consequence the Fourth Dynasty represented the apex of both the Egyptian stonemasonry and the pyramids. There is ample evidence that the Fifth Dynasty kings did not have the unlimited power wielded by those of the Fourth Dynasty (Breasted 1950, p. 129). Besides, the Fifth Dynasty kings shifted their interest from the pyramids to the sun temples dedicated to the worship of the sun. Eserkaf, the founder of the Fifth Dynasty, elevated the cult of Ra to unprecedented importance. Though the pyramids were poorly constructed, the walls and ceilings of the burial chambers were covered by the pyramid texts (the first appearance of the Book of the Dead), magic spells written in hieroglyphics. Also the mortuary complex contained obelisk, a symbol of the sun's rays.

Contrary to the public understanding, the workers at pyramids were not slaves but peasants who were drafted hopefully when there were no works required in their fields for such reasons as out of season or under water inundation (Freeman 1996, p. 25). Egypt had the ingrained system of corvèe labour which was tax paid in labour, apart from the tax paid in goods. The pharaohs made use of the conscripts thereof to build roads, canals, mines, public monuments and pyramids. The majority of the farmers did not own the land they toiled on, and the gods, practically pharaoh, owned; consequently the farmers did not have much choice but to follow what were decreed to them.

The Egyptian famers worked their land from the end of flood in November to the June harvest of the following year. Royal surveyors taxed the land according to the height of the Nile for the year prior, and not according to the yields. The tax rate hovered about 10% of the yields. The buildings of various monuments gave the Egyptian peasantry employment during the four months of the year--July to October--when their agricultural lands were inundated by the flooding of the Nile. Though the employment was corvèe labour, the labourers were fed, clothed and housed. However, the recent research indicated that the convenient hypothesis that the peasants laboured for the pharaoh only during the inundation of the Nile was exaggerated.

Egypt had large bureaucracy with the writing system and the literate class who were called scribes. Contrary to our negative opinion about bureaucracy in general, Egyptian system was noted for its efficiency. The bureaucracy collected revenues and conducted administration by efficient and fair means. As a matter of fact without the bureaucracy Egypt could not have completed the immense construction projects. The scribes recorded the material and the manpower required and the progress status for the pyramids building. The king, the temples and wealthy nobilities employed numerous scribes who had to go through years of apprenticeship. With the directions of bureaucracy tens of thousands of workers of different functions for many years built the pyramids. The designers sought the site where they could get the material for construction and the bedrock capable of withstanding the massive weight of the pyramid. There was an ample supply of high quality limestone in the Giza plateau and it was an ideal place in many ways. (Smith 2004, pp. 87-8)

The Egyptians preferred to use limestone for building pyramids since it was soft and easy to work. Limestone was the major material for the large projects such as pyramids until sandstone which could bear greater load came into vogue in the New Kingdom. When limestone broke because of the heavy load the builders used granite in place. They did not know how to calculate the stress of the member under load neither did they know the bearing strengths of the material. They knew the bearing load of the material only by experience. They carried out trial and error or simply they replaced with stronger material or larger member of the same material when the member gave in. Egypt lacked woods—structural timber or even burning fuel wood. They were imported; particularly timber from Lebanon was well known.

The craftsmen, either utilitarian or artistic, did not receive any public recognition in Egypt. This fact is surprising to us because they created lovely objects in such abundance with the most basic tools, though innovation was out of question in the bureaucratic society as in Egypt. Craftsmen's skills were passed from master to apprentice, in many cases from father to son. Egypt at the time simply did not have the tradition of writing the knowledge of this kind.

At the time of the Khufu's reign the population of Egypt was between 1 and 2 million. Herodotus claimed that 100 000 men worked the Great Pyramid of Khufu at Giza for 20 years. Most likely he misinterpreted that 100 000 were made up of four three-monthly shifts of 25 000 workers a year. (Jackson & Stamp 2003, pp. 51, 54, 113) Even we concur that Herodotus miscalculated the numbers, Egypt supported a large numbers of nobles, priests, scribes, bureaucrats and soldiers apart from the construction workers. It is amazing that Egypt produced a tremendous amount of food to feed these non-productive people thanks to the yearly inundation of the Nile River.

Egypt was famous for producing surplus grains through its history. The eating customs of the people in the Mediterranean coast seem similar all these millenniums. The Bible narrates the following two episodes which took place in the early second millennium. Genesis (12:10) says that Abram (more commonly known as Abraham) and his wife went down to Egypt to live for a while because there was a severe drought in the land of Canaan. Similarly Genesis (42:1-3) relates that Jacob's sons migrated from the Levant to Egypt because the famine was widespread outside Egypt. Also in the latter part of the 1st century BC Caesar and Augustus were anxious to obtain Egypt as the Roman colony because they wanted the huge surplus of grains in Egypt in order to feed the people (soldiers and civilians) in the empire.

It is estimated that over 2 million blocks of limestone each weighing from 1 to 5 metric tons were used to build Khufu's pyramid. Some limestone blocks weigh 10 tons and some granite blocks weigh as much as 40 tons. Since the Giza plateau was uninhabited before the construction of the Great Pyramid, the workers had to build the infrastructure: the workshops, the storehouses, and the housings with the amenities for both the permanent workers of supervisors, stonemasons, artisans, tradesmen; and the temporary workers. It is estimated that there were 5000 permanent workers and their families at the site. The temporary workers of the rotating shifts of three months a year amounted to 20 000 a shift. These figures match with the research results of the recent years. Rotating shifts of limited duration ensures the fresh workers for the hard works and the minimum disruptions to both the workers' life and the national economy. This pyramid was the tomb of the pharaoh Khufu and the sole survivor of the Seven Wonders of the ancient world, as compiled by the Greek poet Antipator of Sidon around 130 BC. This pyramid was exposed to harsh elements for millenniums and lost the gleaming white limestone casing; grave robbers looted the valuables inside; and the builders of later generations helped themselves of the stones for their personal use. What amazes us is not only its size but the accuracy of the shape of the pyramid considering the crude tools used for construction. It is oriented almost true north and south; the angle of inclination of the triangle faces is 51.9 degree: the base is level less than 2 centimetres. The builders constructed the water conduits to make vertical alignments of the building blocks possible. The builders carefully designed the roofs over the resting chamber of Khufu, and the violent earthquakes did not crash the chamber. The earthquakes destroyed many of the Seven Wonders. The robbers made off with all the treasures, the corpse and coffin in the antiquity.

The ancient Egyptians had well-developed mathematics based on decimal system. They had a system of multiplications and divisions, and could calculate areas, angles, volumes and weights. However, they did not develop physics, chemistry and biology to the level to be called science.

I was taught at school that the pharaohs built the pyramids as their tombs or more precisely as places of resurrection, and the pharaohs were entombed inside the pyramids with things they needed after resurrection. However, the evidence points that Sneferu was buried in the modest mortuary temple, mostly destroyed by now, in the vicinity of the North Pyramid. Some pharaohs built more than one pyramid and in the New Kingdom a custom was developed to bury the pharaohs underground. Accordingly, the idea that the pharaohs built the pyramids to entomb their bodies is not necessarily correct. Another interpretation is possible for any other objects such as temples in Egypt: the pyramids were dedicated to the Sun God. Also the pharaohs wanted to impress their subjects and the foreign visitors by the immensity of their creations and to make them admire the pharaohs' authority, thus they could conduct the business of governing more secure. Karl Marx may be at a loss to try to explain why the pharaohs built pyramids spending a vast amount of wealth and man power for no economic gains: he always looked for economic justification for any human ventures. Pharaohs built the pyramid to satisfy a whim of their vanity in the same fashion as a child builds a sand castle on the sandy beach or a rich man builds a large house. The pharaohs wanted to leave the vast wealth in the form of pyramids rather than any other forms. They are all done in the same vain glory to make the builders happy. Today people build the houses for comfortable living or for economic gains, or in many cases for both purposes. The pharaohs did not construct the pyramids to sell them in order to make money. Buildings of the pyramids were sheer economic waste in terms of the intent and the building cost. However, by the irony of the history, Egypt is making a huge amount of money from the tourists who visit the pyramids annually today. In fact it is said that Egypt survives as an economic entity because of a large number of foreign visitors to its various monuments and artefacts. By the time of the New Kingdom, the Egyptian tourists visited the pyramids for curiosity. Also the ancient Greek and Roman tourists made frequent visits to Egypt to have a look at the large number of the temples, antiques and pyramids. Early Greek thinkers, notably Thales, Pythagoras and Herodotus, visited Egypt and obtained the inspirations for their works.

I mentioned earlier that the bureaucracy was the necessary condition for the constructions of huge pyramids and large temples. Also the Egyptians could not have carried out the projects requiring such manpower, cost and skill unless they possessed at the time the advanced knowledge, particularly of agriculture, recording and engineering. Without a fair degree of farming knowledge even we make an allowance for the fertile silt carried by the Nile River, they could not have fed, clothed and sheltered a large number of people working on the pyramids for many years as required. There also had to be a large number of scribes to record the details of constructions, transport, progress and coordination.

I have presented the foregoing paragraphs to highlight my amazement how clever the ancient Egyptians were in those distant years. Because of my amazement and interest I probably expanded the narration on the pyramid buildings beyond what is required as an example showing that the culture results from the excess of the necessities of life. Pyramid construction is also an important piece of history showing an aspect of the unique culture by the unique, racially and linguistically, Egyptians, for three millenniums. The problems are not theoretically challenging in the modern technology but it is remarkable that they used their experience to solve the technical problems among other problems. I am sure that they did not have the theoretical reasoning for many technical problems but they used only the observed results for the constructions of pyramids.

The Egyptians confined education to the practical matters: for example, getting to know the useful equipment for the official career, and they sought the knowledge of nature and the external world solely for practical purpose in mind. It never occurred to them to search for truth for its own sake as the later Greeks did. Their knowledge of astronomy was good enough to develop the rational calendar, and mapped out the heaven with stars. Julius Caesar, advised by the Alexandrian astronomer Sosigenes, made the Roman lunar calendar the solar system in accord with the Egyptian calendar. Thus this new calendar was called Julian calendar, the basis of Gregorian calendar which we use today. Also they developed arithmetic, geometry, mechanics and medicine to carry out the daily businesses. (Breasted 1950, p. 100)

The later Greeks got to know the material aspects of the Egyptian civilisations; however, they did not master the curious writings sufficiently enough to understand the historical or cultural records (p. 578).

Archimedes (?287-212 BC), a Greek scientist of Syracuse, discovered a theory to explain the level surface of the water in a continuous channel. It seems that the ancient Greeks had a fair idea of the reasoning behind material strength as well. However, these theoretical explanations appeared in much later centuries, over 2000 years, than the age of pyramid buildings.

What I am driving at is that the pyramid constructions are non-productive projects and all the people engaged including the farmers while working on the pyramids were the non-productive people. My conclusion here is that the non-productive people who did not produce nor merchandise food, clothes and shelter carried out the constructions of pyramids.

The Egyptian empires, as we know under the rule of pharaohs, had sizable numbers of other non-productive classes such as nobles, priests, bureaucrats and standing army. The army, as in any other countries in any age, were proponents of wars because wars were the reason for their existence. Until the New Kingdom, the army in Egypt was largely a kind of feudal levy that the pharaoh called upon only in time of need. The pharaoh might keep a small cadre of standing troops, but in an emergency he called upon the provincial nobles to conscript the peasants who normally tended the fields, the canals and the quarries. The New Kingdom, beginning at about 1600 BC, saw the nation's zenith as a political power and its acquisition of a quasi-empire mostly in Asia. Before the New Kingdom, Egypt had glorified in isolation. The professional army, which did not arise until the 18th Dynasty in the New Kingdom, grew increasingly stronger as Egypt styled itself as an empire. Because of its size and efficient organisation, Egypt had the free rein to plunder its neighbouring territories.

It is not an exaggeration that the non-productive people in the main decided the characteristics of the ancient Egyptian civilisation, that is, the pharaohs, nobles, priests, army, scribes and construction workers of the various monuments such as the pyramids, temples and palaces. The monuments were a part of the material cultures, and mainly the priests carried the spiritual cultures.

Before the advent of Western technology during the 19th century, Chinese society was predominantly agricultural. It seems that the peasants during the Zhou (Chou) period had a reasonably good life. Feudalism and abundance of arable land for the entire population characterised this era, and the Zhou era lasted nearly one thousand years. Confucius longed for a return to the golden age of Zhou when the peasants reportedly lived a relatively easy life and the inferred ethical level of the general public was high. He himself lived during the Zhou dynasty, though the Zhou rule was in fact only nominal at the time.

Since the earliest times it was a Chinese custom to divide the landed possessions of a man upon his death among all his sons, hence the lands tended to be cut into small holdings which people cultivated intensely. When the land holdings became too small to cultivate, the owners of the holdings sold out and drifted into the towns where they became wage-earners. (Wells 1971, p. 205) In China, for many centuries, there were the mass of wage earning workers in the town; from these the soldiers and gang-labourers were recruited (Wells 1925, p. 145).

Chinese agricultural techniques had not improved substantially since the Zhou era till the 19th century, that is, for over two millenniums. So the marginally improved farming techniques, newly opened lands, the increased productive people and the sheer hard work supported the non-productive class in the successive Chinese empires.

Shih huang-ti unified the region which we today call China for the first time in 221 BC. He was a vigorous and ruthless ruler and instituted various reforms, and thought that his dynasty would last virtually forever, as Adolf Hitler believed that his Third Reich would last for 1000 years. The First Emperor (Shih huang-ti) deployed a large number of people (non-productive people) to complete huge construction works, among which are the Great Wall, the Palaces in the capital Hsien-yang, and the canals. These works are cited as characterising typically Chinese.

Some readers may say that since these construction works had some practical purposes unlike the pyramids, we should class them as productive works. The Great Wall was to fend off the northern barbarians; the palaces were to control the empire; the canals had the military and economic purposes in that they transported soldiers and their equipment during war time, also people and merchandise during war and peace times. However, if readers recall my definition of non-productive class, these people were not engaged in producing or merchandising the necessities of life, hence come under non-productive class. Following the above argument, we can see again, as for Egyptian civilisation, non-productive people, that is, the emperor, his bureaucracy, his army and the people engaged in the huge construction projects, carried the noteworthy material cultures in China at the time.

Reference List with Text Citations Marked

Ali, Abdullah Yusuf (trans.) 2001, *The Qur'an,* US edn, Tahrike Tarsile Qur'an, Inc, New York.
xxi (xxi)

Balkwill, Frances R & Rolph, Mic 1994, *The Egg and Sperm Race: Discover the Human Body,* Harper Collins, London.
160 (160)

Berg, Martin & Litvinoff, Miles 1992, *Ancestors: the Origins of the People and Countries of Europe,* Eurobook Limited, Portugal.
11 42

Blake, Robert (ed.) 1982, *The English World,* Thames and Hudson, London.
125

Boulnois, Luce 2005, *Silk Road: Monks, Warriors & Merchants,* trans. Helen Loveday, Odyssey Books & Guides, Hong Kong.
36 37 37 (37) 39 39 (39) 40 40 48 79 79 132 134

Bowden, Hugh 2002, *Ancient Civilizations,* Times Books, London.
35

Breasted, James Henry 1950, *A History of Egypt: From the Earliest Times to the Persian Conquest, Hodder* & Stoughton, London.
205 208 (208)

Brier, Bob & Hobbs, Hoyt 1999, *Daily Life of the Ancient Egyptians,* Greenwood Press, Westport, Connecticut.
20 21 (22) (23) (23)

Brookesmith, Peter (ed.) 1984, *Life after Death,* Introduction by Brian Inglis, Orbis Publishing Ltd, London.
161 (162)

Brooks, Philip; Fowler, Will & Adams, Simon 2000, *Encyclopedia of Eivilizations, Exploration & Conquest,* Southwater, London.
6

Burenhult, Goran (ed.) 1994, *People of the Stone Age: Hunter-Gatherers and Early Farmers,* Harper, San Francisco.
36 201 (201)

Carmichael, J 1968, *Karl Marx: The Passionate Logician,* Rapp & Whiting, London.
78 178

The Cassell Atlas of World History 2001, Forward by Barry Cunliffe, Orion Publishing Co, London.
4 90

Casson, Lionel 1978, *Ancient Egypt: Great Ages of Man,* revised edn, Time-Life Books, Alexandria, Virginia.
110

Chan, Wing-Tsit (trans. and comp.) 1963, *A Source Book in Chinese Philosophy,* Princeton University Press, Princeton.

153 194

Chang, Chung-li 1974, *The Chinese Gentry; Studies in Their Role in Nineteenth-Century Chinese Society,* University of Washington Press, Seattle.
Reprinted with permission of the University of Washington Press.
xxxiv (xxxiv) (xxxiv) (xxxiv) (xxxiv) (xxxiv) xxxv

Chen, Li Fu 1987, *The Confucian Way: A New and Systematic Study of 'The Four Books',* trans. Shih Shun Liu, KPI Ltd, London.
194

Chien, Szuma 1979, *Selections from Records of the Historian,* this book is generally known as *Shih Chi,* trans Yang Hsien-yi and Gladys Yang, Foreign Languages Press, Peking.
15 18 58 (58) 184

Clark, Herbert H & Clark, Eve V 1977, *Psychology and Language,* Harcourt Brace Jovanovich Inc, New York.
163

Conze, Edward (trans. and ed.) 1975, *The Large Sutra on Perfect Wisdom with the Divisions of the Abhisamayalankara,* University of California Press, Berkeley.
xxii

Cotterell, Arthur (ed.) 1993, *The Penguin Encyclopedia of Classical Civilizations,* Penguin Group, Hong Kong.
32 35 187

Cotterell, Arthur & Morgan, David 1975, *China: An Integrated Study,* Harrap, London.
24 36 41 54 (54) 75 128 129 132 (133) 137 (137)

Davison, Michael Worth (ed.) 1993, *When, Where, Why and How It Happened,* Reader's Digest, London.
5 28 40 58 60 76 91 95 95 102 116 118 119 122 136 190 194

Dudley, Donald R 1968, *The World of Tacitus,* Secker & Warburg, London.
13

Dulbecco, Renato 1987, *The Design of Life,* Yale University Press, New Haven.
160 160

Dutt, Clemens (trans. and ed.) 1961, *Fundamentals of Marxism-Leninism,* Foreign Languages Publication House, Moscow.
182

Early Civilization 1984, Mind Alive Encyclopaedia, Marshall Cavendish Books Ltd, London.
77 96 110

Ebrey, Patricia Buckley 1996, *The Cambridge Illustrated History of China,* Calmann & King Ltd, London.
36 55 59 60 64 65 72 75 80 134 (135) 136 187 201

The Editors of Time-Life Books 1988, *The March of Islam: Time-Life History of the World AD 600-800,* Time-Life Books, Amsterdam.
xxiii 38 66

Eliade, Mircea 1978, *From the Stone Age to the Eleusinian Mysteries,* A History of Religious Ideas, vol. 1, trans. Willard R Trask, University of Chicago Press, Chicago.
26 27 29 184 199 (199) (199) 201

-----1982, *From Gautama Buddha to the Triumph of Christianity,* A History of Religious Ideas, vol. 2, trans. Willard R Trask, University of Chicago Press, Chicago.
xvii (xvii) 40 151

-----1985. *From Muhammad to the Age of Reforms,* A History of Religious Ideas, vol. 3, trans Alf Hiltebeitel and Diane Apostolos-Cappadona, University of Chicago Press, Chicago.
48 103

Fernandez-Armesto, Felipe (ed.) 1994, *Guide to the Peoples of Europe,* Times Books, London.
48 144

Freeman, Charles 1996, *Egypt, Greece and Rome: Civilizations of the Ancient Mediterranean,* Oxford University Press, New York.
18 23 25 32 (32) (32) (32) 32 33 39 43 (43) 105 (105) 148 205 205

Freud, Sigmund 1961, *Beyond the Pleasure Principle,* trans. and ed. James Strachey, WW Norton & Company, New York.
liii

Fryer, Jonathan 1975, *The Great Wall of China,* New English Library, London.
57 59 (59) 129

Galbraith, John Kenneth 1987, *A History of Economics: The Past as the Present,* Hamish Hamilton, London.
119

Goethe, Johann Wolfgang von 1985, *Faust,* trans. John Anster, Harrap Limited, London.
128

Grant, Michael 1969, *The Ancient Mediterranean,* Trinity Press, London.
27 28 32 32 33 36 48 102 106 110 140

Greenberg, Steven & Ainsworth, William A (eds) 2006, *Listening to Speech: An Auditory Perspective,* Lawrence Erlbaum Associates, Mahwah, New Jersey.
32

Grenville, JAS 1994, *The Collins History of the World in the Twentieth Century,* HarperCollins, London.
137 195

Guisso, RWL & Pagani, C 1989, *The First Emperor of China,* ed. D Miller, Sidgwick & Jackson, London.
57 156

Guthrie, WKC 1969, *A History of Greek Philosophy,* vol. 3, Cambridge University Press, Cambridge.
170 (170) 193 (193)

-----1975, *A History of Greek Philosophy,* vol. 4, Cambridge University Press, Cambridge.
33 170 187

Hall, Manly P 1984, *Lectures on Ancient Philosophy,* Philosophical Research Society, INC, Los Angeles.
174 182

Harbottle, Thomas Benfield 1897, *Dictionary of Quotations (Classical) or Classical Quotations, Swan* Sonnenschein & Co Ltd, London.
ii ii 171 174 175 179 (179) 180 (180) (180) (180) 184 (184) 187 187 188 188 190 (190) (190) (190) 191 (191) (191) (191) (191) (191) (191) (191) 191 (191) (191) (191) (191) (191) (191) 192 193 193 (193) (193) (193) (193) 193 (193) (193) (193) 194 (194) 195 (195) 196 (196) 196

Harris, Nathaniel 1999, *Hamlyn History of Imperial China,* Octopus Publishing Group Limited, London.
vii xxxvi xxxvi xxxvii 18 56 64 67 68 (68) 72 72 74 74 80 129 131

Hellum, Jennifer 2007, *The Pyramids,* Greenwood Press, Westport, Connecticut.
20 23

Hitler, A 1992, *Mein Kampf,* trans. Ralph Manheim, Pimlico, London.
13 14 (14) (14)

Ho, Ping-Ti 1976, *The Ladder of Success in Imperial China: Aspects of Social Mobility 1368-1911,* Columbia University Press, New York.
xxxii (xxxii) (xxxiii) xl 194

Hughes-Hallett, Lucy 1990, *Cleopatra,* Bloomsbury, London.
24

Hutchins, Robert Maynard (ed.) 1952, *The Prince by Nicole Machiavelli; Leviathan by Thomas Hobbes,* Great Books of the Western World, vol. 23, Encyclopaedia Britannica series, William Benton, Chicago.
106 156

Jackson, Kevin & Stamp, Jonathan 2003, *Building the Great Pyramid,* Firefly Books Ltd, New York.
25 206

Janaway, Christopher 1994, *Schopenhauer,* Oxford University Press, Oxford.
178

Keen, Maurice 1991, *The Penguin History of Medieval Europe,* Penguin Books, London.
Reproduced by permission of Penguin Books Ltd.
xlix (xlix) 85 (85) (85) 86 (87) (87) 90 (91) (91) (91) 93 (94) 94 (94) (95) 97 (97) (97) (97) (97) 99 (99) (99) 99 (100) (100)

Kenez, Peter 2006, *A History of the Soviet Union from the Beginning to the End,* 2nd edn, Cambridge University Press, New York.
xxxviii

Kennedy, Paul 1987, *The Rise and Fall of the Great Powers,* Random House, New York.
66 67 104 (104) (104) (104) (104) 116 (116) (116) (116) (116) 122 123 (123) (124) 125 128 136 (136) (136) 136 (136) 138 (138) (138) (138) 143

Koller, John M 1985, *Oriental Philosophies,* 2nd edn, Charles Scribner's Sons, New York.
180 181 189 194 195

Konstam, Angus 2004, *Historical Atlas of the Viking World,* Mercury Books, London.
89

Kung, Hans; Ess, Josef van; Stietencron, Heinrich von & Bechert, Heinz 1986, *Christianity and the World Religions,* trans. Peter Heinegg, Doubleday & Co Inc, New York.
151

Lai, TC 1970, *A Scholar in Imperial China,* Kelly & Walsh Ltd, Hong Kong.
xxxiv

Levi, Peter 1980, *Atlas of the Greek World,* Facts on File Inc, New York.
32 41

Loewe, Michael 1990, *The Pride That was China,* Sidgwick and Jackson, London.
54 129 (129) (129) 130 (130) 162 195

Lopez, Donald S Jr (ed.) 1996, *Religions of China in Practice,* Princeton University Press, Princeton.
152

McGreal, Ian P (ed.) 1995, *Great Thinkers of the Eastern World,* Harper Collins Publishers Inc, New York.
56 151 (151) (151)

Martell, Hazel Mary 1995, *The Ancient World,* Kingfisher, London.
6 12 (12)

Marx, Karl 1954, *Capital,* vol. I: *The Process of Production of Capital,* trans Samuel Moore and Edward Aveling and ed. Frederick Engels, Progress publishers, Moscow.
125 182

-----1959, *Capital,* vol. III: *The Process of Capitalist Production as a Whole,* trans. and ed. Frederick Engels, Progress publishers, Moscow.
134 200

-----1968, *Theories of Surplus Value,* part II, (Capital, vol. IV), trans. and ed. S Ryazanskaya, Progress Publishers, Moscow.
125

-----1971, *Theories of Surplus Value,* part III, (Capital, vol. IV), trans Jack Cohen and SW Ryazanskaya and eds SW Ryazanskaya and Richard Dixon, Progress Publishers, Moscow.
125 169

Marx, Karl & Engels, Frederick 1970, *Selected Works,* vol. 3, Progress Publishers, Moscow.
4 127 178 181 181 182 183

-----1989, *Selected Works,* revised edn, vol. 1, Progress Publishers, Moscow.
124 181 181 193

Mathers, Powys (trans.) 1953, *The Thousand Nights and One Night,* vol. 2, Routledge & Kegan Paul Ltd, London.
xxiii (xxiii) (xxiii) (xxiii) xlvii

Mathias, P 1969, *The First Industrial Nation: An Economic History of Britain 1700-1914,* Methuen & Co Ltd, London.
107

Menzel, Johanna M (ed.) 1963, *The Chinese Civil Service,* DC Heath & Co, Lexington, Massachusetts.
xxxv xxxvii xli

Mercer, Derrik (editor-in-chief) 1996, *Chronicle of the World,* Dorling Kindersley, London.
18 110 118 119 119 137 148 170 (170) 187 195

Milston, Gwendda 1978, *A Short History of China,* Cassell Australia, Stanmore, NSW.
xxxi xxxiv xli 41 55 (55) (55) 65 66 109 128

Miyazaki, Ichisada 1976, *China's Examination Hell,* trans. Conrad Schirokauer, Weatherhill Inc, New York.
xl

Montaigne, Michel de 1965, *The Complete Essays of Montaigne,* trans. DM Frame, Stanford University Press, California.
15 (15) (15) (15) 73 (74) (74) 103 147 179 186 190 190 (190) 192 192 (193) (193) (193) (193)

Murowchick, Robert E (ed.) 1994, *China: Ancient Culture, Modern Land,* Cradles of Civilization Series, Weldon Russell Pty Ltd, North Sydney.
xxxvi 39 54 54 56 57 64 75 130 194

Narada, Thera (trans.) 1993, *The Dhammapada,* 4th edn, Buddhist Council of NSW Inc, Eastlakes, NSW.
ii ix 184 193 196 196 (196) (196)

Ostler, Nicholas 2006, *Empires of the World: A Language History of the World,* Harper Perennial, London.
xxx 30 (30) (30) (30) 42 48 51 132 203 (203)

Pfeiffer, John 1976, *The Cell,* Life Science Library Series, Time-Life Books, New York.
160 160 160 (160) 161 (161) (161) (161) (161) (161) 162 (162) (163)

Polo, Marco 1959, *The Travels of Marco Polo,* Andre Deutsch Ltd, London.
80 (80)

Randall, John Herman Jr 1976, *The Making of the Modern Mind,* Columbia University Press, New York.
Reprinted with permission of the publisher.
95 102 105 105 106 106 107 107 117 (117) 143 184 186 (186)

Reader's Digest 1983, *Vanished Civilisation,* Reader's Digest, Sydney.
5 28 32 37 38 38 40 (40) (40) 41

Riasanovsky, Nicholas V 1977, *A History of Russia,* 3rd edn, Oxford University Press, New York.
18 77

Richards, PD & English, FW 1985, *Out of the Dark: A History of Medieval Europe,* Thomas Nelson, Melbourne.
46 93 94 98

Rietbergen, Peter 1998, *Europe: A Cultural History,* Routledge, London.
4 12 34

Robbins, Lionel 1998, *A History of Economic Thought,* Princeton University Press, Princeton.
118

Roberts, Gail 1973, *Atlas of Discovery,* Crown Publishers Inc, New York.
18 40 78 79 108 110 118 (118)

Roberts, JAG 1998, *Modern China: An Illustrated History,* Sutton Publishing Limited, Gloucester, Britain.
xxxv 36 107 129 (129) 131 131 (131) (131) 132

Roebuck, Carl 1966, *The World of Ancient Times,* Charles Scribner's Sons, New York.
178

Roll, Eric 1961, *A History of Economic Thought,* Faber and Faber Ltd, London.
107 122

Rowse, AL 1979, *The Story of Britain,* Artus Publishing Co Ltd, London.
123 138

Schafer, EH 1967, *Ancient China,* Great Ages of Man Series, Time-Life, New York.
40

Schopenhauer, Arthur 1962, *The Essential Schopenhauer,* George Allen & Unwin Ltd, London.
143

Sharma, Arvind (ed.) 1993, *Our Religions,* Harper, San Francisco.
156 161 183

Smith, Adam 1991, *Wealth of Nations,* Great Minds Series, Prometheus Books, Buffalo, New York.
39 118 120 (120) 128 201

Smith, Craig B 2004, *How the Great Pyramid Was Built,* HarperCollins Publishers, New York.
204 206

Spielvogel, Jackson J 1991, *Western Civilization,* West Publishing Co, St Paul.
33 91 105 105 106 107 107 119 163 202

Suzuki, DT 1930, *Studies in the Lankavatara Sutra,* Routledge & Kegan Paul Ltd, London.
157

-----1973, *Outlines of Mahayana Buddhism,* Schocken Books, New York.
xix (xix)

Taylor, Timothy 1996, *The Prehistory of Sex: Four Million Years of Human Sexual Culture,* Fourth Estate, London.
6

Temple, RKG 1986, *China: Land of Discovery and Invention,* introduced by Joseph Needham, Patrick Stephens, Willingborough, Northamps.
vii xxx 72 (72) 72 (72) 74 198 (198)

Thomas A Kempis 1952, *The Imitation of Christ,* Penguin Classics, trans. Leo Sherley-Price, Penguin Books, Middlesex, England.
ii (ii) ii

Thomas a Kempis 1980, *Imitation of Christ,* ed. Paul M Bechtel, Moody Press, Chicago.
190 193 (193)

Thomas A Kempis 1982, *The Imitation of Christ,* With reflections from the documents of Vatican II for each chapter, St Paul Publication, Homebush, NSW.
ii (ii)

Toynbee, AJ 1962, *A Study of History,* Abridged by DC Somervell, Oxford University Press, London.
1 102 146 173

Toynbee, A; Mant, AK; Smart, N; Hinton, J; Yudkin, S; Rhode, E; Heywood, R & Price, HH 1968, *Man's Concern with Death,* Hodder and Stoughton, London.
33

Walker, A 1978, *Marx: His Theory and Its Context,* Longman, London.
125 174

Watson, Burton (trans.) 1993, *The Lotus Sutra,* Columbia University Press, New York.
ii

Wells, HG 1925, *The Outline of History,* revised edn, 2 vols, Cassell and Co Ltd, London.
32 35 40 40 49 49 59 77 78 80 91 95 105 106 118 123 124 142 148 184 201 209

-----1971, *The Outline of History,* Cassell & Co Ltd, London.
54 128 209

Wells, Spencer 2003, *The Journey of Man: A Genetic Odyssey,* Penguin Books, London.
Reproduced by permission of Penguin Books Ltd.
6 7 (7) (7) (7) 11 27 27

Westheimer, Dr Ruth 1994, *Encyclopaedia of Sex,* Element Books, Brisbane, Queensland.
160

Whitehouse, Ruth & Wilkins, John 1986, *The Making of Civilization: History Discovered through Archaeology,* Collins, London.
4 5 (5) 105 142 (143) 182 200 (200) (200) (201) (201)

Williams, Trevar I 1987, *The History of Invention: From Stone Axes to Silicon Chips,* Macdonald & Co Ltd, London.
17 34 38 (38) 67 71 72 73 (73) (73) 74 75 (75) 75 80 102 103 139

Index

www.ingramcontent.com/pod-product-compliance
Lightning Source LLC
LaVergne TN
LVHW081149110826
845149LV00008B/1607
* 9 7 8 0 9 9 2 3 2 9 7 8 5 *